Excavation at Fengate, Peterborough, England: The Third Report

Excavation at Fengate, Peterborough, England: The Third Report

Francis Pryor

With illustrations by Robert Powell, Maisie Taylor and the author

Northamptonshire Archaeological Society Monograph 1
Royal Ontario Museum Archaeology Monograph 6
1980

ISBN: — 0 9507151 07
ISSN: — 0144-5391

This book is published jointly by the Northamptonshire Archaeological Society and the Royal Ontario Museum. A generous grant towards the cost of publication from the Department of the Environment is acknowledged.

The Royal Ontario Museum publishes two series in the field of archaeology: Monographs, a numbered series of original publications, and Papers, a numbered series of primarily shorter original publications. All manuscripts considered for publication are subject to the editorial policies of the Royal Ontario Museum, and to review by persons outside the museum staff who are authorities in the particular field involved. (The Royal Ontario Museum, 100 Queen's Park, Toronto, Canada, M5S 2CS.)

It is distributed in the United Kingdom by the Northamptonshire Archaeological Society and is available from the Society's Editor, A E Brown, Department of Adult Education, The University, Leicester, LE1 7RH, (price on application).

To my Parents

CONTENTS

Foreword   ix
Acknowledgements   ix
List of figures   xi
List of plates   xiii
List of tables   xiii
Terminology, conventions, and abbreviations   xiv
Introduction   1
    Abstract   1
    The site and its setting   1
Chapter 1: Padholme Road subsite   3
    Features   5
        Ditches 1, 2 and associated features   5
        Ditches 3, 4 and associated features   12
    Finds   18
        Pottery   18
        Flint   18
        Miscellaneous   21
Chapter 2: Newark Road subsite   23
    Features   23
        Areas I-VI   23
        Area VII   70
    Finds   87
        Pottery   87
            Fabric Analysis, Dr D F Williams   87
        Flint   106
        Miscellaneous   125
            Metal analysis of the spearhead, Dr P T Craddock   128
            Dating and significance of the spearhead, Dr D G Coombs   129
Chapter 3: Fourth Drove subsite   131
    Features   133
        Second millennium   133
        Post-second millennium   151
    Finds   154
        Pottery   154
        Flint   156
Chapter 4: Cat's Water subsite   158
    Features   158
        Second millennium ditches   158
        Structure 46   163
        Inhumation in F1594   168
Chapter 5: Discussion   169
    The linear ditch system   169
    Non-linear features   173
    Dating   176
    Origins of the ditched enclosures   178
    Economy and Society   180
    Demise of the ditched enclosures   186

Appendices

Methods of Excavation 1975-78   **190**

Sediment analysis of second millennium ditches, C A I French   **190**

Description of terms used in matrix composition of feature fillings, C A I French   **202**

Analysis of molluscs from two second millennium ditches, C A I French   **204**

Report on charcoal from the 'Industrial Area', Maisie Taylor   **212**

Soil phosphate analyses, Newark Road, Dr P T Craddock   **213**

Animal bones from second millennium ditches, Newark Road, Kathleen Biddick   **217**

Human skeletons from Padholme Road and Newark Road subsites, Dr Calvin Wells   **232**

Human skeleton from Cats Water subsite, F V H Powell   **234**

Beaker pottery from the Wyman Abbott collection, Alex Gibson   **234**

Concordance list of field and publication ditch designations   **246**

Radiocarbon dates   **247**

Bibliography   **249**

Plates   **259**

FOREWORD

This report forms part of the scheme of Fengate final publication laid out, in revised form, in the Introduction of the Second Report. It is almost entirely given over to a detailed description of the ditched enclosure system briefly described in two recent publications as being of 'Bronze Age' date (Pryor 1974b; 1976a). This terminology, although a useful abbreviation, is not altogether appropriate for a final report. In terms of the three-age system, as presently understood, the enclosures described below would belong to the Late Neolithic period, Early and Middle Bronze Ages. This is clearly too cumbersome for repeated use, so it has been decided to refer to the enclosures as being of second millennium BC date (for dating evidence see Chapter 5).

All enclosure ditches of this second millennium BC system are described, but those of the Cat's Water subsite are treated in less detail than the rest, as this subsite will form the bulk of the Fourth Report (for an interim report see Pryor and Cranstone 1978). It was considered inadvisable to divide the features of this large and complex subsite on largely subjective chronological criteria; instead, sufficient information is given (in Chapter 4) for readers to obtain a clear understanding of the Cat's Water enclosure system and the way it relates to the rest of Fengate, but details will have to await the Fourth Report.

ACKNOWLEDGEMENTS

Any project as large and long-lived as Fengate must, of necessity, be a team effort. The people mentioned below formed part of that team and I must apologise to those I have not had space to acknowledge here; hopefully I will be able to rectify the worst of those omissions in the Fourth Report.

First, I must acknowledge, with thanks, the efforts of the many specialists who have contributed their work to this report. They are: Charles French (molluscs and sediments); Maisie Taylor (charcoals); Dr Paul Craddock and the British Museum Research Laboratory (soil phosphate analysis and metal analysis); Kathy Biddick (faunal bones); the late Dr Calvin Wells (human bones); Faye Powell (human bones); Alex Gibson (Beakers from the G Wyman Abbott collection); Dr Bob Otlet of the Harwell Radiocarbon Laboratory for processing the C-14 dates; Dr David Williams, of the Department of the Environment Ceramic Petrology Project (pottery fabrics) and finally, Dr David Coombs (the Middle Bronze Age spearhead). A full report on all palaeobotanical material is being prepared for the Fourth Report by Mrs Gay Wilson, palaeobotanist to the Nene Valley Research Committee.

The project has received local assistance from Mr D F Mackreth, Nene Valley Research Committee, Director of Excavations, and the staff at the Ham Lane Field Centre. Mr George Dixon handled our accounts, both in the field and in the office, and continued to perform miracles of financial dexterity. The report was written in Fengate in a cottage overlooking the site, kindly loaned to us by the Peterborough Development Corporation, in no small part through the good offices of David Bath, the Chief Planning Officer. The inhabitants of this cottage (the 'Command Module') during the post-excavation work put up with the present author's deteriorating temper and helped and encouraged him to put pen to paper. Maisie Taylor, Charles French, Bob and Faye Powell and Bob Bourne, therefore, deserve the warmest thanks for their enthusiasm and hard work.

My sincere thanks are due to Tony Brown who has helped with the publication of this volume in so many ways. He has done everything one could ask of an Editor.

Supervision in the field was by Anne Raumann (née Boyle); Bob and Faye Powell; Dermot Bond; David Cranstone; Bill Moss; Chris Evans; Maisie Taylor and Charles French. Boyd Dixon will never be forgotten. Additional drawings for this report were prepared by Chris Evans, Heather Nicol, Charles French and David Crowther.

A final debt of gratitude is to Richard Bradley, Ian Kinnes, David Coombs, David Hall, Doug Tushingham and Tony Fleming all of whom provided much sound advice, refreshingly leavened with humour.

Sources of funds for the seasons 1971-6 are given in the Second Report. Excavation finance for 1977 was provided by the Royal Ontario Museum and the Department of the Environment (via the Nene Valley Research Committee); that for 1978 was provided by the DoE alone. The post-excavation finance has been provided by the Department of the Environment and the Royal Ontario Museum. This report is published with the aid of grants provided by the Department of the Environment and the Publication Services Department of the Royal Ontario Museum, through the courtesy of Mr John Campsie.

Peterborough, April 1979

LIST OF FIGURES

1   Simplified solid geology of the Peterborough area
2   Topographical map of the Peterborough Area, showing location of FIG 3
3   Map showing areas excavated 1971-78
4   General plan of second millennium BC and related cropmarks
5   Plan showing relationship of main second millennium BC excavated ditches
6   Padholme Road subsite: areas excavated and principal second millennium BC ditches
7   Padholme Road subsite: plan of Areas IX and X
8   Padholme Road subsite: plan of Area VII and part of Area II
9   Padholme Road subsite: plan of Area VIII
10 Conventions used in the illustrated sections
11 Padholme Road subsite: sections and profiles
12 Padholme Road subsite: selected sections through second millennium BC ditches
13 Padholme Road subsite: pottery and fired clay from ditches 1 and 2
14 Padholme Road subsite: selected flints from ditches 1-4
15 Padholme Road subsite: axe marks on oak log from ditch 4
16 Newark Road subsite: the grid
17 Newark Road subsite: surface contours
18 Newark Road subsite: general plan
19 Newark Road subsite: plan of south-central second millennium BC features
20 Newark Road subsite: plan of features near the well
21 Newark Road subsite: section through well
22 Newark Road subsite: features at NE corner of enclosure 3
23 Newark Road subsite: plan of features at SE corner of enclosure B
24 Newark Road subsite: section of ditches *i* and 9
25 Newark Road subsite: finds' distribution in SE ditches
26 Newark Road subsite: section through ditch *f*
27 Newark Road subsite: inhumation in ditch *f*
28 Newark Road subsite: ditches at SW corner of enclosure B
29 Newark Road subsite: section through ditches 9 and *m*
30 Newark Road subsite: section through ditch *b*
31 Newark Road subsite: plan of ditches near Structure 1
32 Newark Road subsite: phasing of ditches near Structure 1
33 Newark Road subsite: sections through ditch *n* and associated ditches
34 Newark Road subsite: plan of Area IV settlement
35 Newark Road subsite: plan of Structure 1
36 Newark Road subsite, Structure 1: section location plan
37 Newark Road subsite, Structure 1: ring-gully sections
38 Newark Road subsite, Structure 1: posthole sections
39 Newark Road subsite, Structures 1 and 2: posthole sections
40 Newark Road subsite: plan of Structure 2
41 Newark Road subsite: ditch 8 section and profiles
42 Newark Road subsite: ditch 9 section and profiles
43 Newark Road subsite: ditch 10 section and profiles
44 Newark Road subsite: first millennium BC and Roman features
45 Newark Road subsite: plan of 'industrial area'
46 Newark Road subsite: 'industrial area' sections
47 Newark Road subsite, Area VII: junction of S drove ditches
48 Newark Road subsite, Area VII: plan of N drove ditches
49 Newark Road subsite, Area VII: ditch sections
50 Newark Road subsite, Area VII: ditch sections
51 Newark Road subsite, Area VII: finds' distribution in N drove ditches
52 Newark Road subsite, Area VII: finds' distribution in N drove ditches
53 Newark Road subsite, Areas I-VI: pottery from the ditches
54 Newark Road subsite, Areas I-VI: pottery from the ditches
55 Newark Road subsite, Areas I-VI and VII: pottery from the ditches
56 Newark Road subsite, Area VII: pottery from the ditches
57 Newark Road subsite: pit groups
58 Newark Road subsite: pit groups
59 Newark Road subsite: pit groups
60 Newark Road subsite: pit groups
61 Newark Road subsite: pit groups
62 Newark Road subsite: flints
63 Newark Road subsite: flints

64   Newark Road subsite: flints
65   Newark Road subsite: flints
66   Newark Road subsite: flints
67   Newark Road subsite: flints
68   Newark Road subsite: flints
69   Newark Road subsite: flints
70   Histogram of scraper dimensions (Newark Road)
71   Histogram of scraper dimensions (Storey's Bar Road)
72   Histogram of scraper retouch angles
73   Histogram of utilized flakes' breadth:length ratios
74   Histogram of waste flakes' breadth:length ratios
75   Newark Road subsite: miscellaneous finds
76   Newark Road subsite: antler pick
77   Newark Road subsite: bronze awl
78   Fourth Drove subsite: areas excavated
79   Fourth Drove subsite: surface contours
80   Fourth Drove subsite: Structure 1
81   Plan comparing Newark Road and Fourth Drove structures
82   Fourth Drove subsite: sections
83   Fourth Drove subsite: sections
84   Fourth Drove subsite: sections
85   Fourth Drove subsite: plan of ditch 10 and bank, Area VII
86   Fourth Drove subsite: section through Fen Causeway and ditch 10
87   Fourth Drove subsite: ditch 10 sections
88   Fourth Drove subsite: section through F11
89   Fourth Drove subsite: pottery
90   Fourth Drove subsite: flints
91   Cat's Water subsite: surface contours
92   Cat's Water subsite: stripped surface contours
93   Cat's Water subsite: plan of second millennium BC ditches
94   Cat's Water subsite: plan of Structure 46 and its enclosure
95   Cat's Water subsite: plan of Structure 46
96   Cat's Water subsite: Structure 46 sections
97   Cat's Water subsite: crouched inhumation
98   Appendix 2 (sediment study)
99   Appendix 2 (sediment study)
100 Appendix 2 (sediment study)
101 Appendix 2 (sediment study)
102 Appendix 2 (sediment study)
103 Appendix 2 (sediment study)
104 Appendix 2 (sediment study)
105 Appendix 2 (sediment study)
106 Appendix 2 (sediment study)
107 Appendix 3 (matrix composition terminology)
108 Appendix 4 (molluscs)
109 Appendix 4 (molluscs)
110 Appendix 4 (molluscs)
111 Appendix 6 (soil phosphate analysis)
112 Appendix 6 (soil phosphate analysis)
113 Appendix 7 (animal bones)
114 Appendix 7 (animal bones)
115 Appendix 7 (animal bones)
116 Appendix 7 (animal bones)
117 Appendix 7 (animal bones)
118 Appendix 10 (Wyman Abbott Beakers)
119 Appendix 10 (Wyman Abbott Beakers)
120 Appendix 10 (Wyman Abbott Beakers)
121 Appendix 10 (Wyman Abbott Beakers)
122 Appendix 10 (Wyman Abbott Beakers)
123 Appendix 10 (Wyman Abbott Beakers)
124 Appendix 10 (Wyman Abbott Beakers)
125 Appendix 10 (Wyman Abbott Beakers)
126 Appendix 10 (Wyman Abbott Beakers)
127 Appendix 10 (Wyman Abbott Beakers)
128 Sketch showing interpretation of PL 15

LIST OF PLATES

1   Padholme Road subsite cropmarks
2   Padholme Road subsite, Areas IX and X (ditches 1 and 2)
3   Padholme Road subsite, Area VIII: ditch F4, section
4   Padholme Road subsite: crouched burial in ditch 1
5   Padholme Road subsite: notched log from ditch 4
6   Newark Road subsite cropmarks
7   Aerial view of Newark Road and Cat's Water subsites
8   Newark Road subsite: Areas I-VI
9   Newark Road subsite: Area VII
10 Newark Road subsite: view along drove between ditches 8 and 9
11 Newark Road subsite: view along drove between ditches 8 and 9
12 Newark Road subsite: crouched burial in ditch *f*
13 Newark Road subsite: Structure 1
14 Newark Road subsite: part of Structure 1 and associated ditches
15 Fourth Drove subsite: Area VII, ditch 10 and associated bank
16 The Peterborough logboat (1950 photograph)

LIST OF TABLES

1   Newark Road subsite: feature dimensions, NE enclosure 3
2   Newark Road subsite: features within enclosure C
3   Newark Road subsite: distribution of pottery from enclosure ditches
4   Newark Road utilized flakes: lengths
5   Newark Road utilized flakes: breadths
6   Newark Road waste flakes: lengths
7   Newark Road waste flakes: breadths
8   Cat's Water subsite: details of features comprising Structure 46
9   Textural description of sediments
10 Newark Road subsite, Area III: molluscs from ditch 10
11 Newark Road subsite, Area IV: molluscs from ditch 9
12 Fourth Drove subsite, Area VII: molluscs from ditch 10 and under the Fen Causeway
13 Faunal bone report: species identified (Part 1); bone survival (Part 2)
14 Faunal bone report: skeletal elements
15 Faunal bone report: parts of long bones represented
16 Faunal bone report: epiphyseal fusion record
17 Faunal bone report: epiphyseal fusion and age stages
18 Faunal bone report: tooth wear stages for cattle and sheep
19 Faunal bone report: osteometrics

TERMINOLOGY, CONVENTIONS, AND ABBREVIATIONS

The linear measurements are given in the metric system (wherever possible) and metres are used as the basic unit. In the running text the metre abbreviation (m) is used, but in the catalogues of pottery sherds and flints it is omitted.

Throughout this report radiocarbon dates are given using the 'Libby' half-life for radiocarbon (5,568 years), correct to one standard deviation. Dates in 'radiocarbon years' are indicated by the use of the letters 'ad' and 'bc' to distinguish them from calendar years AD and BC.

The depths of finds in this report are given below the stripped surface (in metres), that is about 0.75 m below the modern ground level (the problem is discussed in the Second Report, Appendix 1). Similarly, sections are drawn with the original ploughsoil removed, but with the stripped surface level indicated in metres above Ordnance Datum. It was thought undesirable to 'reconstruct' the modern soil profile after it had been removed mechanically.

The representation of soil types used in this report follows the standard scheme introduced in 1972 by D F Mackreth, Nene Valley Research Committee Director of Excavations. A few minor modifications, however, have been introduced; the conventions used here are illustrated and explained in FIG 10.

Throughout this report the First Report (Pryor 1974c) is abbreviated to FNG 1, the Second Report (Pryor 1978a) to FNG 2.

INTRODUCTION

ABSTRACT

This report considers a series of ditched enclosures and droves, laid out along, and at right-angles to, the Fen-edge in the second millennium BC. Three small settlements associated with the system are described and evidence for hedges, banks, metalworking, salt-evaporation and possible lime-burning is reviewed. The pottery and flints are of second millennium BC type, and the latter collection is discussed in the light of other assemblages from Fengate (Chapter 2). Post-second millennium BC material is discussed in passing, and a Roman road (the Fen Causeway) is considered in more detail (Chapter 3).

The layout of this report follows the Second Report. The first four chapters are given over to a detailed description of the second millennium BC ditched enclosure system described very briefly in Pryor 1974b and in greater detail in Pryor 1976a. Each of the first four chapters is devoted to a specific subsite (FIG 3 for location): Chapter 1 to Padholme Road; Chapter 2 to Newark Road; Chapter 3 to Fourth Drove and Chapter 4 to second millennum features on Cat's Water (see Foreword). Chapter 5 discusses the system as a whole and attempts to draw some conclusions as to its wider significance. The 34 radiocarbon dates available so far are listed in Appendix 12.

THE SITE AND ITS SETTING (FIGS 1-2)

A few words summarising the detailed description of the site and its setting, given in the Second Report (FNG 2, 1-6), are appropriate here. First, despite its name, Fengate is not a Fen site *sensu stricto*; rather it lies on the extreme edge of the Fen basin on the gravel soils of the Nene First Terrace (FIG 2). The cropmarks (PLS 1 and 6) are mainly confined to land between the 10 and 25-foot contours above OD (FIG 4). Below that range, peats and alluvial clays tend to mask cropmarks and prevent finds from appearing on the surface; the thickness of the clay deposits on the lower parts of the site, combined with the soil's high iron content, make geophysical prospecting extremely difficult, or impossible. Above the 25-foot contour, the urban sprawl of 19th and early 20th century Peterborough covers the land.

The geology of the region is complex (FNG 2, 1-2; Horton *et al* 1974), but in addition to the drift soils of the lower Nene Valley and Fenland, the inhabitants of Fengate would also have had access to the clays and limestones of the principal Upper Jurassic facies which outcrop nearby (FIG 1). The location of so many ancient settlements at Fengate is most probably due to the site's position on the edge of two important ecological zones, namely, the peat (or 'Black') Fens and the low-lying, but seasonally flood-free lands of the Fen Margins. From Fengate, communities could exploit the light soils of the gravels, yet at the same time could take advantage of the many natural inducements offered by the Fenland, the three most important of which were summer pasture (and probably winter hay/fodder), winter protein (fish, eels, wildfowl) and fuel (wood, peat).

1

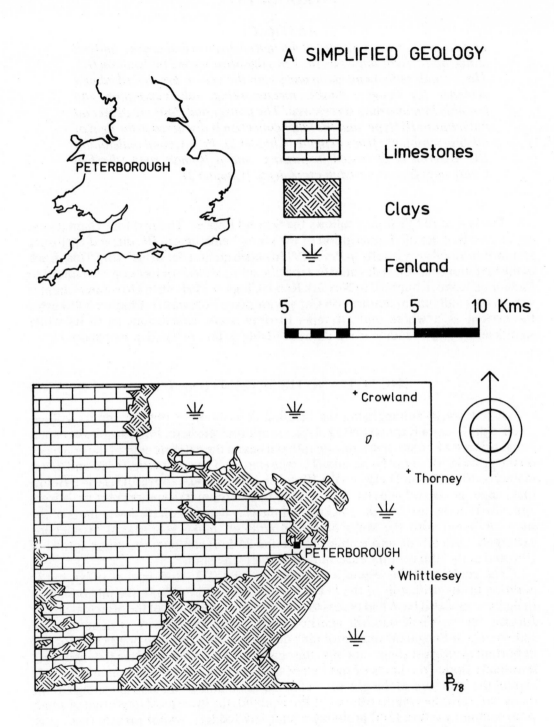

A SIMPLIFIED GEOLOGY

Limestones

Clays

Fenland

5   0   5   10 Kms

Crowland

Thorney

PETERBOROUGH

Whittlesey

Fig. 1   A simplified map of the solid geology of the Peterborough area (after Horton *et al* 1974).

The rôle of the river Nene is at last becoming evident, in large part due to the researches of Dr Robert Evans of the Soil Survey, Cambridge. Evans suggests (*pers comm* and *Durobrivae*, forthcoming) that the original course of the Nene was *south* of Whittlesey 'island' and that the Cat's Water was not one of its original courses: instead, the latter stream is seen as a man-made channel. The implications of this work are considerable, and detailed discussion must await Dr Evans's definitive publication, but the land between Fengate and Whittlesey need not be seen as a complex of watercourses associated with a major Fenland river system. Instead, large areas would have been available for conversion into, or exploitation as, summer meadowland. Whittle's (1977, FIG 4:2) view of Fengate as a riverside settlement, is probably not, therefore, altogether appropriate.

Previous work at Fengate has been discussed in the First Report (FNG 1, 29-31) and it only remains to note here that Miss Mahany's (1969) excavation of an apparently (later?) Neolithic enclosure still awaits detailed publication. Much of the G Wyman Abbott Fengate Neolithic material was illustrated by Dr Smith (1956), and some of the Beakers have been figured by Leeds (1922) and Clarke (1970). The only substantial group of second millennium material from the Abbott collection that had not been published hitherto, was the large group of domestic Beaker pottery, which is now considered in detail by Alex Gibson (Appendix 10).

A final note of explanation is required as to the labelling of the ditches in this report. The principal named ditches (ie ditches 1-10 and *i-iii*) only indicate *alignments*. Thus, the use of the term 'ditch 10' does not indicate that the ditch involved was in use at the same time, nor that it was continuous or contiguous; the label merely indicates an E-W alignment in between ditches 9 and 11 (FIGS 4 and 5).

CHAPTER 1: THE PADHOLME ROAD SUBSITE

INTRODUCTION

The Padholme Road subsite (FIG 3) was excavated in the first two seasons of the Fengate project (1971-2), before excavation methods had been standardised and before the full potential of the site as a whole had been realised. Inevitably this meant that some information was missed. For example, in the early months of the project most attention was paid to the dating of various features and the distribution of finds within those features was not recorded in detail. Every project must have such an initial, exploratory, phase — whether admitted or not — and it would be imprudent to directly compare information from this phase with that obtained during the project proper. Consequently, the reader of the following chapter should bear in mind that ditches 1-4 were excavated in the original belief that they were probably Romano-British (Taylor 1969,6) and that the prehistoric finds from their filling were therefore residual. It was not until the release of radiocarbon dates UB-676 and

Land Above 15 Metres O.D.

Watercourse

The Car Dyke

2 0 2 4 6 8 10 Kms

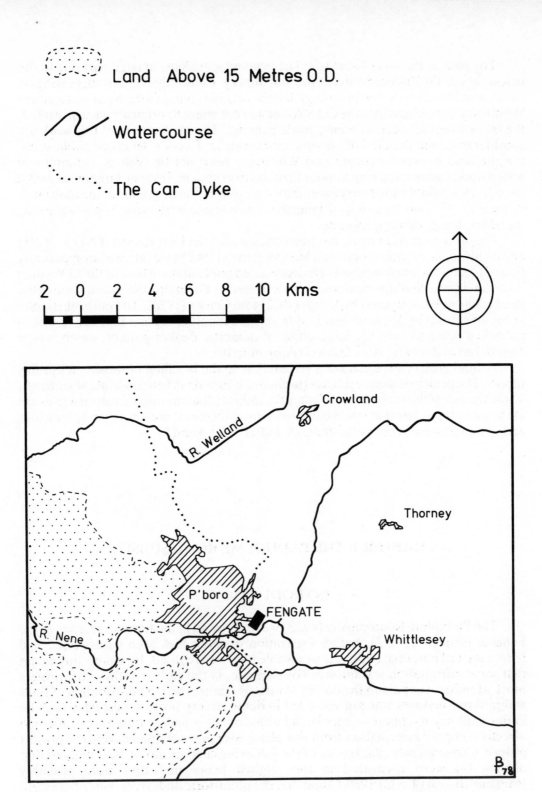

Fig. 2　　Topography of the Peterborough area; the location of FIG 3 is shown in black.

UB-677 (1280 ± 70 bc and 935 ± 135 bc respectively), at the end of the 1972 season, that the true status of these features became apparent. Clearly, no flints, nor any other finds, were discarded, but following Coles's remarks on 'conscience and confession' (1972, 230-2) it must be admitted that the methods used to recover flint and soft Bronze Age pottery were not so sophisticated as those of 1973 and subsequent seasons (FNG 2, Appendix 1). In view of these considerations, it was thought best to illustrate all retouched flints (FIG 14), diagnostic potsherds and fired clay (FIG 13), but not to attempt detailed statistical analyses.

FEATURES (PL 1)

The Padholme Road subsite is traversed from east to west by two pairs of second millennium ditches (FIG 6). The southerly pair (ditches 1 and 2) are joined to the northerly pair (3 and 4) by a slightly sinuous N-S ditch (FIG 6): both pairs of ditches have been traced east of Storey's Bar Road, in the Cat's Water subsite (FIG 5).

DITCHES 1, 2 AND ASSOCIATED FEATURES (FIG 7; PL 2)

Ditches 1 and 2 were more shallow and less regular, in plan or profile, than ditches 3 and 4 (FIG 11). Their filling was generally deposited in one layer of sand-silt, and recuts were not apparent in the stratigraphy; beneath this, a layer, up to 0.10m thick, of more sandy and gravelly rapid silting could sometimes be observed (FIG 12).

The apparent 'gap' in ditch 1 at Grid 112E/220S (FIG 7) is not thought to represent an entranceway; in this area the ditch filling and the natural sand-silt were very hard to distinguish and the ditch itself was most shallow and irregular in profile.

A much-decayed crouched inhumation (PL 4 and FIG 7, for orientation) was found at Grid 134E/219S, along the bottom of ditch 1, 14.5m east of the 'entranceway' just described. The body appears to have been that of a fully mature female (Appendix 8) who had been laid on her right side, aligned NW-SE, hard against the north side of the ditch. The left tibia and fibula were under the right femur, and the left foot lay beneath the right tibia and fibula (ie the legs were crossed); the head was to the NW. There was no trace of a dug grave and the position and alignment of the body suggest that it had simply been dumped in the ditch and, perhaps, covered with topsoil, for there was no clean sand or gravel above or beside the burial, in the ditch filling.

The large circular pit in Area X (FIG 7, F4), should be considered with ditch 1; it formed its westerly excavated extremity and probably represents a pit or well-like terminal enlargement, similar to others described in this report (Chapter 2). Unfortunately, the ditch was shallow and its filling was homogeneous sand-silt at the point where it joined F4, so a stratigraphic relationship could not be seen in longitudinal section. A N-S section across the pit showed no signs of disturbance, so it is probable, on balance, that the pit's upper filling accumulated after the abandonment and subsequent infilling of ditch 1. The spatial relationship of the two features, however, suggests that they may well have been open at the same time and that, therefore, UB-677 (935 ± 135 bc), which was taken from birch twigs found in layer 5 at the bottom of the pit (FIG 12), could represent a *terminus ante quem* for the last recut of ditch 1. There was no other reliable dating evidence from F4, except for a few scraps of soft shell-gritted pottery. The pit's filling appears to have been the result of natural processes, with waterlogged material (layer 5) sealed beneath 'rapid' edge-derived

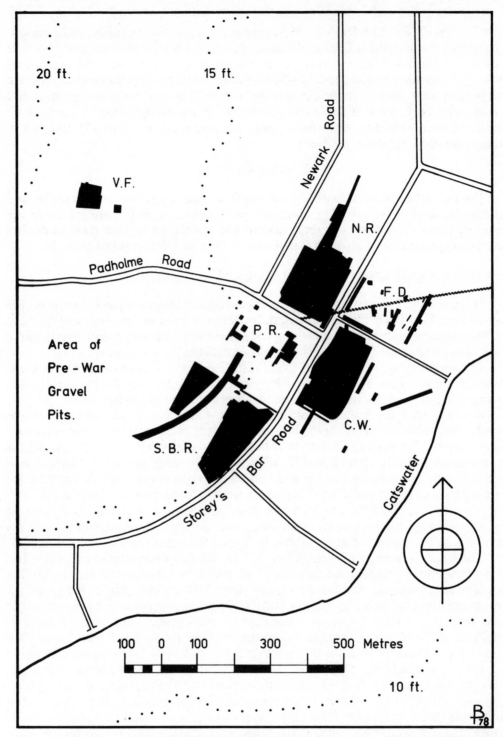

Fig. 3 Areas Excavated 1971-78. Key to subsites: VF, Vicarage Farm; NR, Newark Road; FD, Fourth Drove; PR, Padholme Road; CW, Cat's Water; SBR, Storey's Bar Road. The Fen Causeway (Roman Road) is shown by a slashed line.

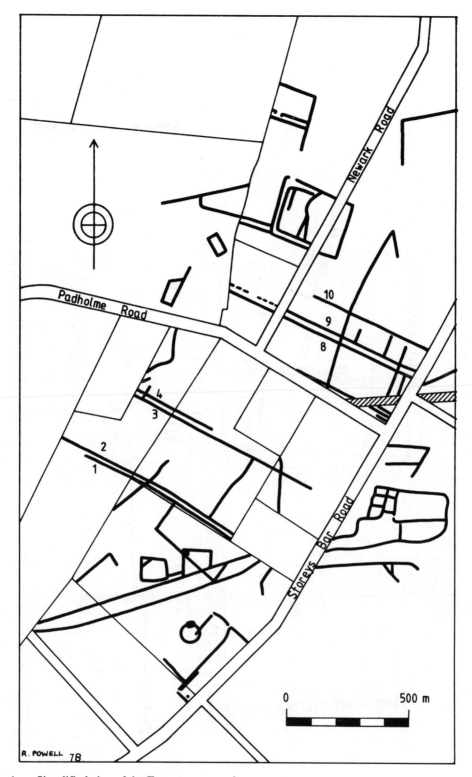

Fig. 4   Simplified plan of the Fengate cropmarks.

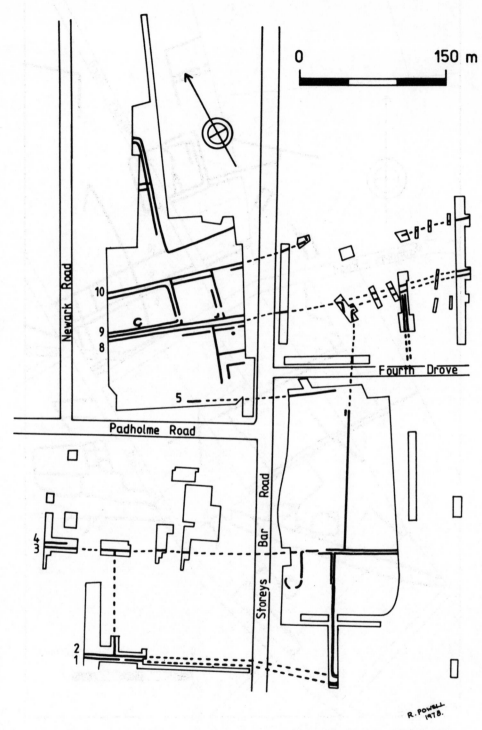

Fig. 5   Plan showing the relationship of principal excavated second millennium BC ditches.

pebbly deposits (layer 4), in turn sealed beneath the more slowly-accumulated silty upper layers (layer 2 may represent a period of stability during which turf formed). The size, shape and depth of this feature strongly suggest that it may once have been used as a well, although no woven wattle lining was found *in situ* (cf FNG 1, FIGS 18 and 19; FNG 2, PL 2). Five layers of filling could be distinguished (FIG 12):

Layer 1 Sand-silt with scattered gravel pebbles (10YR 3/3).

Layer 2 Darker sand-silt, separating layers 1 and 3 and blending evenly with them; minute charcoal flecks and small bone fragments (10YR 3/2).

Layer 3 Sand-silt with scattered gravel pebbles (10YR 4/3).

Layer 4 Sand-silt with sand and gravel, clearly distinguished from layer 3, above (10YR 4/4).

Layer 5 Waterlogged sand-silt with sand and gravel lenses, much organic matter towards bottom (10YR 4/4).

Feature 30, Area IX (FIG 7), was located 23m east of F4, also on the alignment of ditch 1. This feature also appears to have been a pit-like expansion of ditch 1, but not, in this case near a terminal. It was 0.75m deep, circular, about 2.25m in diameter and could, perhaps, have been used as a small well or water-hole, as it extended some 0.10m below the modern water table. No wattle-work or wood was found *in situ* and its homogeneous, stone-free, sand-silt filling blended evenly into that of ditch 1.

The small pit, F3, lay in the 'trackway' between ditches 1 and 2 in Area X at Grid 91E/215S (FIG 7). The filling of this feature was clearly a dumped-in deposit, for there was no 'rapid' silt and the fire-reddened, vertical sides of the pit had not collapsed, nor weathered; it was roughly oval in plan (1.20 × 0.74m), with a flat bottom (depth 0.36m). The filling consisted of blackened sand-silt, much charcoal and calcined bone fragments. Artefacts included S2/3 Beaker potsherds, a barbed and tanged arrowhead and a retouched flint flake illustrated in FNG 1, 14 and FIG 10, 1-8. This feature is best interpreted as a hearth-pit subsequently filled in with soil heavily mixed with settlement debris. It should be noted that the pottery and flint were not burnt.

Ditch 2 ran parallel to ditch 1 and approximately four metres north of it. Its homogeneous sand-silt filling was identical to that of ditch 1 (average colour 10YR 3/3) and neither ditch showed any evidence in their fillings for a collapsed or redeposited bank, either inside or outside the 'trackway' they enclosed. Ditch 2 was in general deeper and wider than ditch 1 (FIG 11) and formed a T-junction with the N-S ditch, F400, in Area IX at Grid 106E/213S. The sand-silt filling of F400 blended evenly into that of ditch 2 and there can be little doubt as to their broad contemporaneity. Aerial photographs show that the N-S ditch ran between ditches 2 and 3; it joined ditch 3 at a T-junction in Area VIII, where it was labelled F4 (FIG 9).

The wattle lined well, F6, Area IX, was located 3m NE of the junction of ditch 2 with F400 (FIG 7). It was fully described in the First Report (FNG 1, FIG 19), where it was considered, on comparative grounds (May 1970, PL XXXIa), to be of probable Iron Age date. The few scraps of pottery found in its filling (FNG 1, 25) are by no means diagnostic, but could as well be of second millennium as of Iron Age date. The principal arguments in favour of an earlier dating include its location at the junction of two major second millennium ditches and the absence of proven Iron Age features in the immediate vicinity.

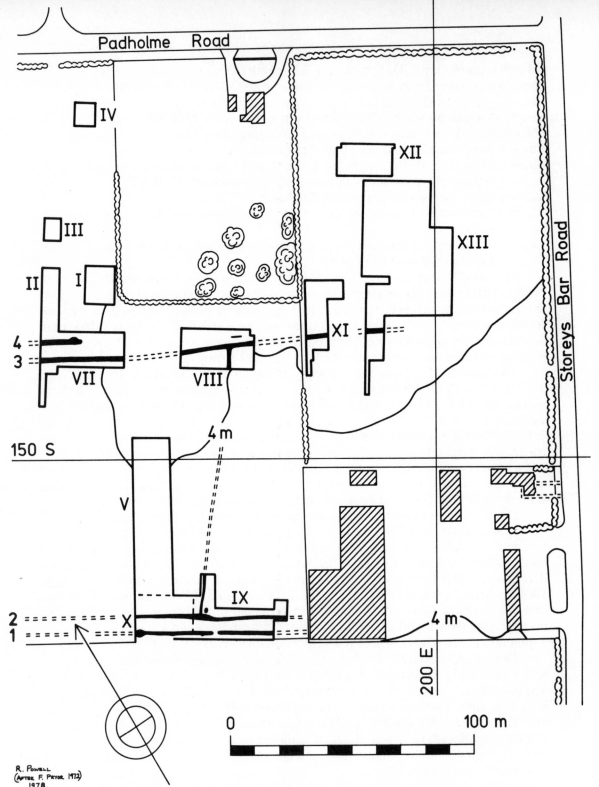

Padholme Road

IV

XII

III

XIII

II I

4
3

VII VIII XI

Storeys Bar Road

150 S

4 m

V

IX

2 X
1

4 m

200 E

0   100 m

R. POWELL
(AFTER F. PRYOR 1972)
1978

Fig. 6.   Part of the Padholme Road subsite showing the alignment of second millennium BC ditches
             1-4 (for complete plan of Padholme Road see FNG 1, FIG 3).

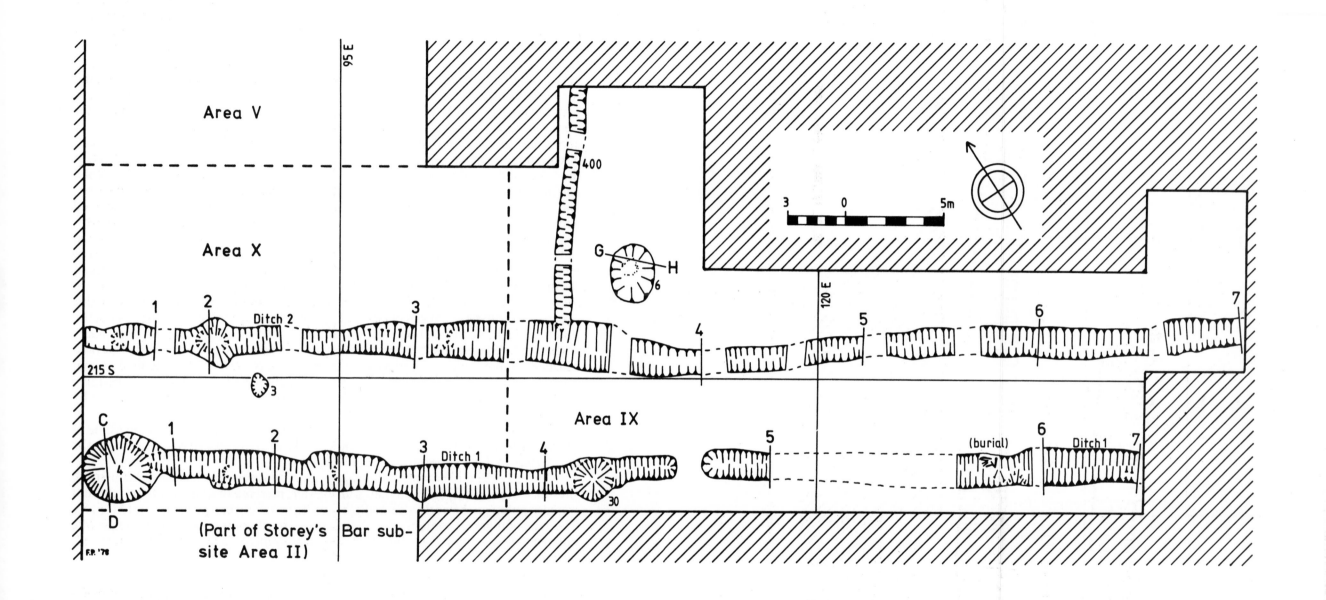

Area V

Area X

95 E

400

G○H
6

1   2   Ditch 2   3   4   120 E   5   6   7

215 S

○3

Area IX

C
1   2   3   Ditch 1   4   5   (burial)   6   Ditch 1   7
4
D   30

(Part of Storey's Bar subsite Area II)

F.P. '78

3   0   5m

Fig. 7   Padholme Road subsite, Areas IX and X: general plan (sections located in bold type).

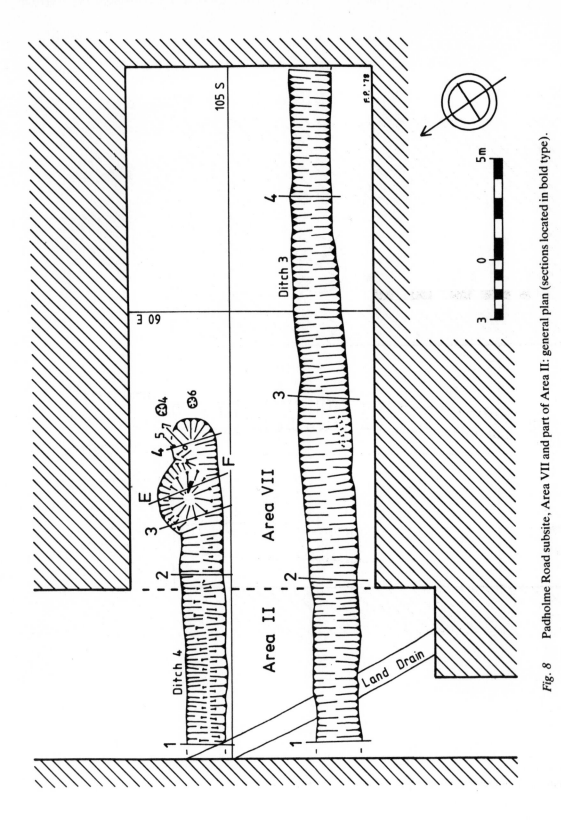

Fig. 8 Padholme Road subsite, Area VII and part of Area II: general plan (sections located in bold type).

DITCHES 3-4 AND ASSOCIATED FEATURES (FIGS 8 and 9)

Ditches 3 and 4 were more regular in profile, deeper and wider than ditches 1 and 2 (FIG 11). Ditch 3 became less substantial as it ran eastwards into Areas XI and XIII, but it still maintained its regular, open V-shaped profile. The filling of both ditches was mainly of sand-silt (layer 1), overlying a more 'rapid' layer of sand-silt with occasional gravel pebbles and lenses of sand and gravel (layer 2). Typical ditch sections are shown in FIG 11. Possible evidence for a collapsed gravel bank was rarely encountered, the two best examples being illustrated in FIG 12 (top left: layer 2; top right: the gravel lens between layers 1 and 2). Finds were generally scarce, but most of those that did occur were found in a charcoal-rich lens of ditch 3 at the bottom of layer 1, immediately above the more 'rapid' silting of layer 2. This darker horizon could be traced discontinuously in Areas II, VII and VIII, but not in the smaller Areas XI and XIII, to the east; it did not re-appear in the Cat's Water excavations east of Storey's Bar Road and may therefore be treated as a localised phenomenon. This deposit was thickest, and most concentrated, at the junction of F4 (Area VIII), the N-S ditch described above (F400, Area IX), with ditch 3. The history of this deposit is important, however, since radiocarbon sample UB-676 (1280 ± 70 bc) was taken from it (FIG 12: section A-B). The discontinuous patches of charcoal and scattered artefacts along ditch 3 are most probably derived from washed-in occupation deposits located along the edge of the ditch, probably on the south side; this material could only provide a *terminus post quem* for a late phase in the ditch's history, and, given the intensity of known Neolithic occupation at Fengate, such a date would be of little practical use. The deposit at the junction of F4 and ditch 3, however, was entirely different. It consisted of large pieces of charcoal, burnt clay daub, burnt sand-silt, minute potsherds, fire-cracked stones and calcined animal bones. The extremely fragile state of some of the calcined animal bones, particularly bones such as scapulae, together with the absence of bedding planes or silt/sand washes would argue that this deposit had been dumped in ditches F4 and 1 when they were still open.

A dark, probably washed-in, occupation horizon was also noted in the filling of ditch 4, again at the bottom of layer 1 (below 0.40m). This deposit was localised to the two metres of ditch either side of profile 2 (FIG 8).

Layer 1 of ditch 4 became increasingly sandy and gravelly, especially on the south side, east of profile 2, and a similar, but slighter, increase in gravel and sand content was also noted on the north side of ditch 3, in layer 1, between profiles 2 and 3 (FIG 8). The sand and gravel content of ditch 3, layer 1, reached its maximum in the pit-like enlargement at section E-F where the following layers could be distinguished (FIG 12, bottom):

Layer 1 Sand-silt with sand and gravel (10YR 5/8).

Layer 2 Sharp transition to layer 1, above. Sand-silt with scattered gravel pebbles (10YR 4/4).

Layer 3 Wet sand-silt with much organic matter, black staining and clay patches (*c* 10YR 3/2). A fast-grown oak log (age *c* 29 years), with clear axe-marks at one end and a V-shaped notch at the centre (PL 5), lay directly on the bottom (FIGS 15 and 12).

The interpretation of this sequence is not straightforward. Layers 2 and 3 appear to have formed as the result of natural weathering processes; the sand and stone

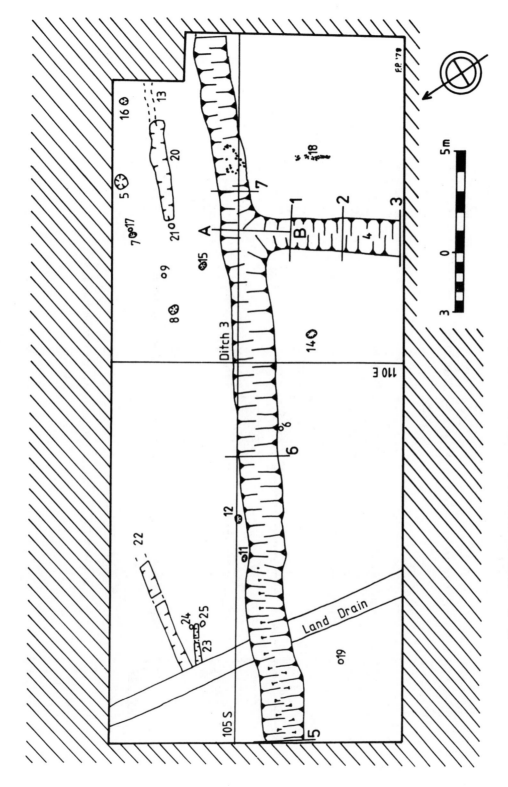

Fig. 9   Padholme Road subsite, Area VIII: general plan (sections located in bold type).

13

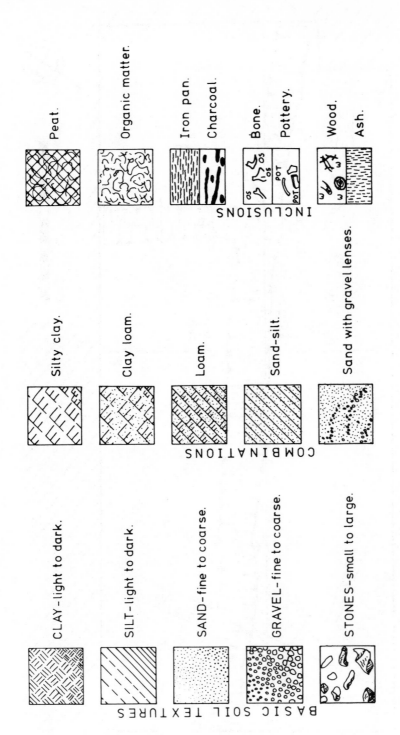

Peat.

Organic matter.

Iron pan.

Charcoal.

Bone.

Pottery.

Wood.

Ash.

INCLUSIONS

Silty clay.

Clay loam.

Loam.

Sand-silt.

Sand with gravel lenses.

COMBINATIONS

CLAY – light to dark.

SILT – light to dark.

SAND – fine to coarse.

GRAVEL – fine to coarse.

STONES – small to large.

BASIC SOIL TEXTURES

Fig. 10   Conventions used in the section drawings.

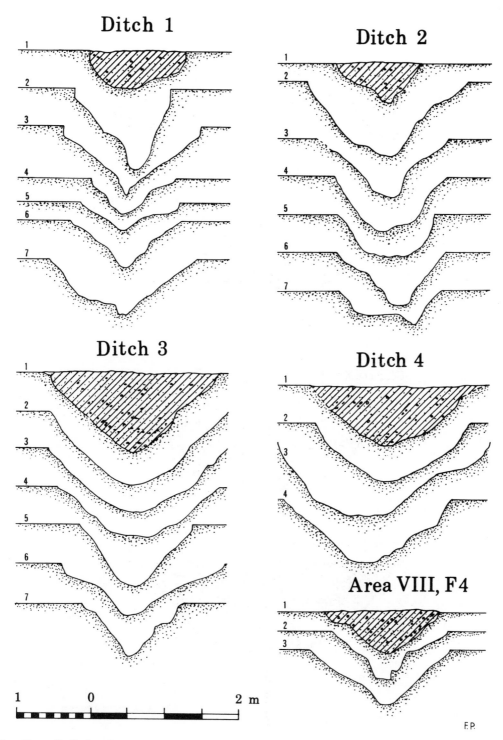

Fig. 11 Padholme Road subsite, profiles and sections: ditches 1-2 (for location see FIG 7); ditches 3-4 and F4, Area VIII (for location see FIGS 8 and 9).

Ditch 3, Area VII, Section 3

Ditch 4, Area VII, Section 1

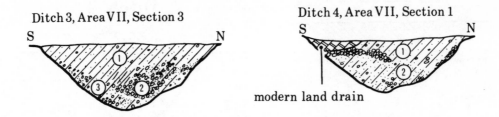

modern land drain

Junction of Ditch 3 and F4, Area VIII, Section A-B

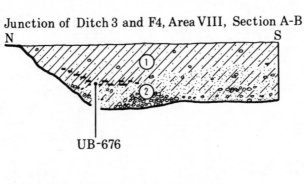

UB-676

F4, Area X (S.W.corner), Section C-D

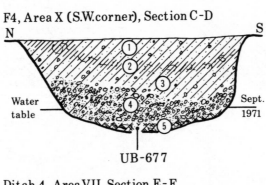

Water table

Sept. 1971

UB-677

Ditch 4, Area VII, Section E-F

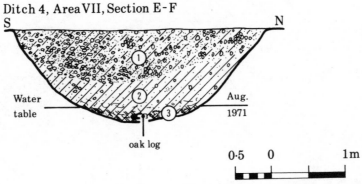

Water table

Aug. 1971

oak log

0·5   0   1m

F. P.

Fig. 12   Padholme Road subsite: selected sections through second millennium BC ditches.

16

content is low, but this could be explained by the open U-shape of the pit's sides. Layer 1, however, is anomalous; its high stone and sand content is not typical of the ditch filling sequence elsewhere, but the absence of tip lines and the even, gradually increasing pebble concentration across the layer from N to S, does not suggest backfilling. We have noted that ditch 3, immediately to the south, showed a similar, but slighter, gravel spread in layer 1, and there can be no doubt that this deposit was washed in from the north, the area of the 'trackway' between ditches 3 and 4. If we assume that the gravel spreads in both ditches were derived from the same source, then we have evidence that both ditches were open at the same time and that, moreover, most of the gravel excavated from the pit-like enlargement of ditch 4 was dumped on the 'trackway' surface, presumably as a deliberate blocking device. The closing of entranceways and droves was a common practice on the later Neolithic site (eg FNG 2, FIG 32) and on the Newark Road subsite, described in the following chapter. It is probably associated with the day-to-day management of livestock (FNG 2, 157).

The reasons for ditch 4 terminating (at Grid 55E/102S, FIG 8) are not clear, and in view of the small area stripped, speculation would be fruitless; however, it should be noted that the small ditch, F20, Area VIII (FIG 9) is on the same alignment. It was 5.10m long, 0.60m wide and about 0.40m deep; its sides were steep, its bottom flat and its filling consisted of homogeneous sand-silt with very few scattered pebbles. The short 'trackway' between F20 and ditch 3 in Area VIII was only 2.50m wide (as opposed to 4.0m at the butt of ditch 4).

Two small pits or postholes were located immediately east of the butt of ditch 4, in Area VII (FIG 8). Feature 6 produced no dating evidence, but the bottle-shaped pit F4 (diameter at surface 0.82m, depth 0.44m) had been backfilled with occupation debris including sherds of Beaker pottery (FNG1, FIG 10; 9, 10) which Clarke (pers comm) considered belonged to his S4 type (FNG 1, 14). Two small weathered Beaker bodysherds, identical in fabric to those found in F4, were found in ditch 4, layer 1, immediately next to F4. The two undated stakeholes (F5 and F7) which had been cut into the surface of ditch 4, layer 1, cannot, therefore, be related on simple stratigraphic grounds, to features 4 and 6.

Feature 18, Area VIII (Grid 120E/109S) was a linear spread of cobblestones (average diameter c 40-70mm), charcoal flecks, clay and burnt clay that had been set into the gravel to a depth of about 0.03-0.05m. It measured about 1.75 × 0.15m and ran precisely parallel to ditch F4 (FIG 9). A deposit of similar small cobblestones and charcoal flecks was found in ditch 3 immediately NE of F18 at Grid 119E/105S; this deposit lay at the intersection of layers 1 and 2 and fanned out into the centre of the ditch, such that the cobbles at the centre of the ditch lay under 0.30m of layer 1 sand-silt, whereas those on the S side were encountered at the stripped surface. The association (and contemporaneity) of F18 and the cobblestone spread in ditch 3 would seem most probable, but the function of this feature is not immediately apparent. Perhaps the cobblestones served some drainage purpose, not unlike the 'brush drain' of the Cat's Water subsite (Pryor and Cranstone 1978, PL 4).

Finally, the remaining small pits, postholes and gullies of Area VIII produced no dateable artifacts, with the exception of ditch F22 which produced a few bodysherds of probable Iron Age type. The small gully, F23, to the NW in Area VIII, could perhaps belong in the second millennium, but its filling is noticeably darker than that of ditch 3 and its alignment is not entirely consistent with other ditches of that period. Similarly, the small pit or posthole F8 (Grid 113E/102S) is on the same alignment as the ditch F20, and may, therefore, be related. The irregular shallow gully F13 which runs into F20 from the E (dashed line, FIG 9) was considered to be an animal burrow when excavated, but could, in the light of subsequent work, possibly be interpreted as a hedge bedding or rooting trench. Its alignment is certainly consistent with such an interpretation; its sides and bottom were heavily encrusted with iron-pan.

FINDS

POTTERY

CATALOGUE OF ILLUSTRATED SHERDS (FIG 13, 1-2)

1. Rimsherd of large vessel (dia 400+mm) with uneven, straight sides and roughly flattened rim. Ext light brown; int light brown/grey mottled. Fabric very hard, well fired with much shell. One side has been sawn ¾ through, after firing, and then broken (in chocolate bar fashion; section A-B in illustration). Area IX, ditch 2, layer 1.
2. Bowl with flat bottom, slightly rounded walls and simple, uneven rim; ht (max) 78 (min) 65; rim dia *c* 95; base dia *c* 90. Fabric very soft (treated with PVA), poorly fired, heavily tempered with coarsely crushed shell (Williams's fabric 1, see Chapter 2). Ext mid-brown; int black. Area IX, ditch 1, (pit-like expansion, F3), layer 1; depth 0.30m.

DISCUSSION

The pottery from ditches 1-4 was similar to that from the ditches of the Newark Road subsite, in its generally poor quality; it was often shell-tempered, and otherwise featureless. Quantities were small, even by Newark Road standards: ditch 1 (excavated length 43.3m) yielded 365gm of pottery; ditch 2 (49.2m), 205gm; ditch 3 (69.3m), 102gm and ditch 4 (16.3m), 18gm.

The two illustrated sherds are of interest, as they provide indirect evidence for salt manufacture. The large sherd (no 1) appears to have been partially sawn through and snapped off after firing, a practice that finds close parallels on prehistoric and Roman saltworks along the Dorset coast (Farrar 1975, 16). The small bowl (no 2) is the only complete vessel found in ditches of the second millennium system. It is very roughly manufactured and no attempt has been made to remove finger impressions or to shape the rim evenly. Such a simple form cannot be used for chronological comparisons, but tentative functional analogies may, perhaps, be sought. The simple, flat-bottomed bowls found on Lincolnshire coastal saltern sites, for example, are considered to have been used as moulds (Baker 1975, FIG 16, nos 4, 10). If this comparison is accepted (and it should be recalled that the dating of the Ingoldmells sites is much later than Fengate (May 1976, 155)), then the occurrence of the small bowl, the large snapped-off sherd and the scatter of briquetage, described below (all found within the same twenty metre square), may provide evidence for second millennium salt extraction. However, the absence of burnt soil, so common on most saltern sites (hence the 'Red Hills' of SE Essex), would suggest that the Fengate salterns were not in the immediate vicinity of the Padholme Road Bronze Age ditches (see Chapter 5 for a discussion). Finally, the hardness and high technical quality of the snapped-off sherd (no 1) is in sharp contrast to the general run of domestic 'Bronze Age' pottery from Fengate. In many respects it recalls the hard, well-fired wares from Billingborough Fen, Lincolnshire (Chowne 1978), and as such refutes the oft-quoted view that the softness of much domestic Bronze Age pottery is the result of technical incompetence.

FLINT

CATALOGUE OF ILLUSTRATED FLINTS (FIG 14)

1. Barbed and tangled arrowhead. Ditch 2, layer 1.
2. Short end scraper. Ditch 1, layer 1.
3. Disc scraper. Ditch 1, layer 1.
4. Short end scraper on broken flake. Ditch 1, layer 1.
5. Short end scraper. Ditch 2, layer 1.
6. Side scraper on broken flake. Ditch 2, layer 1.
7. Short end scraper. Ditch 4, layer 1.
8. Short end scraper with denticulated retouch. Ditch 2, layer 1.
9-10. Long end scrapers. Ditch 3, layer 1.
11. Piercer; worn at 'beak'; unifacial (dorsal) retouch. Ditch 3, layer 1.
12. Core fragment, probably of Clark's (1960) class A (ii). Ditch 3, layer 1.
13. Flake with both sides partially retouched and utilised, on dorsal face only. Ditch 4, layer 1.

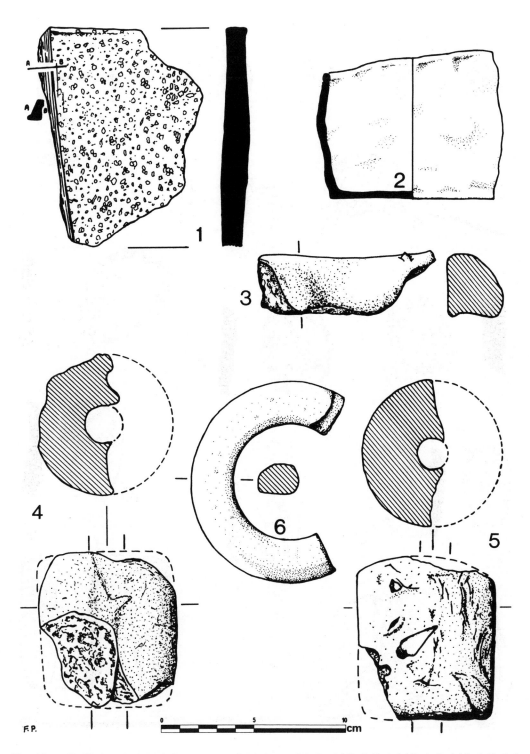

Fig. 13   Padholme Road subsite, pottery, fired clay and shale: 1 (ditch 2); 2-3 (ditch 1); 4 (ditch 2); 5-6 (ditch 1).

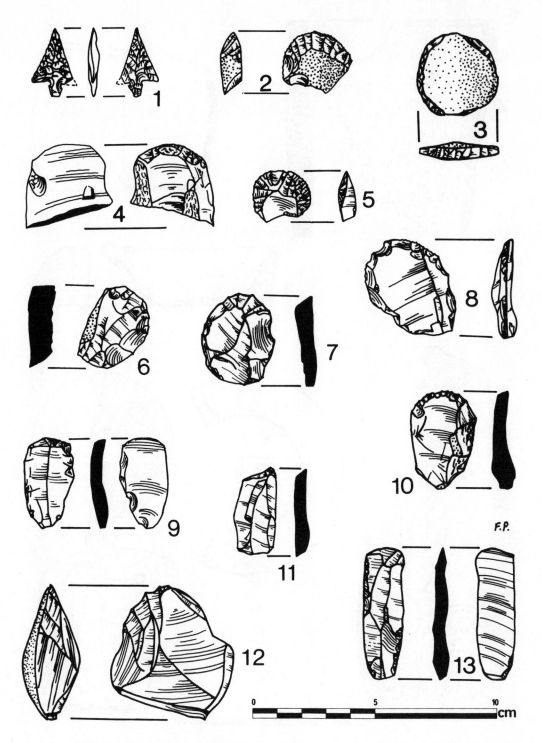

F.P.

Fig. 14 Padholme Road subsite, selected flints: 1 (ditch 2); 2-4 (ditch 1); 5-6 (ditch 2); 7 (ditch 4); 8 (ditch 2); 9-12 (ditch 3); 13 (ditch 4).

All the flint tools and by-products found appear to have been made from local gravel flint, of varying quality, and with the possible exception of the one blade-like flake (no 13), the industry would not be out of place in 'Bronze Age' contexts; the scrapers with flat edge retouch (nos 2, 4 and 5) and the barbed and tanged arrowhead are frequently found on sites of the earlier second millennium BC. The few by-products found include bashed lumps, side-struck flakes and flakes with hinge fracture, again a feature of post-Neolithic flint industries in the area and elsewhere (cf Richards 1978, 19, 'Group 4'). Further comment on the Padholme Road industry could be misleading in view of its small size, but it does not differ significantly from that analysed in greater detail in Chapter 2.

MISCELLANEOUS FINDS

FIRED CLAY (FIG 13, 3-5)

3. Six roughly-shaped fragments of untempered fired clay were found in ditch 1, layer 1, of which the largest and most diagnostic is shown here. The fabric of all pieces is identical; it contains small stones

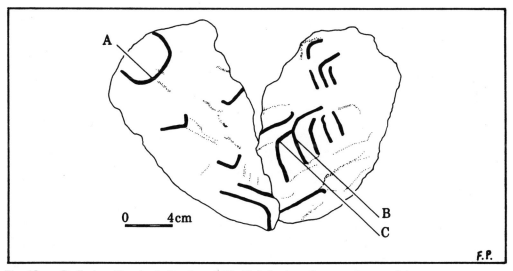

Fig. 15 Padholme Road subsite, Area VII, ditch 4: plan of axe marks on oak log.

(probably derived from the local gravel), both rounded and angular, is pale grey on the exterior (7.5YR 6/ to 5/), has a dark core and shows sign of flame-scorching. The shape and clinker-like feel of these pieces resembles that of supports or hand-bricks from Iron Age and Romano-British saltern sites from south Lincolnshire in the University Museum, Nottingham (Baker 1960). Vegetable temper has not, however, been added to the Fengate briquetage.
4. Parts of an axially-perforated cylindrical clay weight; ht 82; ext dia c 75; perforation dia 21. The clay used is poorly fired and untempered; ext colour uneven; int dark. Ditch 2, layer 1.
5. Axially-perforated cylindrical clay weight; slightly damaged; ht 86; ext dia 78; perforation dia 17. The fabric is identical to no 4, above. An end scraper is incorporated in the clay. Ditch 1, layer 1.
    Fragments of three other probable axially-perforated cylindrical clay weights were found in ditches 1 and 2. The function of these objects is briefly discussed in the next chapter.

SHALE (FIG 13, 6)

A black circular shale bracelet or pendant was found in ditch 1, layer 1, depth 0.07m. It is broken and only survives over approximately 2/3 of its original circumference; ext dia 107; width 23; thickness 16. Although now conserved, the shale was very loosely laminated when excavated, so the thickness given here may include a slight expansion factor. Surface inspection is unable to determine whether this piece has been lathe-turned or hand-cut (Calkin 1955, Radley 1969), but its early date would strongly favour the latter. It was located near a transverse baulk which showed no signs of disturbance in its upper levels, so there are strong grounds for accepting that it is contemporary with, or earlier than (unlikely, in view of its fragile state), the latest recut of the ditch in which it was found (cf Brewster 1963, FIG 66, no 4; Cunliffe and Phillipson 1968, PL VI (lower); Rahtz and ApSimon 1962, 323 and FIG 23, no 7).

WOOD (FIG 15)

The log discussed here was found in layer 3 of the pit-like enlargement of ditch 4, Area VII, described in detail above. It has been identified by Ruth Morgan (pers comm) as a log of oak (*Quercus robur/petraea*), fast grown and aged about 29 years when felled. Seventeen axe-marks were visible on the V-shaped cut end, of which three (FIG 15, A-C), were especially distinct; these showed that the log had been axed by a blade with slightly rounded corners and a width of 32mm.

CHAPTER 2: THE NEWARK ROAD SUBSITE

INTRODUCTION (FIGS 16-18)

The Newark Road subsite (FIG 3) revealed the largest and most complex arrangement of second millennium BC ditches yet excavated at Fengate. Excavations began in 1972 with a small trench (Area I) in the extreme SE corner of the subsite. This was a salvage operation carried out in advance of sewer and cable-laying works along Storey's Bar Road. The year 1974 saw the first large-scale excavation on the subsite, with the opening of Area II. This was enlarged to the north in 1975 (Area III) and the remaining areas were excavated in 1976, with the exception of the extreme north end of Area VII which was dug in the Spring of 1977.

The grid was surveyed in 1974 and follows the NE edge of Area II. Grid references are given in metres west and north.

The following chapter is arranged in two halves: features and finds. The arrangement of the first half generally follows the order in which the features were dug: thus the features of Areas I-VI, ie the features associated with enclosures A-C and 1-3 (FIG 19), are described first, working from south to north. A description of the features of Area VII occupies the latter part of the first section, which closes with a general consideration of first millennium and later features.

The finds are considered by artifact-type and, in the case of the flint, comparisons are made with other flint assemblages from Fengate. The discussion of the pottery in general follows the system adopted in the feature description.

FEATURES (FIG 18; PLS 5-7)

AREAS I-VI (FIG 19; PLS 6-8)

GENERAL

The features of Areas I-VI are divided into two 'territories' by the main E-W drove between ditches 8 and 9. Enclosures south of the drove are in general defined by smaller ditches than those to the north. An interesting element in the layout of the southern enclosures is the presence of internal droves within each enclosed area. Thus enclosure 1 is served by the subsidiary drove defined by ditches u/v and 8; enclosure 3 has the small (?) internal drove defined by ditches s and 8; enclosure 2 — if it is an enclosure — would have been served by the wide right-angled drove defined by ditches w-z.

Enclosures north of the main droveway also appear to have their internal drove system, although the status of the 'droves' defined in enclosure A by ditches g, h and 10; and in enclosure B by ditches c and 10 is not clear. Internal droves in enclosure B are defined by ditches e and f and i, j, k. Droves within enclosure C are more complicated, but are principally defined by ditches 9, n, m, a, b and 10. Enclosure C differs from others in the completeness of its surrounding internal drove and in the multiplicity of recuts visible in the smaller ditches just south of Structure 1; the presence of two structures and other settlement features also contributes to the enclosure's unique status.

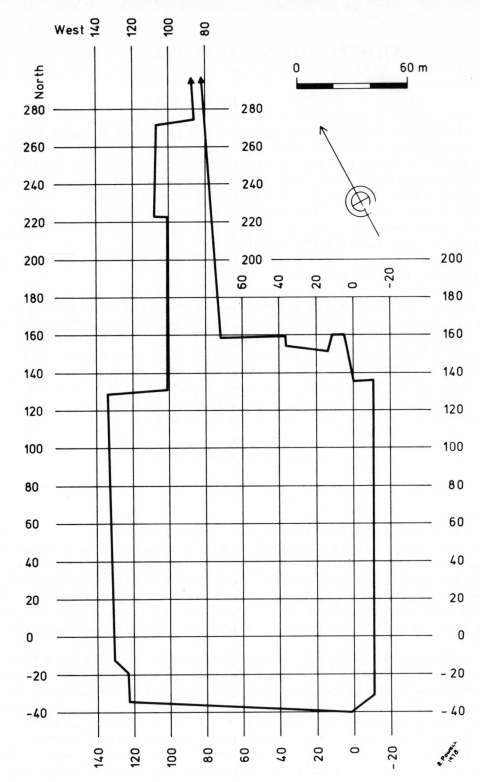

Fig. 16   Newark Road subsite: the Grid (in metres).

The well ordered rectilinear layout of these enclosures and droves strongly suggests some form of controlled planning and surveying. There is very little good evidence for extensive modification or for abandonment of different areas at various times. The whole system seems to have been in use at more or less the same time and there can be little doubt that Structures 1 and 2 were built and used after the main elements of the enclosure system had been laid out, and in use, for some time.

The detailed description of second millennium features is based on the arrangement of the ditch system. Part I considers features south of the main E-W drove and Part II treats features between ditches 9 and 10. Ditches 8, 9, 10 and features that post-date the second millennium are discussed in Parts III and IV.

1. FEATURES SOUTH OF MAIN E-W DROVE

1. DITCHES 5-7 (FIG 4)

These three ditches show up clearly on Professor St Joseph's aerial photographs as cropmarks underlying the Roman road — the Fen Causeway — which traverses the extreme southern corner of the subsite from NE to SW. Trench I, which was excavated under salvage conditions, was opened in order to date these features more closely. The results of this work were, however, somewhat ambiguous. Only two linear ditches of the size and orientation suggested by the air photographs were discovered and both of these contained coarse, shell-gritted 'scored' Iron Age pottery. They are probably best seen, therefore, in the contexts of the Iron Age settlement of the Cat's Water subsite, perhaps as outlying drains or boundary ditches (Pryor and Cranstone 1978). The picture was further complicated by disturbance associated with gravel scoops on either side of the Roman road which made the differentiation of pre-Roman features most difficult. In addition, modern surface water drains alongside Storey's Bar Road had cut into the gravel and the whole disturbed area had been thickly blanketed with flood clays, probably laid down in the third century AD (Pryor and Cranstone 1978, 13). The absence of ditch 5, which must have run well to the south of the two ditches just described, is hardly surprising, therefore.

Ditches 6 and 7 do not belong to the second millennium enclosure system considered in this report. The evidence for ditch 5, is however, much better. The short length (c 22.1m — FIG 5) of ditch 5 in Area V was located in an area much disturbed by flood deposits and activity associated with the Fen Causeway, so a reliable section or profile could not be obtained. Its filling, however, was pale and free from clay, like other second millennium features on the subsite, and there seemed no good reason to doubt that it formed part of the main ditch system. The strongest argument for such an attribution, however, lies in its precise alignment on a well-dated E-W ditch at the extreme NW corner of the Cat's Water subsite (FIG 5). The short length of ditch at the extreme S of the excavated area (Area V) is on the correct alignment for ditch 5, but cannot be defined or dated with any precision owing to post-depositional disturbance.

2. DITCHES W, X, Y, Z (FIG 19)

Ditches w-z enclosed a short length (c 30m N-S; c 39m E-W) of L-shaped droveway noticeably wider (c 11m) than other droves of the system. It was entered laterally by at least two clearly defined entranceways, one 2.2m wide between ditches w and x, and another, 1.6m wide, between ditches z and t. These entrances gave access

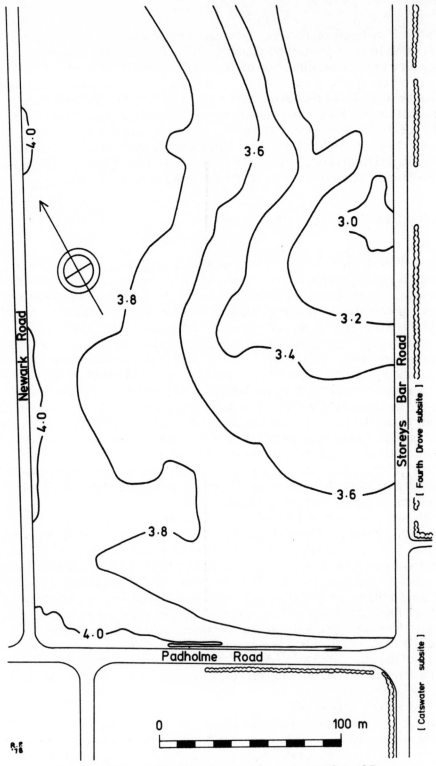

Fig. 17 Newark Road subsite, south half: surface contours in metres above OD.

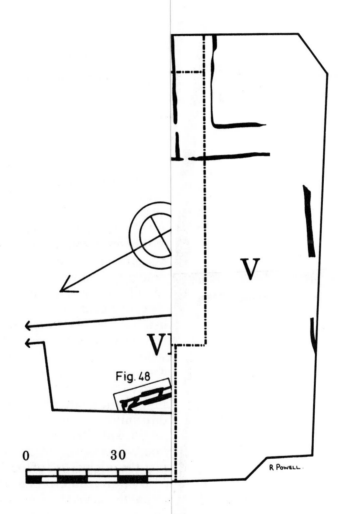

V

VI

Fig. 48

0   30

R Powell

to enclosures 1 and 3. Access to the possible enclosure 2 was probably provided by an entranceway, of similar width to those just mentioned, which was located in ditch *y* about 5m from the edge of the excavated area. This entranceway appeared to have been blocked by a smaller ditch in a manner frequently encountered elsewhere on the subsite (eg FIG 25); this area, however, was so extensively disturbed by subsequent flooding, that ditch *y* could not be traced across Area I.

All four ditches were of similar width, depth and open U-shaped profile and all, too, had been disturbed by flood action and/or Roman road building work. Width was typically 0.8-1.0m; depth varied between 0.2 and 0.5m and the usual homogeneous sand-silt (average colour 10YR 4/3) comprised the filling. There was no evidence for recutting in the ditches' stratigraphy, although the possible entranceway in ditch *y* strongly suggests that this took place, and evidence for slipped gravel banks was nowhere clear-cut. Again, it should be emphasised that flooding and post-depositional disturbance make any firm conclusions difficult.

3. THE WELL AND ENCLOSURE 1 (FIG 19)

Enclosure 1 is located immediately north of the drove defined by ditches *w-z*, just described, and is separated from the main E-W drove (defined by ditches 8 and 9), by a parallel, subsidiary drove to the south, defined by ditches 8 and *u/v*. The latter drove is approximately 1.6-2.0m wide and has an excavated length of 41m. Its NW end is blocked off by ditch *t* which is very slightly (*c* 0.05m) deeper NE of ditch *u*, suggesting, perhaps, that the length of ditch blocking the droveway could be later, or more recut, than the remainder of the ditch along the NW side of enclosure 1. The two points where ditches *t* and 8, and *t* and *u* intersect were stratigraphically obscure.

Ditch *u* was a continuation, to the NW, of ditch *v*. The gap between the two ditches was 2.8m wide and must have formed a convenient entranceway into enclosure 1 and the well nearby. Access from the main drove, defined by ditches 8 and 9, to the well and enclosure 1, would have been provided by an entranceway through ditch 8, immediately north of the gap between ditches *u* and *v* (FIG 20). Evidence for such an entrance is provided by the slight narrowing of ditch 8 at this point and by the distribution of finds immediately SW of this slight constriction (FIG 25). The filling of ditch 8 was very homogeneous at this point, so little could be learned from simple stratigraphy; but the constriction, and the distribution of finds at the point where the ditch became slightly deeper (compare FIG 25 with 20), suggest that an original entranceway, *c* 2.8m wide, had been cut through a narrower ditch (width 1.0m), and that this had been allowed to silt up, whereupon the original line of the ditch, SW of the gap, had been recut. This may, perhaps, be an over-interpretation of the finds' distribution, but the large numbers of finds from the sieved half-metre of ditch to the SW of the blocked entranceway, reflects the general increase in finds' density at this point. The fact that the finds' density does not increase on the other side of the blocked entranceway might suggest that the ditch deposits on either side are not contemporary. Again, the two sieved half-metres, NW of the blocked entranceway, tend to reflect the slighter distribution of finds in this area. Finally, although the evidence is slight, the increase in finds' density in ditch 8, immediately SW of ditch *i*, could perhaps indicate the position of the other side of the late recut entranceway; if this idea is accepted, the late entranceway from the main drove, measured between the two finds' concentrations in ditch 8, would be about 16m wide.

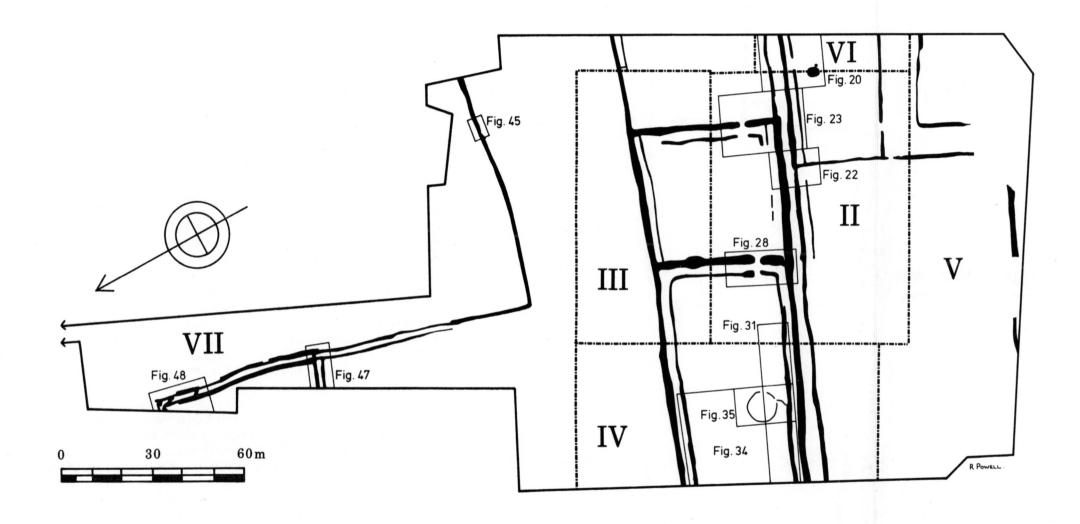

Fig. 18   Newark Road subsite: general plan of second millennium BC ditches.

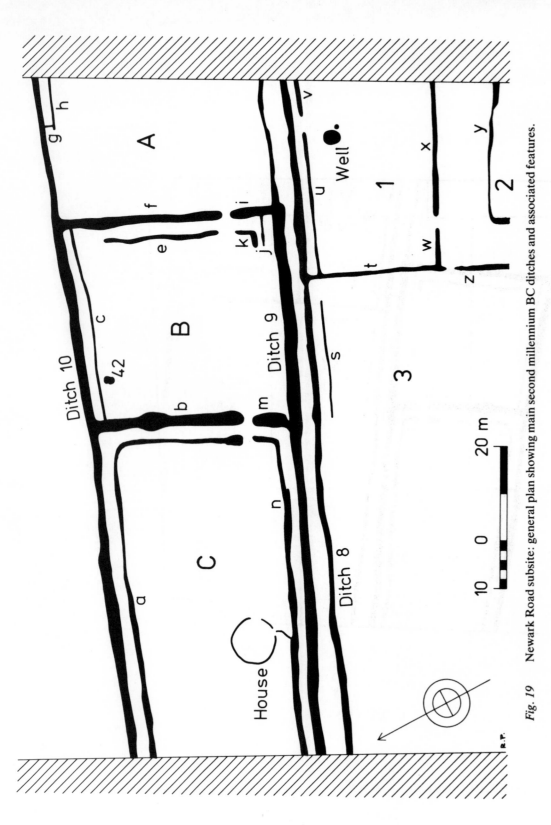

Fig. 19   Newark Road subsite: general plan showing main second millennium BC ditches and associated features.

to enclosures 1 and 3. Access to the possible enclosure 2 was probably provided by an entranceway, of similar width to those just mentioned, which was located in ditch *y* about 5m from the edge of the excavated area. This entranceway appeared to have been blocked by a smaller ditch in a manner frequently encountered elsewhere on the subsite (eg FIG 25); this area, however, was so extensively disturbed by subsequent flooding, that ditch *y* could not be traced across Area I.

All four ditches were of similar width, depth and open U-shaped profile and all, too, had been disturbed by flood action and/or Roman road building work. Width was typically 0.8-1.0m; depth varied between 0.2 and 0.5m and the usual homogeneous sand-silt (average colour 10YR 4/3) comprised the filling. There was no evidence for recutting in the ditches' stratigraphy, although the possible entranceway in ditch *y* strongly suggests that this took place, and evidence for slipped gravel banks was nowhere clear-cut. Again, it should be emphasised that flooding and post-depositional disturbance make any firm conclusions difficult.

3. THE WELL AND ENCLOSURE 1 (FIG 19)

Enclosure 1 is located immediately north of the drove defined by ditches *w-z*, just described, and is separated from the main E-W drove (defined by ditches 8 and 9), by a parallel, subsidiary drove to the south, defined by ditches 8 and *u/v*. The latter drove is approximately 1.6-2.0m wide and has an excavated length of 41m. Its NW end is blocked off by ditch *t* which is very slightly (*c* 0.05m) deeper NE of ditch *u*, suggesting, perhaps, that the length of ditch blocking the droveway could be later, or more recut, than the remainder of the ditch along the NW side of enclosure 1. The two points where ditches *t* and 8, and *t* and *u* intersect were stratigraphically obscure.

Ditch *u* was a continuation, to the NW, of ditch *v*. The gap between the two ditches was 2.8m wide and must have formed a convenient entranceway into enclosure 1 and the well nearby. Access from the main drove, defined by ditches 8 and 9, to the well and enclosure 1, would have been provided by an entranceway through ditch 8, immediately north of the gap between ditches *u* and *v* (FIG 20). Evidence for such an entrance is provided by the slight narrowing of ditch 8 at this point and by the distribution of finds immediately SW of this slight constriction (FIG 25). The filling of ditch 8 was very homogeneous at this point, so little could be learned from simple stratigraphy; but the constriction, and the distribution of finds at the point where the ditch became slightly deeper (compare FIG 25 with 20), suggest that an original entranceway, *c* 2.8m wide, had been cut through a narrower ditch (width 1.0m), and that this had been allowed to silt up, whereupon the original line of the ditch, SW of the gap, had been recut. This may, perhaps, be an over-interpretation of the finds' distribution, but the large numbers of finds from the sieved half-metre of ditch to the SW of the blocked entranceway, reflects the general increase in finds' density at this point. The fact that the finds' density does not increase on the other side of the blocked entranceway might suggest that the ditch deposits on either side are not contemporary. Again, the two sieved half-metres, NW of the blocked entranceway, tend to reflect the slighter distribution of finds in this area. Finally, although the evidence is slight, the increase in finds' density in ditch 8, immediately SW of ditch *i*, could perhaps indicate the position of the other side of the late recut entranceway; if this idea is accepted, the late entranceway from the main drove, measured between the two finds' concentrations in ditch 8, would be about 16m wide.

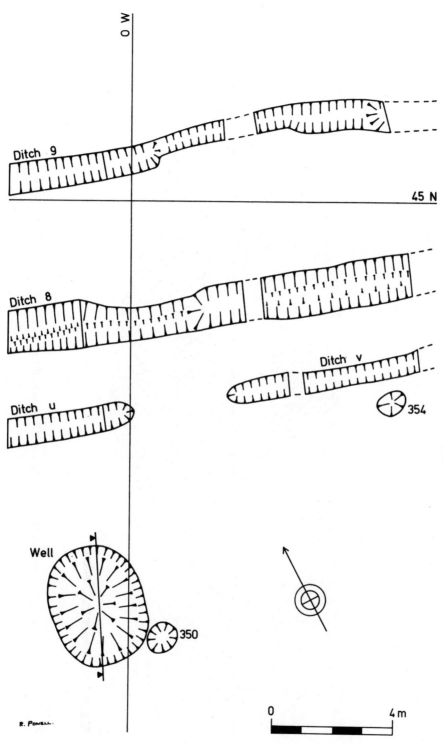

O W

Ditch 9

45 N

Ditch 8

Ditch V

Ditch U

354

Well

350

R. POWELL.

0   4 m

Fig. 20   Newark Road subsite, Areas II and VI: plan of features in the vicinity of the well.

29

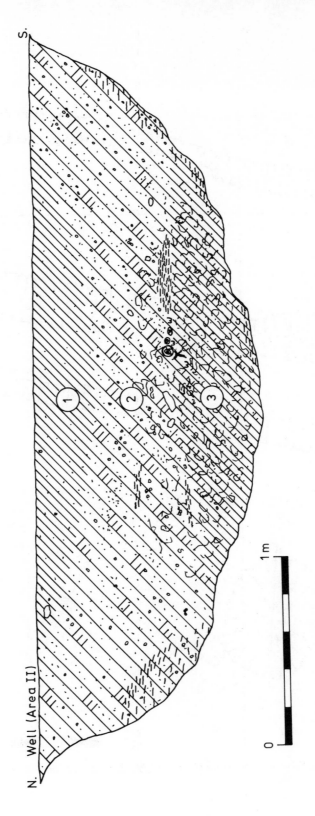

Fig. 21   Newark Road subsite, Area II: section through the well (for location see FIG 20).

The ditches that surrounded enclosure 1 were of similar size, filling and profile to ditches *w-z*, described above. Ditch *v* ran out of the excavated area and was 7.5m long and *c* 0.7m wide; ditch *u* was 15m long and less regularly dug than ditch *v*: its width varied between *c* 1.0 and 0.4m; ditch *t* was 15m long and *c* 0.8m wide (FIG 22); ditches *w* and *x* were more disturbed than the others and have been described above. With the exception of the NE extension of ditch *t*, discussed above, there was no evidence, either in the distribution of finds, or in the stratigraphy, to suggest major episodes of re-digging in any of these ditches. Profiles were open U-shaped, fillings were of homogeneous sand-silt with scattered gravel pebbles (average colour 10YR 4/3) and depths usually varied with width, such that the depth was half the width. This 'law' was seen to hold true for most of the shallower second millennium ditches on the Newark Road, Fourth Drove and Cat's Water subsites; but below depths of about 0.5m regularities were less readily observed. The depth to width ratio of a naturally weathered ditch profile, on a gravel site, will, of course, be a reflection of the gravel's angle of repose (discussed in Horton *et al* 1974, 70).

Only three features within enclosure 1 could be placed in the second millennium BC with any confidence. A shallow (0.13m), dished-profile oblong pit (1.0 × 0.7m), F354, was located at Grid 9E/38N (FIG 20). Its filling was of homogeneous sand-silt and scattered gravel pebbles and it contained three flints and shell-gritted pottery of Dr Williams's Fabric 1. Its location, alongside ditch *v*, and its soft, shell-gritted pottery, tend to suggest a second millennium BC date. Feature 350 was located immediately S of the well, at Grid 1E/30N. Like F354, it was a shallow pit (depth 0.32m), approximately circular (dia 1.07m), with dished sides and a homogeneous sand-silt filling (10YR 3/3) and scattered gravel pebbles. Two fresh flint flakes were found, but there was no pottery. Its dating rests with its location immediately alongside the well. The well itself, however, can be dated with greater precision.

The feature known here as the well was located on the boundary of Areas II and VI (F26 and 355 respectively), at Grid 1W/32N. A N-S section revealed the following stratigraphy (FIG 21):

Layer 1. Sand-silt with scattered gravel pebbles in an even, homogeneous mix (10YR 3/3).

Layer 2. Sand-silt with scattered gravel pebbles and few gravel lenses; blends gradually into layers 1, above, and 3, below (10YR 3/2). Some iron-pan and clay.

Layer 3. Sand-silt with very few gravel pebbles, twigs and other organic matter, iron-pan and charcoal flecks (10YR 2.5/1). The organic matter is most concentrated towards the centre of this layer.

Although no traces of a wattlework lining survived (*c* FNG 1, PL 6; FNG 2, PL 2), the depth and shape of this feature are most distinctive and its original use as a well seems in little doubt. The 'slow', homogeneous, largely sand-silt filling must have accumulated as the result of natural weathering and the latest finds within it therefore provide a *terminus ante quem* for its abandonment. The two sherds of Late Bronze/Early Iron Age type (FIG 61, nos 40-41) were found in layers 2 and 3 (depth 0.57 and 0.84m respectively) and probably found their way into the feature shortly after its last period of use. The more than usually open U-shaped profile of this well might perhaps suggest that it had been gradually enlarged, probably as the result of continuous use over many centuries, as the natural gravel was not noticeably looser at this point than elsewhere on the subsite.

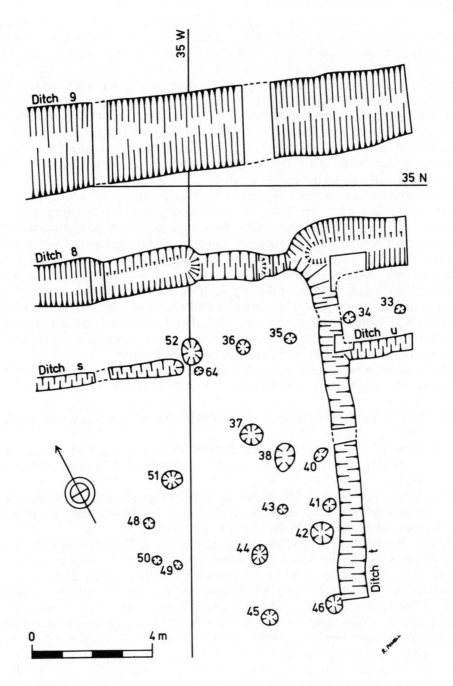

Fig. 22   Newark Road subsite, Area II: features at north-east corner of enclosure 3.

4. ENCLOSURE 3 AND ASSOCIATED FEATURES (FIGS 18 and 22)

This rather enigmatic, large enclosure can be defined with reasonable certainty on only two of its sides; to the SW, the two much disturbed lengths of ditch 5 form a southern boundary, which, if it is accepted, would make the enclosure about 66m wide. Its SE boundary is formed by ditches z and t, described in detail above, but its NW boundary was not discovered; it must, however, be over 101m long. Its northern boundary is formed by ditches s and 8. Ditch s is about 25m long; its eastern end is rounded and definite (FIG 19), but its western end is gradual and indistinct. The ditch is nowhere deeper than about 0.3m and is usually much shallower (c 0.1m); its width is fairly even (c 0.4m) and its sides, insofar as they can be clearly determined, are steep. Its filling was of homogeneous sand-silt with scattered gravel pebbles. This feature is clearly not a land boundary in its own right and seems far too slight to have been used as even a small hedge bank quarry. It would seem most probable, therefore, that the trench itself was used for bedding a hedge; this might explain why the ditch peters out to the west.

Apart from its NE corner, described shortly, enclosure 3 was devoid of second millennium BC features. It should again be emphasised, however, that the southern part of the subsite was low-lying and considerably disturbed by flooding and other subsequent activity (FIG 17). Too much significance should not be attached to such negative evidence, especially in view of the slight nature of the settlement features revealed in Area IV (described below).

The principal area of activity in enclosure 3 seems to have been in the extreme NE corner (FIG 22). At this point ditch 8 was pierced by an entranceway about 2.8m wide; this was then narrowed by a slighter ditch to a gap of just 1m in width (the stratigraphy, however, was not at all clear and the sequence could be *vice versa*). The gaps of the first two phases, whatever their order, were finally blocked by a shallow, off-centre recut (0.3m deep, 0.3m wide) which was clearly visible in the entranceway area, but which became rapidly indistinguishable to the west; it could be followed for about 10m to the east.

The non-linear features in the NE portion of enclosure 3 formed three distinct groups (Table 1). A group of five postholes (nos 33-36 and 52) formed a row just 10°N, off the alignment of ditch s. They seemed to respect the presence of ditch u, but not the northerly extension of ditch t where it blocks the E-W drove (defined by ditches u and 8). A chronological explanation for this apparently sequential layout may seem the most probable, but the broad contemporaneity of the posthole alignment and the linear ditches seems in little doubt. A row of three postholes (37, 44, 45) is aligned on posthole 36, of the E-W row just described, and at an angle of 100° to the SW. This row of postholes runs precisely parallel to ditch t, perhaps to form some kind of temporary 'drove' 2.2m wide. The pottery from F37 (FIG 60, nos 35-38) finds its closest parallels among domestic wares of the Neolithic/Bronze Age transition (see below, this chapter) and the large posthole F52 yielded a large rimsherd of Collared Urn type (FIG 58, no 21). This slight ceramic evidence, together with the better evidence of their spatial arrangement, suggests that the two posthole rows are contemporary with each other and, most probably, with the ditch system as well. The small pit, F37, gave a radiocarbon date (HAR-774) of 2030 ± 100 bc.

The third element in the posthole scatter consists of a possible four-post structure (nos 42, 44-46) at the southern end of the NE-SW posthole row. Clearly this arrangement is hard to explain, as its layout is not altogether satisfactory. It would perhaps be feasible to reject F42, in view of its larger size and slightly off-centre location, and instead to posit an arrangement in which postholes 45 and 46 form possible gateposts at the head of the temporary drove suggested above.

The fourth element consists of postholes arranged in an amorphous group around the centre of the NE-SW 'drove' (nos 40-3, 48-9, 50-1). The strict contemporaneity of this group of postholes and the 'drove' is clearly impossible, but some degree of chronological association seems, on the whole, probable. Finally, the stakehole F64 could, on grounds of alignment, be associated in some way with ditch s.

TABLE 1

Newark Road subsite, Area II: dimensions of non-linear features in the NE corner of enclosure 3 (*all measurements in mm*).

Number	Diameter	Depth
33	450	300
34	400	120
35	370	200
36	500	220
37	700	200
38	760	250
40	450	c200
41	440	170
42	750	400
43	350	75
44	560	340
45	590	400
46	c600	450
48	400	120
49	330	100
50	350	190
51	580	300
52	690	400
64	300	120

II. FEATURES BETWEEN DITCHES 9 AND 10

1. ENCLOSURE A AND ASSOCIATED FEATURES (FIGS 19, 23 and 25)

Enclosure A is the most easterly of the three enclosures north of the main drove. It is defined to the north by ditch 10, with ditches g and j; to the west by ditches f and i, and to the south by ditch 9. Its western side lies beyond the limits of the excavated area. Its width is approximately 47m.

The filling of ditch 9 in the vicinity of enclosure A was, unfortunately, entirely homogeneous and evenly coloured; this meant that vertical stratigraphy would not unravel its stages of development. The problem had, therefore, to be approached from a different point of view. First, the surface plan of the ditch strongly suggests at least three phases and the distribution of finds gives some indication as to their sequence. Phase plans, however, have not been drawn as these would tend to give the interpretation offered here greater weight than it warrants. It is also especially

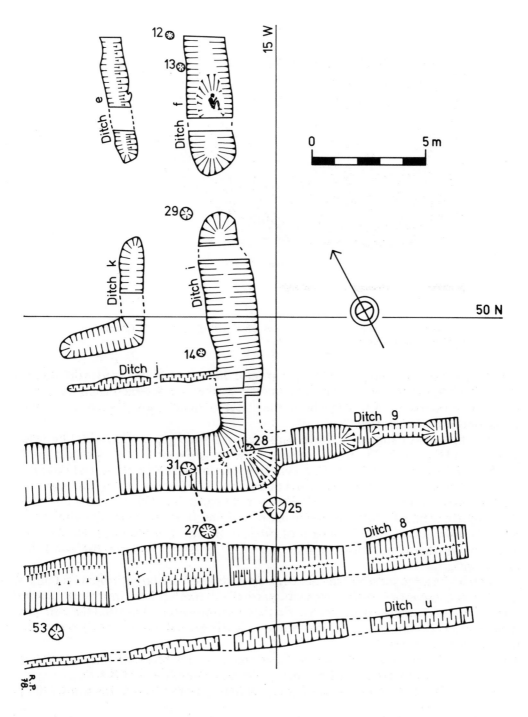

Fig. 23   Newark Road subsite, Area II: detailed plan of ditches at the south-east corner of enclosure B and the main E-W drove (ditches 8 and 9).

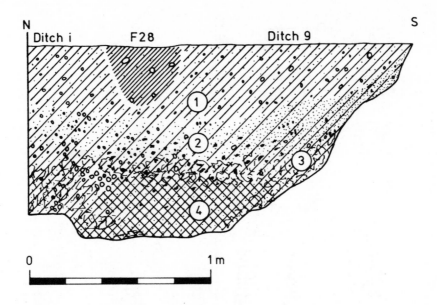

Fig. 24   Newark Road subsite, Area II: section at junction of ditches *i* and 9 (posthole F28 is part of a later four-post structure — see FIG 44).

important to resist the temptation to synchronise the sequence observed in ditch 8 with that of ditch 9, below. At present the sequence worked out for each ditch is relative, and there is no means of telling whether the developments took place over months, years, decades or centuries.

The first phase appears to have consisted of a wide gap (*c* 21m wide) between points A and E (FIG 25). During the second phase the gap was blocked by a short length (*c* 9.5m) of ditch between C and D, leaving narrow entranceways between D and E (*c* 5.0m) and A and C (*c* 6.5m). The final phase sees the blocking of the two gaps by a narrow, discontinuous trench which does not appear to have involved the complete recutting of existing ditches. The last phase post-dates the reduction of the width of the westerly entranceway by the length of ditch A-B, but it is not clear whether this extension was dug at the same time as the ditch C-D, or later. The gap at B-C is only two metres wide.

Ditch 9 became substantially deeper west of its intersection with ditch *i* at point A (FIG 25). A transverse section across the centre of this intersection from north to south showed that both ditches were open when they were abandoned and that the four-post structure (FIG 23) was clearly cut into the completely filled ditch. The section revealed the following layers (FIG 24):

Layer 1.   Even mix of sand-silt with scattered gravel pebbles. Slightly more stony towards layer 2, with which it blended smoothly (10YR 4/3).

Layer 2.   Sand-silt with scattered gravel pebbles; more sandy to the south (10YR 4/4).

Layer 3.   Sand-silt with scattered gravel pebbles, sand and iron-pan; located between layers 2 and 4, to the S (10YR 2.5/1).

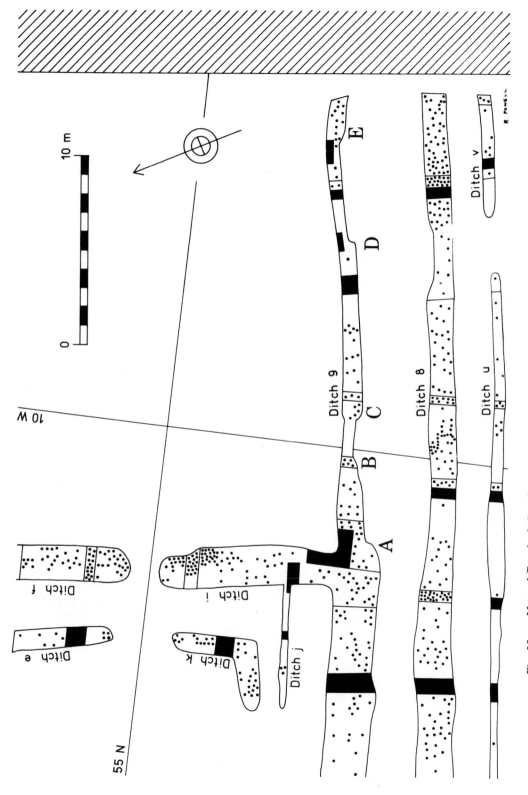

Fig. 25   Newark Road subsite: plan showing distribution of finds in south-easterly ditches. Baulks are shown in black. Finds' locations in sieved half-metres of ditch are approximate only.

37

Layer 4.   Peaty organic material with numerous twigs, semi-rotten leaves etc; scattered gravel pebbles and a fairly high sand content (10YR 4/1?). Heavy iron-pan immediately on bottom.

Feature 28.   This posthole was cut into layer 1, above. Its filling was of sand-silt with scattered gravel pebbles and large quantities of charcoal which had not been burned *in situ* (10YR 3/2). The even mix of this filling and the steep angle of the feature's sides (bearing in mind they were cut into very soft ditch fill) suggest that this deposit had been dumped into the empty posthole.

The droveway formed by ditches *e, f, i, j, k,* although strictly speaking within enclosure B, is best described at this point. It is *c* 34m long, from NE to SW and *c* 2.4m wide. It is pierced by an entranceway *c* 9m NE of ditch 9; this entranceway is 1.6m wide between ditches *f* and *i*, and 3.1m wide between ditches *k* and *e*. Both entrances are arranged about the same E-W axis and accurately aligned. There can be little doubt as to their general contemporaneity. The droveway passes through a right-angle at its intersection with ditch 9, at which point it appears to have been deliberately narrowed by the small, irregular ditch *j*. Ditches *j* and *k* butt together 6.6m NE of ditch *i*. Ditch *j* was faint, irregular and shallow (0.3m-0.1m), but its rounded termination was clear. Its relationship to ditch *i*, however, could not be determined, although it certainly did not continue SW of the latter ditch. An extremely indistinct length of ditch, which was too faint to be excavated, was observed on the same alignment as ditch *j*, about 15m to the W (FIG 18). This tiny ditch, like ditches *s, g* and *h* might well have been used as a hedge bedding trench.

An irregular row of postholes (from N-S, nos 12, 13, 29, 14) could possibly be interpreted as the remains of a fence or palisade, but apart from their rough alignment along the western edge of ditches *i* and *f*, there is little to recommend this hypothesis. They are best seen as the southern extension of the demonstrably later group of postholes discussed at greater length below (FIG 44).

The distribution of finds is of some interest, as it shows a significant concentration in ditches *i* and *f* on either side of the entranceway. Finds in the N-S length of ditch *k* tend towards the inside of the droveway, but those in ditches *i* and *f* are strongly concentrated towards the outside. It is difficult to say whether this patterning is the result of different areas of activity — in the case of ditches *i* and *f* this would be in enclosure A — or of off-centre recutting. The problem is that the upper layers of the deeper second millennium ditches on the Newark Road subsite are remarkably uniform in composition and rarely show details of stratigraphy clearly. The slight rise and fall in the interface of layers 1 and 2 in the illustrated section of ditch *f* (FIG 26) could indicate the sort of shallow recutting that would tend to distort finds' distribution plans (this is a fine example of Schiffer's (1976) c-transforms). The crouched inhumation, described below, was located immediately north of the sieved half-metre baulk at the S end of ditch *f* (FIG 25) and the finds' distribution shows no signs of disturbance in this area. This would strongly support the hypothesis, advanced below, that the burial took place at an early stage in the ditch's history.

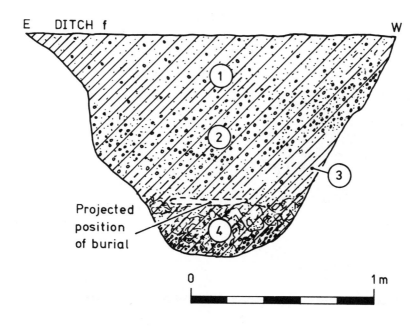

E   DITCH f   W

Projected
position
of burial

0   1 m

Fig. 26   Newark Road subsite, Area II: section through ditch *f* at Grid 17W/59N, immediately S of the
              inhumation (FIG 27).

The section of ditch *f*, taken immediately S of the burial (FIG 23) showed the
following sequence (FIG 26):

Layer 1. Sand-silt with scattered gravel pebbles and a few gravel lenses towards the
layer 2 interface (10YR 4/3)

Layer 2. Sand-silt with gravel lenses and some iron-pan (10YR 5/3).

Layer 3. Sand-silt with sand, gravel lenses and iron-pan (10YR 4/2). This layer
contained the crouched skeleton (described below). It lay at the bottom of
layer 3, separated from layer 4 by 0.02-0.03m of sand-silt and gravel pebbles.
Iron-pan had formed over the bones and there was no sign of a grave having
been cut through ditch layers 1 or 2. Charcoal pieces from the immediate
vicinity of the body gave a C-14 date (HAR-780) of 1900 ± 120 bc. This
provides a *terminus post quem* for the burial.

Layer 4. Gravel with peaty organic matter overlying sand and gravel lenses with
iron-pan; natural bedding or sinking lines were visible (these could also,
perhaps, represent tip-lines).

A crouched inhumation was found in ditch *f*, layer 3, Grid 17W/59N, at a depth of
c 0.85m (FIG 27; PL 12). Dr. Calvin Wells judged (Appendix 8) this individual to be
probably female, aged between 20-23. The body lay near the bottom of the deepest
part of ditch *f*, just a few centimetres above the permanent water table. The
orientation was NE (head)-SW, with the arms laid across the chest (left arm) and
abdomen (right arm); the legs were drawn up to the left side of the body, but were not
crossed. Slight traces of green staining and bronze/copper corrosion products on the
third finger of the right hand suggest the presence of a ring.

The NE corner of enclosure A, as excavated, was the location of the two
enigmatic ditches, *h* and *g* (FIG 19). They were very slight and pale, but their layout

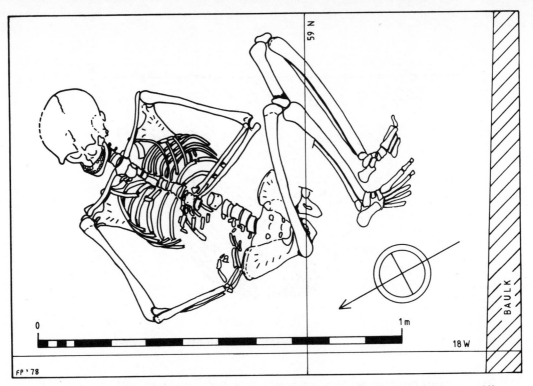

Fig. 27   Newark Road subsite, Area II, ditch *f*: crouched inhumation (for location see FIG 23).

clearly respected ditch 10. The intersection of ditch *h* with *g* was as undiagnostic as that of ditches *g* and 10; their pale, sand-silt fillings blended evenly into each other. Ditches *g* and *h* were both very narrow (*c* 0.2m) and, in the dry summer of 1976, proved almost impossible to excavate accurately as their filling and the natural sub-soil were sun-bleached and difficult to distinguish. A subjective impression of depth would be about 0.2m. Ditch *h* was aligned on ditch *c* (FIG 19) in the adjoining westerly enclosure, B. It is most probable that ditch *h* represents the remains of a hedge bedding trench (see discussion above), but ditch *g* is less straightforward to explain: its morphology suggests a hedge, but its alignment does not.

No non-linear features from the interior of enclosure A could be assigned to the second millennium BC with any confidence.

2. ENCLOSURE B AND ASSOCIATED FEATURES (FIGS 19, 28-30)

Enclosure B is the central enclosure of the three excavated between ditches 9 and 10. It is defined by ditches *c* and 10 to the north, ditches *e, f, i, j, k* to the east, ditch 9 to the south and ditches *m* and *b* to the west. Its widest E-W measurement is *c* 42m and its widest N-S is *c* 46m. Its E and SE side is formed by a droveway (ditches *e, f, k, i,* and *j*) which has been described in detail above. This droveway is breached *c* 10m N of ditch 9 by an entranceway, giving access to enclosure A, enclosure B and the N and S lengths of the drove itself; this arrangement, which is echoed on the other, westerly, side of the enclosure would appear to be deliberate and might have been used as a means of sorting or inspecting livestock. A broadly similar feature was excavated in the settlement on Area I of the Storey's Bar Road subsite (FNG 2, FIG 6: drove formed by ditches B21 and B38).

The short length of ditch aligned on ditch *j*, but to the west, has been discussed at

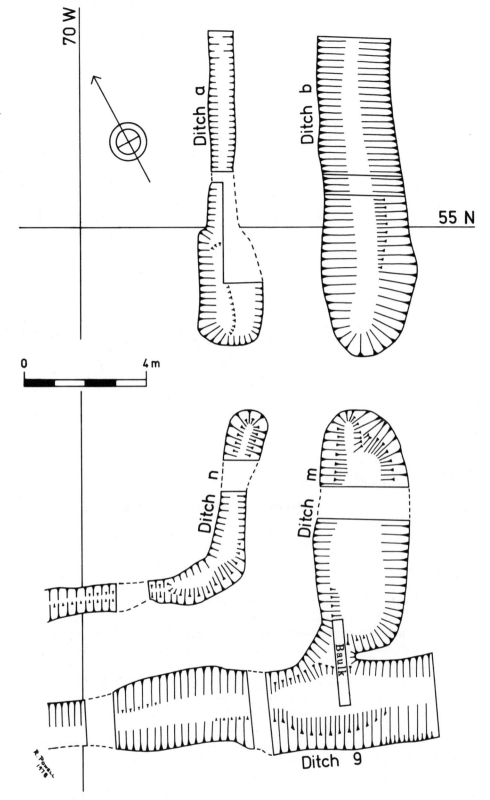

Fig. 28   Newark Road subsite, Area II: ditches at the south-west corner of enclosure B.

41

length above.

Turning now to the SW corner of the enclosure, the relationship of ditch *m* to ditch 9 is of considerable interest (FIG 28). Ditch *m* is short (7.8m), wide (*c* 3.0m) and deep (0.75m) and, as such, is atypical. It is joined to ditch 9 by a short NE-SW extension, which the section (FIG 29) clearly shows to be contemporary with both major ditches. The N butt of ditch *m* has an uneven bottom which might indicate at least one period of recutting. No recuts were visible in the section, however. The short length of NE-SW ditch, just referred to, appears to have been cut through a very narrow (*c* 0.2m) gravel 'baulk' which ran parallel to, and N of, ditch 9, and which appears to have separated ditch 9 from ditch *m*. It is difficult to suggest an explanation for this gravel 'baulk' which does not occur on any other intersection on the site. The best hypothesis is that it was left because the hedge along ditch 9 was particularly tough and difficult to remove at that particular spot.

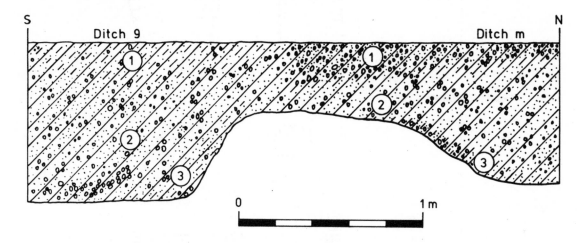

Fig. 29   Newark Road subsite, Area II: section at the junction of ditches 9 and *m*.

The section at the junction of ditches 9 and *m* showed the following succession (FIG 29):

Layer 1. Sand-silt with scattered gravel pebbles in an even, homogeneous mix (10YR 6/4-6/6). The stone content of layer 1 in ditch *m* was slightly higher than that of ditch 9. The stone concentration between the two ditches was aligned on the narrow gravel 'baulk' discussed above and may represent the collapsed remnants of a bank.

Layer 2. Sand-silt with scattered gravel pebles and gravel lenses near ditch sides (10YR 5/4-4/4). Scattered charcoal flecks were common.

Layer 3. Sand-silt with scattered gravel pebbles, sand and gravel lenses near ditch sides and bottom (10YR 4/3); charcoal was very rare.

All the layers of both ditches tended to blend evenly into each other and there were no signs of recutting, turf formation or backfilling.

The entranceway between ditches *b* and *m* was 1.6m wide and that between ditches *a* and *n* was 2.0m; the latter entranceway was positioned very slightly NE of the former. The droveway formed by ditches *a-b* and *n-m* will be discussed with other features of enclosure C; it is sufficient to note here that despite the alignment of the gap just described, with the entranceway through the drove on the other (E) side of enclosure B, and the superficial resemblance of both droves, they nonetheless probably had different functions. Ditches *n* and *a* have expanded or slightly inturned butts at the entranceway, suggesting, perhaps, that livestock traffic flowed east-west, across the drove, rather than along it. Furthermore, the drove around enclosure C is probably too long to have been used as a sorting feature, as was suggested (above) for the drove on the east side of enclosure B.

Ditch *b* was clearly a feature of some importance, to judge by its size; it was approximately 32.5m long and about 2.6m wide. A section across its widest point, slightly north of midway along it, revealed the following sequence (FIG 30):

Layer 1. Sand-silt with scattered gravel pebbles (10YR 5/6). At the centre and east, layers 1 and 2 were separated by a distinctive stone-free layer of darker (7.5YR 4/1) sand-silt with a high proportion of charcoal; this layer is only found in the expanded part of the ditch and was probably washed in from the east.

Layer 2. Sand-silt with iron-pan near the 1/2 interface, lenses of stone-free sand-silt; lenses of sand and lenses of gravel (7.5YR 5/2). This layer blended into layers 1 (above) and 3 (below) without an obvious pause in the depositional sequence.

Layer 3. Sand-silt with scattered gravel pebbles and organic matter in a semi-decayed state (10YR 3/1). Decayed woody plant roots were found growing into the clean gravel sub-soil near the bottom of the feature. This would suggest that the ditch at this point was somehow kept open long enough for plants to grow. Experience suggests that some physical means of restraining the sides must have been employed, as the gravel at this depth (*c*1.1m) is wet and free-running. No traces of wattle-work were found, despite a careful search. A thick deposit of iron-pan had formed immediately above the undisturbed gravel bottom.

The NE side of the enclosure was defined by two more or less parallel ditches (10 and *c*) which did *not* define a drove. Ditch *c* was very slight (depth *c* 0.25m; width 0.55m) and was filled with uniform sand-silt with very few scattered gravel pebbles (10YR 4/3). It joined ditch *f*, to the east, and *b*, to the west, at T-junctions which showed no stratigraphic priority. The profile of ditch *c* was uniform throughout and there were no traces of recuts or of blocked entranceways. It is suggested that this small ditch perhaps represents an early phase in the system's arrangement. It may alternatively, and less probably, have formed some kind of revetment for a bank immediately south of ditch 10; the absence of postholes along this ditch (which was completely excavated) makes this hypothesis improbable.

The only non-linear feature of probable second millennium BC date was the pit F42 (FIG 19) which was situated in the NW portion of enclosure B at Grid 53W/80N. It was cut by the N-S Romano-British ditch (FIG 44) and was amorphous in both plan and section. The filling was of pale sand-silt with few scattered gravel pebbles (10YR 5/2) and apart from Beaker pottery (FIG 59, no 31), a few undiagnostic bodysherds, and four weathered flints which were found in the filling, there was nothing about this

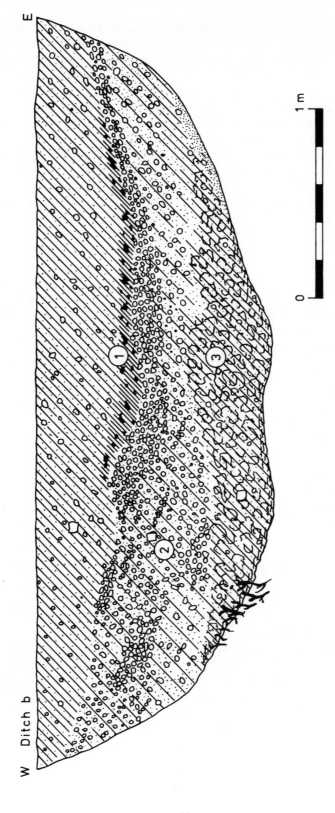

W Ditch b

E

1 m

0

Fig. 30   Newark Road subsite, Area II: section through pit-like enlargement of ditch *b* at Grid 60W/71N.

feature to distinguish it from other silt patches in the area. It seems, therefore, most probable that this 'feature' is not man-made, but instead represents the truncated remains of a once undulating land surface upon which secondary rubbish (discussed in Schiffer 1976, 30) had been allowed to accumulate. A similar situation was encountered on the Storey's Bar Road subsite (Pryor 1979).

3. ENCLOSURE C AND ASSOCIATED FEATURES (FIGS 19 and 34)

The Drove and Enclosure Ditches (FIGS 31-33)

Enclosure C was the most westerly of the three excavated between ditches 9 and 10. Its westerly edge was not discovered, but its known length (E-W) was 66m and its width (N-S) 35m. These measurements are taken from the internal ditch of the surrounding, external, drove formed by ditches 10 with *a* (to the N), *a* and *b* (to the E), and *n* and 9 or *m* (to the S and SW). This drove is remarkably uniform in width (*c* 2.0-2.5m) and most probably served to divert livestock around the edges of the enclosure, possibly to enclosures further W, without having to use the main droveway defined by ditches 8 and 9. Ditch *a* is similar in every respect to ditch *n* which will be considered in greater detail below. Attention should be drawn, however, to Dr Paul Craddock's study of soil phosphate levels in this area, where it will be seen that the small enclosure ditches, such as *n* and *a* have a markedly higher phosphate level than the larger ditches (eg 9 and 10). Dr Craddock notes that this may be the result of the small ditches having been abandoned shortly after the period of occupation discussed below; the larger ditches, on the other hand, may have stayed open for longer. It may be that the surrounding drove became redundant once the small settlement was abandoned. Given the length of time a small gravel-cut ditch would take to fill-in naturally, a causal link between settlement and ditch abandonment seems quite plausible. Alternatively, any hedge that may have been planted alongside ditches *a* and/or *n* could have become impenetrable to livestock during the short life of the settlement, and the constant maintenance of the small ditch may thus have been deemed unnecessary; as ever, simple explanations will probably prove inadequate.

It was decided to treat ditch *n* in some detail, both because it is typical, in size and profile, of the many small ditches of the enclosure system and because it is the only ditch that clearly demonstrates a series of recuts. These recuts are confined to the area near the round house, Structure 1 (FIG 34), a location that must have a functional explanation; in this case, it would seem that the efficient removal of water from the house and the land around it were the ditches' principal function. Again, hedges may well have had a role to play, for it is difficult otherwise to account for the consistent band of undisturbed gravel to the SW of ditch *n*, between it and ditches *p*, *o* and *r* (FIG 31). Ditch *d*, which appears to have drained the round house's eavesdrip gully, also runs parallel to ditch *n* (for *c* 4.5m), but to the NW; again, given that there are at least 4 phases involved (FIG 32), a recent or relict hedge-line could be the explanation for the gap between the various ditches. It should be recalled that hedges are easier to cut and lay than to remove, and once well established are difficult and time-consuming to root out (Pollard *et al* (1974, 213) quote the modern, mechanised, cost of removing a hedge as £200 per mile).

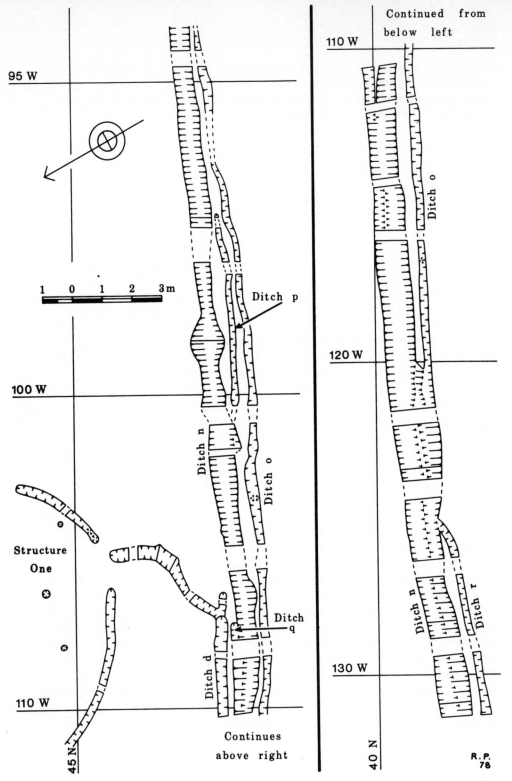

95 W

100 W

110 W

110 W

120 W

130 W

1 0 1 2 3 m

Ditch p

Ditch p

Ditch n

Ditch o

Ditch o

Structure
One

Ditch
q

Ditch d

Ditch n

Ditch r

Continued from
below left

45 N

40 N

R.P.
78

Continues
above right

Fig. 31   Newark Road subsite, Area IV: plan of ditches adjacent to Structure 1 (note orientation of this plan).

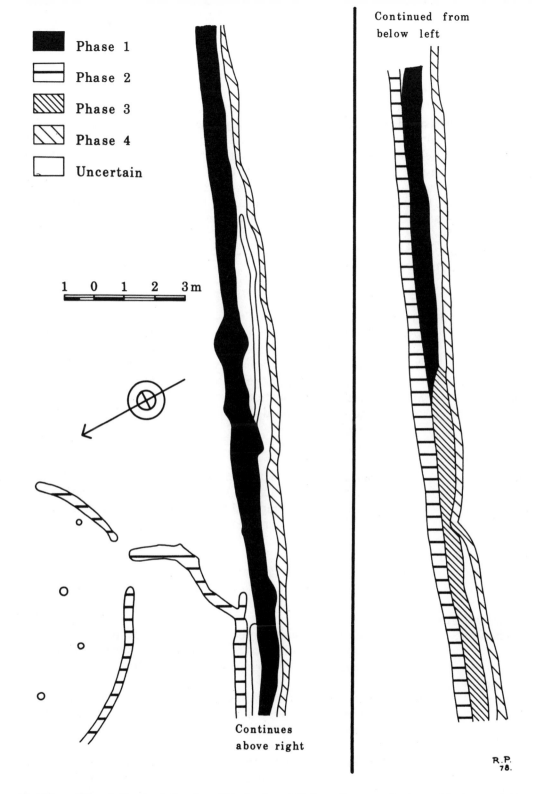

Continued from
below left

Phase 1
Phase 2
Phase 3
Phase 4
Uncertain

1 0 1 2 3m

Continues
above right

R.P.
78.

Fig. 32   Newark Road subsite, Area IV: phasing of ditches adjacent to Structure 1 (at bottom left).
Orientation as FIG 31.

47

FIG 31 shows the general layout of ditches in the region of Structure 1, and FIG 32 shows the stratigraphic relationship of the various ditches. It should be emphasised, however, that the interpretation offered here, although sequentially sound, probably only represents a small number of the recuts actually involved: recuts that followed the precise alignment of ditch *n*, even if substantially smaller, would not have been detected in the field. This is due both to the homogeneity of the ditch fillings involved and to the dry summer of 1976 which tended to bleach most soil colours.

The sections illustrated here (FIG 33) are taken from E to W, along ditch *n*. The first section was located 1.6m SW of the entranceway between ditches *n* and *a* and is deeper as the result of the enlargement of the ditches on either side of the gap discussed above (FIG 28).

The detailed stratigraphy of ditch *n* and associated ditches (*d, o, p, q* and *r*) was as follows (FIG 33):

Section 1 (Grid 63W/48N)

Ditch *n*   *layer 1* Sand-silt with scattered gravel pebbles (10YR 5/4). Charcoal flecks rare. The slight concentration of pebbles towards the surface may represent the remains of a collapsed bank. Layers 1 and 2 blend together.

Ditch *n*   *layer 2* Sand-silt with scattered gravel pebbles with lenses of sand and gravel towards bottom (7.5YR 5/6). Charcoal flecks rare.

Section 2 (Grid 68W/43N)

Ditch *n*   *layer 1* Sand-silt with scattered gravel pebbles (7.5YR 5/6). Charcoal flecks absent. Layers 1 and 2 blend together.

Ditch *n*   *layer 2* Sand-silt with sand and fewer gravel pebbles than layer 1 (7.5YR 3/2). Charcoal rare.

Section 3 (Grid 85W/41N)

Ditch *n/o*   *layer 1* Sand-silt with scattered gravel pebbles (7.5YR 5/8). Charcoal flecks very rare. Relationship between ditches *n* and *o* was not apparent.

Section 4 (Grid 88W/41N)

Ditches *n/o*   *layer 1* Sandy loam with scattered gravel pebbles (10YR 3/2). Very dense concentrations of charcoal flecks were evenly mixed in the matrix of ditch *n* in the upper 0.3m.

Section 5 (Grid 105W/39N)

Ditch *n*   *layer 1* Sand-silt with an even mix of gravel pebbles (10YR 4/3). Charcoal was very dense in the top 0.25m (*cf* Section 4, above).

Section 6 (Grid 108W/39N)

Ditches *n/q*   *layer 1* Sandy loam with an even gravel mix (10YR 4/3). The relationship of ditches *q* and *n* was not clear at this point. Charcoal, less dense than in previous sections (4 and 5) was confined to the upper 0.20m of filling in the N half of ditch *n*.

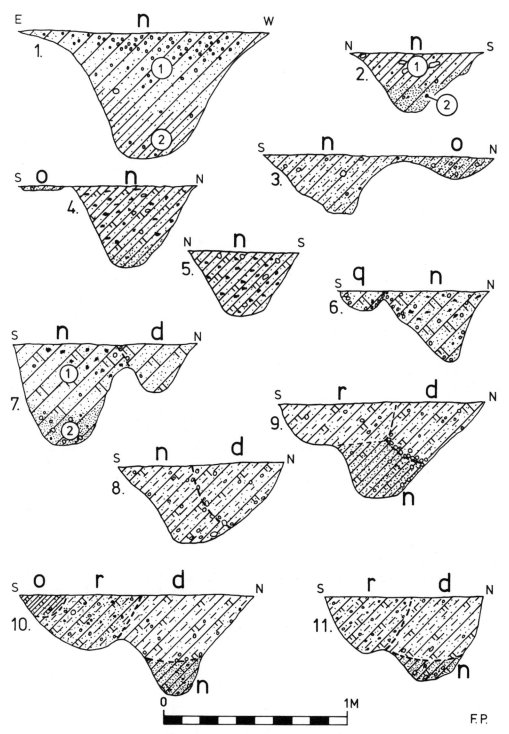

Fig. 33   Newark Road subsite: sections through ditch *n* and associated second millennium BC ditches of Areas I-VI.

Section 7 (Grid 111W/39N)

Ditches *n*/*d*	*layer 1*	Sandy loam with an even gravel mix (10YR 4/3). Dense charcoal (extends 0.35m from surface) is mainly concentrated to the north of ditch *n*. Ditch *n* was cut by ditch *d*.
Ditch *n*	*layer 2*	Silty sand with gravel pebbles, the rapid silting beneath layer 1.

Section 8 (Grid 114W/38N)

Ditches *n*/*d*	*layer 1*	Sandy loam with an even gravel mix (10YR 4/3). Charcoal common, but evenly distributed through the filling of both ditches.

Section 9 (Grid 121W/38N)

Ditch *r*	*layer 1*	Sandy loam with an even gravel mix (10YR 5/3). Charcoal common. Ditch *r* cuts ditches *n* (below) and *d* (to N).
Ditch *d*	*layer 1*	as ditch *r* layer 1. Cut by ditch *r* (a very slight colour and texture difference). Cuts ditch *n*. Charcoal rare.
Ditch *n*	*layer 1*	(and 2?) Sandy loam (with more sand than ditches *r* and *d*) with an even gravel mix (10YR 4/3). Charcoal flecks common. Cut by ditches *r* and *d*.

Section 10 (Grid 123W/38N)

Ditches *r*, *d*, *n*	same as ditches *r*, *d*, *n* in section 9, above. Ditch *o* (darkness exaggerated in FIG 33) cuts ditch *r*. The filling of ditch *o* was similar to the other ditches, but very slightly darker; traces of a (?) weathered edge were visible between it and ditch *r*. This was the only section where the distinction between ditches *o* and *r* could be made. An alternative interpretation, based on spatial criteria, is that ditches *o* and *r* are different phases of the same ditch; this explanation is offered in the phase plan (FIG 32). It should be emphasised that ditches *d*, *n*, *r* and *o* were extremely difficult to differentiate.

Section 11 (Grid 126W/38N)

Ditches *r* and *d*	*layer 1*	Sandy loam with scattered gravel pebbles (10YR 5/3). Charcoal rare. Ditch *r* (textural difference) cuts ditch *d*; both cut ditch *n*.
Ditch *n*	*layer 1*	(and 2?) Sandy loam with more sand than ditches *r* and *d* (10YR 4/3). Cut by ditches *r* and *d*.

THE SETTLEMENT (FIG 34)

Introduction

The settlement area was located at the western end of enclosure C and almost certainly extended into the unexcavated area beside Newark Road. As the size of the settlement is unknown, no estimates of area can be offered. The settlement, as

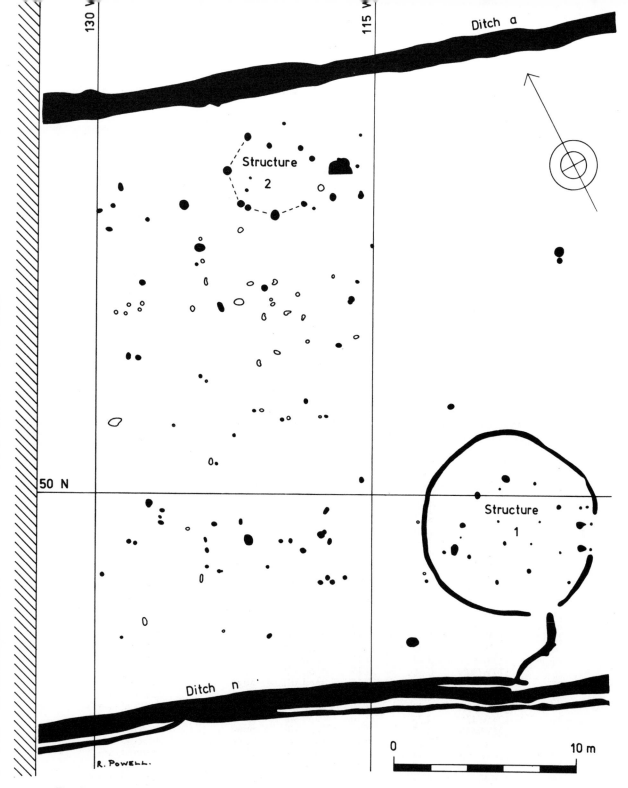

130 W

115 W

Ditch a

Structure 2

50 N

Structure 1

Ditch n

R. POWELL.

0   10 m

Fig. 34   Newark Road subsite, Area IV: general plan of occupation features between ditches 9 and 10 (doubtful features shown in outline).

excavated, consisted of three main elements: Structure 1, a round house, Structure 2, a roughly circular probable animal byre and a wide scatter of very small pits, post and stakeholes forming no discernible pattern.

Scattered Pits and Postholes (FIG 34; Table 2)

The scattered small features were very slight, most being no more than shallow scoops of 0.1-0.3m depth (finds were also slight and in the main undiagnostic). Three points of interest arise from their spatial distribution. First, none are found north of ditch *a* or south of ditch *n*. This suggests that the droveway around enclosure C was in use at the same time as the settlement, and that the isolated features may reasonably be associated with Structures 1 and 2 which can be linked to the ditched enclosure system by vertical and horizontal stratigraphy. Second, there does seem to be an area (width *c* 2.0-4.0m) devoid of these small features around both structures, the only exception being a small group of pits and postholes, perhaps themselves forming some part of the building, immediately E of Structure 2. Third, Grid line 115W forms an eastern boundary to this feature scatter; the point should not be over-stressed, but a hedge could reasonably be suggested to account for this clear-cut limit. Table 2 lists the attributes of principal non-linear features not considered with Structures 1 and 2, below.

TABLE 2

Newark Road subsite, Area IV: scattered features within Enclosure C, west of Grid 115W (not including Structure 2). All measurements in metres.

Feature Number	Grid	Diameter	Depth	Filling	Finds	Notes
8	128W/66N	0.32	0.10	sand-silt	potsherds	charcoal rare
10	129W/46N	0.24	0.21	sand-silt	1 potsherd; daub	charcoal common
11	128W/43N	0.20	0.15	sand-silt	wattle imp. daub	charcoal rare
13	120W/42N	0.23	0.06	sand-silt	none	charcoal very rare
14	116W/46N	0.20	0.09	sand-silt	none	charcoal rare
15	121W/46N	0.18	0.16	sand-silt	none	charcoal very rare
16	118W/46N	0.26	0.11	sand-silt	none	charcoal very rare
17	120W/47N	0.21	0.06	sand-silt	none	charcoal very rare
18	118W/48N	0.38	0.16	sand-silt	1 potsherd	charcoal rare
19	118W/48N	0.26	0.07	sand-silt	none	charcoal very rare
20	118W/45N	0.24	0.10	sand-silt	none	charcoal rare
21	120W/47N	0.23	0.05	sand-silt	none	charcoal very rare
22	118W/45N	0.31	0.16	sand-silt	none	charcoal very rare
23	119W/47N	0.31	0.11	sand-silt	none	charcoal common
24	117W/48N	0.30	0.10	sand-silt	none	charcoal very rare
25	123W/45N	0.34	0.11	sand-silt	none	charcoal rare
26	117W/50N	0.35	0.15	sand-silt	none	charcoal very rare
27	123W/43N	0.46	0.15	sand-silt	none	charcoal rare
29	122W/49N	0.20	0.07	sand-silt	none	charcoal rare
30	124W/45N	0.23	0.10	sand-silt	none	charcoal very rare
31	124W/47N	0.25	0.16	sand-silt	none	charcoal rare
33	126W/48N	0.22	0.15	sand-silt	none	charcoal common
35	124W/49N	0.34	0.11	sand-silt	none	charcoal rare
36	126W/48N	0.16	0.09	sand-silt	none	charcoal rare
37	128W/47N	0.29	0.16	sand-silt	1 potsherd	charcoal common
38	126W/53N	0.18	0.09	sand-silt	none	charcoal very rare

TABLE 2 (continued)

Feature Number	Grid	Diameter	Depth	Filling	Finds	Notes
39	126W/49N	0.22	0.05	sand-silt	none	charcoal very rare
40	123W/52N	0.18	0.08	sand-silt	daub	charcoal very rare
41	127W/50N	0.36	0.11	sand-silt	pot/daub frags	charcoal rare
43	128W/47N	0.22	0.06	sand-silt	1 flint	charcoal very rare
45	123W/53N	0.16	0.09	sand-silt	none	charcoal rare
46	120W/54N	0.22	0.05	sand-silt	none	charcoal very rare
47	121W/54N	0.20	0.07	sand-silt	none	charcoal rare
49	117W/54N	0.15	0.05	sand-silt	none	charcoal very rare
53	118W/55N	0.26	0.08	sand-silt	none	charcoal very rare
54	124W/56N	0.17	0.07	sand-silt	daub	charcoal rare
57	116W/57N	0.34	0.08	sand-silt	none	charcoal rare
61	128W/57N	0.28	0.16	sand-silt	none	charcoal common
64	128W/57N	0.27	0.10	sand-silt	none	charcoal common
66	115W/60N	0.48	0.11	sand-silt	pot	charcoal rare
67	123W/60N	0.62*	0.08	sand-silt	none	charcoal rare
69	115W/61N	0.18	0.07	clay-silt	none	charcoal very rare
82	121W/61N	0.32	0.07	sand-silt	none	charcoal very rare
83	128W/61N	0.22	0.12	sand-silt	1 potsherd	charcoal rare
85	115W/63N	0.20	0.07	sand-silt	none	charcoal rare
86	125W/62N	0.19	0.09	sand-silt	none	charcoal rare
90	125W/63N	0.22	0.11	sand-silt	1 potsherd	charcoal rare
91	129W/64N	0.33	0.12	sand-silt	none	charcoal very rare
92	127W/65N	0.20	0.09	sand-silt	none	charcoal rare
93	129W/65N	0.22	0.11	sand-silt	1 flint	charcoal rare
95	126W/66N	0.55	0.11	sand-silt	none	charcoal rare
96	130W/65N	0.30	0.10	sand-silt	none	charcoal rare

* Length

Structure 1 and Associated Features (FIGS 35-39; PLS 13 and 14)

Structure 1 is a fine example of a round-house. Its external eaves-drip gully (F324) was *c* 0.25-0.40m wide and varied in depth from less than 0.05m to *c* 0.15m. These dimensions are less substantial than those of similar Iron Age round-house ring-gullies on the nearby Cat's Water subsite (Pryor and Cranstone 1978); too much emphasis should not, however, be given to this apparent contrast, which may be more the result of differential plough damage or erosion than different construction techniques. The approximate internal diameter of the ring-gully was 9.25m. Its filling was of uniform sandy loam (10YR 4/3) with scattered gravel pebbles. Its profile was in general an open U-shape (FIG 37: 2-17) and the botton was rather irregular, as the depths of the different transverse sections attest. The ring-gully was broken at the entranceway, which faced E. The entranceway gap was 2.1m wide and the undulations in the ring-gully on either side of it are illustrated by the two longitudinal sections (FIG 37: nos. 4 and 5). It is suggested that the external ring-rully was an eavesdrip drain, and that it was in turn drained by the short length of S-shaped ditch F320 which fed into the main drove ditch *d* (FIG 31; PL 14). The only objection to this argument is that the ring-gully and F320 do not appear to join one another. This may, at first, seem an insuperable objection until it is realised, first, that both ditches are extremely shallow at the point where they ought to join: FIG 39 (top) shows a longitudinal section between the two ditches which are a maximum of six (F320) and seven (F324) centimetres deep in the illustrated profile. Such depths barely constitute hard and fast butt-ends. Second, feature 320 becomes steadily deeper as it approaches ditch *d* which in turn

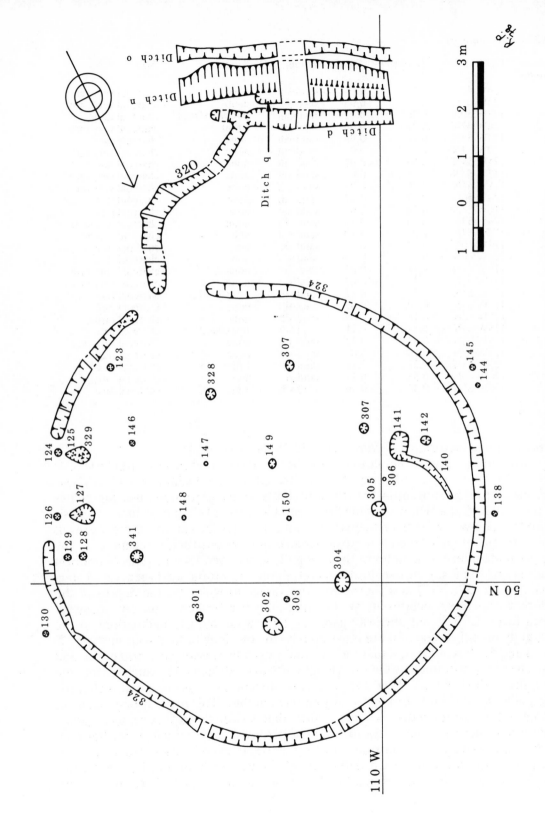

Fig. 35 Newark Road subsite, Area IV: plan of Structure 1 and associated features.

54

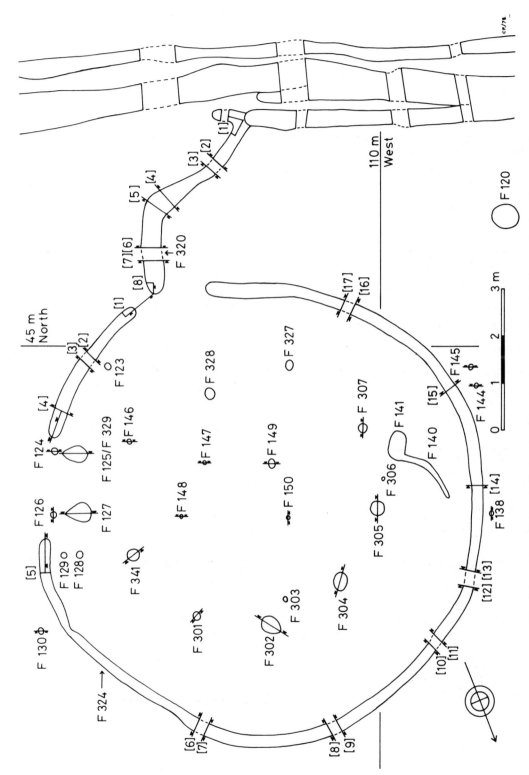

Fig. 36   Newark Road subsite, Area IV, Structure 1: plan, showing section locations.

55

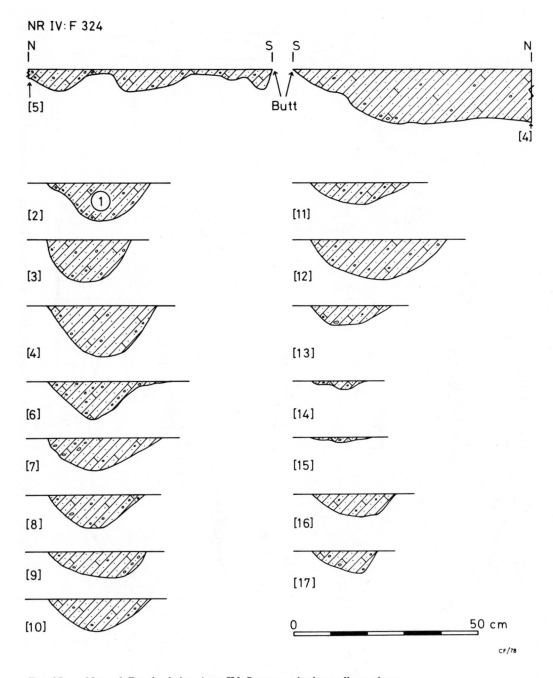

Fig. 37   Newark Road subsite, Area IV, Structure 1: ring-gully sections.

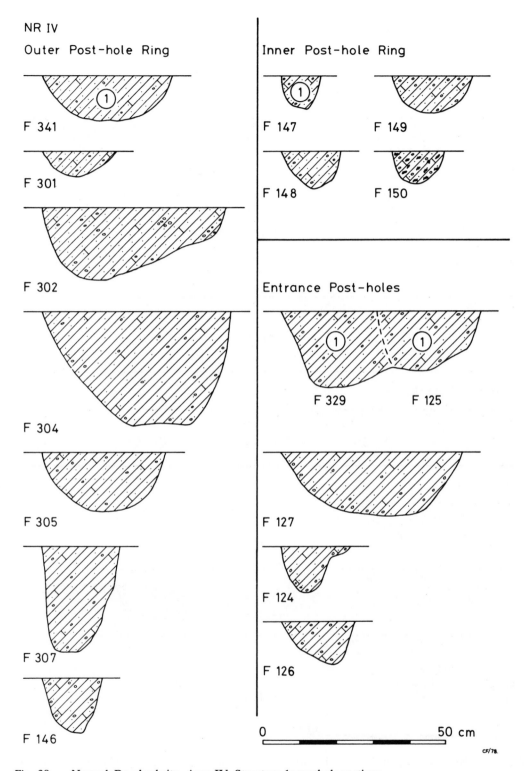

Fig. 38   Newark Road subsite, Area IV, Structure 1: posthole sections.

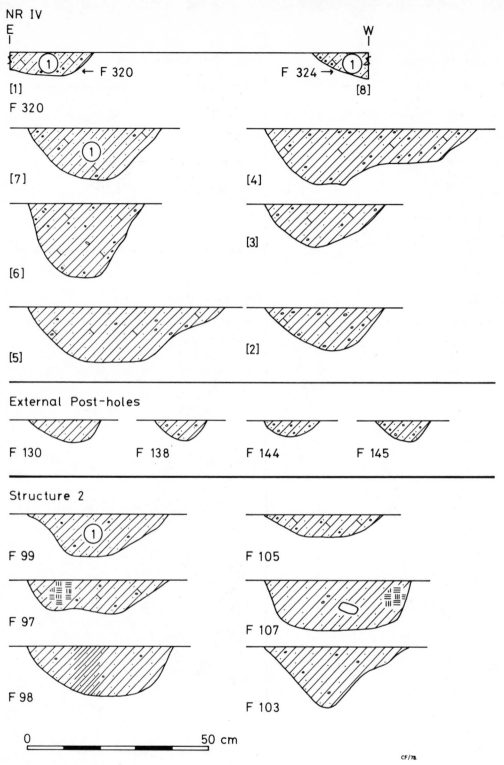

Fig. 39   Newark Road subsite, Area IV, Structure 1: posthole sections (contd). Structure 2: posthole sections.

becomes rapidly deeper further west. The drainage function of these two features can be in no doubt. The apparent gaps between the ring-gully and its supposed drain, F320, can therefore be explained by the slight nature of the available evidence, for we are here considering features which have been severely truncated by the plough, and by the nature of the actual drainage involved: for F320 might only have held running water after, or during, persistent rain. The gravel subsoil drains well on this part of the site and seepage would probably dispose of roof run-off after heavy dews or light showers. Under such circumstances a low transverse ridge at the bottom of a much deeper ditch would scarcely be noticed.

The undulating bottom of the ring-gully is probably caused by the undulation of the gravel subsoil, as no certain postholes could be discerned either in the gully bottom or in its filling. It is of course also quite probable that the eavesdrip trench could have been used to secure the feet of temporary post or stake wall-props, in the manner of an angled buttress. The outward thrust of the roof, which is taken by the walls, is always a problem with round houses, and temporary buttresses would have provided a simple, quick and effective solution. In this regard it is perhaps worth noting the presence of four small postholes immediately outside the ring-gully (FIG 39). Their connection with the building cannot be demonstrated, but they may well have provided footings for longer wall buttress poles. Their irregular spacing suggests that they were dug when and where they were required, and did not form part of the building's original design.

Turning now to internal features, there were six principal elements: an outer ring of postholes; an inner approximate ring of postholes; door and porch postholes; possible wall stakeholes and a few apparently random postholes. No post-stains or stone post-packing were found.

The postholes of the outer ring (features 341, 301, 302, 304, 305, 307, 327, 328, 146) formed a circle, diameter c 5.5m. Their depths varied, but their filling, sand-silt with scattered gravel pebbles (10YR 5/4), was consistent and uniform. Two postholes (nos 328 and 327), however, could not be excavated as the dry conditions allied with the silty nature of the local subsoil, made excavation impossible. They were, however, clearly visible from the photographic tower and their existence is not in doubt.

The inner 'ring' (dia c 2.2m) of postholes consisted of features 147-50. These postholes were more uniform in depth than the outer ring. The filling of the inner ring was similar to that of the outer ring — sand-silt with scattered gravel pebbles (10YR 4/3) — but one feature, F150, had a markedly higher concentration of charcoal. This material was not burned *in situ* and probably derived from a central hearth.

The entrance postholes consisted of two slight external porch posts (F126 and 124) and two more substantial door posts (F127 and 129), one of which had been replaced by F125 (FIG 38: bottom right). The greater size of the door posts is the result of the outward thrust of the roof, discussed above.

Iron Age houses excavated at Fengate generally leave very slight traces of wall foundations, so it is not surprising that the structure considered here, which seems to have suffered severe plough-damage, has yielded such scanty evidence. Apart from the two large door posts, which must certainly indicate the position of the walls, only two other stakeholes (F128 and (?)F123) could have been involved in their construction. If we take the distance from the centre of the door posts to the centre of the ring-gully as a guide to the width of the eaves, then the roof overhang was about 0.9m. This is almost exactly the eaves width observed on Iron Age houses at the Cat's Water settlement.

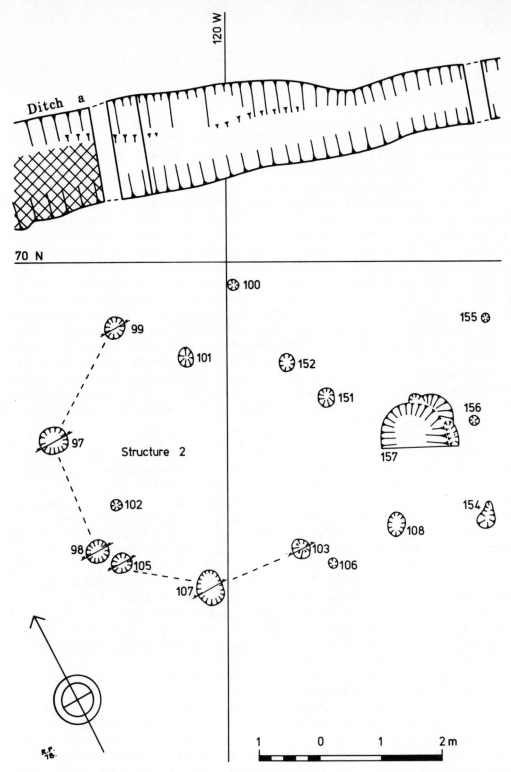

120 W

Ditch a

70 N

100

155

99

101

152

151

156

97

Structure 2

157

102

154

98

108

105

103

106

107

Fig. 40 Newark Road subsite, Area IV, Structure 2. Charcoal spread in ditch *a* indicated by cross-hatching.

Finally, features 129, 140, 141 and 306 find no ready explanation. The two stakeholes, F129 and 306 could be associated with the internal arrangements of the house, and F140 is most probably an animal burrow, albeit an ancient one.

Structure 2 and Associated Features (FIGS 39 and 40)

The postholes of Structure 2, which was situated 15m north of Structure 1, were located in a rough arc immediately south of ditch *a*. We will consider reasons for selecting the six features in greater detail below, but first it is necessary to give other evidence for the existence of the structure.

The best reason for supposing the existence of a structure in the area was provided by the independent results of the soil phosphate survey carried out by Dr Craddock and the British Museum Research Laboratory (Appendix 6). This survey shows a marked increase in soil phosphate concentration in ditch *a* alongside and to the west of the hypothetical structure. This increase in soil phosphate level could result from the discard of domestic rubbish in the nearby ditch or, more plausibly, from the run-off of animal manure which would be the result if the building were used to house livestock.

Ditch *a* runs gently downhill west of Structure 2, and it is at that point that a pronounced spread of charcoal was observed in the ditch filling, significantly, on the south side of the ditch.

The third argument runs the risk of circularity, but is nonetheless important. It is simply that another probable structure of closely analogous form, size and construction was located, also just south of a drove ditch (8), in the Fourth Drove subsite, Area VII. The two suggested buildings are compared in FIG 81.

The six postholes which together are seen to comprise Structure 2 have many points in common (the only exception being F99 whose peripheral location may be fortuitous). It will be seen that the spacing between the various postholes is very regular (FIGS 40 and 81). Their size and depths, too, are similar and they all, with the exception of F99, contained much charcoal which had not burned *in situ*. The salient points of each feature are given below:

F97. Sand-silt with scattered gravel pebbles, lumps of blue clay (collapsed post packing?) and much charcoal (10YR 3/2). Round (?) post-pipe (dia 0.07m) clearly visible.

F98. Identical in every respect to F97, but no post-pipe.

F99. Sand-silt with scattered gravel pebbles; charcoal rare (10YR 4/3).

F103. Sand-silt with scattered gravel pebbles and substantial quantities of blue clay (?packing) on the S side of the posthole (10YR 3/3). Much charcoal.

F105. Sand-silt with scattered gravel pebbles, charcoal and blue clay (10YR 5/3). This feature had less charcoal than the other features which also contained blue clay.

F107. Sand-silt with scattered gravel pebbles, large quantities of charcoal and a few pieces of burnt clay (10YR 4/2).

It will be seen that the above features, with the possible exception of F99, have many points in common, especially their size, depth, and filling rich in charcoal and distinctive blue clay. The morphology and filling of features 100, 101, 151 and 152 were significantly different from those just described and they are not considered to have formed part of the structure.

III. DITCHES 8, 9 AND 10

DITCH 8 (FIG 41)

Ditch 8 ran E-W across Areas VI, II and IV for a distance of 142m. It was in general the slightest of the three main E-W ditches and shows evidence, particularly N of enclosure 1, for repeated recutting. This evidence is considered in greater detail above, and may be seen in the ridged profiles 2, 3 and 4 (FIG 41). There is no evidence in any of the main E-W ditches for deliberate in-filling by man, and it may therefore be assumed that the layers, illustrated in FIGS 41-42, accumulated as the result of natural weathering processes (see also Appendix 2). The following sequence was observed in section 1, FIG 41:

Layer 1. Sand-silt with scattered gravel pebbles (10YR 4/4).

Layer 2. Sand-silt with fewer pebbles than 1, but more sand (10YR 4/2). Layers 1 and 2 blended together evenly.

Layer 3. (Not visible in the drawn section). A darker sand-silt layer separating the 'rapid' layer 4 from layer 2, above (10YR 3/3).

Layer 4. Silty sand with many gravel lenses (10YR 3/3).

The profiles illustrated in FIG 41 are taken at roughly ten metre intervals across the large excavated area, from E (no 1) to W. Different feature and section numbers were used in the field and these are given below for reference purposes. Grid references indicate the southern edge of the section line in question.

1. Grid 9E/43N. Area VI, F359 section 4.
2. Grid 1W/41N. Area VI, F359 sieve section 1.
3. Grid 10W/40N. Area II, F2 section 2.
4. Grid 21W/39N. Area II, F2 sieve section 4.
5. Grid 32W/38N. Area II, F2 section 7.
6. Grid 43W/37N. Area II, F2 section 9.
7. Grid 57W/35N. Area II, F2 sieve section 11.
8. Grid 68W35N. Area II, F2 sieve section 13.
9. Grid 78W/34N. Area II, F2 sieve section 14.
10. Grid 87W/32N. Area II, F2 sieve section 16.
11. Grid 94W/32N. Area IV, F7 section 3.
12. Grid 106W/31N. Area IV, F7 section 6.
13. Grid 118W/29N. Area IV, F7 section 10.
14. Grid 129W/26N. Area IV, F7 section 14.

DITCH 9 (FIG 42)

Ditch 9 ran E-W across Areas VI, II and IV for a distance of 145m, *c* 2.0-5.0m N of ditch 8, and parallel to it. Ditch 9 was in general much deeper and wider than ditch 8, except where it forms the SW boundary of enclosure A. Section 1 showed the following succession (FIG 42):

Layer 1. Sand-silt with scattered gravel pebbles (10YR 3/3).

Layer 2. Sand-silt with fewer pebbles than layer 1 (10YR 4/3). The two layers were separated by a lens of gravel pebbles (but this was not observed elsewhere where the layers tended to blend together).

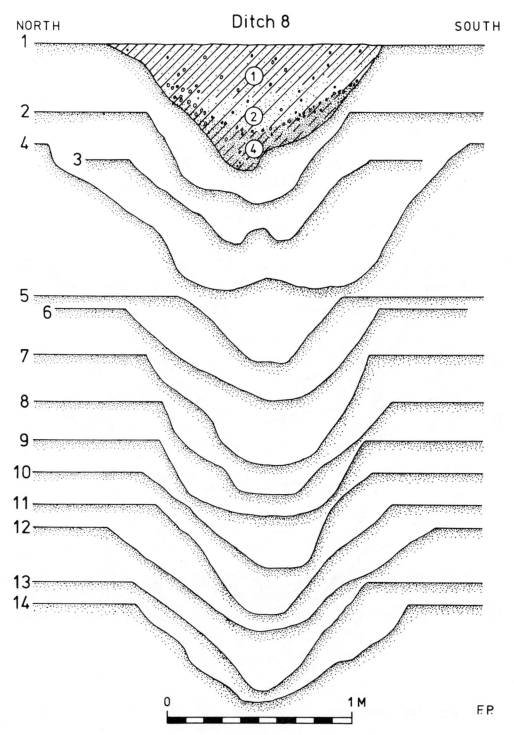

NORTH   Ditch 8   SOUTH

0   1 M

F. P.

Fig. 41   Newark Road subsite, Areas II, IV and VI: profiles and section of ditch 8. Profiles are drawn at approximate 10m intervals from E (no 1) to W (no 14).

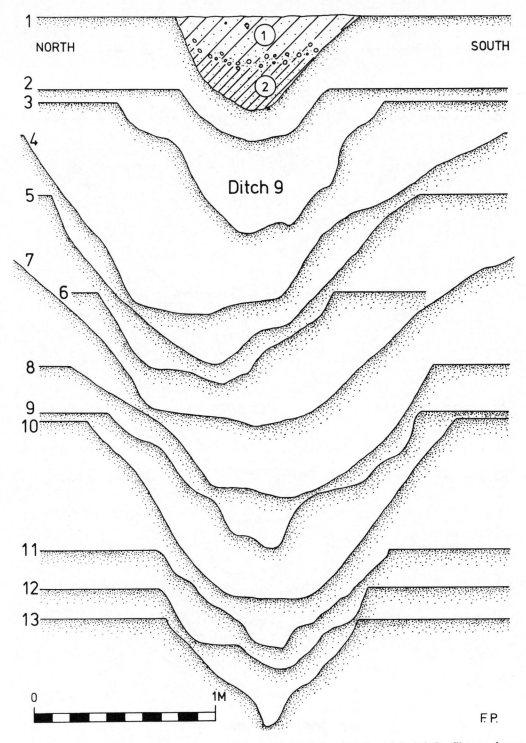

NORTH

SOUTH

Ditch 9

0   1M

F. P.

Fig. 42   Newark Road subsite, Areas II, IV and VI: profiles and section of ditch 9. Profiles are drawn at approximate 10m intervals from E (no 1) to W (no 13).

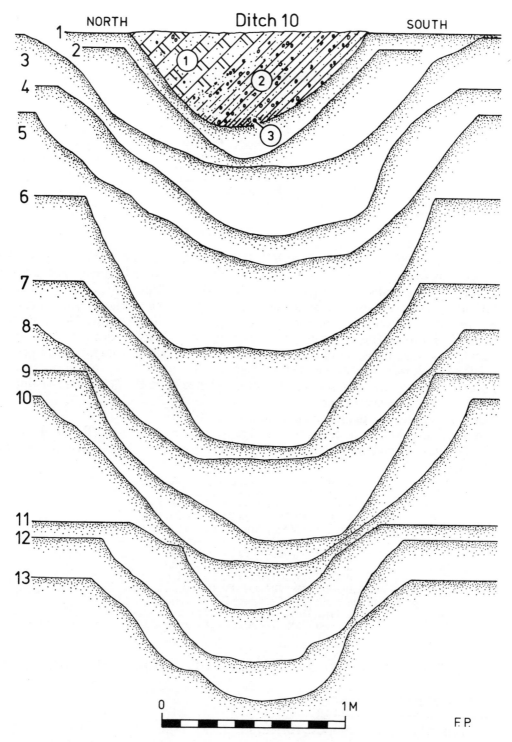

NORTH

Ditch 10

SOUTH

0   1 M

F.P.

Fig. 43   Newark Road subsite, Areas III, IV and VII: profiles and section of ditch 10. Profiles are drawn at approximate 10m intervals from E (no 1) to W (no 13).

Profiles were taken at approximately ten-metre intervals across the excavated area, from E (no 1) to W:

1. Grid 9E/48N Area VI, F358 section 2.
2. Grid 1W/48N Area VI, F356 section 1.
3. Grid 11W/47N Area II, F3 section 4.
4. Grid 21 W/45N Area II, F3 section 6.
5. Grid 31W/44N Area II, F3 sieve section 6.
6. Grid 41W/41N Area II, F3 section 9.
7. Grid 52W/40N Area II, F3 section 12.
8. Grid 68W/39N Area II, F3 sieve section 13.
9. Grid 79W/38N Area II, F3 section 18.
10. Grid 89W/38N Area VI, F6 section 1.
11. Grid 101W/37N Area VI, F6 section 3.
12. Grid 113W/35N Area VI, F6 section 5.
13. Grid 129W/35N Area VI, F6 section 8.

DITCH 10 (FIG 43)

Ditch 10 ran E-W across Areas VII, III and IV for a distance of 144m. It was less extensively sampled than either ditches 8 or 9, but still showed a remarkably uniform profile (FIG 43). Unlike the other two main E-W ditches, ditch 10 showed no evidence for entranceways, open or cut-through. Despite limited excavation, some evidence was revealed for recutting, but individual recuts could rarely be traced for more than about 10 metres. These recuts probably represent cleaning out following storm damage, or something similar, rather than major phases of occupation. Layer 1 in section 1, below, is a recut (FIG 43):

Layer 1. Clay-loam with scattered gravel pebbles (10YR 5/4). Clear distinction between layers 1 and 2.

Layer 2. Sand-silt with an even gravel mix (10YR 6/6).

Layer 3. Silty sand with scattered gravel pebbles; 'rapid' silting (10YR 4/7).

Profiles were taken at *c* ten-metre intervals across the excavated area, from E (no 1) to W:

1. Grid 4W/96N Area III, F2 section 19.
2. Grid 13W/94N Area III, F2 section 17.
3. Grid 30W/90N Area III, F2 section 13.
4. Grid 39W/89N Area III, F2 section 11.
5. Grid 47W/86N Area III, F2 section 9.
6. Grid 53W/86N Area III, F2 section 8B.
7. Grid 59W/85N Area III, F2 section 7.
8. Grid 70W/84N Area III, F2 section 4B.
9. Grid 87W/81N Area III, F2 section 1.
10. Grid 94W/80N Area IV, F1 section 2.
11. Grid 105W/78N Area IV, F1 section 3.
12. Grid 118W/77N Area IV, F1 section 6.
13. Grid 126W/76N Area IV, F1 section 7.

IV. FEATURES THAT POST-DATE THE DITCHED ENCLOSURE SYSTEM (FIG 44)

1. NON-LINEAR FEATURES

Four-post Structure (FIG 44A)

This structure was composed of features 25, 27, 28 and 31 and was situated in Area II at the junction of ditches 9 and *i*. The arrangement of the postholes was an almost precise square, with sides (measured from posthole centres), of 3m. No dateable

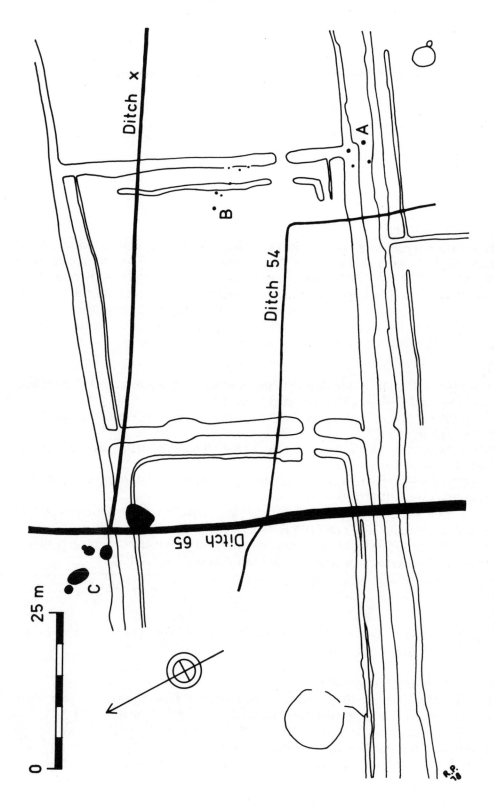

Fig. 44 Newark Road subsite, Areas I-VI: first millennium BC and Roman features.

artifacts were found, but features 28 (FIG 24) and 31 clearly cut layer 1 of ditch 9. Feature 28 is fully described in the discussion of FIG 24, above. The remaining three features were as follows:

F25. Dia 0.70m; depth 1.05m (over-dug?). Sand-silt with scattered gravel pebbles, two burnt stones, dense concentration of charcoal, not burnt *in situ*.

F27. Dia 0.55m; depth 0.4m. Sand-silt with scattered gravel pebbles, two burnt cobblestones, much charcoal, not burnt *in situ* (10YR 3/3).

F31. Dia 0.55m; depth 0.53m. Sand-silt with scattered gravel pebbles and dense concentration of charcoal, not burnt *in situ*, evenly mixed through the filling (10YR 3/1).

Posthole scatter (FIG 44B)

This scatter of postholes overlay ditches *e* and *f*, and (on the basis of pottery from one posthole, F17, Area II (FIG 61, no 39) and an associated radiocarbon date, also from F17 (HAR-773 790 ± 80 bc)) may tentatively be dated to the Late Bronze Age. Seven postholes are shown in FIG 44 and are described below. Five doubtful ones are omitted. The natural subsoil at this part of the subsite was badly disturbed by frost action. No post-pipes were visible and the shapes of individual features were undiagnostic. The following information should therefore suffice.

Area II

F11. Grid 19W/63N. Dia 0.4m; depth 0.2m. Sand-silt with scattered gravel pebbles; rare charcoal (10YR 3/3). Cuts ditch *f*, layer 1.

F12. Grid 19W/62N. Dia 0.35m; depth 0.3m. Sand-silt with scattered gravel pebbles; no charcoal (10YR 3/3).

F13. Grid 18W/60N. Dia 0.35m; depth 0.15m. Sand-silt with scattered gravel pebbles; rare charcoal (10YR 4/3).

F15. Grid 26W/66N. Dia 0.5m; depth 0.35m. Sand-silt with scattered gravel pebbles; charcoal rare (10YR 4/3).

F16. Grid 23W/64N. Dia 0.37m; depth 0.16m. Sand-silt with scattered gravel pebbles; charcoal very rare (10YR 4/4).

F17. Grid 22W/64N. Dia 0.5m; depth 0.33m. Sand-silt with scattered gravel pebbles; dense concentrations of charcoal, not burnt *in situ* (10YR 4/3).

Area III

F13. Grid 27W/69N. Dia 0.35m; depth 0.35m. Sand-silt with scattered gravel pebbles; charcoal rare (10YR 4/3).

Pits NE of Enclosure C (FIG 44C)

Five large (and one small) pits were found in Area III, overlying and to the north of ditches *a* and 10. Their precise contemporaneity would be difficult to prove, but their location in a group and their consistent N-S alignment, suggest a degree of chronological, if not functional, association. Fillings were generally similar and only one example is described below (see archive for F4, F23, F24, F25 and F27):

F26. Grid 80W/86N. Dia 1.9m; depth 0.57m. Sand-silt with clay (10YR 4/2). This pit probably dates to the earliest Iron Age/Late Bronze Age on the basis of two rim sherds from layers 2 and 3 (FIG 61, 40, 41). It is cut, to the NE, by the small pit F27, described below.

Layer 1. Sand-silt with clay (10YR 4/2). Find: 1 flint.

Layer 2. Sand-silt with even gravel mix (10YR 5/4). Find: 1 potsherd.

Layer 3. Sand-silt with scattered gravel pebbles (10YR 5/1). Find: 1 potsherd.

Other Non-Linear Features

In closing this section on non-linear features that post-date the ditch enclosures, it should be noted that there were 37 small pits or postholes scattered haphazardly over Area I-VI. None of these revealed dateable artifacts and the generally rather dark colour of their filling suggests a post-'Bronze Age' date (feature filling colour is briefly discussed in Pryor 1976b). They have been omitted from the plans for the sake of clarity.

2. DITCHES (FIG 44)

Only three ditches could be shown to post-date the second millennium enclosure system. They are all illustrated in FIG 44:

F54. This was a very shallow (*c* 0.05-0.35m), narrow (0.2-0.4m) ditch which ran N-S for *c* 24m, passed through a corner of *c* 107°, to run SE-NW for *c* 60m. It cut all ditches of the second millennium ditched enclosure system, but was cut by the Roman ditch F65. It yielded no dateable finds other than a spatulate bronze awl which was found on the stripped surface (and should, therefore, be treated with caution). The filling was distinctly darker than that of the second millennium ditches and was uniformly composed of sand-silt with scattered gravel pebbles (10YR 4/3). It did not end abruptly to the S or W, but 'petered out'. It may well have continued further in either direction. Its function is not clear, but its size would argue against drainage. An Iron Age date would seem probable but not certain (the awl is probably residual).

F65. This ditch ran across the site from NE-SW (PL 9). It cut all second millennium ditches and later prehistoric features. Its upper layer, as revealed on the stripped surface, was filled with flood clay which shows up as a dark line on the air photographs of the crop-marks (PL 6) and stripped surface (PL 9). This flood clay is most probably that discussed below (Chapter 3) and would have been laid down in the third century AD. This is in accord with the pottery (Nene Valley Grey Ware) found in the ditch filling immediately below the clay. The ditch would, therefore, have been visible as a slight depression at the time the flooding took place.

Turning to the question of function, there can be little doubt that the ditch served as a drain in its more northerly length (PL 9), which was not excavated. Here a series of subsidiary ditches joined the main ditch at angles of 10°-20°, very much in the manner of feeder drains, and not at all typical of the rectilinear arrangement of boundary ditches. The small ditch *x* (FIG 44), on the other hand, does join F65 at an approximate right-angle and it is probable, therefore, that the ditch served the dual role of drain and boundary, as is commonly found in the area to this day.

AREA VII (FIGS 18, 45, 47, 48; PL 9)

INTRODUCTION (FIG 18; PL 9)

The linear ditches that comprise the northern element of the Newark Road second millennium system cannot actually be demonstrated to form the sides of enclosures. This, however, is almost certainly the result of our inability to strip areas of a suitable size and does not reflect differential patterns of land management. On the contrary, the arrangement of the archaeological features suggests that a broadly similar pattern of land management was practised over the whole subsite.

The most southerly ditch of the northern system, F254, runs E-W for a distance of about 76m, whereupon it passes through a right-angle and extends N for about 126m; its N-S length is F186 (FIG 47), up to, but not beyond the first of two T-junctions with ditched E-W droves, one of which is encountered just S of Grid 200N and the other of which is located at the extreme N end of the system. Both these droves appear to be composed of parallel ditches which pass out of the excavated area, westwards. Unfortunately none of these features appeared on aerial photographs and the spoil heaps were accordingly sited directly on top of them, effectively preventing further investigation of land to the west.

Feature 254 ran approximately parallel (40-50m) to ditch 10 in an ENE direction; the divergence from ditch 10 reflected the general divergence, of all the main E-W ditches (best seen in FIG 5), and is a strong argument for their general contemporaneity (Chapter 5). The principal interest in feature 254 lies in the occurrence of a large area of charcoal and burnt limestone (the 'industrial area') in its NE length. This area is examined in detail first. Attention will then turn to the northern drove ditches and their associated features.

1. THE 'INDUSTRIAL AREA' (FIGS 45-46)

The 'industrial area' consisted of a layer of redeposited rubbish in an off-centre recut on the south side of ditch 254, mainly concentrated between Grid lines 15 and 21W (FIG 45). Charcoal staining affected the stripped natural gravel subsoil for about 5m south of the ditch; in addition, a narrow band of similar staining (c 1-2m) was found to the north of the ditch. There was no evidence for *in situ* burning, but this is explained by the loss of about 0.3m of ancient land surface through modern ploughing (see Chapter 3 for more detailed discussion of plough damage). The charcoal that was observed on the stripped surface most probably reached its present location through the action of earthworms. This would incidate that the industrial activity took place on the surface and did not involve the use of sunken hearths or kilns.

We shall consider the recut and its filling below, but first we must describe the ditch in its un-recut form.

Ditch 254 was in general U-shaped and of regular width, depth and profile, becoming somewhat wider and deeper towards the east. A typical transverse section (taken at the extreme E edge of the excavated area) showed the following succession (FIG 46, no 2):

Layer 1. Clay-silt with much gravel in an even mix; charcoal absent. Many of the features in the S part of Area VII were capped by this thin gravel layer which probably represents water-sorting. A similar deposit was encountered on

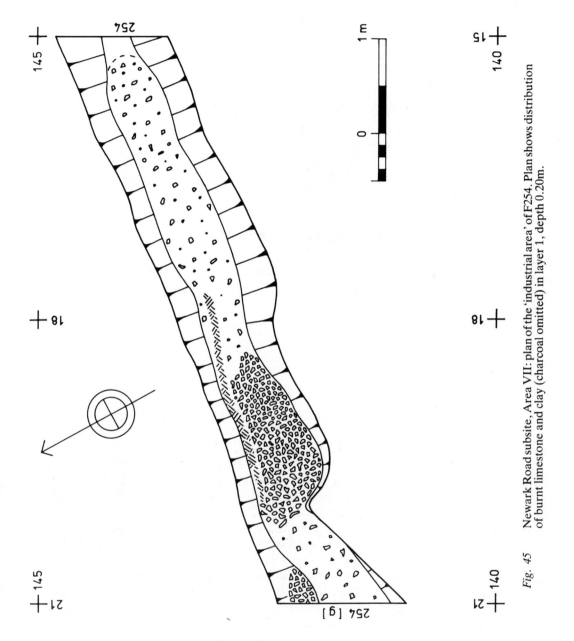

Fig. 45   Newark Road subsite, Area VII: plan of the 'industrial area' of F254. Plan shows distribution of burnt limestone and clay (charcoal omitted) in layer 1, depth 0.20m.

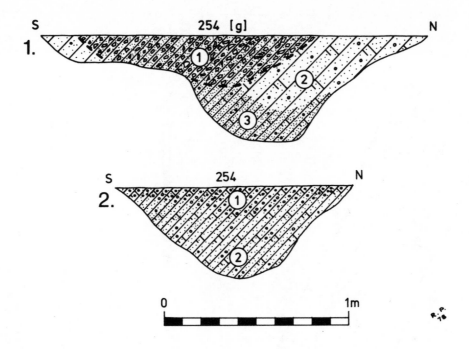

Fig. 46   Newark Road subsite, Area VII: 'industrial area' sections.

        lower parts of the Cat's Water subsite where its alluvial nature was not in doubt.

Layer 2. Silt with clay and scattered gravel pebbles (10YR 3/3); charcoal very rare.

    The principal deposit of the 'industrial area' was confined between Grid lines 21W and 15W (FIG 45). It was contained in a recut of F254 which had a stepped profile in this area. The bulk of the deposit consisted of burnt limestone fragments, derived from Cornbrash outcrops to the west (cf FNG 1, Vicarage Farm subsite). It also contained large quantities of charcoal (described in detail in Appendix 5 below) and a few pieces of burnt clay and pottery. A typical section through this deposit showed the following succession (FIG 46; for location see FIG 45):

Layer 1. (the recut containing the 'industrial' deposit) Dark sand-silt with much charcoal, burnt, and unburnt, Cornbrash limestone, gravel pebbles (some burnt) and clay (10YR 2.5/1). This layer cut through layers 2 and 3 and could be clearly distinguished from them.

Layer 2. Clay-silt with scattered gravel pebbles (10YR 5/3).

Layer 3. Clay-silt with more sand than layer 2; a few gravel lenses were also found (10YR 4/1). This is a more 'rapid' deposit than layer 2, above it.

Discussion

The principal points of interest may be summarised thus. The 'industrial area' consisted of a deposit of secondary rubbish which had been dumped into a late, off-centre, recut of the first millennium ditch, F254. The area around the ditch was extensively stained with charcoal which it is suggested found its way to the B/C horizon through worm action. This spread, therefore, probably indicates the approximate area where the industrial activity took place. The deposit, mainly limestone and charcoal, would not have been unpleasant-smelling or noxious and there seemed no good reason to suppose that it was not produced very close to where it was found.

The nature of the deposit itself calls for comment. First, although a few burnt gravel pebbles were encountered, the vast majority of burnt stones were of limestone. A few unburnt fragments of limestone were compared with Cornbrash from the Vicarage Farm subsite, and the two were identical. Cornbrash is the only limestone series which outcrops at Fengate. In its weathered state it is brown, flaggy, with some vertical fissuring (Horton *et al* 1974, 81) and its only modern use appears to have been for lime-burning or crushing; it is certainly too soft and prone to frost damage to have been used for building (Horton *et al* 1974, 61 and 66). In this regard, it should be recalled that there is as yet no evidence at Fengate for stone-built buildings.

The limestone fragments found amounted to a total estimated weight of about one half imperial ton. Fragment size varied from the minute to fist-sized, but the majority were sub-angular in shape with well-rounded edges and average length/breadth of *c* 50mm. A grab sample of 10 typical fragments weighed 505gm. Over 90% of the sample showed signs of extensive burning (reddening, fire-cracking etc) on all faces.

Other non-organic material included a few pieces of burnt clay, some of which showed wattle-impressions (FIG 75, 5, 6). One piece of burnt pottery was also found (FIG 56, 45).

The charcoal is described in detail below (Appendix 5), but the principal point to arise from this study is that typical Fenland wood was used in the 'industrial' process. The precise position of the second millennium Fen-edge is still in some doubt, but Mr David Hall, Cambridgeshire Archeological Committee Fenland Field Officer (pers comm), agrees that the location of the 'industrial area' is very approximately midway between the contemporary Fen-edge and the Vicarage Farm outcrop of the Cornbrash. Mrs Taylor's study of the charcoals further points out that the timber used was from logs *c* 200-300mm in diameter; there was virtually no evidence for brushwood or twigs. It would appear then that the siting of the 'industrial area' was intended to minimise the time and effort involved in transporting both logs and limestone.

Three radiocarbon samples were taken from charcoal from this deposit. They gave dates of (HAR-1970-2) 960 ± 70 bc; 1030 ± 70 bc; 1000 ± 70 bc. These dates would agree well with the chronology of the ditched enclosure system suggested here (Chapter 5) and the size of the timbers involved would rule out the serious chronological distortion that would result from the use of mature trunks (Coles and Jones 1975, 124). The use of ancient 'bog oaks' is highly improbable because of the species of trees involved: nobody would attempt to dig up fossil alder and willow when these trees would have been growing in large numbers in the Fen, for it should be recalled that 'bog oak' is extremely hard, heavy and difficult to cut. The fact that Fen species were almost exclusively used for fuel in the 'industrial area' might be taken to imply that the gravel soils of the Fen margin were largely cleared of tree cover. An incidental effect of clearing the Fen-edge and skirtland, where willow and alder flourish, would be to open more ground suitable for summer pasture (Darby 1940, 61ff).

We must now consider the nature of the industrial activity which required the transportation of large quantities of stone and timber, assuming, that is, that the secondary deposit in the recut is only a small sample of the quantities used in antiquity. Metalworking may be discounted because (a) no moulds, crucibles, bronze spills or semi-finished artifacts were found and, (b) the small quantities of burnt clay found show no evidence for vitrification. The role of the limestone is also not clear in this explanation.

It could, perhaps, be argued that the deposit represents the collapsed remains of a house which had burnt down. Against this, it must be argued that the quantities of wattle-impressed daub found are very small and that, as noted above, stone-built buildings are unknown at Fengate. It could be suggested that Cornbrash might have been used to provide the bedding for walls, or the packing for postholes, but if that were the case, one would not expect burning to be as severe as that encountered here. Other hypotheses that involve the use of fire (for example meat or fish smoking; salt evaporation; charcoal burning) fail to account for the limestone and its transportation for at least a quarter of a mile, and probably farther. There is also no evidence for saltern briquetage, and willow burns without smoke (see Appendix 5).

The only explanation which can so far be advanced is that the industrial activity involved is lime burning. We have noted above that the burning probably took place in the vicinity of the ditch and that there is no evidence for a deeply sunken kiln. Lime burning in a surface clamp or bonfire would not have been a particularly efficient process and it is suggested here that the burnt limestone fragments found are merely the cores of the larger pieces which the heat was not able to reach. This might account for their sub-angular and rounded appearance. It must be emphasised here that this, very surprising, explanation of the 'industrial area' is not intended to be final or conclusive, but it does seem to fit the available data best. Possible uses for the lime are considered in Chapter 5.

2. THE NORTHERN DROVEWAYS AND THEIR ASSOCIATED FEATURES (FIGS 47-52)

INTRODUCTION

The ditches that comprise the northern droves show the clearest evidence at Fengate for recuts and more than one period of use. They also give some idea of the way in which a ditched drove system could be altered and adapted to meet the different needs of day-to-day land management and stock control. This is particularly evident in the blocking and unblocking of entranceways and subsidiary droves. The first part of this section will be given over to a description of the ditches and their fillings, while the second part will consider evidence for phasing.

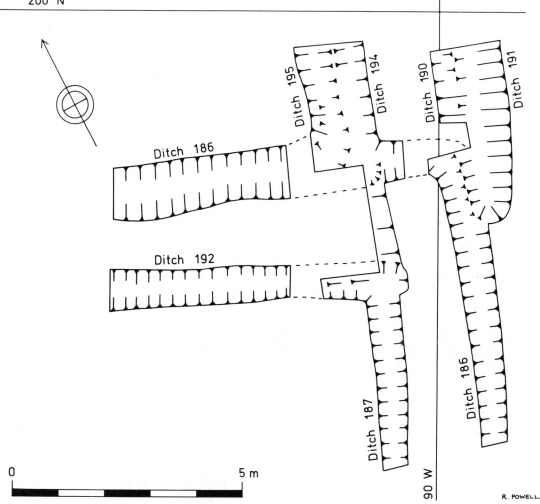

Ditch 195
Ditch 194
Ditch 190
Ditch 191
Ditch 186
Ditch 192
Ditch 187
Ditch 186

90 W

R. POWELL

0   5 m

Fig. 47   Newark Road subsite, Area VII: junction of southerly droves.

DESCRIPTION OF THE DITCHES

Ditch 186 (FIGS 47, 49, nos 3 and 5; 51)

This ditch runs N-S (73m) for most of its excavated length (84m). To the south, it is contemporary and continuous with ditch 254 which it joins at a right-angle (at Grid 75W/126N). To the north (FIG 47) it passes through another right-angle and runs E-W for 11m, to leave the excavated area at Grid 100W/195N. The profile of ditch 186 was, on the whole, regular, except for a short (*c* 10m) stretch between Grid 150 and160N. Here the apparent irregularity of plan, evident in FIG 18, is probably caused by

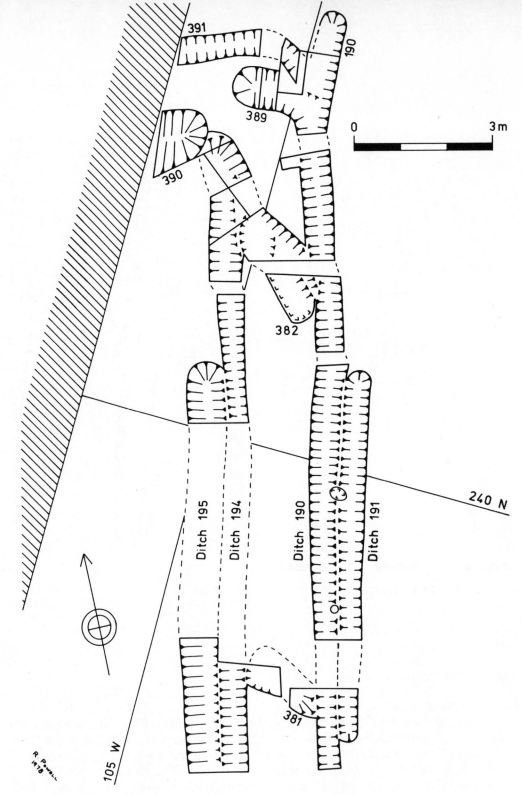

391

190

389

390

382

240 N

Ditch 195

Ditch 194

Ditch 190

Ditch 191

381

105 W

R Powell
1978

Fig. 48   Newark Road subsite, Area VII: northerly droveway ditches.

problems experienced by the excavators in accurately locating the correct working level. It was at this point that ditch 187 was located, *c* 1.5m W of, and parallel to, ditch 186, with which it formed a N-S droveway. The apparent butt-end to ditch 187 may, therefore, not be 'real' and it is quite possible that it originally extended further southwards. The problems in this area were caused by a sudden thinning-out of the 'B' soil horizon (discussed in FNG 2, Appendix 1). North of approximate Grid line 160N, however, the correct level was established with fair confidence.

Two sections are shown here, one (FIG 49, no 3) in the deeper, wider length of E-W ditch, the other in the main, N-S, length at Grid *c* 190N (FIG 49, no 5). Most sections were drawn during the height of the 1976 drought, so Munsell colours are frequently not given. The sections showed the following stratigraphy:

FIG 49, no 3:

Layer 1. Sand-silt with even gravel mix; charcoal very rare.

Layer 2. Gravel with sand-silt lenses; charcoal absent. A 'rapid' deposit.

FIG 49, no 5:

Layer 1. Sand-silt with scattered gravel pebbles; charcoal rare. There was no rapid silting visible.

Ditch 187

This ditch ran parallel to 186, to the W, from Grid *c* 150N to Grid 193N, a distance of *c* 44m. It may originally have continued further south, but could not be traced, due to the practical problems discussed above. To the north, the E-W element could not be linked with any great certainty to the N-S element, so a new feature number (192) was allocated to this ditch (FIG 47). Ditch 187 was, in the main, slighter than ditch 186, as the illustrated section, taken at Grid 191N, shows:

FIG 49, no 6:

Layer 1. Sand-silt with scattered gravel pebbles; charcoal rare.

Ditch 190

This ditch continues the alignment of ditch 186 northwards, but is slightly off-set, *c* 0.5m to the W (FIG 47). Its total excavated length was *c* 52m and it appeared to be continuous, without any obvious signs of recutting. Its course in the extreme north was not clear, but it may well have passed through a right-angle westwards (as 391) as indicated in FIG 48. It certainly did not continue further northwards beyond its possible butt at Grid 104W/249N in the excavated area. It was, in general, steep-sided and uniform in both width and profile. The two sections illustrated here will be described below (with ditch 191).

Ditch 191

This ditch was contiguous with ditch 190, immediately to the E. It was arranged in three separate lengths, each broken by a 'causeway'-style gap or entranceway. The southerly length ran from Grid 195N to 212N, a length of *c* 17m; the central length ran from Grid 214N to 227N, a length of *c* 14.5m, and the gap between each section was 2.2m wide. The northern length was shorter than the other two. It ran from Grid 234N to 242N, for a distance of *c* 7.7m; the gap separating it from the central length of ditch was *c* 7.5m wide. Both the butt-ends of each length of ditch were sharp and clear and there can be no doubt about the layout of the ditch, as shown here (FIGS 51 and 52). Despite the dry conditions under which most of the ditch was excavated, the great length of intersecting ditch filling allowed the relationship of ditches 190 to 191 to be established with confidence. Two sections of the double ditch are described below:

FIG 49, no 1 (Grid 201N)

Ditch 190

Layer 1. Sand-silt with even gravel mix. Darker than ditch 191, layer 2, which it cuts.

Layer 2. Sand-silt with scattered gravel pebbles, above lenses of sand and gravel 'rapid' silting. Appeared to cut 191 layer 3, but this not very clear.

Ditch 191

Layer 1. Sand-silt with scattered gravel pebbles, similar to 190, layer 1.

Layer 2. Sand-silt with even gravel mix, paler than layers 1 (above) and 3 (below, to W) and cut by 190, layer 1.

Layer 3. Sand-silt with scattered gravel pebbles; colour as layer 1. Possibly cut by 190, layer 2, certainly cut by 190, layer 1.

Layer 4. Sand-silt with even gravel mix and gravel lenses. A 'rapid' deposit.

This southerly section of ditch 191 is the only one to show possible evidence for recutting. Layers 3 and 4 show the familiar sequence of rapid and slow silting which seems to be truncated by a slightly off-centre sequence (represented by layers 1 and 2), of renewed rapid and slow silting. There was, however, no clear surface evidence for off-centre recutting, but this could be explained by the dry conditions under which the feature was excavated. An alternative explanation for layer 2 is that it represents the collapsed remains of a bank; the direction and location of slip, however, does not favour this hypothesis. Whatever the explanation, all layers of ditch 191 were cut by ditch 190.

FIG 50, no 1 (Grid 236N)

Ditches 190 and 191

Layer 1. Sand-silt with scattered gravel pebbles. This section was excavated in 1977 and a Munsell colour of 10YR 4/3 was obtained for both ditches. Ditch 190 cut 191.

Ditch 192

This ditch ran parallel to the E-W length of 186, *c* 1.0-1.5m south of it. It was excavated for a length of 9.7m and joined the N extremity of ditch 187 (FIG 47) at right-angles. A slight heel-like projection E of 187 at the junction possibly suggests that the two ditches were not originally contemporary, although no hint of this was provided by their uniform sand-silt filling. A single section is illustrated here. It had the following filling:

FIG 49, no 4 (Grid 97W/193N)

Layer 1. Sand-silt with scattered gravel pebbles; charcoal very rare.

Ditch 194

This ditch continued the alignment of ditch 187 northwards, for an excavated length of *c* 52m. It ran parallel to ditches 190 and 191, but *c* 1.0-1.5m west, for the whole

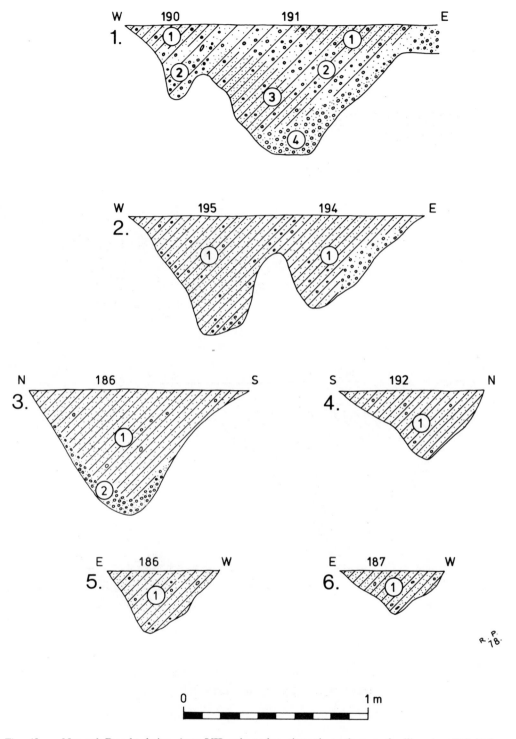

Fig. 49   Newark Road subsite, Area VII: selected sections through second millennium BC ditches.

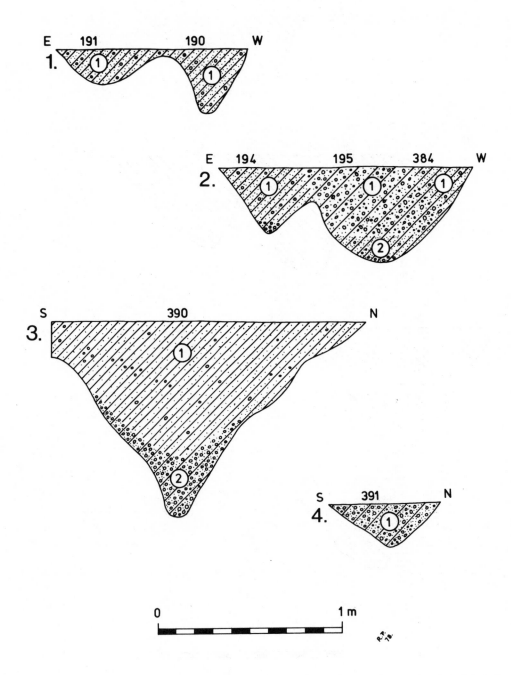

Fig. 50   Newark Road subsite, Area VII: selected sections through second millennium BC ditches.

of its length. It was remarkably uniform in width and profile, and showed no obvious signs of recutting, except at the extreme north where the sequence of events was very difficult to establish, as will be discussed below. The two sections which are reproduced here will be described with those of ditch 195 which cut it.

Ditch 195

Ditch 195 was the most westerly of the main N-S drove ditches, and was clearly demonstrated to cut ditch 194 with which it was contiguous and parallel for the whole of its length (*c* 57m). Its southern end adjoined ditch 186, as it swung westwards; and its N end was rounded, clearly defined and level with the northern end of ditch 191 (at Grid 105W/241N). Its width, depth and profile were, in general, uniform. Two sections are illustrated:

FIG 49, no 2 (Grid 93W/199N)

Ditches 194 and 195

Layer 1. Sand-silt with scattered gravel pebbles; charcoal very rare or absent. Although their fillings were usually identical, a thin line of gravel pebbles and a slight change in 'feel' during excavation clearly showed that 195 cut 194.

FIG 50, no 2 (Grid 104W/240N)

Ditch 194

Layer 1. Sand-silt with scattered gravel pebbles; charcoal absent (10YR 4/3). Some rapid silting at very bottom. Cut by 195 layer 1.

Ditch 195

Layer 1. Gravel with some sand-silt and iron-pan (10YR 4/4). Over layer 2; cuts ditch 194; cut by ditch 384 layer 1.

Layer 2. Sand-silt with scattered gravel pebbles; iron-pan (10YR 4/3). A more sandy, 'rapid' deposit.

Layer 1. Sand-silt with scattered gravel pebbles (10YR 4/3). Cuts 195 layer 1.

Ditch 384

This is a problematic feature. It could not be seen in plan, but could be seen in sections to cover the most northerly 17m of ditch 195. It contained a noticeably slighter concentration of gravel pebbles and was confined to the western edge of the ditch. The main argument against its interpretation as a recut of ditch 195 is the fact that at no point was it seen to cut into the natural subsoil (to give ditch 195 a stepped profile). It is illustrated in section in FIG 50, no 2 which is described in detail above.

Feature 390 (FIG 48)

This feature cannot be interpreted as a ditch with any confidence as so little of it could be excavated (*c* 1.5m, E-W). However, arguments in favour of it being a ditch are strong. They include its location on the W side of a probable butt of ditch 194; its elongated shape and orientation; and its filling (and finds) which were indistinguishable from other second millennium ditches in the area. It should also, perhaps, be noted that it was too shallow for a well and that pits of its size and depth are unknown in second millennium contexts at Fengate. In view of the above, the feature is perhaps best explained as a substantially enlarged butt-end of an E-W ditch, contiguous with the N-S ditch 194. If this is accepted, it would have formed a drove with ditch 391 which is a probable E-W extension of ditch 190. Only one section was exposed:

FIG 50, no 3 (Grid 107W/245N)

Layer 1. Sand-silt with scattered gravel pebbles, occasional gravel lenses and sand; charcoal very rare (10YR 4/3-3/3). An evenly graded deposit with no indication of recutting.

Layer 2. Sand-silt and fine sand with a heavy gravel admixture; charcoal absent (10YR 5/4). A rapid deposit under layer 1; the sides of the ditch were difficult to determine in the limited space available and the section shown may be slightly over-dug at the very bottom.

Ditch 391

Ditch 391 ran E-W for an excavated length of *c* 3m. It probably represents an E-W extension of the N-S ditch 190. Its profile, width and depth are certainly consistent with such an interpretation (compare FIG 50, nos 1 and 4). One section is illustrated:

FIG 50, no 4 (Grid 103W/247N)

Ditch 391

Layer 1. Sand-silt with sand and scattered gravel pebbles; charcoal rare (10YR 4/3).

DISCUSSION AND PHASING OF THE DITCHES (FIGS 51-2)

This section is best introduced by giving the relationships which can be stratigraphically demonstrated with confidence. Finds' distributions, spatial relationships and other data will later be used to support the observations noted below.

Of the main N-S ditches, ditch 190 cut 191, and ditch 195 cut 194. These relationships were observed at numerous sections. The only other area where the stratigraphic relationships could be observed was at the junction of the southern ditches 186 and 187 with those from the north and those forming the E-W drove (FIG 47). Here 194 was cut by the E-W length of 186 which was, in turn, cut by 195 which then continued westwards along the alignment of 186. No other relationships could be stratigraphically demonstrated.

The following detailed observations should amplify the above (the results are summarised at the end of the section). The earliest two ditches of the series appear to be nos 191 and 194. Ditch 191 butted near the N end of 186, but the relationship between the two was obscured by the cutting-through of the later ditch 190. A slight deepening in the ditch bottom at the appropriate spot suggests that ditch 194 may well have originally ended at the south edge of what was to become the E-W length of 186 (at Grid 91.5W/96.5N). The earliest phase, then, is represented by a simple N-S droveway which ended with ditches 191 and 194 and which was probably entered via the 'causeways' in ditch 191. These 'causeways' indicate that the drove primarily serviced land to the east.

The droveway formed by ditches 191 and 194 then appears to have been blocked at its southern end by a new droveway from the south, formed by ditches 186 and 187/192. The relationship of the latter two ditches is not altogether clear; the heel-like projection at the point where they both meet might indicate that they were laid out in

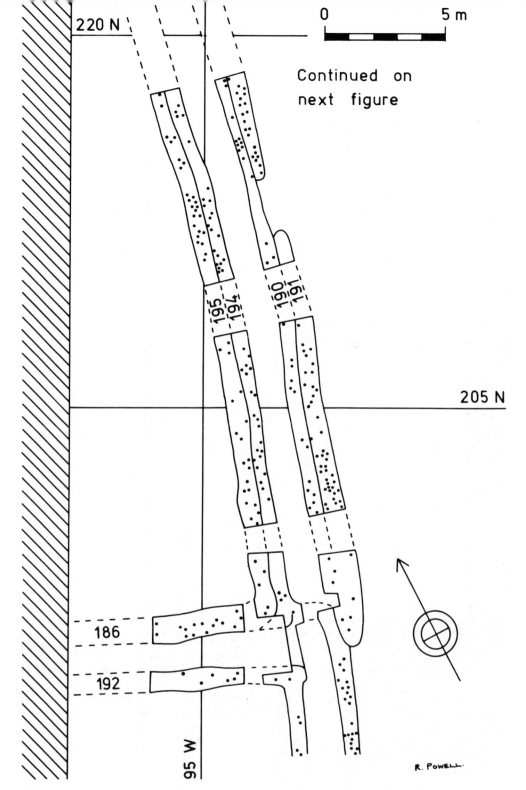

Fig. 51 Newark Road subsite, Area VII: distribution of finds in the northerly drove, S half (continued on FIG 52, below).

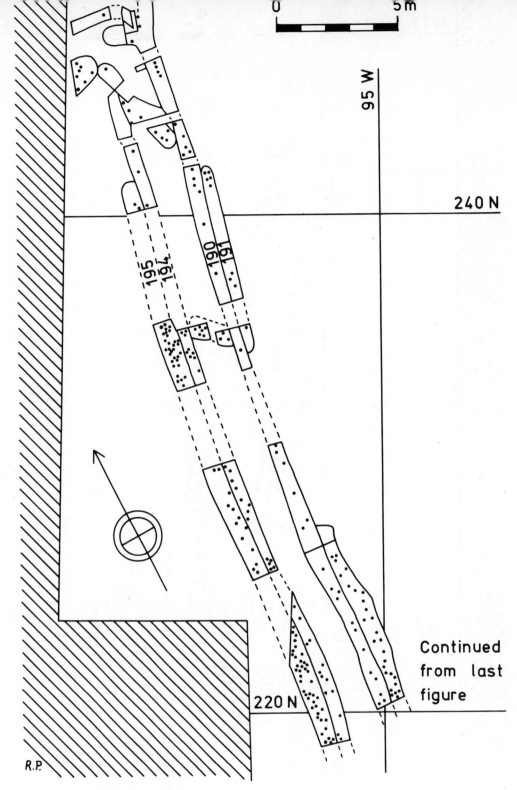

Fig. 52   Newark Road subsite, Area VII: distribution of finds in the northerly drove, N half (continued from FIG 51, above).

two operations; but if that is the case, there is no means of establishing which of the two droves thus formed has chronological priority. The short length of ditch joining 187 with 194 presents many problems of interpretation (FIG 47). It could be seen as a simple, first phase, extension of 194 which would have given better access to livestock coming from the east. On the other hand, it could be seen as a blocking ditch dug between the earliest phase and the latest phase represented by the digging of ditch 195. Indeed, other interpretations are possible.

The third major phase sees the cutting of ditches 190 and 195, presumably to form a droveway. The northern part of the site showed little soil colour differentiation, so interpretation is difficult. Nonetheless, of the three courses open to it, ditch 190 is best seen as having turned through a right-angle, along the course of 391 (FIG 48). The two alternative courses, both of which terminate in butt-ends could represent earlier or later phases of use, but are, perhaps, best seen as non-man-made—this, certainly, was the subjective impression gained in the field. Turning to ditch 195, this terminates at Grid 241N (FIG 52); it has already been suggested that feature 390 may be a pit-like expansion of an E-W ditch which would have run parallel to 391 and formed a drove with it. If 194 did, in fact, butt immediately next to 390 (and this was not altogether clear in the field), then the contemporaneity of the two features would seem most improbable. A better explanation that fits all the facts is that feature 390 and ditch 195 are contemporary, and that the gap between them is a corner entranceway (width 4.5m), giving access into the third phase droveway (ditches 195 and 190). At its southern end, it is not clear whether ditches 192 and 187 were still in use, but the fact that 195 can be seen to swing west, along the alignment of 186 strongly suggests that they were. Ditch 186 can be shown to have filled-in by this stage and it is unfortunate that the section at the junction of 186 and 190 was inconclusive; however, the precise alignment of 190 and 186 does suggest that the former was extended along the course of the latter, thus totally re-cutting it. Ditch 186, in both its suggested phases was the same depth and width as 190.

Only two features could not be seen to form any part of the ditch system. These are the two oblong 'pits' 381 and 382, located in the northern part of the main N-S droveway (FIG 48). Their filling was identical to that of the ditches with which they were contiguous and their finds, insofar as they could be dated, were of probable second millennium date. Their sides were too steep to suggest that they may have been formed by trampling livestock and their profiles were not at all typical of weathered ditches. Their location with respect to the most northerly segment of ditch 191 may be significant, but this cannot be proved. Their role must remain enigmatic until a better explanation can be offered.

Finally, the finds' distribution is less revealing than might be expected: the two phases (represented by ditches 191-194 and 190-195) of droveway are reflected in different patterns of finds' distribution. It is interesting to note, however, that finds do not tend to concentrate around entranceways into, or out of, droveways. The lack of sharp changes in finds' distribution suggests that the ditches were not cleaned, apart from the major phases noted above. This impression is certainly borne out by the even, regular plan and profile of the ditches concerned and is in sharp contrast with the pattern noted in many of the droveway ditches of Areas I-VI.

The phasing may be briefly summarised thus: a simple N-S droveway, formed by ditches 191 and 194, was followed by an L-shaped droveway, formed by ditches 186 and 187/192; this was, in turn, replaced by a new N-S drove, just half a metre west of the original drove, formed by ditches 190 and 195. This latter drove was probably extended west, along the existing alignment of 186 and 192, and south, along 186 and 187. In the first phase, access to the drove was from the south, perhaps also from the north-east, but mainly from 'causeways' in ditch 191. Access to the second phase, southerly drove, remains unclear, but access to the final phase seems to have been via a wide entranceway to the north, between the north butt-end of ditch 195 and the possible E-W ditch 390.

General implications of the above will be considered in Chapter 5, but a few specific points should be mentioned here. First, the precise alignment of different phases of ditch, as seen, for example, in the total recutting of ditch 186 (west) by ditch 195, and the equally precise off-centre alignment of the first and third phases of the northerly N-S drove, strongly suggests that some form of surface marker was present for the diggers of the later phase ditches to follow. It can be shown statigraphically that the early phase ditches had filled in when the latter phase ditches were dug. A hedge would seem the most obvious solution to this problem. Second, the sequence, as outlined here, indicates a gradual, progressive increase in the area of land subjected to intensive management. Third, although the basic structure of the physical features remains the same, ditches are recut and entranceways are moved around, suggesting that day-to-day land management measures were constantly changing, as on any well-run modern farm. Fourth, it must again be emphasised that the length of time involved is still not clear, although the complete silting-up of ditches between various phases might suggest that decades, rather than years, separated the major phases of extension and reconstruction.

TABLE 3

Newark Road subsite: distribution, by weight (in grammes), of second millennium BC pottery from linear ditches. Fabric types after D F Williams.

	Fabric 1	Fabric 2	Fabric 3	Fabric 4	Total	% (of total)
(Areas I-VI)						
Ditch 8	27	168	93	84	372	12.3
Ditch 9	170	264	36	38	508	16.8
Ditch 10	56	52	3	16	127	4.2
Ditch a	26	138	3	—	167	5.5
Ditch b	152	16	14	—	182	6.0
Ditch c	—	—	11	—	11	0.4
Ditch e	5	15	—	8	28	0.9
Ditch f	267	2	5	15	289	9.5
Ditch i	—	27	18	—	45	1.5
Ditch j	—	—	1	—	1	—
Ditch k	—	1	32	—	33	1.1
Ditch m	63	—	—	—	63	2.1
Ditch n	—	426	—	33	459	15.2
Ditch q	—	2	—	23	25	0.8
Ditch t	—	55	3	7	65	2.1
Ditch u	—	7	2	—	9	0.3
Ditch x	—	15	—	—	15	0.5
Ditch z	—	2	3	—	5	0.2
(Area VII)						

Ditch 186	—	—	59	—	59	1.9
Ditch 190	—	70	1	—	71	2.3
Ditch 191	—	31	86	—	117	3.9
Ditch 194	—	6	19	30	55	1.8
Ditch 195	—	26	69	—	95	3.2
Ditch 254	191	—	—	—	191	6.3
Ditch 384	—	24	—	—	24	0.8
Ditch 390	—	—	5	—	5	0.2
Ditch 391	—	6	—	—	6	0.2
Totals:	957	1353	463	254	3027	
%	31.6	44.7	15.3	8.4		

FINDS

1. POTTERY (FIGS 53-61)

INTRODUCTION

Pottery from the Newark Road subsite will be described under two general headings. First, that from the ditches of the second millennium enclosure system (Areas I-VI followed by Area VII), then that from pits of all periods. It was not thought advisable to subdivide the finds from these small pits, so some non-ceramic material is also briefly considered in this section. The Catalogue is preceded by a report on Newark Road second millennium pottery fabrics by Dr D F Williams, Ph D, of the DoE Ceramic Petrology Project, Department of Archaeology, Southampton University. The fabric types distinguished in this study are used throughout the Report. Table 3 lists the distribution of Dr Williams' four fabrics in the second millenium ditches.

SECOND MILLENNIUM BC POTTERY FROM THE NEWARK ROAD SUBSITE, FENGATE, PETERBORUGH
Dr D F Williams

A representative selection of second millennium BC sherds from the Newark Road subsite, Fengate, was submitted for fabric analysis. All the sherds were studied macroscopically with the aid of a binocular microscope, and many were thin sectioned and examined under the petrological microscope. This allowed a number of fabric groupings to be made on the basis of the type of inclusions present in each sherd.

Fabric 1

Soft, slightly soapy fabric, normally dark grey (Munsell 2.5Y N4/) throughout, with numerous fragments of shell protruding through the surfaces. Thin sectioning shows recrystallization of calcite in some of the shell, suggesting that it is fossiliferous. A little limestone was also present. The local Cornbrash or Oxford Clay and Kellaways Beds, for example, would be a suitable source for the raw materials used in the pottery.

Fabric 2

Soft, friable fabric, variable in colour. Thin sectioning revealed a large number of voids making up the matrix (the samples submitted were too small to see if this was a feature of the sherds in the hand-specimen). In some cases the blade-like nature of the vesicles suggests vegetable matter that has burnt out during firing. However, it is difficult to say whether this applies to all the voids, some of which may represent shell or limestone fragments which have disappeared due to adverse soil conditions.

Fabric 3

Fairly soft fabric, tending towards reddish-brown (5YR 5/3) surfaces, with a darker core. Small fragments of grog (crushed up pieces of pottery) can be easily distinguished in the hand-specimen.

Fabric 4
Soft, friable fabric, brown (7.5YR 5/4) throughout, with infrequent large fragments of flint. Thin sectioning shows that besides flint, there are numerous subangular grains of quartz, average size 0.40-0.60mm.

CATALOGUE OF ILLUSTRATED POTTERY (FIGS 53-61)

DITCHES OF AREAS I-VI (FIGS 53-55)

Ditch 8 (FIG 53, 1-7)
1. Rimsherd. Fabric 3.
    Decoration: light, diagonal punctate impressions (not comb).
    Area VI, F359, layer 2, (Grid 7E/42N) depth 0.26. 76:770
2. Two rimsherds. Fabric 2. Flat-topped, inturned, smoothed rim.
    Undecorated.
    Area II, F2, layer 1, (Grid 25W/38N) depth 0.25. 74:1933
3. Rimsherd. Fabric 2.
    Decoration: slight, horizontal (?) twisted cord impression below rim.
    Area II, F2, layer 1, (Grid 19W/39N) depth 0.27. 74:1206
4. Rimsherd. Fabric 2. A weathered scrap.
    Undecorated.
    Area II, F2, layer 1, (Grid 17W/39N) depth 0.30. 74:2239
5. Rimsherd. Fabric 3.
    Decoration: one, low, pinched-up cordon below simple rim; sherd has broken along lower cordon (or carination?). Light, diagonal grooves.
    Area II, F2, layer 2, (Grid 26W/38N) depth 0.50. 74:1952
6. Simple base angle of slightly splay-sided vessel. Fabric 2.
    Undecorated.
    Area II, F2, layer 2, (Grid 20W/38N) depth 0.24. 74:1201
7. Simple base angle of steep-sided vessel. Fabric 2.
    Undecorated.
    Area II, layer 1, (Grid 85W/32N) depth 0.10. 74:2379

Ditch 9 (FIG 53, 8-11)
8. Rimsherds of closed bowl. Fabric 2.
    Undecorated.
    Area II, F3, layer 4, (Grid 16W/44N) depth 0.78. 74:1614
9. Rimsherd. Fabric 1. Much weathered.
    Undecorated.
    Area IV, F6, layer 2, (Grid 116W/36N) depth 0.50. 76:318
10. Rimsherd, flat-topped, unweathered.
    Undecorated.
    Area II, F3, layer 2, (Grid 75W/38N) depth 0.35. 74:2118
11. Wall sherd. Fabric 2. Weathered.
    Decoration: three fingertip impressions.
    Area II, F3, layer 1, (Grid 31W/43N) depth 0.15. 74:698

Ditch 10 (FIG 53, 12)
12. Rimsherd of straight-sided vessel; roughly smoothed, flat-topped and unweathered. Fabric 2.
    Decoration: single (?) bird-bone impression on rim top.
    Area IV, F1, layer 2, (Grid 109W/79N) depth 0.65. 76:31

Ditch a (FIG 54, 13-14)
13. Rimsherd of straight-sided vessel. Fabric 2.
    Undecorated.
    Area IV, F2, layer 1, (Grid 129W/71N) depth 0.05. 76:91
14. Rim and wall sherds of straight-sided vessel; flattened, smoothed rim top. Fabric 1 ('corky' surfaces).
    Area IV, F2, layer 1, (Grid 115W/73N) depth 0.20. 76:126

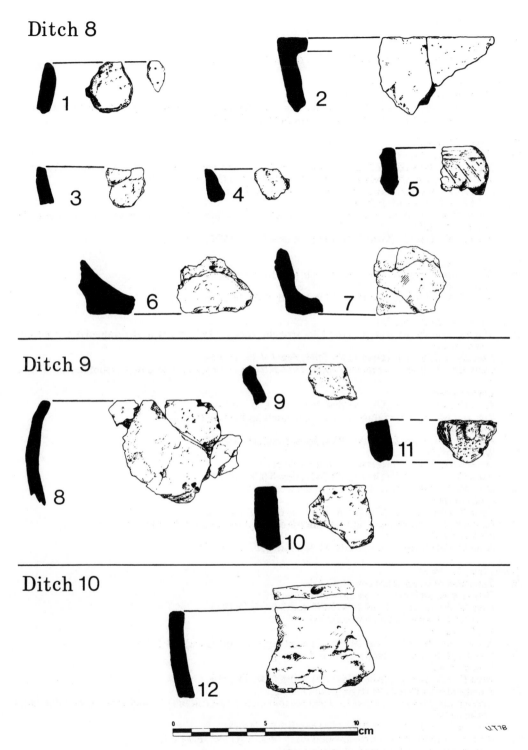

Ditch 8

Ditch 9

Ditch 10

Fig. 53   Newark Road subsite, Areas I-VI, second millennium BC ditches: pottery.

Ditch f (FIG 54, 15)
15. Base angle of large (dia *c* 24) steep-sided vessel. Fabric 3.
    Undecorated.
    Area II, F10, layer 1, (Grid 18W/57N) depth 0.50. 74:1504

Ditch i (FIG 54, 16)
16. Cordoned bodysherd. Fabric 3.
    Decoration: the cordon is probably the angle of a Collared Urn-type vessel, exterior rimsherd.
    Area II, F10, layer 2, (Grid 16W/52N) depth 0.25. 74:1627

Ditch k (FIG 54, 17-18)
17. Wall sherd. Fabric 3.
    Decoration: twisted cord impressions. Another sherd (not illus, no 76:1661) with very slight probable cord impressions was also found. Probably a Collared Urn-type vessel.
    Area II, F9, layer 2, (Grid 21W/49N) depth 0.45. 74:1657
18. Cordoned bodysherd. Fabric 3.
    Decoration: raised cordon could be the collar of a Collared Urn-type vessel. Fabric, firing and colour identical to nos 16 and 17, above.
    Area II, F9, layer 2, (Grid 21W/49N) depth 0.35. 74:1650

Ditch m (FIG 54,19)
19. Rimsherds of straight-sided bowl or jar (dia 160). Fabric 1.
    Undecorated.
    Area II, F55, layer 2, (Grid 60W/43N) depth 0.40. 74:2071

Ditch n (FIG 54, 20-24; 55, 25)
20. Rim and wall sherds of large (dia *c* 230), straight-sided jar with inturned, flat-topped rim. Fabric 2.
    Undecorated.
    Area IV, F5, layer 1, (Grid 119W/39N) depth 0.35. 76:203
21. Rimsherd, T-shaped, formed by applied bands to ext and int; gently rounded, smoothed top. Fabric 2.
    Undecorated.
    Area IV, F5, layer 1, (Grid 98W/41N) depth 0.10. 76:144
22. Rim and wall sherds of thin- and straight-sided jar/bowl. Fabric 2.
    Undecorated.
    Area II, F56, layer 2, (Grid 81W/41N) depth 0.20. 74:2186
23. Wall sherd. Ware 2.
    Decoration: row of fingertip/nail impressions.
    Area IV, F5, layer 1, (Grid 116W/39N) depth 0.30. 76:209
24. Base angle, simple type. Fabric 2. Much weathered.
    Undecorated.
    Area II, F56, layer 2, (Grid 85W/42N) depth 0.30. 74:2192
25. Base angle, concave type, and wall sherds of splay-sided vessel. Fabric 2.
    Undecorated.
    Area II, F56, layer 2, (Grid 86W/41N) depth 0.40. 74:2197/8

Ditch t (FIG 55, 26-32)
26. Rimsherd of steep-sided vessel. Fabric 2.
    Decoration: wide groove on internal rim bevel.
    Area II, F5, layer 1, (Grid 29W/24N) depth 0.04. 74:1923
27. Rimsherd. Fabric 3. Much weathered.
    Undecorated.
    Area II, F5, layer 1, (Grid 29W/15N) near surface (from sieve). 74:2215
28. Rimsherd. Fabric 2. Much weathered.
    Undecorated.
    Area II, F5, layer 1, (Grid 28W/17N) depth 0.04. 74:1919
29. Rimsherd of Collared Urn-type vessel. Fabric 2.
    Decoration: diagonal twisted cord impressions on ext; two (three?) twisted cord impressions along int rim bevel.
    Area II, F5, layer 1, (Grid 29W/28N) depth 0.10. 74:2151
30. Rim and wall sherds of vertical-sided small (dia 110) bowl. Fabric 4.
    Decoration: random fingernail impressions.

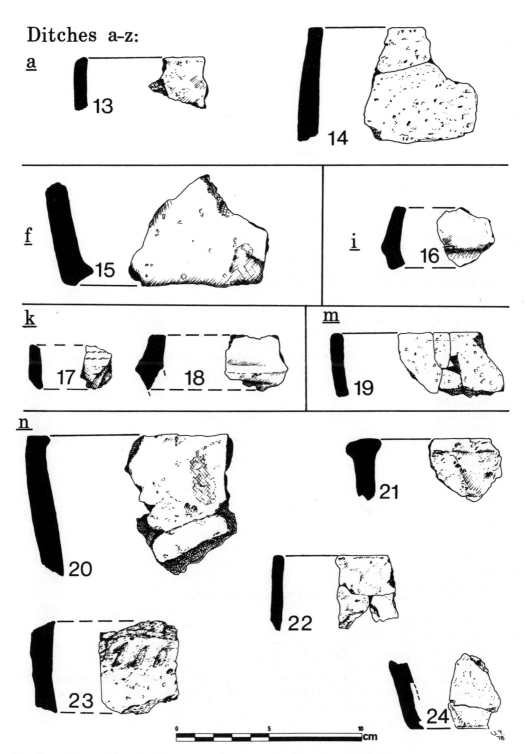

Ditches a–z:

a

13

14

f

15

i

16

k

17

18

m

19

n

20

21

22

23

24

0   5   10 cm

Fig. 54   Newark Road subsite, Areas I-VI, second millennium BC ditches: pottery.

Area II, F5, layer 1, (Grid 28W/10N) depth 0.15. 74:2158
31. Wall sherd. Fabric 2.
    Decoration: opposed diagonal twisted cord impressions. Collared Urn-type fabric and finish.
    Area II, F5, layer 1, (Grid 29W/29N) depth 0.05. 74:1973
32. Wall sherd. Fabric 3.
    Decoration: twisted cord impression. Collared Urn fabric and decoration.
    Area II, F5, layer 1, (Grid 29W/27N) depth 0.15. 74:2154

Ditch u (FIG 55, 33-34)
33. Rimsherd. Fabric 2. Much weathered.
    Undecorated.
    Area II, F1, layer 1, (Grid 8W/37N) depth 0.10. 74:1073
34. Rimsherd. Fabric 2. Much weathered.
    Undecorated.
    Area II, F1, layer 1, (Grid 7W/37N) near surface (from sieve). 74:2201

DITCHES OF AREA VII (FIG 55, 35-37: FIG 56)

Ditch 186 (FIG 55, 35)
35. Rimsherd. Fabric 3.
    Decoration: horizontal and diagonal twisted cord impressions on ext; two twisted cord impressions along int rim bevel. Collared Urn-type vessel.
    Area VII, F186, layer 1, (Grid 85W/176N) depth 0.02. 76:341

Ditch 190 (FIG 55, 36-37)
36. Rimsherd. Fabric 2. Very soft (PVA added). Possibly same vessel as no 37.
    Decoration: two lines of pseudo-cord incised decoration on rim top.
    Area VII, F190, layer 1, (Grid 99W/230N) depth 0.10. 77:5
37. Wall sherd. Fabric 2. Very soft (PVA added). Possibly same vessel as no 36.
    Decoration: deep (3mm) fingernail impressions on ext.
    Area VII, F190, layer 1, (Grid 99W/230N) depth 0.30. 77:6

Ditch 191 (FIG 56, 38-40)
38. Rimsherd of large vessel; rim externally thickened. Fabric 3, very similar to Collared Urn-type vessels.
    Decoration: ext: two rows of deep (*c* 3mm) sub-triangular spatulate impressions; rim top impressed with similar, deeper (5mm), punctate impressions.
    Area VII, F191, layer 1, (Grid 94W/221N) depth 0.10. 76:1000
39. Rimsherd, thickened and flared. Fabric 2.
    Decoration: coarse, angled twisted cord impressions across rim top.
    Area VII, F191, layer 1, (Grid 101W/237N) depth 0.05. 77:12
40. Wall sherd. Fabric 2. Weathered.
    Decoration: deeply grooved ext furrows.
    Area VII, F191, layer 1, (Grid 95W/221N) depth 0.02. 76:873

Ditch 194 (FIG 56, 41)
41. Wall sherd. Fabric 4 (very coarse). Weathered.
    Decoration: deep furrows on ext.
    Area VII, F194, layer 1, (Grid 105W/242N) depth 0.05. 77:182

Ditch 195 (FIG 56, 42-43)
42. Cordoned wall sherd. Fabric 3.
    Decoration: raised cordon (collar) of Collared Urn-type vessel in characteristic grog-filled fabric.
    Area VII, F195, layer 1, (Grid 99W/225N) depth 0.15. 77:67
43. Cordoned wall sherd. Fabric 3, but slightly finer than usual.
    Decoration: collar sherd of Collared Urn-type vessel with two rows of star-shaped (reed?) impressions; sherd has broken (to R) along diagonal row of similar, deeper, impressions.
    Area VII, F195, layer 1, (Grid 97W/219N) depth 0.35. 76:1082

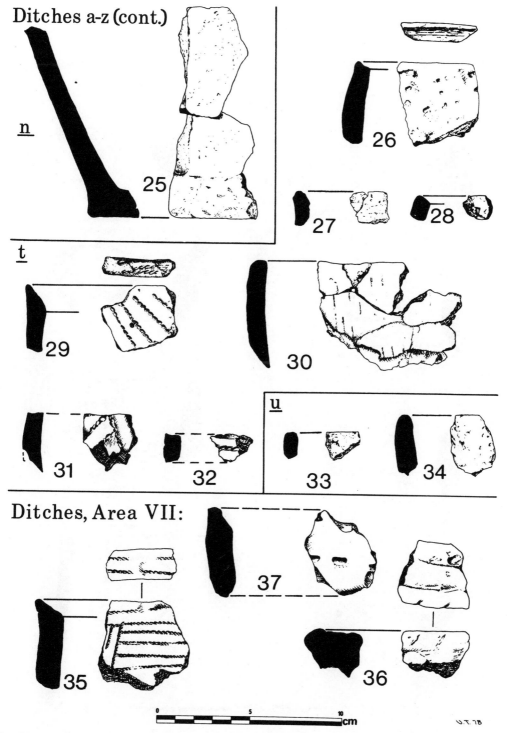

Ditches a-z (cont.)

n

t

u

Ditches, Area VII:

25 26 27 28 29 30 31 32 33 34 35 36 37

0   5   10
cm

U.T. 78

Fig. 55   Newark Road subsite, Areas I-VI and VII, second millennium BC ditches: pottery. Nos 25-34 (ditches *a-z*); 35 (VII, F186); 36-37 (VII, F190).

93

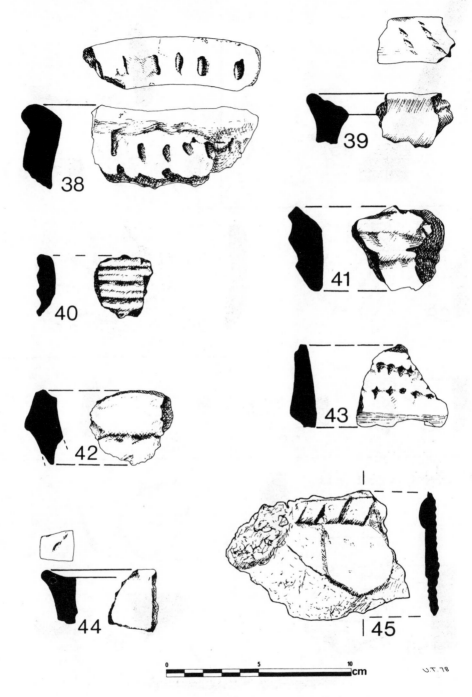

Fig. 56   Newark Road subsite, Area VII, pottery from second millennium BC ditches. 38-40 (F191); 41 (F194); 42 (F195); 43 (F193); 44 (F384); 45 (F254).

Ditch 384 (FIG 56, 44)
44. Rimsherd, flared, ext thickened. Fabric 2.
    Decoration: two light impressions on rim top.
    Area VII, F384, layer 1, (Grid 100W/227N) depth 0.10. 77:54

Ditch 254, 'Industrial Area' (FIG 56, 45)
45. Cordoned wall sherd. Fabric 1 (extremely soft, PVA added *in situ*).
    Decoration: rounded, slashed horizontal (?) cordon applied to ext; note: int surface lacking.
    Area VII, F254, layer 1, (Grid 20W/142N) depth 0.10. 76:1272

PIT GROUPS (ALL NEWARK ROAD AREAS) (FIGS 57-61)

EARLIER NEOLITHIC (FIG 57, 1-4)
Area II, F7 (FIG 57, 1-2)
1. Rimsherd, everted. Vesicular fabric, fine grits and sand; dark reddish-brown ext colour; fabric and colour very like Grimston/Lyles Hill pottery from the E Neolithic house, Padholme Road subsite (FNG 1, FIG 6).
    Undecorated.
    Area II, F7, layer 1, (Grid 4W/29N) depth 0.05. 74:1045
2. Rimsherd, everted. fabric as no 1, above, but from different vessel.
    Undecorated.
    Provenance etc as no 1. 74:1037

Area VII, F268 (FIG 57, 3-4)
3. Rimsherd, everted. Fabric as no 1, above, but colour dark brown.
    Undecorated.
    Area VII, F268, layer 1, (Grid 10W/134N) depth 0.05. 76:1249
4. Rim and wall sherds (not drawn) of Grimston/Lyles Hill style everted rim bowl. Fabric and colour as no 1, above.
    Undecorated.
    Area VII, F268, layer 2, (Grid 9W/135N) depth 0.24. 76:1248

LATER NEOLITHIC (FIG 57, 5-13; FIG 58, 14-20)
Area VII, F393 (FIG 57, 5-8)
5. Wall sherds of Grooved Ware. Granular fabric with vacuoles (vegetable?) and small grogs. Ext dark brown; core and int black.
    Decoration: opposed diagonal grooves separate zones of pinched rustication.
    Area VII, F393, layer 1, (Grid 106W/257N) depth 0.05. 77:36
6. Wall sherd, probably same vessel as no 5, above.
    Decoration: single scored line and pinched rustication on ext
    Provenance etc as no 5. 77:33
7. Wall sherd, probably same vessel as no 5, above, but slightly softer.
    Decoration: single diagonal groove.
    Provenance etc as no 5. 77:37
8. Wall sherd, probably same vessel as no 5, above, but ext and int light brown; uneven black core.
    Decoration: rough vertical cordon with fingertip impressions.
    Provenance etc as no 5. 77:31

Area VII, F397 (FIG 57, 9)
9. Wall sherd. Fabric etc as no 5, above; probably Grooved Ware.
    Decoration: two parallel scored lines.
    Area VII, F397, layer 1, (Grid 102W/258N) depth 0.10. 77:49

Area VII, F209 (FIG 57, 10-13; FIG 58, 14-15)
10. Rim sherd of closed, straight-sided vessel with internally thickened rim moulding; dia *c* 180. Fabric hard, evenly fired, with core and int black; ext mid-brown. Small grits, shell and grog temper.
    Decoration: complex series of panels: 5 vertical grooves separate, to L, rows of comb-impressions and, to R, rows of punctate impressions above rows of comb-impressions; two grooves below rim on either side of vertical grooved zone.
    Area VII, F209, layer 1 (Grid 78W/222N) depth 0.05. 76:691

Pit Groups

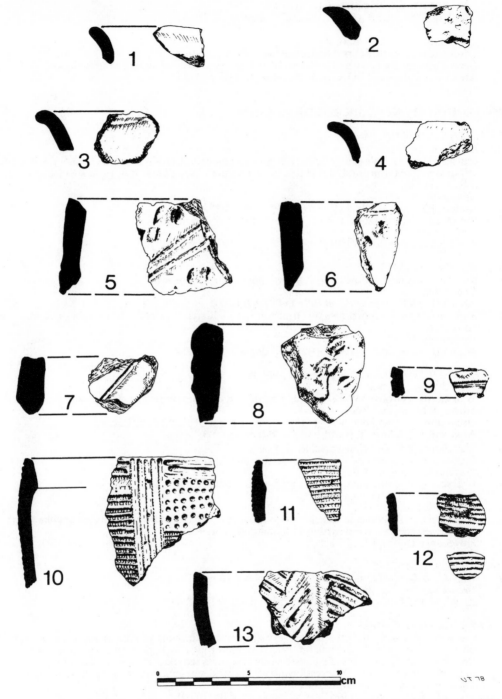

Fig. 57   Newark Road subsite, pit groups. Nos. 1-2 (II F7); 3-4 (VII F268); 5-8 (VII F393); 9(VII F397); 10-13 (VII F203).

Pits (cont.)

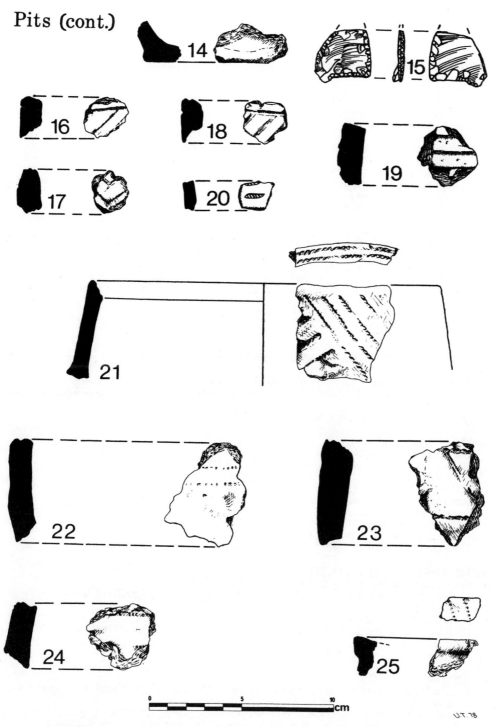

Fig. 58 Newark Road subsite, pit groups. Nos 14-15 (VII F209); 16-20 (VII F394); 21 (II F52); 22-24 (VII F188); 25 (VII F189).

11. Rim sherd with internal, hollow, bevel. Fabric hard, well-fired with pale brown ext, int and core; fine grits, no shell. Slight internal thickening (applied?) below bevel.
Decoration: rows of comb-impressed lines.
Provenance etc as no 10. 76:922

12. Two wall sherds. Fabric soft, poorly-fired; fine grits; int dark brown; ext red brown; core black.
Decoration: rows of fine lines.
Provenance etc as no 10. 76:933

13. Wall sherd. Fabric hard, well-fired; int and core black; ext grey-brown. Flint grits, no shell.
Decoration: (orientation uncertain) low (2mm) stepped cordon separates zones of wide diagonal grooves (herringbone?)
Provenance etc as no 10. 76:923

14. Externally thickened base angle. Fabric and colour as no 13, above.
Undecorated.
Provenance etc as no 10. 76:929

15. Damaged 'petit tranchet derivative' arrowhead of single barbed or tranverse type. Fine bifacial retouch; condition fresh and unweathered. Dark flint.
Provenance etc as no 10. 76:935

Area VII, F394 (FIG 58, 16-20)

16-19 Wall sherds from the same vessel. Soft, crumbly fabric with grog, crushed shell and flint; ext mid-brown; core and int black.
Decoration: grooved lines.
Area VII, F394, layer 1, (102W/258N) depth 0.15. 77:42, 44, 46, 48

20. Wall sherd. Crumbly fabric with grog, shell and flint, but surface smoother and fabric harder than nos 16-19, above.
Decoration: two whipped cord 'maggot' impressions.
Provenance etc as nos 16-19. 77:41

EARLY/MIDDLE BRONZE AGE AND BEAKER (FIGS 58, 21-25; 59-60)
Area II, F52 (FIG 58, 21)

21. Rimsherd of Collared Urn-type vessel (dia 190). Fabric 3.
Decoration: two lines of twisted cord impressions along int rim bevel; ext opposed diagonal twisted cord impressions.
Area II, F52, layer 1, (Grid 35W/34N) depth 0.15. 74:1985

Area VII, F188 (FIG 58, 22-24)

22. Wall sherd of Collared Urn-type vessel. Fabric 3.
Decoration: two rows of very light, punctate stabs above a low, applied, boss.
Area VII, F188, layer 1, (Grid 88W/173N) depth 0.15. 76:362

23. Wall sherd of Collared Urn-type vessel. Fabric 3.
Decoration: two horizontal and one diagonal twisted cord impressions.
Provenance etc as no 22. 76:378

24. Wall sherd of Collared Urn-type vessel. Fabric 3.
Decoration: one row of closely-spaced small stabs.
Provenance etc as no 22. 76:364

Area VII, F189 (FIG 58, 25; FIG 59, 26)

25. Fragment of flat-topped rim in Collared Urn fabric (3).
Decoration: two diagonal rows of shallow punctate impressions (cf no 22) on rim top.
Area VII, F189, layer 1, (Grid 88W/173N) depth 0.15. 76:372

26. Rimsherd of Collared Urn-type vessel: dia 240. Fabric 3.
Decoration: confined to ext surface: small, punctate stabs (cf nos 22, 25) in three rows below rim; these above similarly executed opposed diagonal lines.
Provenance etc as no 25. 76:372

Area VII, F193 (FIG 59, 27)

27. Collared Urn-type vessel; almost complete: rim dia 133; base dia 90; height 163. Fabric 3, evenly fired, friable.
Decoration: rim bevel — diagonal rows of light, punctate impressions/stabs (cf nos 22, 25, 26); above collar — similarly executed irregular lozenges (design highlighted with deeper stabs); below collar — single zone of regular lozenges above row of fingertip impressions.
Area VII, F193, layer 1, (Grid 87W/173N) depth 0.10. 76:665

Pits (cont.)

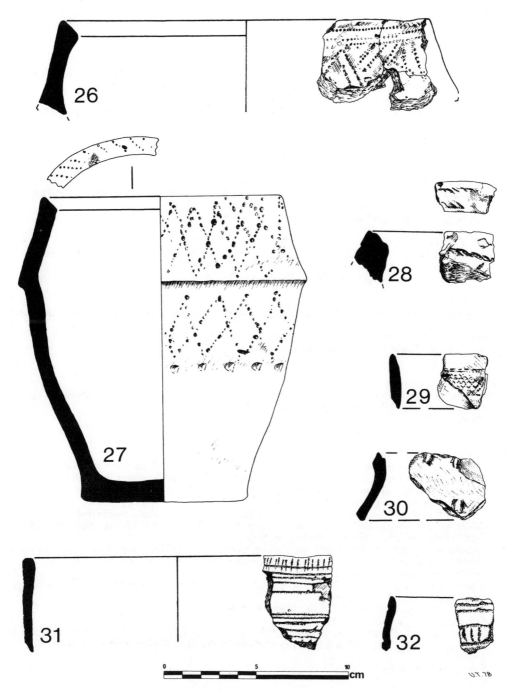

Fig. 59 Newark Road subsite, pit groups. No 26 (VII F189); 27 (VII F193); 28 (VII F222); 29-30 (VII F217); 31 (III F42); 32 (VII F219).

Area VII, F222 (FIG 59, 28)

28. Rimsherd. Collared urn fabric (3).
Decoration: two lines of twisted cord along rim top; two more lines of coarse twisted cord on ext below rim (the orientation is uncertain; this could be the flange of a Food Vessel-type thickened rim).
Area VII, F222, layer 1, (Grid 78W/183N) depth 0.01. No finds no.

Area VII, F217 (FIG 59, 29-30)

29. Rimsherd of Beaker. Fabric medium hard with fine sand; ext, int and core pale pinkish brown.
Decoration: horizontally zoned comb-impressed linear and cross-hatched motif.
Area VII, F217, layer 1, (Grid 82W/189N) depth 0.05. 76:937

30. Concave wall sherd. Fabric similar to no 29, but sand slightly coarser; core and int light brown; ext light reddish brown.
Decoration: pinched spaced rustication.
Provenance etc as no 29. 76:937

Area III, F42 (FIG 59, 31)

31. Rimsherd of Beaker (dia 170). Soft fabric with fine sand; thin black core; ext and int light brown.
Decoration: two zones of close-toothed comb impressions in horizontal rows, separated by reserved band; vertical comb impressions define rim.
Area III, F42, layer 1, (Grid 53W/80N) depth 0.10. 75:3566

Area VII, F219 (FIG 59, 32)

32. Rimsherd of Beaker. Soft fabric with fine sand; ext brown; int and core black. Weathered.
Decoration: horizontally-zoned coarse-toothed comb impressions.
Area VII, F219, layer 1, (Grid 85W/189N) depth 0.15. 76:940

Area IV, F10 (FIG 60, 33)

33. Fragment of axially-perforated cylindrical clay loomweight (dia *c* 120). Poorly-fired untempered clay.
Decoration: two deep (8+mm) punctate impressions (cf FIG 75, no 4)
Area IV, F10, layer 1, (Grid 129W/46N) depth 0.15. 76:72

Area IV, F112 (FIG 60, 34)

34. Slightly damaged axially-perforated cylindrical clay loomweight (ext dia 85; perforation dia 14; length 76; weight 715gm). Poorly-fired untempered clay.
Undecorated.
Area IV, F112, layer 1, (Grid 98W/41N) depth 0.55. 76:112

Area II, F37 (FIG 60, 35-38)

35. Rimsherd of straight-sided vessel; rim slightly everted and thickened on ext; low, rounded cordon 45mm below rim. Fabric soft, with large grogs and vegetable temper; ext int and core light brown.
Decoration: rough, all-over punctate impressions, more frequent below cordon.
Area II, F37, layer 1, (Grid 33W/32N) depth 0.17. 74:1869

36. Rimsherds of large (dia *c* 440) straight-sided vessel. Flattened, everted rim with low cordon 45mm below rim. Fabric very soft (+PVA) with grog, grits and vegetable temper; int and core black; ext light brown (this is not the same vessel as no 35).
Decoration apparently haphazard fingertip rustication, but with closer row along cordon. (Note; a rimsherd from the same vessel was found in the small pit F57 (Grid 35W/30N); 74:1979).
Provenance etc as no 35. 74:1852

37. Wall sherds of large vessel. Soft fabric with shell, sand and vegetable temper; ext and half core light brown; int black-light brown mottled.
Decoration: haphazard, rough, fingertip pinched rustication.
Provenance etc as no 35. 74:1874

38. Base of splay-sided vessel (base dia 60). Fabric very soft with grog and coarse grits; ext and int light brown; core black. The walls are thin, the base heavy, reinforced and pinched-out externally.
Undecorated.
Provenance etc as no 35. 74:1873

Pits (cont.)

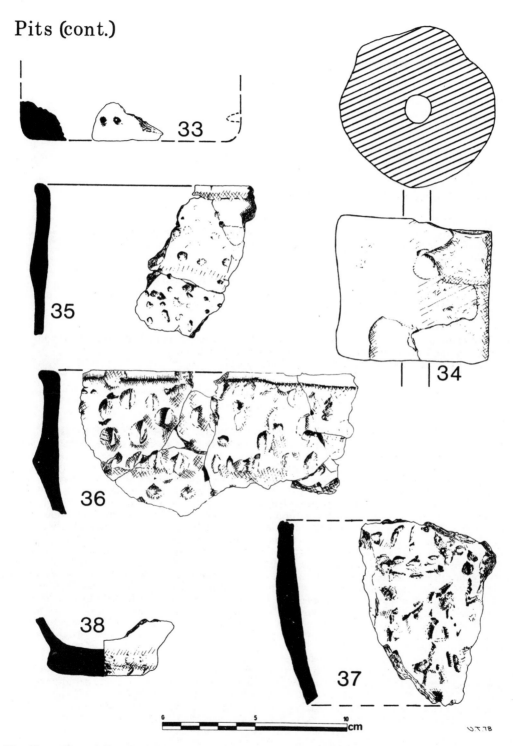

Fig. 60   Newark Road subsite, pit groups. No 33 (IV F10); 34 (IV F112); 35-38 (II F37).

101

FIRST MILLENNIUM BC (FIG 61)
Area II, F17 (FIG 61, 39)
39. Rimsherds of flared vessel (dia 225). Hard fabric with crushed flint, grog and sand; half core and int, black; ext mid-brown. (Previously published in Pryor 1976a, FIG 3.5 no 12).
Undecorated.
Area II, F17, layer 1, (Grid 22W/63N) depth 0.13. 74:1169

Area II, F26 (FIG 61, 40-41)
40. Rimsherd (angle uncertain). Hard, black, burnished fabric with crushed shell temper (FNG 4, fabric 1B).
Undecorated.
Area II, F26, layer 2, (Grid 1W/32N) depth 0.57. 74:1438
41. Rimsherd of flared vessel. Fabric similar to no 40, but smooth, not burnished; ext and int brown; core black.
Undecorated.
Area II, F26, layer 3, (Grid 1W/32N) depth 0.84. 74:1446

Area IV, F180 (FIG 61, 42-43)
42. Rimsherd of vertical-rimmed high-shouldered vessel. Hard fabric with crushed shell (FNG 4, fabric 1B). Extra light brown; int and core black; smooth surface.
Undecorated.
Area IV, F180, layer 1, (Grid 121W/22N) depth 0.20. 76:243
43. Rimsherd of slack-shouldered vessel (dia *c* 220). Fabric and colour as no 41, above.
Undecorated.
Provenance etc as no 42. 76:245

Area VII, F241 (FIG 61, 44)
44. Wall sherd (dia 140). Fabric hard, with fine sand; grey-brown core and int; ext paler grey-brown.
Decoration: light horizontal grooves above rounded carination.
Area VII, F241, layer 1, (Grid 89W/191N) depth 0.05. 76:947

DISCUSSION

1. POTTERY FROM THE DITCH SYSTEM AND CLOSELY ASSOCIATED FEATURES

It should be noted from the outset of this brief discussion that few attempts will be made to produce parallels for individual potsherds. This is for two reasons. First, reliably excavated local parallels are notoriously elusive and, second, the Newark Road material is not composed of primary rubbish, deposited *in situ*, nor is most of it composed even of secondary rubbish, that which has been redeposited from primary sources in antiquity (Schiffer 1976; Pryor 1979). The vast majority of potsherds (and other artifacts) found in the second millennium BC ditch fillings found their way into the archaeological record (Schiffer's (1976, 30) S-A processes) by natural means. None of the ditch fillings show evidence for deliberate back-filling, nor of redeposited domestic refuse (with the probable exception of the 'industrial area' of F254); rather, the finds are located evenly throughout the generally homogeneous sand-silts. Sudden and dramatic changes in finds' density are rare, and where they do occur can usually be attributed to ditch recutting. The finds' distribution in any ditch, therefore, probably gives a fair reflection of the artifact concentration in the nearby topsoil which had slipped into the ditch after its last period of maintenance. Finds from ditch fillings thus provide a *terminus post quem*, strictly speaking, for the ditch's last period of use (although it must be remembered that any hedge would substantially extend the useful life of a filled-in ditch). In view of the above, it is best to regard the material under consideration here as comprising a loose *collection* and certainly not an *assemblage*, in the sense of 'an associated set of contemporary artefact-types' (Clarke 1978, 489). General, rather than specific vessel-to-vessel, *comparanda* will therefore be sought.

Evidence for placing the rectilinear ditched enclosure system within the second millennium BC will be summarised in Chapter 5, but there is no pottery from the Newark Road ditches that conflicts with that hypothesis. Mindful of the limitations of the evidence, it is probably reasonable to suggest that the pottery shown in FIGS 53-56 dates to the second millennium BC, and that some may even be earlier.

In the absence of any indications to the contrary, we will assume that all of the pottery to be described in this chapter derives from domestic contexts. Stylistically, a number of traditions can be distinguished.

Vessels in the Collared Urn tradition from the ditches are represented by nos 5(?), 16-18, 29, 31, 32, 35, 42 and 43. One small pit, which can be linked to the ditches on spatial grounds (F52 in the NE corner of enclosure 3), yielded a similar sherd (FIG 58, 21).

Pits (cont.)

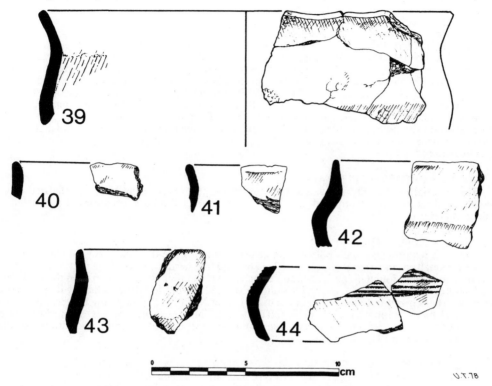

Fig. 61   Newark Road subsite, pit groups. No 39 (II F17); 40-41 (II F26); 42-43 (IV F180); 44 (VII 241).

Pottery in other traditions is less straightforward to identify. The splayed, decorated rims of nos 39 and 44 recall Food Vessel usage and the poorly defined (in E England) Deverel-Rimbury domestic tradition could be represented by nos 12, 20, 23, 45 and, from a pit (F37) in the NE corner of enclosure 3, by FIG 60, nos 35-37. The latter three sherds are of importance as they derive from back-filled secondary refuse, *sensu stricto*, and gain much chronological significance from the radiocarbon date (HAR-774) of 2030 ± 100 bc which was taken from the charcoal with which they are directly associated. The rusticated sherds could, possibly, be seen as having points in common with so-called Deverel-Rimbury pottery, but the narrow, thickened, splayed base appears to reflect classic Late Neolithic Fengate usage (Smith 1956, FIGS 67 and 69).

Recent finds of Collared Urns in the region have almost invariably been from funerary contexts, except for a few isolated scraps which may have derived from domestic situations (eg Aldwincle, Area B — Jackson 1976, FIG 20). Important recent finds of Collared Urns include, in the Nene Valley, Fengate (Storey's Bar Road subsite (FNG 2, FIG 41, 26a and b)), and Weldon (Manby 1974, 11); in the Welland Valley, Pilsgate, near Barnack (Pryor 1974a); in the Ouse Valley, Cotton Valley Farm (Green 1974).

Fengate is located south of the main distribution of Food Vessel pottery (D D A Simpson 1968, FIG 48), but material in this tradition is known locally at Pilsgate (Pryor 1974a), Barnack (Donaldson *et al* 1977, FIG 10, no 3) and Tallington (W G Simpson 1976, FIG 7, no 2), all of which are located in the Welland

Valley, north of Fengate.

The vessels considered here to have points in common with the so-called Deverel-Rimbury tradition, as found in the east of England, and as exemplified by the cemetery at Ardleigh, Essex (Erith and Longworth 1960) and the Middlesex cemeteries at Acton, Ashford, Littleton and Teddington (Barrett 1974), do not have good, recently excavated, local parallels; although the quantities of material that could be found if a thorough search through local collections was made, is illustrated by the region's only published synthesis of earlier Bronze Age pottery (Smedley and Owles 1962).

The Fengate collection finds its best parallels among the few well excavated Bronze Age settlements of the Fen-edge, especially, to the south, at Plantation Farm, Shippea Hill (Clark 1933, PLS 45-6) and Mildenhall Fen (Clark 1936, PL 7; FIGS 4-7; Leaf 1935, FIG 4). It is perhaps worth noting here that the straight-sided, bossed jar, loosely stratigraphically associated with the Fordy, Little Thetford, wooden trackway (Lethbridge 1935, FIG 1) could be perhaps seen as having features in common with the Newark Road material. Turning to the large and important stretches of Fen-edge in Lincolnshire, field walking has recently revealed numerous sites (Chowne 1977) of which Billingborough Fen is, as yet, the only excavated example (Chowne 1978). Stylistically Billingborough Phase 1 vessels have many points in common with those from the Fengate second millennium BC ditches (Chowne 1978, FIG 5-6), but the fabrics are, on the whole, dissimilar: those from Billingborough being much harder, and mainly grog tempered. Further field survey and excavation along the 40, or so, kilometres that separate the two sites is urgently required.

2. POTTERY FROM THE PITS (FIGS 57-61)

This material may broadly be divided into three groups: that of the earlier Neolithic, that of the Late Neolithic and second millennium and that of the 'Post-Deverel-Rimbury' traditions of the early first millennium (Barrett 1976).

3. EARLIER NEOLITHIC (FIG 57, 1-4)

Only two features produced pottery that could reasonably pre-date the second millennium BC. These were small pits in Areas II (F7) and VIII (F268) and the sherds concerned are very similar in form and fabric to pottery found in the foundation trenches of the earlier Neolithic house on the Padholme Road subsite, Area XIII (FNG 1, FIG 6). Dr Smith (FNG 1, 31ff) considered the Padholme Road material to belong to her Grimston/Lyles Hill tradition of the earlier Neolithic period (or the Eastern style of the earlier Neolithic, in Whittle's recent (1977, 82ff) scheme). This pottery is, however, a notoriously poor means of dating, as it seems to have been made and used throughout the third, and into the second millennium bc (Green 1976, table 3).

4. LATE NEOLITHIC AND SECOND MILLENNIUM BC (FIGS 57, nos 5-13; 58-59)

Two pits which produced material of this type have already been discussed (FIG 58, no 21; 60, nos 35-38) in the context of the ditched enclosures, above. Again, a number of different pottery traditions appear to be represented.

Sherds in the Grooved Ware tradition were found in Area VII, F393, F397, F209 and F394 (FIG 57, nos 5-15; FIG 58, nos 14, 16-19). Sherds from the latter feature were too fragmentary for certain identification and the presence of a sherd with whipped cord 'maggot' impressions from the same small pit throws doubt on the attribution suggested here. The vessels from F209 (FIG 57, nos 10-13; FIG 58, no 14) are of particular interest, in that three sherds (nos 10-12) make use of fine-toothed comb-impressions. This might suggest that they belong to the Beaker tradition, but the rim forms of nos 10 and 11 strongly recall Clacton usage (Longworth et al 1971). The frequent use of deep grooving, especially in no 13 (cf Green 1976, FIG 2.5, no 14), and the presence of a 'petit tranchet derivative' arrowhead support a Grooved Ware attribution for the assemblage, for there can be little doubt that the filling of this small pit was deliberately dumped in, as secondary rubbish, and that the finds from it are probably therefore broadly contemporary. They certainly all exhibit the same degree of very slight weathering.

Sherds in the Collared Urn tradition were found in Area VII pits F188, F189, F193 and F222 (FIG 58, nos 22-25; FIG 59, nos 26-28). Although the terms Primary and Secondary, as defined by Longworth (1961) have been shown to have no chronological significance (eg FNG 2, 97, with refs; Burgess and Varndell 1978) it is important to note that diagnostic material from Newark Road and Storey's Bar Road (FNG 2, FIG 41 nos 26a and b) all belong to the Secondary Series. Only one Primary Series vessel (Longworth 1961, no 122) is known to have come from Peterborough itself, and this is perhaps of interest in view of the well accepted view that Collared Urns evolved from Late Neolithic Peterborough, especially Fengate, ceramic traditions. The nature of this 'evolution' is still very vague, and the evidence from the type site would not suggest that it took place in the immediate vicinity. A convincing explanation of the evolutionary process will be difficult to suggest, as most Primary Collared Urns derive from funerary contexts, whereas most Late Neolithic Peterborough sherds come from domestic sites. There is a serious danger, therefore, of attributing too much to a comparison of like with unlike.

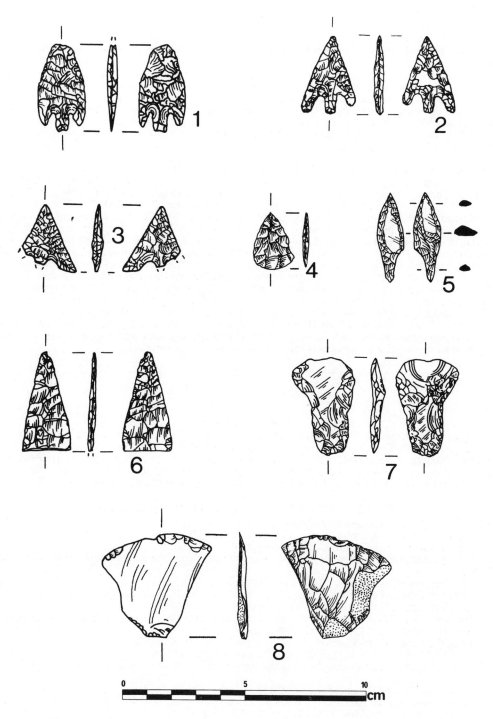

Fig. 62   Newark Road subsite, second millennnium BC ditches, flint: projectile points and arrowheads.

Turning now to Beaker material, only four sherds, from three small pits—Area VII, F217; Area III, F42; Area VII, F219 — can be reliably attributed to this tradition (FIG 59, nos 29-32). Alex Gibson (Appendix 10) has noted that the Newark Road Beaker material is weathered, unlike that in the Wyman Abbott collections. Dumped-in domestic Beaker material was found in small pits on the Padholme Road subsite (FNG 1, FIG 10). Apart from Fengate, massive assemblages of domestic Beaker pottery have been found at America Farm, on the Fen-edge just 2 miles NE of Newark Road (Clarke 1970, 490). The common occurrence of dumped, secondary, Beaker rubbish together with less reliably associated material from weathered deposits (Newark Road; see also FNG 2, 96) argues for a strong Beaker presence in the area. The role of Beaker-pottery-using communities in the construction and subsequent operation of the ditched enclosure system must, however, still remain enigmatic. Simple explanations, however plausible at first sight (eg Burgess and Shennan 1976), might partially account for the spread and arrival of the Beaker phenomenon, but are unlikely to explain the subsequent Beaker *presence* (to use Kinnes' (1977, 214) useful phrase).

5. 'POST-DEVEREL-RIMBURY' FIRST MILLENNIUM BC (FIG 61)

Only six sherds could be attributed to this group with any reliability. They all belong to a tradition which has generally been described as 'Early Iron Age' in the literature, but which is now seen to have many points in common with later Bronze Age wares. The radiocarbon date, (HAR-773) 790 ± 80 bc, for charcoal from a backfilled deposit, which contained the sherd illustrated in FIG 61, no 39, tends to support this early dating. The problems associated with the dating of much of the Wyman Abbott 'Iron Age' material, discussed by Hawkes and Fell (1945), have recently been reviewed by Champion (1975), who considers that many of the decorated globular jars of Hawkes and Fell's 'Middle and Later Phases' find good parallels in late Urnfield contexts in the Low Countries. Much of the material illustrated here would not be out of place in such contexts. A full review of the problem will be attempted in the Fourth Report (FNG 4, Group 1) when considerably larger assemblages will be discussed in detail. The important point to note here is that the partial vessel illustrated in FIG 61, no 39 was reconstructed from sherds which had broken in antiquity and which showed no traces of weathering. It would appear that the charcoal and the potsherds are from a back-filled deposit and are, therefore, probably contemporary. The filled-in pit or posthole in which they were found had been cut into the completely filled ditch *e*. In this case, then, the vessel's post-Deverel-Rimbury status can be demonstrated stratigraphically.

2. THE FLINTS (FIG 62-74)

INTRODUCTION

The flintwork from the Newark Road subsite derives from ditches of the second millennium BC enclosure system. All flints are considered in the analysis and discussion, below, but only a sample of the types found has been illustrated; the only exceptions to this are the arrowheads and projectile points which are illustrated in full. The final discussion compares the Newark Road flints with those from the earlier Neolithic house (FNG 1) and the later Neolithic Storey's Bar Road settlement (FNG 2).

CATALOGUE OF ILLUSTRATED FLINTS (FIGS 62-69)

Fig 62, 1-8. Projectile points and arrowheads of various types
1. Barbed and tanged arrowhead; thin, finely retouched. Tip broken.
    Area II, ditch 9, layer 2, (Grid 59W/39N) depth 0.80. 74:1582
2. Barbed and tanged arrowhead; thin, finely retouched; barbs of unequal length. From 'industrial area'.
    Area VII, ditch 254, layer 1, (Grid 5E/147N) depth 0.15. 76:1142
3. Barbed and tanged arrowhead; thin, finely retouched. One barb and tang broken.
    Area VII, ditch 191, layer 1, (89W/199N) depth 0.50. 76:1111
4. Triangular (small leaf shaped) arrowhead; thin, generally finely retouched. Right side damaged.
    Area II, ditch 8, layer 1, (Grid 26W/38N) depth 0.01. 74:1746
5. Tanged arrowhead; thick, generally crude retouch except for the tang.
    Area IV, ditch 10, layer 1, (Grid 117W/77N) depth 0.35. 76:111
6. Point of large leaf shaped arrowhead; cf Mortimer (1905, PLS 2, 3, 51 etc); very finely retouched. To W of 'industrial area'.
    Area VII, ditch 254, layer 1, (Grid 37W/135N) depth 0.20. 76:1133
7. Transverse arrowhead; thin, bifacial, crude, retouch. Residual in R-B ditch.
    Area III, F6, layer 1, (Grid 23W/78N) depth 0.02. 75:4385
8. Transverse arrowhead; thin, uneven bifacial retouch.
    Area II, ditch 9, layer 2, (Grid 41W/41N) depth 0.45. 74:2439

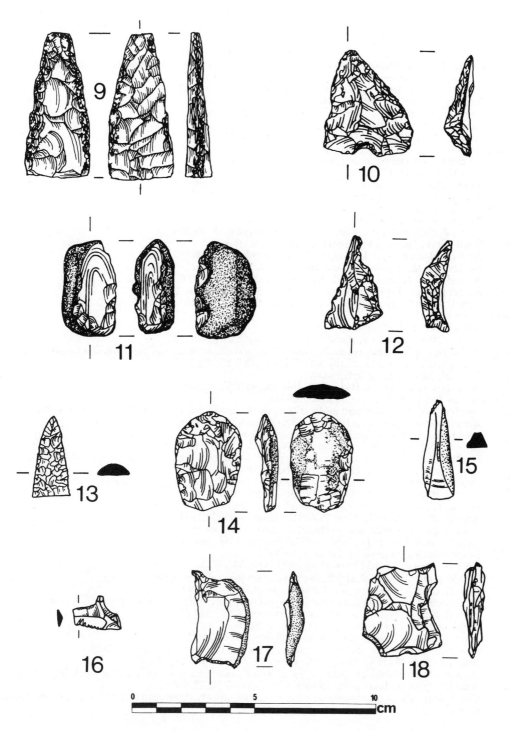

Fig. 63 Newark Road subsite, second millennium BC ditches, flint: 9, single piece sickle fragment; 10-12, retouched flakes; 13-14, plano-convex 'knives'; 15-18, piercers.

Single Piece Sickle (FIG 63, 9)
9. Tip portion of single piece crescentic sickle — note the slight off-centre skewing of the blade (Clark 1932). Tip missing; cutting edges severely battered.
Area II, ditch 9, layer 1, (Grid 56W/40N) depth 0.60. 74:2530

Retouched flake tools (FIG 63, 10-12)
10 Unifacially retouched flake with steeply retouched notch. Battered.
Area II, ditch 9, layer 1, (Grid 45W/42N) depth 0.15. 74:2362
11. Bifacially retouched thermal flake.
Area II, ditch *f*, layer 1, (Grid 17W/63N) depth 0.14. 74:2395
12. Unifacially retouched flake.
Area II, ditch 9, layer 1, (Grid 60W/38N) depth 0.30. 74:2317

Plano-convex 'Knives' (FIG 63, 13-14)
13. Unifacially retouched tip of (?) plano-convex 'knife'.
Area II, small pit, F7, layer 1, (Grid 91W/33N) depth 0.10. 74:37
14. Short, bifacially retouched plano-convex implement ('knife'?).
Area II, ditch *f*, layer 1 (Grid 18W/58N) depth 0.08. 74:1677

Piercers (FIG 63, 15-18)
15. Piercer; single, worn, point; unifacially retouched.
Area IV, ditch *n*, layer 1, (Grid 120W/38N) depth 0.15. 76:258
16. Small, beaked piercer with unifacial retouch; on flake.
Area III, ditch *a*, layer 1, (Grid 66W/74N) depth 0.01. 75:4070
17. Piercer with three points, all unifacially retouched and worn.
Area II, ditch 9, layer 1, (Grid 16W/43N) depth 0.25. 74:1606
18. Piercer with single point, unifacially retouched and worn; on flake.
Area II, ditch 9, layer 1, (Grid 3W/45N) depth 0.25. 74:1016

Awls (FIG 64, 19-21)
19. Awl with bifacial retouch; tip worn (?)
Area IV, ditch *a*, layer 1, (Grid 110W/74N) depth 0.10. 76:108
20. Awl/burin; tip bifacially retouched and worn *before* the removal of the burin flake (arrowed).
Area III, ditch *f*, layer 1, (Grid 20W/87N) depth 0.15. 75:3543
21. Awl with bifacial retouch; tip worn.
Area II, ditch *k*, layer 2, (Grid 21W/48N) depth 0.50. 74:1659

Denticulated Tools (FIG 64, 22-32; FIG 65, 33-41)
22. Denticulated tool; worn and unifacially retouched; on a piece of irregular workshop waste.
Area II, ditch 9, layer 2, (Grid 36W/42N) depth 0.50. 74:2296
23. Core fragment with unifacial retouch; points worn.
Area II, ditch 9, layer 1, (Grid 16W/43N) depth 0.25. 74:1607
24. Denticulated tool with bifacial retouch; points worn; on a piece of irregular workshop waste.
Area II, ditch 8, layer 1, (Grid 63W/34N) depth 0.15. 74:2046
25. Denticulated tool with heavy bifacial retouch; on a piece of irregular workshop waste.
Area II, ditch 9, layer 1, (Grid 31W/43N) depth 0.15. 74:697
26. Denticulated tool with unifacial retouch and point heavily worn; on flake.
Area II, ditch *t*, layer 1, (Grid 29W/31N) depth 0.05. 74:1967
27. Denticulated tool with heavy bifacial retouch; points worn.
Area II, ditch 9, layer 1, (Grid 16W/43N) depth 0.20. 74:1608
28. Denticulated tool; unifacial retouch; on flake.
Area II, ditch *i*, 2, (Grid 16W/47N) depth 0.60. 74:1711
29. Pebble denticulated tool with heavy bifacial retouch; all points heavily worn.
Area II, ditch 8, layer 1, (Grid 8W/40N) depth 0.03. 74:1143
30. Denticulated tool; unifacial retouch and points heavily worn; on core rejuvenation flake.
Area II, ditch *n*, layer 1, (Grid 76W/42N) depth 0.12. 74:2171
31. Denticulated tool with unifacial retouch; on blade.
Area II, ditch 9, layer 2, (Grid 36W/42N) depth 0.50. 74:2296
32. Denticulated tool with unifacial retouch and points very heavily worn; on flake.
Area III, ditch 254 (F5), layer 1, (Grid 67W/127N) depth 0.15. 75:3571
33. Denticulated tool with unifacial retouch; points worn; on a piece of irregular workshop waste.
Area III, ditch 10, layer 3, (Grid 64W/83N) depth 0.50. 75:4453
34. Core fragment with discontinuous scraper retouch and heavy retouch on the denticulations; points severely worn.

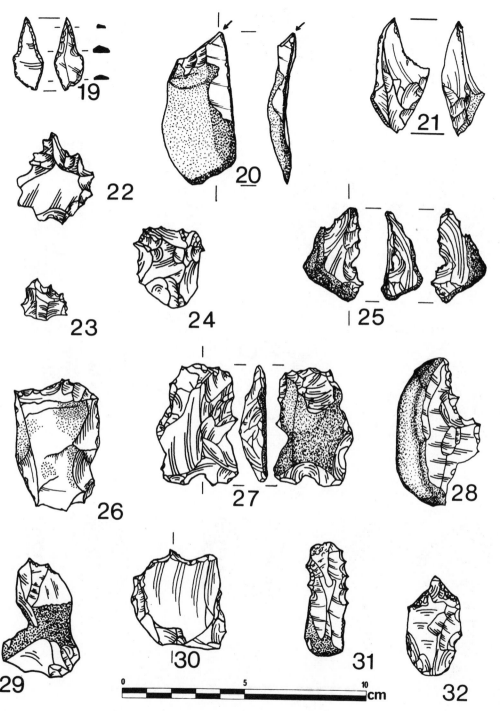

Fig. 64 Newark Road subsite, second millennium BC ditches, flint: 19-21, awls; 22-32, denticulated tools.

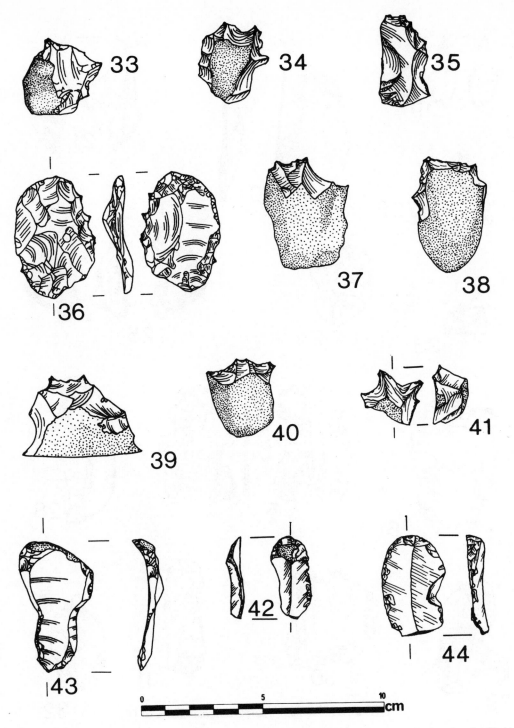

Fig. 65   Newark Road subsite, second millennium BC ditches, flint: 33-41, denticulated tools; 42-44, long-end scrapers.

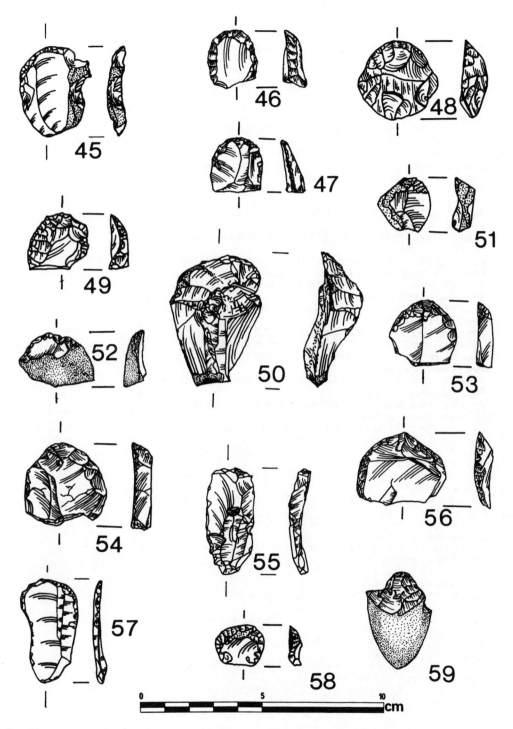

Fig. 66   Newark Road subsite, second millennium BC ditches, flint: short-end scrapers.

111

Area IV, ditch *a*, layer 1, (Grid 110W/74N) depth 0.10. 76:108

35. Denticulated tool, with unifacial retouch; points heavily worn; on flake.
    Area VII, ditch 186, layer 1, (Grid 84W/172N) depth 0.08. 76:339
36. Denticulated tool with bifacial retouch; sides and points heavily worn; on flake.
    Area III, ditch *b*, layer 3, (Grid 61W/77N) depth 0.80. 75:4319
37. Denticulated tool made from bashed pebble; points heavily worn.
    Area VII, ditch 191, layer 1, (Grid 93W/217N) depth 0.25. 76:867
38. Denticulated tool made from bashed pebble; points worn.
    Area VI, ditch 8, layer 1, (Grid 5E/42N) depth 0.12. 76:760
39. Denticulated tool with crude bifacial retouch; points heavily worn; on piece of irregular workshop waste.
    Area VII, ditch 186, layer 1, (Grid 84W/172N) depth 0.30. 76:348
40. Denticulated tool made from bashed pebble; crude unifacial retouch; points heavily worn.
    Area IV, ditch 10, layer 1, (Grid 128W/75N) depth 0.10. 76:34
41. Core fragment with unifacial retouch; points heavily worn.
    Area IV, ditch 9, layer 2, (Grid 103W/35N) depth 0.50. 76:477

Scrapers (FIG 65-66)

42. Long-end scraper on flake.
    Area II, ditch *v*, layer 1, (Grid 14W/9N) depth 0.10. 74:2165
43. Long-end scraper on flake.
    Area III, ditch *f*, layer 2, (Grid 20W/80N) depth 0.45. 75:4282
44. Long-end scraper on flake.
    Area II, ditch *t*, layer 1, (Grid 29W/34N) depth 0.08. 74:1960
45. Short-end scraper on flake (with denticulations to right).
    Area III, ditch *c*, layer 1, (Grid 32W/85N) depth 0.05. 75:3541
46. Short-end scraper on flake.
    Area VII, ditch 187, layer 1, (Grid 85W/166N) depth 0.10. 76:350
47. Short-end scraper on flake.
    Area VII, ditch 195, layer 1, (Grid 95W/213N) stripped surface. 76:789
48. Short-end scraper on piece of irregular workshop waste.
    Area III, ditch *c*, layer 1, (Grid 41W/84N) depth 0.10. 75:3535
49. Short-end scraper on flake.
    Area VII, ditch 191, layer 1, (Grid 90W/205N) depth 0.05. 76:648
50. Short-end scraper on flake.
    Area II, ditch *a*, layer 1, (Grid 65W/51N) depth 0.10. 74:1895
51. Short-end scraper on flake.
    Area VII, ditch 195, layer 1, (Grid 96W/214N) depth 0.15. 76:823
52. Short-end scraper on flake.
    Area II, ditch *x*, layer 1, (Grid 13W/9N) depth 0.05. 74:2163
53. Short-end scraper on flake.
    Area II, ditch 8, layer 1, (Grid 43W/40N) depth 0.25. 74:1880
54. Short-end scraper on flake; partially calcined.
    Area II, ditch 8, layer 1, (Grid 70W/34N) depth 0.10. 74:1816
55. Short-end scraper; steep retouch; edges damaged; probably residual.
    Area II, ditch 9, layer 1, (Grid 28W/43N) depth 0.10. 74:693
56. Short-end scraper on flake.
    Area II, ditch 8, layer 1, (Grid 47/36) depth 0.20. 74:2576
57. Short-end scraper on flake.
    Area II, ditch *i*, layer 1, (Grid 17W/53N) depth 0.05. 74:2580
58. Short-end scraper on flake.
    Area II, ditch 8, layer 1, (Grid 47W/36N) depth 0.10. 74:2575
59. Bashed pebble with steep scraper retouch.
    Area II, ditch 8, layer 1, (Grid 71W/34N) depth 0.10. 74:1817
60. End scraper on broken flake.
    Area II, ditch 9, layer 3, (Grid 45W/40N) depth 0.85. 74:2610
61. Short-end scraper on flake.
    Area II, ditch 9, layer 1, (Grid 45W/40N) depth 0.30. 74:2364
62. Short-end scraper ; 'nibble' retouch; on flake.
    Area II, ditch *u*, layer 1, (Grid 17W/37N) depth 0.12. 74:1080
63. Disc scraper on flake.
    Area III, ditch 10, layer 2, (Grid 51W/86N) depth 0.35. 75:4398

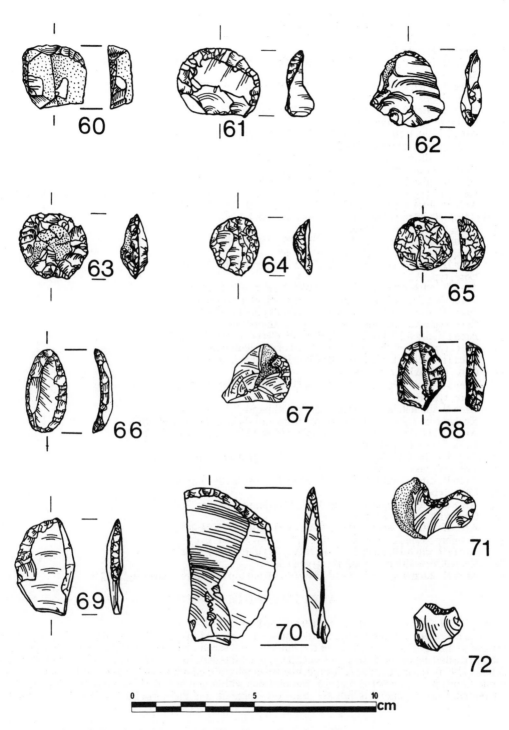

Fig. 67   Newark Road subsite, second millennium BC ditches, flint: scrapers, various types.

64. Disc scraper on flake.
   Area III, ditch *b*, layer 1, (Grid 62W/69N) depth 0.45. 75:4063
65. Disc scraper on flake; partially calcined.
   Area VII, ditch 187, layer 1, (Grid 91W/197N) depth 0.20. 76:490
66. Oval scraper on flake.
   Area II, ditch 8, layer 1, (Grid 17W/39N) depth 0.10. 74:1345
67. Side scraper on flake.
   Area II, ditch 9, layer 1, (Grid 46W/41N) depth 0.05. 74:2358
68. End scraper on broken flake.
   Area II, ditch 8, layer 1, (Grid 28W/39N) depth 0.25. 74:1732
69. End/side scraper on broken flake.
   Area III, ditch 10, layer 1, (Grid 64W/83N) depth 0.20. 75:4450
70. End scraper on broken flake.
   Area IV, ditch *n*, layer 1, (Grid 122W/38N) depth 0.10. 76:237
71. Hollow scraper on flake; vertical retouch.
   Area II, ditch 9, layer 1, (Grid 7W/45N) depth 0.15. 74:1059
72. Piece of irregular workshop waste with concave scraping edge carrying steep 'nibble' retouch.
   Area II, ditch 8, layer 1, (Grid 27W/38N) depth 0.10. 74:2244

Cores (FIGS 68 and 69) (The types are those of Clark 1960)
73. Core, type A1, on pebble.
   Area II, ditch *i*, layer 2, (Grid 17W/53N) depth 0.40. 74:2585
74. Core, type A2, with light scraper retouch.
   Area II, ditch *a*, layer 1, (Grid 64W/51N) depth 0.10. 74:2100
75. Core, type A2.
   Area II, ditch 9, layer 1, (Grid 21W/44N) depth 0.05. 74:964
76. Core, type A2, with subsequent wear scars; platform renewed.
   Area III, ditch 10, layer 1, (Grid 28W/90N) depth 0.05. 75:4458
77. Core, type A2; subsequently used as hammerstone.
   Area IV, ditch 10, layer 1, (Grid 107W/77N) depth 0.25. 76:27
78. Core, type A2, with slight wear at tips of denticulations.
   Area II, ditch *a*, layer 1, (Grid 60W/53N) depth 0.10. 74:2335
79. Core, type A1; a remnant; worn.
   Area II, ditch 9, layer 1, (Grid 79W/37N) depth 0.02. 74:2106
80. Core, type B1.
   Area II, ditch 9, layer 2, (Grid 42W/40N) depth 0.35. 74:2443
81. Keeled core (type B2) with one platform and slight traces of utilisation.
   Area III, (F5) ditch 254, layer 1, (Grid 66W/127N) depth 0.15. 75:3572
82. Keeled core, type B2; utilised.
   Area III, ditch 10, layer 1, (Grid 49W/87N) stripped surface. 75:4482
83. Core, type B3; surfaces abraded.
   Area II, ditch *a*, layer 1, (Grid 65W/52N) depth 0.10. 74:1897
84. Core, type B3.
   Area II, ditch 9, layer 1, (Grid 35W/40N) depth 0.04. 74:2280
85. Core with three platforms (type C).
   Area II, ditch *a*, layer 2, (Grid 81W/41N) depth 0.05. 74:2182
86. Roughly bashed core with (?) three platforms (type C).
   Area III, ditch 10, layer 3, (Grid 70W/83N) depth 0.46. 75:4293
87. Keeled core with two platforms (type E).
   Area II, ditch 9, layer 1, (Grid 35W/40N) from top of stripped surface. 74:2276

ANALYSIS AND DISCUSSION

A NOTE ON THE CIRCUMSTANCES OF DEPOSITION

It is necessary to briefly reiterate the cautionary remarks made in the introduction to the pottery discussion above. Flintwork found in the fillings of the second millennium BC ditches is not primary rubbish (ie that deposited during flint-knapping) nor is it redeposited, secondary, rubbish, as defined by Schiffer (1976). It is instead a redeposited, biassed, haphazard sample of such rubbish and is consequently prone to distortion. Detailed metrical comparisons within and outside Fengate cannot therefore be attempted. Certain general trends are, however, apparent and these will be considered following the

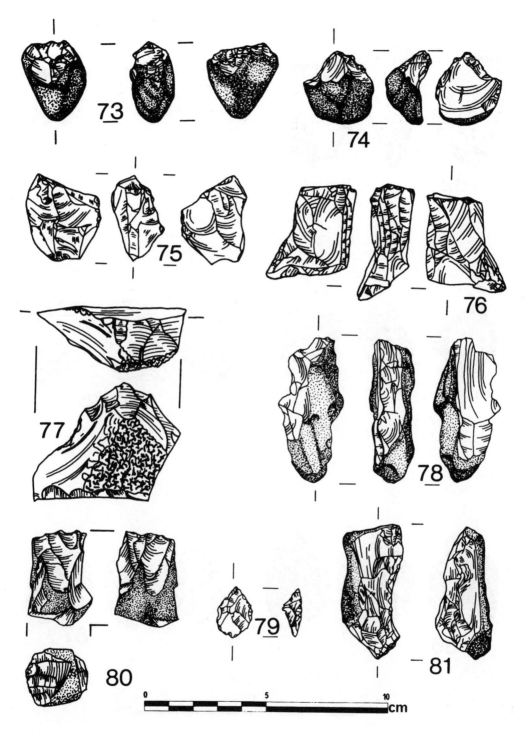

Fig. 68   Newark Road subsite, second millennium BC ditches, flint: cores.

115

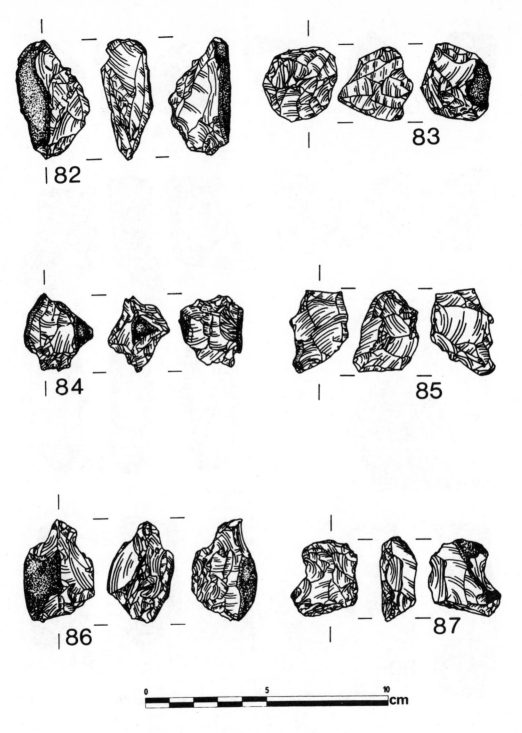

Fig. 69   Newark Road subsite, second millennium BC ditches, flint: cores.

116

general description of the various flint types found at Newark Road. Throughout the discussion the term 'Bronze Age' (as distinguished by Pitts 1978a, 191-2) will be used to differentiate the Newark Road from the Storey's Bar Road (Late Neolithic) flintwork. Finally, in the same way that the term 'assemblage' was not used to describe the pottery from Newark Road, the even more specific term 'industry' (Clarke 1978, 492) seems inappropriate for the flints considered here; instead, the less specific 'collection' is preferred.

THE FLINT ANALYSIS

The layout of this section follows that adopted in the Second Report (FNG 2, 136-143). A total of 1681 flints were found (total weight 8707.4gm; average weight 5.18gm), of which all appeared to have been made from local gravel pebbles. Attempts were made in the Second Report to describe the colour and surface appearance of this source material, but these are not considered to have been successful and the effort has been abandoned in the catalogue and description of this report.

IMPLEMENTS (37.8% of total)

The 635 implements were of the following types:

		(percentage of total implements)
Scrapers	65	10.2%
Arrowheads/projectile points	7	1.1%
Utilized flakes	499	78.6%
Serrated flakes	1	0.2%
Retouched flakes	15	2.4%
Denticulated tools	36	5.7%
Piercers	6	0.9%
Awls	3	0.5%
Plano-convex knives (?)	2	0.3%
Single piece sickle	1	0.2%

1. *Scrapers* (FIGS 65-67)

The 65 scrapers could be classed after Clark's (1960), Hurst Fen, scheme, as follows:

Class A (i) Long-end	5	7.7%
Class A (ii) Short-end	37	56.9%
Class B Double ended	*nil*	
Class C Disc	4	6.1%
Class D (i) Long-side	1	1.5%
Class D (ii) Short-side	3	4.6%
Class E On broken flakes	7	10.8%
Class F Hollow scrapers	2	3.1%
Damaged beyond classification	6	9.2%

The total weight of the scrapers was 501.5gm, giving an average weight per scraper of 7.8gm. This figure is considerably less than the average (19.9gm) for the 131 scrapers from Feature Divisions 1-9 of the Storey's Bar Road subsite. The earlier Neolithic house did not produce a statistically significant quantity of scrapers. The generally smaller size of the Bronze Age scraper collection is emphasised in the comparative histograms of length, width and thickness (FIGS 70 and 71). Bronze Age scrapers are, on the whole, significantly shorter, narrower and much thinner than those from Late Neolithic contexts at Fengate. Working edge retouch angles, on the other hand are steeper, and form a markedly skewed distribution, when compared with the even, normal, distribution of the Late Neolithic assemblage. This might suggest that the Bronze Age scraper working edge retouch angles are from more than one variety of scraper. The illustrations, however, with the possible exception of the 'bashed pebbles' variety of scraper, do not show the clear distinction into two types, as seen at Micheldever Wood, site R4, phase 4 — henceforward to be known as R4 (Fasham and Ross 1978). The skewed and irregular shape of the Bronze Age retouch angle histogram (FIG 72) tends to confirm the strong subjective impression that a degree of control was lacking and that knapping technique was inferior to that of Late Neolithic times. Possible reasons for this will be briefly considered below.

The composition of the scraper collection is generally similar to that of the Late Neolithic assemblage, with short-end scrapers by far the commonest type found. No double ended scrapers occurred on either subsite and the Late Neolithic industry produced more scrapers of Class E, than Newark Road.

2. *Arrowheads and Projectile Points* (FIG 62)

The following eight arrowheads were found in the linear ditch system (excepting no 7 which was from a Roman ditch immediately next to a second millennium ditch):

Small leaf, or triangular	1 (No. 4)
Transverse	2 (Nos. 7, 8)
Barbed and tanged	3 (Nos. 1-3)
Tanged	1 (No. 5)
Leaf (?)	1 (No. 6)

In addition, one single barb, '*petit tranchet* derivative' projectile point of Clark's (1948) type E (or, possibly, I), was found in the small pit F209, Area VII (FIG 58, no 15).

This collection is very unlike that of the Storey's Bar Road subsite (FNG 2, FIGS 43, 44 and 45, 1-5). Single barb projectile points (this terminology is defined in FNG 2, 138) were absent in the ditches, and transverse types were proportionally rarer. Barbed and tanged arrowheads were the commonest types found at Newark Road, whereas only one example was found on Storey's Bar Road, and that came from a small posthole only doubtfully associated with the Late Neolithic settlement. Types hitherto not represented at Fengate include the tanged arrowhead (no 5), the fragment of large leaf-shaped arrowhead (no 6) and the small sub-triangular arrowhead (no 4). The fragment of large leaf shaped arrowhead (no 6) is particularly thin and finely manufactured. It is difficult to parallel exactly, but its size and shape would argue for affinities with earlier Bronze Age large leaf shaped arrowheads, such as those illustrated by Mortimer (1905) from barrows of the Towthorpe (PL 2) and Calais Wold Groups (especially PL 51, FIGS 413 and 414). The other two new types, particularly the more diagnostic no 5, would not be out of place in post-Neolithic contexts (eg I F Smith 1965, 105 FIG 50).

In sum, the arrowheads from Newark Road are, in general, typologically later than those from the Grooved Ware settlement at Storey's Bar Road. In round terms, an earlier Bronze Age /Beaker context would seem to be indicated.

3. *Utilised Flakes* (FIG 73; Tables 4 and 5)

TABLE 4

Lengths (mm) of unbroken utilised flakes from Newark Road (Bronze Age) subsite, Areas I-VII.

0-10	10-20	20-30	30-40	40-50	50-60	Total
5	126	136	65	24	3	359

TABLE 5

Breadths (mm) of unbroken utilised flakes from Newark Road (Bronze Age) subsite, Areas I-VII.

0-5	5-10	10-15	15-20	20-25	25-30	30-35	35-40	40-45	45-50	Total
—	10	68	114	76	58	15	10	7	1	359

Utilised flakes were differentiated from waste flakes by simple inspection with a x10 hand-lens (the validity of the method is briefly discussed in FNG 2, 115). A total of 499 flakes showed signs of utilisation (total weight 1823gm; average weight 3.6gm); the 768 utilised flakes from the late Late Neolithic industry at Storey's Bar Road weighed on average 5.06gm. This tended to confirm the subjective impression that the Newark Road utilised flakes were in general smaller than those from Storey's Bar Road. One hundred and forty (28%) of the 499 utilised flakes were broken and have not been included in the breadth/length ratio histogram. The Storey's Bar Road assemblage produced a far higher (46%) percentage figure for broken utilised flakes; this would add additional significance to the figures for average weights referred to above, and would emphasise the marked dissimilarity of flake size on the two subsites. The breadth/length histogram (FIG 73) reflects the trend away from the long, narrow, blades of the earlier Neolithic industry, to the shorter, squat flakes of the Storey's Bar Road assemblage. This trend is continued at Newark Road, but with an even greater emphasis on short, squat flakes; the bimodal tendency of the histogram is also somewhat exaggerated, but no convincing explanation for this can be offered (cf FNG 2, 142). Cortical to non-cortical ratios remain approximately the same in both groups.

4. *Denticulated Tools* (FIG 64, nos 22-32; FIG 65, nos 33-41)

Thirty-six denticulated tools were found, and this represents an unusually high proportion of the total number of implements recovered. The 20 illustrated examples show that this class of implement falls into two broad groups: those made on flakes, core remnants or irregular workshop waste (it is often hard

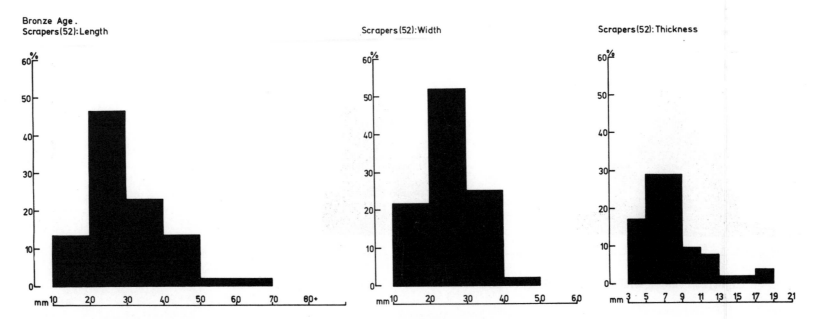

Fig. 70   Histograms showing various dimensions of scrapers from second millennium BC ditches of the Newark Road subsite.

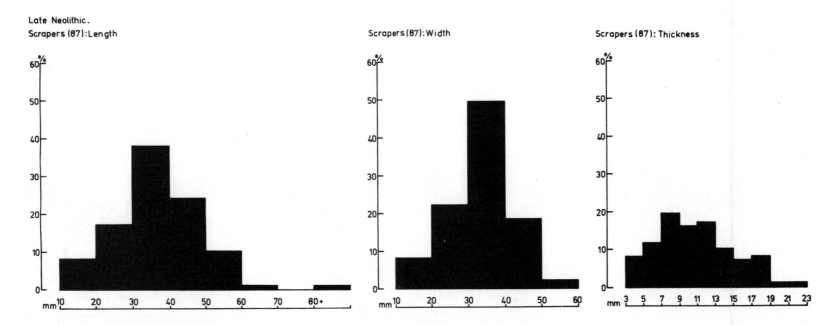

Fig. 71   Histograms showing various dimensions of Late Neolithic scrapers from the Storey's Bar Road subsite (FNG 2).

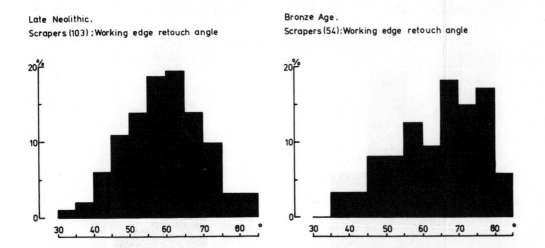

Late Neolithic.
Scrapers (103) : Working edge retouch angle

Bronze Age.
Scrapers (54) : Working edge retouch angle

Fig. 72   Histograms showing scraper retouch angles (Newark Road and Storey's Bar Road subsites).

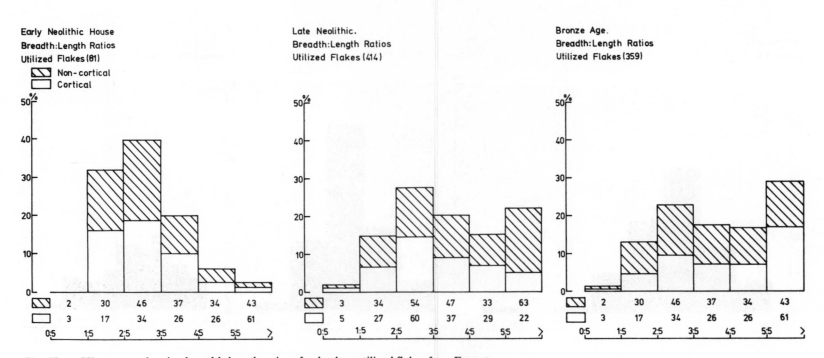

Early Neolithic House
Breadth:Length Ratios
Utilized Flakes (81)

Non-cortical
Cortical

Late Neolithic.
Breadth:Length Ratios
Utilized Flakes (414)

Bronze Age.
Breadth:Length Ratios
Utilized Flakes (359)

Fig. 73   Histograms showing breadth:length ratios of unbroken utilized flakes from Fengate.

to distinguish the types of implement or by-product that have been reworked or selected for subsequent re-use) and those made from crudely bashed pebbles (eg FIG 65, nos 37-41). The isolation of this category of implements is open to question, as it is, at best, somewhat ill-defined, the only morphological requirement being the presence of more than two denticulations. Its main distinguishing feature is the presence of clear signs of wear polish on the points of the denticulations. In common with other, qualitative, aspects of this collection, however, there is a strong subjective impression that any pointed and denticulated bashed flint was selected for subsequent use or re-use. Indeed, it is probable that the distinction between piercers (as distinct from awls) and denticulated tools is one of morphology rather than function. The Newark Road piercers and denticulated tools compare well with the borers of R4 (Fasham and Ross 1978, FIG 6) which the authors point out represent a tool type of increasing importance in the Early Middle Bronze Age. Mercer (1976, 109) has suggested that the piercing tools found in the secondary rubbish of the 'Middle Bronze Age' resettlement at Grimes Graves may have been used in the treatment of leather or wood; but microwear study of this implement-type is required to test this hypothesis.

5. Other Implement Types

Single piece sickle (FIG 63, no 9)
This is the second example of this uncommon artifact-type to have been found at Fengate (cf FNG 1, FIG 6, no 3). Unlike that from the earlier Neolithic house, the Newark Road sickle is in poor condition: it is broken at either end and its cutting edges are damaged; it is hardly surprising, therefore, that diffuse lustre is not visible. Its condition suggests that it had lain on the ground surface for some considerable time before being incorporated within the filling of ditch 9. Its slightly skewed shape is distinctive (Clark 1932).

Retouched Flake Tools (FIG 63, nos 10-12)
Fifteen retouched flake tools were recovered. None of these could be placed within any generally accepted tool class, and most showed signs of utilisation, which was generally confined to the dorsal surface only. This suggests that many of these tools were not used for cutting or sawing, but rather for scraping in one direction (Tringham et al 1974). Prominent points of retouched flakes often showed signs of wear polish similar, macroscopically, to that observed on denticulated flakes and piercers.

Piercers (FIG 63, nos 15-18)
Six piercers were recovered. Five showed signs of wear similar to that seen on the denticulated tools discussed above. Wear scars on convenient cutting edges suggest that these tools could have performed a number of different functions. Retouch, as opposed to wear scars, was unifacial, often slight and uneven.

Awls (FIG 64, nos 19-21)
Three implements can be classed as awls with some confidence, but this may be a misleadingly low figure, as retouch and utilisation scars are frequently hard to differentiate. The term 'awl' is used here to describe an implement carrying often very slight bifacial retouch which has been applied in such a way as to allow the tool to be used as a gimlet, or hand drill. In one case (no 20), a worn awl has been retouched by the removal of a burin spall, indicating a change in function from drilling to scoring or scribing.

Serrated Flakes
One worn serrated flake was found. The rarity of this implement type in all periods at Fengate is in marked contrast to the earlier Neolithic industry at Windmill Hill (I F Smith 1965, FIG 38). Serrated flakes were similarly rare at Hurst Fen (Clark 1960, 217) and it may be tentatively suggested that the rarity of this implement type on the Fen-edge could have economic significance; nearly all examples from Fengate showed clear signs of lustre in a narrow band along the cutting edge.

Plano-convex 'knives' (FIG 63, nos 13-14)
The classification of the two implements illustrated here is only a tentative suggestion, for want of any better alternative: both are plano-convex in section, and both could be considered knives. Objections to this hypothesis are clear: no 13 is very fragmentary and retouched on the dorsal face only; no 14 is both too short and irregularly retouched to be classed as a 'classic' plano-convex knife, as seen in funerary contexts. It might be suggested that no 14 is a 'domestic' plano-convex knife (cf Wainwright and Longworth 1971, FIG 76, nos 75-6).

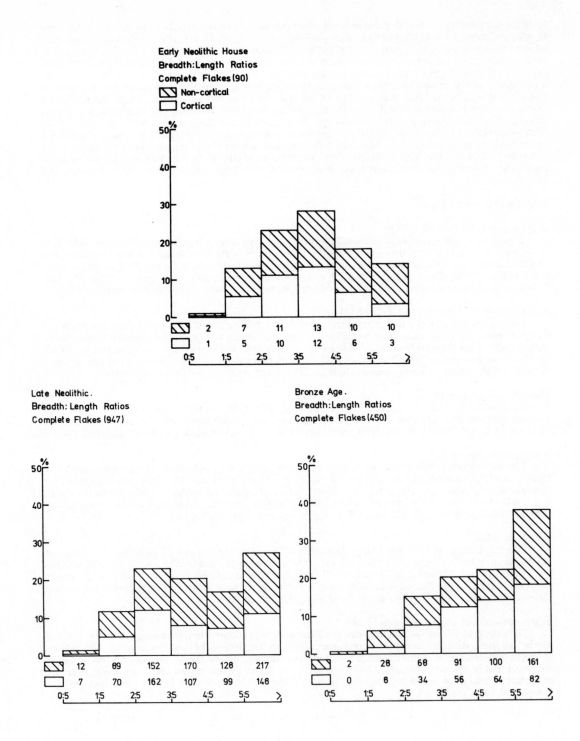

Fig. 74   Histograms showing breadth:length ratios of unbroken waste flakes from Fengate.

BY-PRODUCTS (62.2% of total)
    There were 1046 pieces of flint-working by-products. These could be grouped as follows:

		(percentage of total by-products)
Waste Flakes	666	63.7%
Cores	55	5.3%
Irregular workshop waste	325	31.1%

1. *Waste Flakes* (FIG 74: Tables 6 and 7)

TABLE 6
Lengths (mm) of unbroken waste flakes from Newark Road (Bronze Age) subsite, Areas I-VII.

0-10	10-20	20-30	30-40	40-50	50-60	*Total*
35	260	117	36	1	1	450

TABLE 7
Breadths (mm) of unbroken waste flakes from Newark Road (Bronze Age) subsite, Areas I-VII.

0-5	5-10	10-15	15-20	20-25	25-30	30-35	35-40	40-45	*Total*
1	46	137	136	66	35	21	6	2	450

    Breadth to length ratios of the 450 unbroken waste flakes from Newark Road show a pronounced trend away from narrow blades (as in the earlier Neolithic industry) towards squat flakes — a trend also observed in the Late Neolithic assemblage from Storey's Bar Road. Although it is difficult to define at what point hinge fracture may be so described, it is estimated that 30-50% of the complete flakes show good evidence for excessive and uncontrolled force in their removal (it must however, be emphasised that hinge fracture or short, squat flakes, could have been intentionally produced; some hinge fracture surfaces showed signs of utilisation). Approximately 54.4% of the Storey's Bar Road waste flakes remained unbroken, whereas complete flakes at Newark Road formed 67.6% of the flake total. It would seem probable, however, that the different circumstances of deposition and redeposition at each subsite might play a significant rôle in producing this apparent discrepancy. The Newark Road waste flakes showed an appreciable tendency towards more cortex cover (FIG 74), although this again, may be due to post-depositional distortion. In general, the Newark Road waste flakes are smaller than those from Storey's Bar Road, an observation that is supported by the low average weight figures: the 666 waste flakes from Newark Road weighed 1269gm (average 1.9gm); whereas the 1742 from Storey's Bar Road weighed 3811gm (average 2.2gm) and this is despite the fact that the Newark Road collection contains a lower proportion of broken flakes. Again, as we have noted elsewhere, the figures support a strong subjective impression that the Newark Road material is slighter than that from the two earlier assemblages. It should also be noted that the size difference between Newark Road waste (average 1.9gm) and utilised flakes (average 3.6gm) is considerable. The figures also show a tendency to select more blade-like flakes for utilisation; cortex cover, on the other hand, does not seem to have affected the selection of flakes for use as tools (compare FIGS 73 and 74).

2. *Cores* (FIGS 68 and 69)
    It should be noted that the designation of any particular piece of flint as a core was often a highly subjective affair: the nature of the collection was such that many bashed pieces of irregular workshop waste had had flakes removed from them and could, strictly speaking, be classed as cores. The pieces illustrated here thus represent a sample of flint waste whose classification is mostly based on studies of Earlier Neolithic sites (Clark 1960; I F Smith 1965). Following the system of Clark (1960), the following cores could be distinguished:

		Percentage of Total
Type A1 (single platform, flakes removed all round)	4	5.4%
Type A2 (single platform, flakes removed part of way round)	22	40.0%
Type B1 (two platforms, parallel)	6	10.9%
Type B2 (two platforms, one at oblique angle)	6	10.9%
Type B3 (two platforms at right angles)	7	12.7%
Type C (three or more platforms)	6	10.9%
Type D (keeled, flakes struck from two directions)	2	3.6%
Type E (keeled, but with one or more platform)	3	5.4%

These 55 cores weighed a total of 1130gm (average 20.5gm), whereas the 41 from Storey's Bar Road were on average about 20% heavier (total weight 1051.9gm; average 25.6gm). None of the cores had been used for making blades and the preponderance of Type A2 cores follows the well-established pattern (Fasham and Ross 1978, table 10).

3. *Irregular Workshop Waste*

The criteria defining this group are discussed in greater detail in the Second Report (FNG 2, 8). In essence it consists of flint which shows clear signs of having been worked by man, but which cannot be classed under any of the accepted categories of implements or by-products. The 325 pieces of irregular workshop waste weighed 3349.7gm, giving an average weight of 10.3gm; that from Storey's Bar Road (349 pieces), on the other hand, weighed 4170.2gm, giving an average of 11.9gm. Irregular workshop waste is the only numerically significant category of flint not to show a pronounced decrease in weight from Storey's Bar to Newark Road.

GENERAL CONSIDERATIONS OF THE NEWARK ROAD FLINTS

The preceding paragraphs have discussed individual implement and by-product categories in their Fengate context, and two general trends could be observed: first, a decrease in weight of individual flints and, second, a strong impression that technical standards of flintworking had declined. One minor trend of some importance was the recognition that boring or piercing tools, particularly the multi-pointed denticulated tool, were more common in the Newark Road collection than in the earlier and Late Neolithic assemblages at Fengate.

Modern, published, studies of flint industries in the region are rare and it is difficult to find adequate contemporary comparative material. Professor Clark's work in the southern Fenland must still, therefore, provide the standard by which others are judged. Clark's pre-War excavations at Plantation Farm, Shippea Hill (1933) and Mildenhall Fen (1936) provide well-dated parallels, from a very similar environment, for most of the implement types found at Newark Road. His post-War excavations (1960) at Hurst Fen, Mildenhall, also a Fen-edge site, but of earlier Neolithic date, provide the important quantitative data which serve to emphasise the differences between Fenland flint industries of the third and second millennia BC. These differences have been touched on above and in the Second Report, and it must be emphasised that great caution is necessary when attempting to compare two sites so far apart in time and distance. The sites also differ substantially in the way in which their deposits accumulated. The processes that caused the Newark Road collection to accumulate in the ditch fillings have been considered at length above; Hurst Fen on the other hand, is a very well preserved site which had not been cultivated 'at least during the historic period' (Clark 1960, 203). Furthermore, whereas Newark Road represents redeposited secondary rubbish, much of Hurst Fen, especially the 'compacted brownish culture layer' (*ibid*, 203) comprised actual *in situ* primary rubbish.

Hurst Fen, however, clearly differs significantly from Newark Road and should not be used for comparative purposes; but Professor Clark's earlier excavation at Mildenhall Fen (Clark 1936) does provide an excellent contemporary, and local, comparative flint industry. This important excavation was undertaken before the widespread adoption of detailed metrical analysis of British Bronze Age flintwork, but despite this, the two groups are closely comparable. Many of the Mildenhall Fen end scrapers are broken transversely, a phenomenon that was also observed at Newark Road (cf Clark 1936, FIG 9, no 6). Clark's pseudo-awls compare well with the Fengate piercers and the true awls from both sites are also similar. Comparisons of this sort are, perhaps, too subjective and of only passing interest; but of greater significance is Clark's note that much of the waste has a 'bashed' appearance. Clark also notes that the Mildenhall Bronze Age flints are of a lower standard of workmanship than those from the Chalcolithic (to interpose Pitts's 1978a term) settlement site at Plantation Farm, nearby (Clark 1933). Similar sites to Mildenhall Fen are known to exist on the Fen islands and skirtland in Cambridgeshire and many of these are being seriously damaged by peat 'shrinkage' and deep ploughing (David Hall, pers comm). Modern excavation of at least one of these sites is urgently required.

The site at R4 has already been discussed at some length as it provides the best published comparative material for Newark Road. Other recently excavated comparable sites, mainly from Wessex and Berkshire, include Ram's Hill, Itford Hill and Oakley Down. Ram's Hill (Bradley 1975a) did not produce a large stratified flint assemblage of Bronze Age date, but what was found clearly resembles Newark Road in many important respects, particularly 'the tendency towards crude broad flakes' and 'a perceptible decline in technical competence'. Itford Hill (Holden 1975; Bradley in Holden 1972, 93-102), like Ram's Hill (but unlike Newark Road), produced an assemblage where waste flakes, which again were short and squat, vastly outnumbered finished, retouched implements (Bradley, *ibid* notes that there were over 40,000 waste flakes, but only 37 finished implements — excluding the *c* 12% of utilised flakes). As at Fengate (Newark Road), and elsewhere, cores of Clark's (1960) type A2 were the most commonly found. Finally, this brief review of the Wessex material must make note of the general similarity of the 'several hundred' flint flakes recovered from Oakley Down (White and Reed 1971).

124

Returning to the western Fen-edge and east midlands, the only approximately contemporary site in the region to have been recently excavated and published is that at Ecton, near Northampton (Moore and Williams 1975). This settlement site produced Late Neolithic pottery in the Mortlake and Ebbsfleet styles and is probably, therefore, somewhat earlier than Newark Road. A few Beaker sherds were also found, but at a slightly higher stratigraphic level, so the chronological difference between the two sites may not be as large as might first appear.

The raw material used in the Ecton assemblage was Nene gravel flint. Moore based his classification of cores on Clark's (1960) system but noted that 'classification was difficult because of their small size and irregular nature' (*ibid* 20). The small flake assemblage was more blade-like than other Late Neolithic industries, but the high proportion of borers and the fact that the scrapers had few common features (and had, therefore, to be described individually), recalls Newark Road. Moore rightly emphasises the dangers of attaching too much weight to so small a flint industry (809 struck flints), but Ecton does, nonetheless, seem to have many qualitative points in common with Newark Road (cf, for example, *ibid* FIG 9). The Ecton assemblage is important in that it implies that the typically 'Bronze Age' features of the Newark Road flint collection could also be found locally in the later Neolithic period. Its chief importance, however, is that, with Fengate, it provides good evidence for spatial and chronological variability in the domestic flint assemblages of the region. This variability must be set against a more or less uniform flint source (Welland or Nene gravel).

This brief review of the Newark Road collection has shown that there was significant change — from our standpoint perhaps a 'decline' — in flint working techniques between the Late Neolithic (Pitts's (1978a) 'Chalcolithic'), as represented at Storey's Bar Road, and the full Bronze Age. The apparent 'decline' may accompany the more widespread use of metal (Bradley 1975a, 87); it may reflect the gradual exhaustion of high quality sources of flint (Pitts and Jacobi 1979), and in this regard it is interesting to note the re-use of 'at least one' flint saddle quern at Mildenhall Fen (Clark 1936, 44); it may also reflect a change in flint technology where control over flake or blade 'blanks' was given less emphasis; instead, attention was given to the retouch of suitable material selected from debitage (Pitts 1978 a and b). Most probably the explanation lies in a combination of these and other factors, and the recent studies mentioned above have shown exciting new possibilities for future research.

3. MISCELLANEOUS FINDS

CATALOGUE OF ILLUSTRATED MISCELLANEOUS FINDS

BURNT CLAY

Loomweights (FIG 75, nos 1-4)

1. Large fragment of axially-perforated cylindrical clay loomweight (est dia 88; perforation dia 25). Well-fired untempered clay with light striations (wear marks?) on end and sides.
    Undecorated
    Area II, ditch 9, layer 3, (Grid 48W/42N) depth 0.40. 74:2373
2. Large fragment of axially-perforated cylindrical clay loomweight (ext dia *c* 75; perforation dia 18; length 102). Well-fired untempered clay.
    Decoration: light longitudinal parallel scratches on ext.
    Area III, ditch *a*, layer 2, (Grid 64W/84N) depth 0.35. 76:2
3. Large fragment of axially-perforated cylindrical clay loomweight (ext dia 85; perforation dia 21). Poorly fired, soft, untempered clay.
    Undecorated
    Area III, ditch *b*, layer 2, (Grid 61W/66N) depth 0.40. 75:4467
4. Fragment of axially-perforated cylindrical clay loomweight (ext dia *c* 100; perforation dia *c* 25). Poorly fired, soft untempered clay.
    Decoration: vertical and horizontal rows of deep (5+mm) punctate impressions on ext.
    Area III, ditch *b*, layer 2, (Grid 63W/80N) depth 0.50. 75:4312

Burnt Clay 'Daub' (FIG 75, nos 5-6)

5. Poorly fired, untempered burnt clay with wattle impression. 'Industrial area'.
    Area VII, F254, layer 2, (Grid 18W/143N) depth 0.11. 76:1173
6. As No 5, above.
    Area VII, F254, layer 1, (Grid 20W/142N) depth 0.24. 76:1268

BRONZE (FIG 75, no 7; FIG 77)

7. Tip portion of socketed spearhead (see reports by Drs Coombs and Craddock, below). Length 89; max width 24; thickness 9.
    Area II, ditch 8, layer 1, (Grid 5W/40N) depth 0.18. 74:1122
Fig 77 Complete awl (weight 3gm); length 54; max width 4; thickness 3.5.
    Area II, ditch F54, (Grid 36W/54N) from top of stripped surface. 74:1812

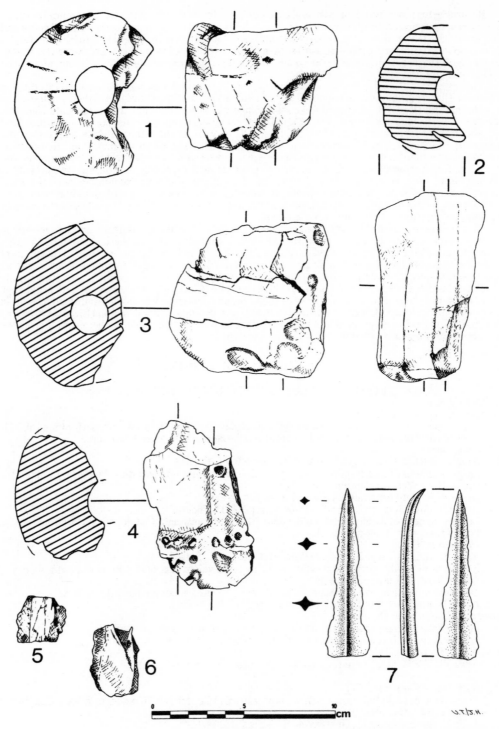

Fig. 75 Newark Road subsite, second millennium BC ditches: miscellaneous finds. No 1 (ditch 9); 2 (ditch *a*); 3-4 (ditch *b*); 5-6 (VII F254); 7 (ditch 8).

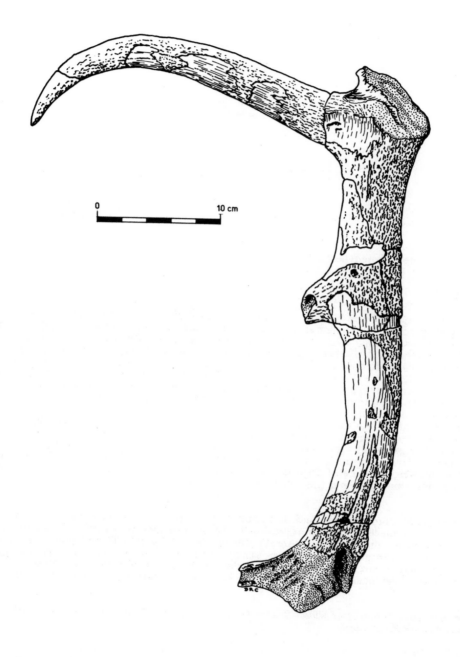

Fig. 76   Newark Road subsite, Area VII, ditch 10: antler pick from layer 1 at Grid 73W/83N.

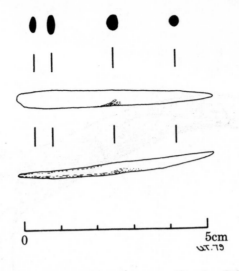

Fig. 77   Newark Road subsite, Area II, ditch F54 (? first millennium BC): bronze awl.

ANTLER
Fig 76 Complete (restored) pick of Red Deer antler.
Area III, ditch 10, layer 1, (Grid 74W/83N). 75:4553

DISCUSSION
1. *Burnt Clay*
Roughly fired or burnt clay was used to fashion cylindrical, axially-perforated weights. These weights are generally interpreted as loomweights and there seems little reason to doubt this view: certainly the Newark Road weights are too poorly fired to have been used as net weights for fishing, nor are they heavy enough to have been used as thatch weights. Slight evidence in support of the loomweight hypothesis is provided by the two weights found in small pits, or postholes, within the settlement area near Structures 1 and 2, in Area IV (FIG 60, nos 33 and 34). At least one weight (FIG 75, no 4) has been crudely decorated with a row of deep punctate stabs. Possible warp-impressions, or other signs of wear likely to be associated with weaving were not encountered. The Newark Road weights may be closely paralleled on the Padholme Road subsite (see Chapter 1).

Burnt clay 'daub' was found in small quantities in most of the second millennium BC enclosure ditches. It was most frequently encountered in the off-centre recut of ditch 254 in the 'industrial area', Area VII. Approximately four pieces of 'industrial area' burnt clay daub showed traces of wattle impressions and the two clearest of these are illustrated in FIG 75, nos 5-6. This area produced about 85 pieces of daub weighing a total of 926gm (average per piece: 10.9gm); approximately 50% of these pieces showed signs of smoothing on at least one face.

2. *Bronze*
Three pieces of bronze were found: the tip portion of a socketed spearhead; a small spill and a tanged awl. The first two objects were found in ditches of the second millennium system, the spearhead (74:1122) from Area II, ditch 8, and the spill from Area IV, ditch *a*, layer 1, (Grid 109W/74N) depth 0.25m (76:106), some 104m W of the spearhead. Dr Craddock's analysis of the metal composition of both pieces suggests that the spill 'may be part of the debris of casting the spearhead, evidence that it was cast on site'. The wider contexts of the spearhead are considered by Dr Coombs following Dr Craddock's metallurgical analysis.

A note on the composition of the Middle Bronze Age spearhead (74:1122) and spill of metal (76:106) from Fengate, Newark Road subsite.

Dr P T Craddock

The spearhead was drilled from the junction of the socket and blade, and the spill from its centre, using a portable jeweller's drill mounted with a size 60 (1mm diameter) bit. Surface and corroded metal was rejected and 10mgm of clean metal turnings were collected for analysis.

The sample was analysed by Atomic Absorption Spectrometry; precise details of the methodology have been fully published elsewhere (Hughes et al 1976) and need not be repeated here. The results quoted below have a precision of ± 1% for the major elements, copper and tin, and ± 20% for the remaining trace elements. The detection limit was at least 0.005% for each element.

	Cu	Sn	Pb	Ag	Fe	Sb	Ni	Co	As	Bi
Spearhead	88.5	10.8	0.13	0.04	0.18	0.05	0.3	0.005	0.15	0.005
Spill	88.5	11.1	0.5	0.04	0.06	0.05	0.3	0.01		0.005
										0.005

Mn, Au, Zn and Cd were also sought but not detected.

Comment

The composition of the spearhead is a 10% tin bronze with traces of other metals, entirely typical of Middle Bronze Age metalwork in general (Craddock 1978). The spill of metal has an almost identical composition, especially the tin nickel, silver and antimony. This suggests the spill may be part of the debris of casting the spearhead, evidence that it was cast on site.

A note on the dating and archaeological significance of the Fengate, Newark Road subsite, spearhead fragment

Dr D G Coombs

The bronze fragment can be identified as the tip of a spearhead. It has badly damaged edges but still retains a sharp point. It is totally solid throughout its length and has a very prominent sharp midrib. The cross section is star shaped and there is a marked concavity to the wings of the blade (Rowlands 1976, 58, blade section a).

It is difficult to be too precise about such a small and damaged piece, but comparisons suggest a few broad classes.

Spearheads in use during the Late Bronze Age had the socket extending almost to the tip, and a rounded midrib; thus it can be said, with some confidence, that the fragment is not from a leaf-shaped peg-hole spearhead of that period.

As 89mm of the spearhead survive, all solid, this indicates that the socket ended lower down the blade, which would indicate a spearhead of large dimensions. Star-shaped cross sections are present on side-loop spearheads (eg Ehrenberg 1977, 11, 25, 26, 28, 35, 108, 140, 143, 146), often with the wing concavity as seen on the Fengate piece. Side-loop spearheads, however, rarely exceed 150-160mm in length.

The Fengate tip probably best fits the large basal-loop class of spearhead, many of which have a similar cross section, with prominent narrow midrib (Rowlands 1976, PLS 39-41; Ehrenberg 1977, FIGS 13-17).

Although we still lack a comprehensive survey of Bronze Age spearheads in the British Isles, recent studies (Burgess et al 1972; Coombs 1975; Rowlands 1976; Ehrenberg 1977) have added greatly to our knowledge of the origins, chronology and development of the various classes.

Basal-loop spearheads represent an insular tradition with an origin in Ireland. They seem to have been introduced into southern Britain at the end of the Middle Bronze Age, with the earliest association in the Ornament Horizon (M A Smith 1959). The very large examples appear to be confined to the end of the Middle Bronze Age (Middle Bronze Age 3 (Burgess 1968), or Late Bronze Age 1, as it has recently been defined (Jockenhövel 1975)), where they formed an essential element in the weapon hoards (eg Ambleside, Westmorland (Fell and Coles 1965); Isle of Axholme, Lincolnshire (Davey 1973); Appleby, Lincolnshire (Davey and Knowles 1971); Maentwrog, Merioneth (Hawkes and Smith 1955)). According to Rowlands (1976) basal-loop spearheads are all over 150mm in length, and fall into two groups based on size, between a) 150-250mm and b) 250-450mm, in length.

The spill of metal from the same subsite, which shows similar trace elements to the spearhead fragment, suggests metalworking on the site; published distribution maps, however, would suggest the Thames Valley was the major production area of basal-loop spearheads.

If the Fengate fragment is indeed from a basal-loop spearhead, then it represents the first example from a definite settlement location. Rowlands (1976) mentions two finds from possible settlements: Walthamstow, Essex, said to have been from a crannog site; and 'between Kempsey and Dixham Ferries, River Severn', said to have been found amongst some oak piles on the river foreshore.

A date just prior to 1000 BC would best fit the fragment.

The Awl

The small bronze awl (74:1812) was found on the stripped surface of the pre-Roman, but post-second millennium BC ditch F54 (FIG 44). It is almost certainly a residual find, as its dubiously stratified contexts clearly post-date the second millennium ditches. Awls of this sort are not found in Late Bronze Age hoards, being more commonly found in Early and Middle Bronze Age contexts (eg Annable and Simpson 1964, no 364; Rowlands 1976, PL 35).

3. *Antler Pick* (FIG 76)

One antler pick was found, in a fragmentary, but restorable, state in layer 1 of ditch 10, Area III. It is made from shed Red Deer antler and the pick is formed out of the brow tine. Other tines have been removed and the brow tine tip shows evidence (polish and striations) of wear.

CHAPTER 3: THE FOURTH DROVE SUBSITE

INTRODUCTION (FIGs 78 and 79)

The Fourth Drove subsite (FIG 3) was excavated in 1977 and 1978. The field in question had been put down to permanent pasture shortly after the Second World War and did not, therefore, show any positive cropmarks from the air; the Fen Causeway, which runs diagonally across the subsite from E-W, did, however, stand out as a clear negative mark (PL 6). In the absence of aerial evidence for prehistoric occupation, it was decided to excavate the Newark Road and Cat's Water subsites first, in the hope that ditch alignments might suggest suitable areas for subsequent exploration. Fourth Drove was also the least severely threatened subsite at Fengate and was known to be thickly blanketed by flood clays. These considerations, among others, led to a change of excavation strategy in which large open areas were abandoned in favour of smaller trenches (FIG 3). These trenches therefore represent a 'judgement sample' (Cherry *et al* 1978, 409) of the subsite's archaeology which, by definition, is neither complete nor unbiased.

It should be stressed here that the ditch numbers used represent alignments only, and do not imply actual physical continuity; this is particularly apparent in the two lengths of ditch 10 (FIG 78) and in the lengths of ditches 8 and 9 on either side of Storey's Bar Road (FIG 5).

Turning to the Grid, it was decided that subsites to the east of Storey's Bar Road (ie Cat's Water and Fourth Drove) should be laid out on a common grid. This grid is aligned on Ordnance Survey grid north and has a false origin to the SE of the Cat's Water subsite, beyond the Designated Area of Peterborough New Town. Grid references are given to the nearest metre and indicate the SE corner of each metre square. Two grid lines are shown in FIG 78.

The trenches were laid out with three aims in mind. Trench I was located as close to the Cat's Water subsite as possible in order to determine whether the Iron Age settlement extended significantly further north — which it clearly proved was not the case. Trench II was placed as near to the Newark Road subsite as possible in order to locate ditches 8-10. Trench VII was placed along the Fen-ward edge of the subsite to determine the eastward extent of the second millennium ditches; its location was also determined by the presence of a low bank (which ran along the W side of the drainage dyke that formed the eastern boundary of the subsite), as it was hoped that this bank would protect any archaeological features from plough damage. The remaining trenches were positioned to confirm suspected alignments or to investigate probable intersections.

The ground surface prior to excavation was almost flat, there being a slight rise (*c* 1.20m) from NE to SW. The course of the Fen Causeway was visible as a very wide, low *agger*, best seen in the 3.0 and 3.2m contours (FIG 79).

This chapter is arranged in two parts: features followed by finds. Both sections follow the pattern of the previous chapter, in which ditches and other features of the second millennium are described before later features.

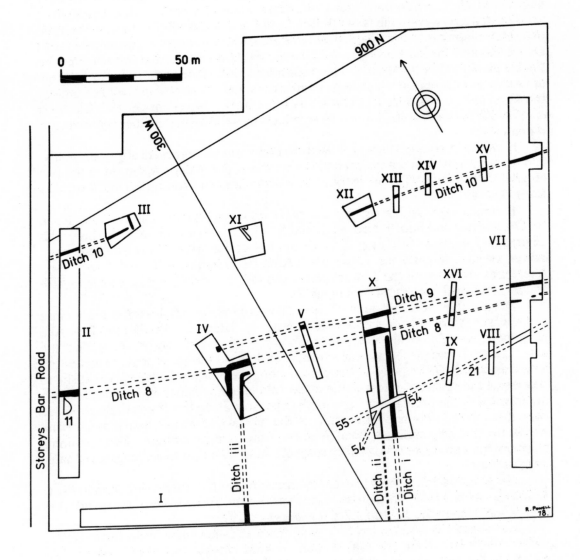

Fig. 78   Fourth Drove subsite: general plan of excavated area.

SECOND MILLENNIUM BC DITCHES AND ASSOCIATED FEATURES

GENERAL

It has already been noted that this subsite was excavated using small trenches and it cannot, therefore, be guaranteed that the lengths of ditch represented by the dashed line in FIG 78 actually exist. Some assumptions must be made, however, to avoid repeated qualification, so the hypothetical lengths of ditch are treated as 'real' in the description that follows.

The Fourth Drove subsite is important because it ties together the two large open-area excavations of the Cat's Water and Newark Road subsites. It is also important in that it has been less severely ploughed than any other subsite at Fengate. The thick accumulations of flood clay in the topsoil are also likely to have protected the underlying archaeological features from severe damage. Further, some indication of the extent of post-depositional damage is given by the survival of the bank which originally accompanied ditch 10 in Area VII. These factors, taken together, suggest that ditch sections and fillings on Fourth Drove should be considered in some detail.

The description that follows is in two parts: part 1 considers ditches S of, and including, ditch 9, and part 2 considers the two lengths of ditch 10.

1. DITCHES 8-9, i-iii AND ASSOCIATED FEATURES

General description (FIGS 78, 80-1).

This general description of the excavated features has been separated from the detailed description of sections (below) because of the fragmentary nature of the excavations themselves, and the decision, discussed above, to describe the sections in greater than usual detail.

The layout of the Fourth Drove ditched enclosures is consistent with that observed on Newark Road and Cat's Water (FIG 5). The gradual divergence of ditches 8-9 and 10, seen on Newark Road, is continued on Fourth Drove, as is the perfectly straight N-S alignment of Cat's Water ditch *iii*.

The ditches of the southern half of the subsite can be seen to form the sides of (?) three enclosures. These enclosures are bounded to the N by ditch 8; ditch 9 runs parallel to, and N of, ditch 8 to form an E-W droveway 138m long, 5-7m wide; this droveway runs off the subsite to the E. Only the central (?) enclosure can be defined on three sides (width *c* 55m); the other two are defined by discontinuous lengths of ditch and their size and subdivisions are unknown. The easterly enclosure is of interest, however, as it shows evidence for settlement near its northern edge, in Area VII. These occupation features will be considered in greater detail below.

Ditch 9 ran approximately E-W across the E half of the subsite, for a distance of 138m. Its profile was open U-shaped and its depth was quite constant (FIG 83, nos 4, 5). It showed no evidence for recutting or blocking and appeared to terminate in an indistinct butt-end in Area IV at Grid 324W/827N.

Ditch 8 was an E-W ditch which ran across the subsite for a distance of about 209m. Unlike ditch 9, ditch 8 was variable in profile and showed considerable evidence for recutting and blocking. The variability of profile is well illustrated in the two sections of ditch shown from Area II (FIG 84, nos 1-2). Approximately 60m E, (in Area

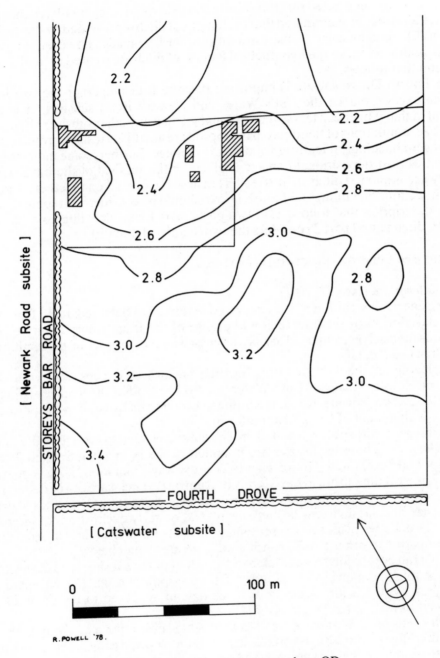

Fig. 79   Fourth Drove subsite: surface contours in metres above OD.

IV), ditch 8 joined the W ditch of a N-S drove aligned on ditch *iii*; the intersection of the two ditches was unclear, and they may well have been originally contemporary. A slight kink in the N edge of ditch 8 at this point indicates that its eastward extension was of a different phase. Close inspection of this kink revealed it to be a true butt-end; FIG 84, no 3 shows a longitudinal section of ditch 8 east of, and including, the butt-end and it should be noted that the ditch has at this point become considerably slighter than hitherto (compare FIG 84, nos 1, 2 with 3). No stratigraphic relationship between the two lengths of ditch could be seen, but the slight change in depth and alignment might suggest that the E length of ditch 8 is somewhat earlier. In Area X, immediately opposite the butt-end of ditch *i* (at Grid 265W/800N), ditch 8 showed clear stratigraphic evidence for recutting. FIG 84, no 4 is a longitudinal section at this point and it can be seen that a shallow, early phase, represented by layer 2, is cut by two later recuts to E (layer 3) and W (layer 1). The relationship of the two recuts cannot be demonstrated stratigraphically, but their contemporaneity is doubtful in view of the narrow gap (*c* 0.50m) between them; this would be a very poor entranceway.

The best example of recutting and modification on the subsite is provided by ditch 8 in Area VII, immediately north of Structure 1 (FIG 80). At this point the ditch has a rather irregular, stretched S-shaped course which could, perhaps, be seen to respect the postholes of Structure 1. The clear evidence for recutting, and its slightly meandering course, recall the many phases of ditch *n* in the vicinity of Structure 1, Newark Road (FIG 31). This twisting course is in sharp contrast to the straight, uninterrupted length of ditch 9, just 4.0-5.2m to the NE. Ditch 8, N of Structure 1, showed evidence for at least two phases. The first phase is represented by three lengths of deeper ditch, forming two entranceways of width 4m and 1.5m; these two entranceways were subsequently blocked by a very shallow (0-0.20m) sinuous recut which followed the alignment of the earlier phase, except where it passed out of the excavated area, to the E. A broadly similar pattern of blocked entranceways, also confined to one side only of a droveway, was observed in Areas II and VI of the Newark Road subsite, immediately north of the well, in enclosure 1 (FIG 25).

Settlement features are represented by the four postholes of Structure 1 (FIG 80); the postholes between ditches 8 and 9 are doubtful, as is the small pit just north of ditch 8 near the E edge of the excavated area. The four postholes of Structure 1 are arranged in an arc of diameter *c* 4.7m. The arrangement of the postholes, their spacing and location alongside an enclosure boundary ditch are factors which are closely paralleled by Structure 2, in Area IV of Newark Road (FIG 40, 81). Ditches 8 and 9 in Area VII produced more finds (including sherds in the Collared Urn tradition — FIG 89, nos 2, 3) than any other second millennium features on the subsite; this would indicate settlement in the vicinity. None of the four postholes produced artifacts, although charcoal was commonly found; they are described below:

F27. Posthole (0.4 x 0.35) with steep, vertical sides (depth 0.18), flat bottom and filling of silty loam with scattered gravel pebbles (10YR 3/2); charcoal common.

F28. Recut posthole (first phase: dia 0.21, depth 0.14; second phase: dia 0.18, depth 0.06); filling of first phase: sand-silt with scattered gravel pebbles; no charcoal (10YR 3/2); filling of second phase: silty loam with charcoal commonly occurring (10YR 2.5/1).

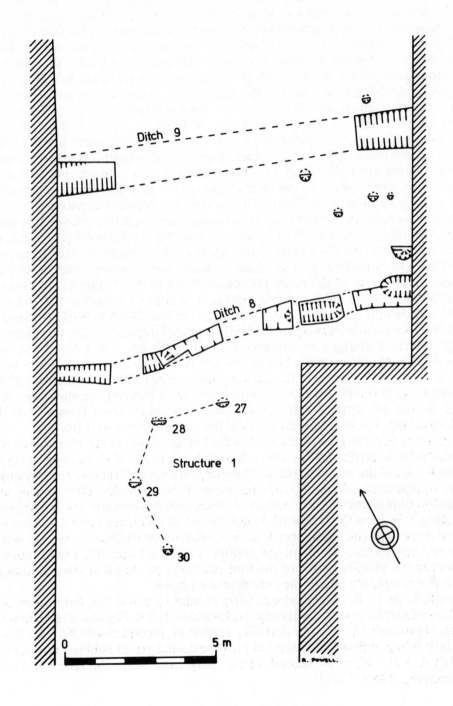

Ditch 9

Ditch 8

27

28

Structure 1

29

30

0　　　　　　　　　　　5 m

R. POWELL.

Fig. 80　　Fourth Drove subsite, Area VII: ditches 8-9 and Structure 1.

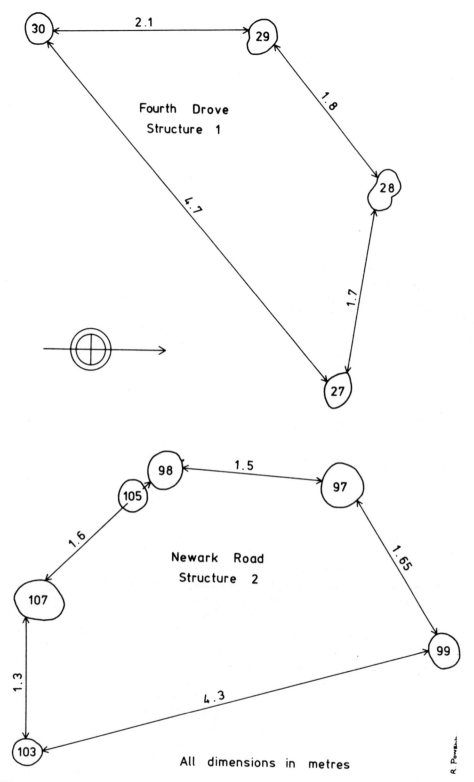

Fourth Drove
Structure 1

Newark Road
Structure 2

All dimensions in metres

R. Powell

Fig. 81   Comparative plans of two second millennium BC semi-circular structures.

137

F29. Oblong posthole (possibly recut?) (0.40 x 0.30) with steep sides (depth 0.23) and filling of silty loam with scattered gravel pebbles (10YR 3/3); charcoal fairly common.

F30. Posthole (dia 0.30) with vertical sides (depth 0.12) and flat bottom; filling of sand-silt with scattered gravel pebbles (10YR 3/1); charcoal common.

Turning to the ditches south of ditches 8 and 9, ditches *i* and *ii* ran NE-SW to form a straight drove (width 3.5m) which divided the central from the eastern (?) enclosure. Both ditches terminated 1.0m south of ditch 8, to form narrow corner entranceways at the head of the drove; the various recuts of ditch 8 at this point may once have provided access, from the N-S drove, into the main E-W drove. Both ditches were cut by the later (Iron Age) ditches F21/54 and F55 (FIG 82, nos 1 and 2). The course of both ditches southwards was confirmed by the cleaning-out of the modern field boundary ditch that ran along the north side of Fourth Drove itself.

Finally, the westerly side of the central enclosure was marked by a length of drove defined, to the E, by ditch *i*, and, 3.5 to the W, by the N-S extension of ditch 8, briefly mentioned above. The latter ditch was not present in Area I. Ditch *i*, however, ran southwards for a total length of 240m (to its junction with ditches 3 and 4 on the Cat's Water subsite). Two sections of this ditch are illustrated in FIG 83 (nos 2 and 3).

Detailed descriptions of illustrated sections (FIGS 82-84)

FIG 82

1. F21 (Iron Age ditch continuous with F54); transverse section in Area VII at Grid 218W/769N:

    F21 layer 1.   Clay-silt with gravel lenses and iron pan (10YR 4/3); charcoal very rare. Cuts layer 3, overlies layer 2, which it blends into.

    F21 layer 2.   Silty loam and gravel with sand lenses and iron pan (10YR 4/2); charcoal very rare.

    F21 layer 3.   Silty loam with scattered gravel pebbles and sand lenses (10YR 3/2); charcoal rare. An early phase of the ditch.

2. Ditch *i* and F54 (Iron Age ditch continuous with F21); longitudinal section along ditch *i* in Area X at Grid 272W/771N. F54 cuts ditch *i* (all layers):

    F54 layer 3.   Sand-silt with scattered gravel pebbles and clay (10YR 4/2); charcoal rare.

    F54 layer 4.   Sand-silt with even gravel mix (10YR 5/8); charcoal absent.

    F54 layer 5.   Clay-silt with some sand-silt and scattered gravel pebbles (10YR 4/2); charcoal very rare.

    F54 layer 6.   Clay-silt with scattered gravel pebbles (10YR 2.5/1); charcoal common, also organic material including wood, twigs.

    This intersection was hard to interpret with any confidence. The dashed line represents the clear indication that ditch F54 cuts ditch *i*; this probably represents a later recut (layers 1, 2, 4) of F54 whose earlier phase is seen in layers 3, 5 and 6.

    Ditch i layer 1.   Clay-silt with much sand-silt and scattered gravel pebbles (10YR 4/2); charcoal rare.

    Ditch i layer 2.   Clay-silt with even gravel mix (10YR 3/3); charcoal absent.

3. Ditch *ii* and F54 and F55 (Iron Age ditches); transverse section across the Iron Age ditches at the point (in area X) where they cut ditch *ii* (Grid 280W/770N). F54 (continuous with F21 to the E) cuts ditch *ii* and F55; F55 cuts ditch *ii* (not shown in this section):

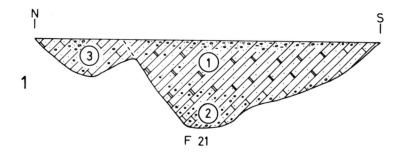

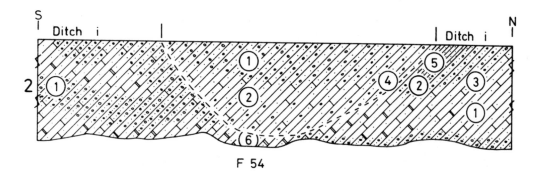

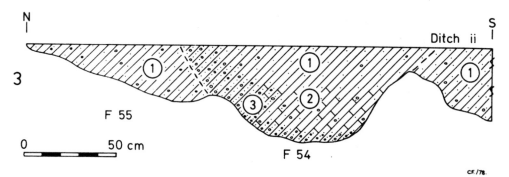

Fig. 82   Fourth Drove subsite: sections through selected features.

F54 layer 1.	Sand-silt with scattered gravel pebbles (10YR 4/3); possibly back-filled; charcoal very rare.
F54 layer 2.	Clay-silt with scattered gravel pebbles and gravel lenses (10YR 4/2); charcoal very rare.
F54 layer 3.	Sand-silt with an even gravel mix (10YR 3/3); charcoal very rare. Possibly a slipped-in bank? Clearly overlies F55 layer 1.
F55 layer 1.	Sand-silt with clay and scattered gravel pebbles (10YR 3/3); charcoal very rare. Underlies, and is cut by, F54 layer 3.
Ditch ii layer 1.	Sand-silt with clay and scattered gravel pebbles (10YR 4/3); charcoal absent. Cut by F54 layer 1.

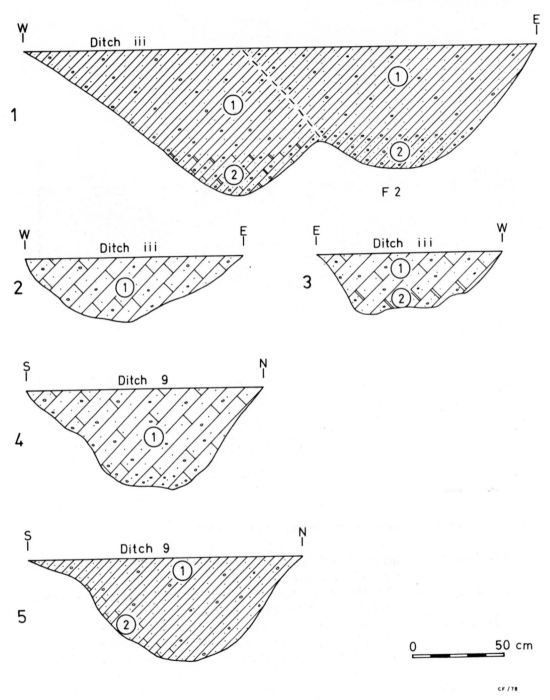

Fig. 83   Fourth Drove subsite: sections through selected features.

FIG 83

1. Ditch *iii* and the pit (undated F2); transverse section in Area I at Grid 345W/767N. The pit, F2, cuts ditch *iii*:

F2 layer 1. Sand-silt with scattered gravel pebbles (10YR 6/4); charcoal very rare. Cuts ditch *iii*, layer 1, blends into layer 2, below.

F2 layer 2. Sand-silt with even gravel mix and iron pan (10YR 6/8); charcoal absent. Relationship to ditch *iii* not clear.

Ditch iii layer 1. Silty loam with even gravel mix (10YR 6/6); charcoal very rare. Cut by F2, layer 1; blends into layer 2, below.

Ditch iii layer 2. Silty loam with even gravel mix and iron pan (10YR 5/4); charcoal very rare. Relationship to F2 layer 2 not clear.

2. Ditch *iii*; transverse section in Area IV, south end, at Grid 328W/799N:

Ditch iii layer 1. Clay-loam with scattered gravel pebbles and sand (10YR 5/2); charcoal rare.

3. Ditch *iii*; transverse section in Area IV, east-centre, at Grid 320W/811N:

Ditch iii layer 1. Loam with scattered gravel pebbles (10YR 4/3); charcoal rare. Blends evenly into layer 2, below.

Ditch iii layer 2. Clay-loam with scattered gravel pebbles and flecks of iron-pan (10YR 5/2); charcoal rare.

4. Ditch 9; transverse section in Area V at Grid 289W/818N:

Ditch 9 layer 1. Clay-silt with scattered gravel pebbles and sand (10YR 4/3); charcoal very rare. Slight gravel spread at bottom ('rapid' silting).

5. Ditch 9; transverse section in Area XVI at Grid 232W/798N:

Ditch 9 layer 1. Sand-silt with few clay lenses, scattered gravel pebbles and redeposited iron-pan (7.5YR 4/2); charcoal rare. Blends into layer 2, to the S.

Ditch 9 layer 2. Clay-silt with sand (10YR 5/2); charcoal rare. This layer is a slipped deposit from the S, clay, side of the ditch.

FIG 84

1. Ditch 8; transverse section in Area II (NW edge) at Grid 388W/845N:

Ditch 8 layer 1. Silty loam with some sand-silt and scattered gravel pebbles (10YR 5/1); charcoal rare. Blends evenly into layer 2, below.

Ditch 8 layer 2. Silty loam with clay, an even gravel mix and iron-pan (10YR 6/8); charcoal rare. Blends evenly into layer 3, below.

Ditch 8 layer 3. Clay-silt with much sand-silt, an even gravel mix and iron-pan (10YR 4/1); charcoal rare.

2. Ditch 8; transverse section in Area II (SE edge) at Grid 382W/840N:

Ditch 8 layer 1. Silty loam with some sand-silt in an even gravel mix (10YR 4/1); charcoal rare. Blends evenly into layer 2, below.

Ditch 8 layer 2. Silty loam with clay, some iron-pan, and an even gravel mix (10YR 6/8); charcoal rare. Blends evenly into layer 3, below.

Ditch 8 layer 3. Clay-silt with some sand-silt and iron-pan in an even gravel mix (10YR 5/1); charcoal rare.

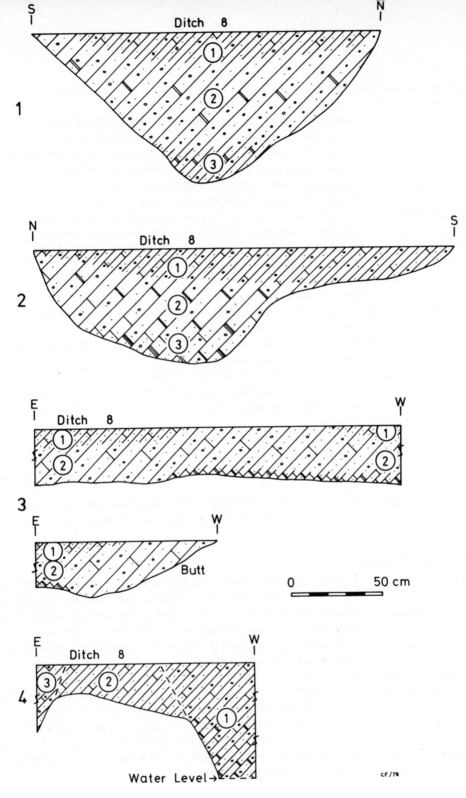

Fig. 84   Fourth Drove subsite: sections through selected features.

3. Ditch 8; longitudinal section in Area IV, east-centre, at Grid 320W/820N. This section passes through the butt-end of an earlier (?) phase of ditch 8:

Ditch 8 layer 1. Sand-silt with scattered gravel pebbles (10YR 4/1); charcoal absent. Blends evenly into layer 2, below.

Ditch 8 layer 2. Sand-silt with clay lenses, scattered gravel pebbles and iron-pan (10YR 4/2); charcoal absent.

4. Ditch 8; longitudinal section in Area X at Grid 265W/800N. This section is placed at a point in the ditch where the surface plan showed evidence for at least two phases of recutting, perhaps associated with entranceway creation and replacement.

Ditch 8 layer 1. Clay-loam with scattered gravel pebbles (10YR 3/2); charcoal absent. The section was very homogeneous at this point, but surface indications suggest this layer cuts layer 2, to the E. Layer 1 could not be completely excavated owing to repeated waterlogging.

Ditch 8 layer 2. Loam with scattered gravel pebbles (10YR 3/3); charcoal very rare. Clearly cut by layer 3; relationship to layer 1 discussed above.

Ditch 8 layer 3. Silty loam with even gravel mix (10YR 3/2); charcoal very rare. Cuts layer 2.

2. DITCH 10 AND ASSOCIATED FEATURES

General description (FIGS 78, 85, 86, 128; PL 15)

Ditch 10 was represented by two lengths, to E and W, which were separated by about 90m of apparently open, unenclosed land. Both lengths were orientated in the same direction, but their alignments were slightly displaced (FIG 78). The westerly length will be considered first.

Ditch 10 entered the subsite from Newark Road at the NW end of trench II, at Grid 360W/890N. At this point the ditch was U-shaped and steep sided, but generally slighter than ditch 9, with which it ran parallel some 54m to the SW (cf FIG 87, no 1 and FIG 84, no 1); the subsoil in the NW part of the subsite was more clay-rich than elsewhere, which explains the steepness of ditches' sides in this area. Ditch 10 was much less substantial to the E, in Area III (FIG 87, no 2), but was seen to terminate in a well defined butt-end at Grid 332W/979N. Ditch F70 ran N from ditch 10 at this point; its butt-end (located at Grid 329W/977N) extended 1.5m S of ditch 10 and the gap between the two ditches was 1.4m wide; this entranceway (like those between ditch 8 and ditches *i* and *ii*) was narrower than was the usual second millennium practice at Fengate. The ditch F70 had steep sides and a flat bottom (FIG 87, no 3), similar to ditch 10 in Area II.

The small trench, Area XI, was positioned to locate any junction between the easterly length of ditch 10 and ditch *iii*, coming from the S. One very doubtful ditch was observed (outlined in FIG 78) on the wrong alignment, but there was no good evidence for second millennium activity in the vicinity (this illustrates the dangers of using small trenches, as Area XI might well be positioned over a wide drove or corner entranceway).

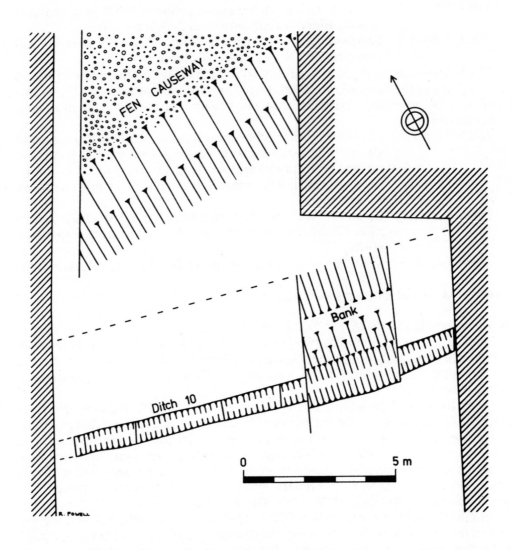

Fig. 85 Fourth Drove subsite, Area VII, NE end, showing Fen Causeway (Romano-British), ditch 10 (second millennium BC) and its associated bank.

Moving eastwards, ditch 10 was relocated in Area XII where it terminated in a clear butt-end (at Grid 249W/848N); a section some 5m to the E showed a slight open U-shaped ditch which gradually deepened as it ran downhill to the E (FIG 87, nos 5 and 6). Ditch 10 passed under the Fen Causeway in Areas XIII, XIV, and XV and emerged in Area VII immediately south of the road; it ran out of the subsite, to the E, at Grid 167W/829N. The short (13m) length of ditch 10 excavated in Area VII was of the greatest interest and will be considered in detail.

The NE end of trench VII was at the lowest point above OD yet excavated at Fengate (see FIG 79); this low level, moreover, coincided with an exceptionally thick accumulation of superficial deposits which resulted from gravel-wash off the road surface, upcast from the modern drainage dyke (discussed at the beginning of the chapter), and flood action. The thickness of these deposits and the hardness of the iron-pan-bound gravel road surface necessitated their removal by machine. A mechanical trench through the Fen Causeway revealed ditch 10 running in a slightly divergent course immediately south of it. This was at first taken to be a side ditch to the road, but a close inspection of the section (FIG 86) showed that this hypothesis was invalid, as gravel which had washed down from the road surface (layer 2) was seen not only to overlie the low bank (layer 4) which accompanied ditch 10, but also to be separated from it by a layer (3) of flood clay, which ran under the road for its entire width. On strictly stratigraphic grounds, therefore, the road and the ditch cannot be contemporary. This discovery led to the excavation of Areas XIII-XV which conclusively showed the ditch to antedate the road. These three narrow trenches again provided evidence for a low bank immediately N of the ditch; excavation of this bank, however, was made extremely difficult by the presence, above it, of the road gravel and it was therefore decided to move eastwards and extend Area VII further into the much softer upcast of the modern drainage dyke.

The easterly extension of Area VII revealed a length (c 3.5m) of low gravel bank immediately north of ditch 10. The bank is shown in section in FIG 86 and, behind the standing figure, in FIG 128 and PL 15. As excavated, it stood c 0.35m above the old land surface and was approximately 1.5m wide. Three levels, taken along the top of the bank shown in PL 15, at the E, centre and W respectively, gave heights above OD of 2.29m, 2.28m and 2.44m. The bottom of the ditch would therefore be at about 1.5m OD.

The bank was completely excavated and showed no signs of post- or stakeholes either in its filling, in the old land surface, or below it. It is suggested that the bank was used as the basis for a hedge which would have been planted along its top. Three points must, however, be stressed. First, although sealed beneath a flood clay which must, on stratigraphic grounds, be pre-Roman, it is quite possible that the bank may have been higher in prehistoric times. It can, however, be stated with confidence that the bank has not suffered the depredations of modern or medieval ploughing. Second, the small amount of gravel visible in the bank make-up does not accord with the size of the ditch. There are at least two possible explanations for this: gravel could have been broadcast on either side of the ditch at various stages in its excavation or, perhaps more reasonably, the ditch could have been frequently dug and re-dug as part of normal day-to-day farming practice. This would have caused gravel pebbles to become mixed with topsoil and for the gravel to loose its otherwise distinctive orange/yellow appearance: there were, for example, very slight hints in the walls of trenches XIII-XV for a low bank S of the ditch. The rich organic material from the ditch bottom when cleaned out and thrown on top of the bank, would have provided the hedge roots with valuable nourishment. The third, and perhaps most important point, is that the filling of the ditch showed no sign whatsoever of a collapsed gravel bank. The reason for this is quite simple: if it is assumed that the bank had a functional purpose, as an enclosure boundary, then experience would quickly show the

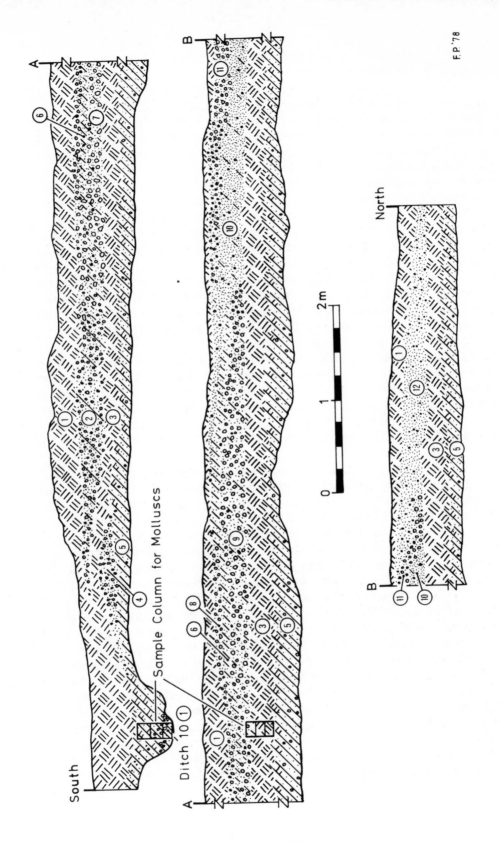

Fig. 86   Fourth Drove subsite, Area VII: section through Roman road and second millennium BC ditch (10) and bank.

146

importance of locating it sufficiently far away from the ditch to prevent it slipping back into the ditch after heavy rain or frost. By the same token, it would be important not to place it so far away from the ditch that it lost the benefit of the latter's drainage. This ideal position would also minimise labour and effort, both in transporting gravel from the ditch and in avoiding unnecessary recutting. It is suggested that the rarity of obvious slipped-in bank deposits in Fengate ditch sections is an indication of efficient land management; this negative evidence does not indicate flat, ditched, unembanked enclosures.

Detailed Descriptions of Illustrated Sections (FIGS 86 and 87)
FIG 86
The general sequence

This section is drawn along the west edge of Area VII, from ditch 10, across the Roman Fen Causeway, to the northern edge of the excavated area. The general sequence (illustrated in three dimensions in FIG 128) is as follows.

Layer 5, which runs beneath all others and is cut by ditch 10, is the old land surface (topsoil). This is overlain by a freshwater deposit (Appendix 4), layer 3, which underlies the road (layers 9-12), but which overlies the bank of ditch 10 (layer 4) and dips into ditch 10, at which point it is indistinguishable from the later (c third century AD), Roman, freshwater deposit, layer 1, which in turn forms the bulk of the modern topsoil. The junction of the bank (layer 4) and the pre-Roman freshwater deposit is clean and sharp and there is no evidence for soil formation. Furthermore, the fact that this early freshwater deposit dips into the partially silted (c 0.30m) ditch 10 indicates that it was the result of flooding which took place when the ditch was still open and in use. The absence of this deposit elsewhere on the subsite can be explained by the general rise of the land surface away from the NE corner of the subsite. There is also slight evidence (FIG 84, no 4) that some of the more easterly lengths of ditch were not maintained open for as long as those on higher ground. It should also be noted that the pre-Roman and Roman freshwater deposits are very similar in composition, being produced as the result of identical causes; they are therefore hard to differentiate (Turnbaugh 1978). They are also stiff, hard to dig and tend to mask archaeological features, and are, therefore, generally removed mechanically.

The Fen Causeway is represented by a number of gravel deposits dumped, or redeposited, directly on top of the underlying freshwater layer, 3. The interpretation of these layers is very problematic in view of the absence of obvious wear or resurfacing horizons. Layer 2, which passes over the second millennium bank and serves to separate the two freshwater deposits, probably represents wash from layers 7 and 9, which form the first phase of road building. The thin silty layer 6, which separates the second (layers 10-12) from the first phase, may represent a period of disuse when a thin soil was allowed to form. The sandy gravel of the second phase is quite unlike that of the first phase, so any hypothesis of slip or spread may be discounted. The second phase is, therefore, a northerly, off-centre, rebuild of the original road. Sherds of late first/early second century Romano-British pottery were found 0.10-0.15 into the gravel of layer 12; these sherds covered an area of about 2 sq m and come from the same vessel (FIG 89, no 7). The road was capped by a freshwater deposit (layer 1) which probably dates from the early third century AD (Bromwich 1970). This deposit which covers much of Fengate is discussed in greater detail by CAI French in the Fourth Report.

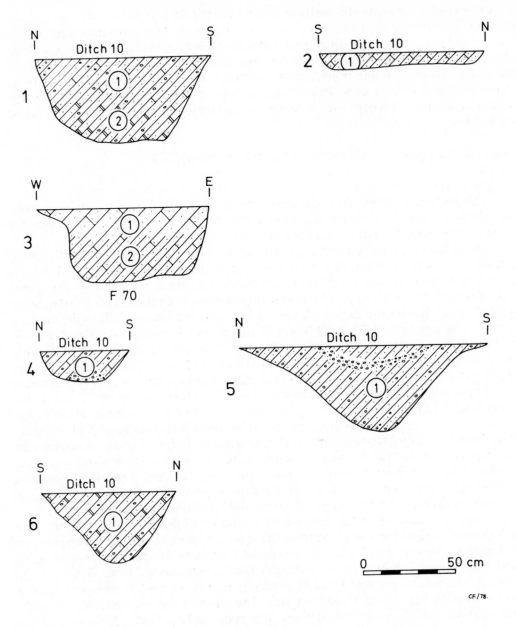

Fig. 87 Fourth Drove subsite: selected sections through ditch 10 and associated features.

The composition of the various layers was as follows:

Ditch 10:

Layer 1. Clay-silt with some sand (10YR 3/3); charcoal rare. Blends into layer 3, above. Interpretation: naturally accumulated ditch filling.

Other layers (charcoal very rare or absent in all):

Layer 1. Disturbed clay with few scattered gravel pebbles (10YR 4/1). Interpretation: Roman freshwater deposit.

Layer 2. Sand and gravel with iron-pan (10YR 5/8). Interpretation: spread of first period road make-up.

Layer 3. Clay with some sand-silt and few scattered gravel pebbles (10YR 4/2). Interpretation: first, pre-Roman (?early first millennium BC), freshwater deposit.

Layer 4. Sand-silt with gravel and iron-pan (10YR 5/4). Interpretation: bank of ditch 10.

Layer 5. Silt, with few scattered gravel pebbles (10YR 5/2). Interpretation: buried old land surface; cut by ditch 10.

Layer 6. Clay-silt with clay lenses, sand, gravel and iron-pan (10YR 5/3). Interpretation: period of abandonment between Fen Causeway phases 1 and 2.

Layer 7. Sand and gravel with iron-pan (10YR 6/6). Interpretation: first phase of Fen Causeway.

Layer 8. Sand, gravel and iron-pan (10YR 5/8). Interpretation: probably represents phase 1 spread over abandonment layer, 6.

Layer 9. Same as layer 7, but slightly more stoney.

Layer 10. Sand with gravel, slightly disturbed by plant roots (10YR 5/6). Interpretation: second phase of Fen Causeway.

Layer 11. Sand, gravel and iron-pan (10YR 5/8). Interpretation: possibly represents slip from phase one surface; or re-use of same.

Layer 12. Sand and gravel mixed with clay and clay-loam from layer 1 at their interface (10YR 4/3). Interpretation: either a second phase road surface or slip from layer 10.

FIG 87

1. Ditch 10; transverse section in Area II at Grid 358W/892N:

   Ditch 10 layer 1. Clay-silt with some sand-silt and scattered gravel pebbles (10YR 4/2); charcoal very rare. Blends into layer 2, below.

   Ditch 10 layer 2. Clay-silt with some sand-silt and scattered gravel pebbles (10YR 2.5/1); charcoal rare.

2. Ditch 10; transverse section in Area III at Grid 332W/887N:

   Ditch 10 layer 1. Clay-loam with sand-silt (5YR 3/2); charcoal absent.

3. Ditch F70; second millennium ditch associated with ditch in Area III; transverse section at Grid 328W/893N:

   F70 layer 1. Clay-loam with scattered gravel pebbles and some sand (10YR 4/2); charcoal rare. Blends into layer 2, below.

   F70 layer 2. Clay-silt with scattered gravel pebbles (10YR 2.5/1); charcoal very rare.

4. Ditch 10; transverse section in Area XII at Grid 245W/845N:

   Ditch 10 layer 1. Silty loam with scattered gravel pebbles (10YR 3/2); charcoal very rare.

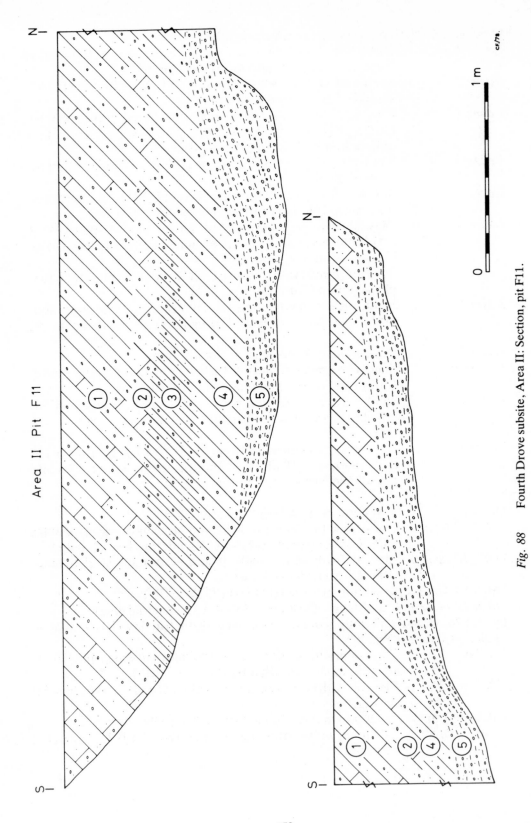

Area II Pit F 11

Fig. 88   Fourth Drove subsite, Area II: Section, pit F11.

5. Ditch 10; transverse section in Area XIII at Grid 229W/844N:
    Ditch 10 layer 1. Silty loam with some sand-silt and scattered gravel pebbles
    (10YR 4/1); charcoal absent. Thin gravel lens near surface.
6. Ditch 10; transverse section in Area XV at Grid 195W/836N:
    Ditch 10 layer 1. Clay silt with a few scattered gravel silt, sand lenses and
    iron-pan (10YR 4/4); charcoal rare.

FEATURES THAT POST-DATE THE SECOND MILLENNIUM BC DITCHES

These can be divided into two groups: pre-Roman features and the Fen Causeway.

1. *Pre-Roman features*

Only two demonstrably pre-Roman features merit detailed description. First, the ditch F21/54 which was observed in Areas VII-X, is of Iron Age date and is best seen as a drainage ditch in some way associated with the large Iron Age settlement on the Cat's Water subsite (Pryor and Cranstone 1978). Its use as a drain is indicated by its alignment, which seems to respect the ground's contours, and its association with Cat's Water seems reasonable in view of the latter settlement's close proximity to Fourth Drove. The fact that the ditch was not found in Area I could argue against this hypothesis, however. Its relationship to ditches of the second millennium system is shown in FIG 82, nos 1-3.

The second important later feature is the large pit in Area II, F11 (Grid 586W/837N). This large pit (or collapsed well?) contained sherds of 'post-Deverel-Rimbury' type (FIG 89, nos 4-5); a similar sherd (FIG 89, no 6) was found in the small scoop or hollow, F17, 17m NE of F11. A transverse section through F11 revealed the following layers (FIG 88):

Layer 1. Silty loam with scattered gravel pebbles, some clay (10YR 4/1); charcoal common. Blends into layer 2, below.

Layer 2. Silty loam with scattered gravel pebbles, some clay (10YR 6/2-5/1); charcoal common.

Layer 3. Silt, with some sand-silt and scattered gravel pebbles (10YR 3/1); charcoal common.

Layer 4. Silt, with some sand-silt, scattered gravel pebbles and iron-pan (10YR 4/2); charcoal and partially burnt wood.

Layer 5. Gravel and iron-pan with waterlogged wood (5YR 4/4-10YR 5/1); charcoal absent. This layer is shown schematically in the illustration.

Finally, it should be noted that the rarity of Iron Age and Roman settlement features on the Fourth Drove subsite provides clear negative evidence that the large Cat's Water Iron Age and Roman settlement did not extend north of the Fourth Drove itself.

2. *The Fen Causeway* (FIGS 3; 86; PL 6)

Margary's (1957, 292-3) route 25, the Fen Road, survives in two lengths. The shorter length, running from Milton Park to Ermine Street via Upton is immediately west of Peterborough. This portion of the road is separated from the main length, the

Fen Causeway proper, by modern Peterborough. The easterly length of this road ran across the Fens, more or less due E-W, from Fengate, via Whittlesey, March and Nordelph to Denver (Norfolk) (Browne 1978, 22-3, for a summary of the Cambridgeshire route). The precise course of the road in Fengate is important, as this would give some indication of its subsequent route westwards through modern Peterborough. Its path NE of Padholme Road, across the Newark Road and Fourth Drove subsites is clear (FIG 3, PL 6), but there is no evidence of it further south or west. This negative evidence is, however, of importance: the Padholme Road subsite was freshly ploughed when first visited by the present writer (in 1971) and there was no trace of gravel on the surface (unlike the clear surface indications NE of Padholme Road itself). Further, Padholme Road Areas I and II (FIG 6) were specifically laid out to locate the road, which they failed to do. It can be stated with some confidence, therefore, that the Fen Causeway does not continue south of Padholme Road and that the route proposed by Salway (in Phillips 1970, 185), *along* Padholme Road, would seem most probable. Examination of aerial photographs in the Vicarage Farm area (FIG 3) again proved to be negative, which might suggest that the modern road follows the course of the Roman road quite precisely.

The actual construction of the road, as seen at Fengate, is similar to that observed in the Fens proper (Kenny 1933, 439), where gravel was simply dumped on the old ground surface. Two sections were exposed at Fengate. The first, in Area I of the Newark Road subsite, was excavated under salvage conditons in 1972. This part of the subsite was heavily disturbed, but the road's simple gravel-dump construction was clearly visible; its width at this point was about 5m. Irregular scoops 3-4m wide seem to have been used to provide the gravel required and these had subsequently been filled with alluvial clays. At one point, a natural hollow in the ground, 2m across and 0.75m deep, had been roughly filled with Cornbrash limestone, and the road built directly over the top.

The second section through the road was that of Fourth Drove Area VII. This section is described in detail in the discussion of FIG 86, above. It raises various points of interest. First, there is evidence that two phases of road building (and use) are involved. The second phase (layers 10-12) is separated from the first phase (layers 7 and 9) by a thin silty layer (6) which is thought to represent a period of disuse. Second, there is no evidence for side ditches or scoops (even though excavation north of the road was not extensive). Third, despite modern plough-damage, it was apparent that the whole road surface had once been buried beneath a deposit of alluvial clay.

Although no datable artifacts were found in secure contexts from within the road metalling itself, the available evidence suggests a first century date (Hallam 1970, 74). The evidence may be summarised thus: a *terminus post quem* is provided by the second millennium ditch and bank which underlie it; a *terminus ante quem* is provided by the alluvial clay (layer 1) which covers it and which most probably belongs in the earlier third century AD (see discussion above). More precise dating is provided by the 20 fresh, unabraded, sherds of first, or early second, century Romano-British pottery which were found stratified within layer 12 (they are discussed below, see also FIG 89, no 7). The problem with this layer is that its origin is poorly understood; its location on the northern edge of the road would indicate that it was a secondary deposit, perhaps

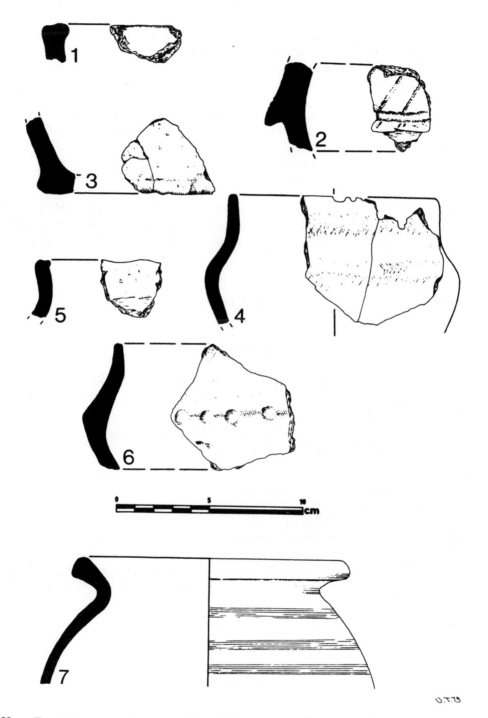

Fig. 89   Fourth Drove subsite pottery (all periods): 1, ditch 8; 2, ditch 9: 3, ditch 8; 4-5, pit F11, Area II; 6, pit F17, Area II; 7, Fen Causeway layer 12.

153

resulting from slip or wash. The clean gravel and the absence of any abandonment deposits, between layer 12 and the other layers of the second phase, would, however, argue against this hypothesis. On balance, the nature of the deposit and of the pottery itself, would favour the suggestion that the vessel provides dating evidence for the second phase of the road's use. One final, indirect, strand of evidence in favour of a first century date is provided by the relationship of the Cat's Water settlement to the nearby road.

The settlement features of the Cat's Water subsite seem not to respect the Fen Causeway. The road passes a few paces north of this substantial settlement, yet no subsidiary tracks, droves or roads are seen to connect with it. This pattern is most unlike that observed elsewhere in the Fenland, where the road is usually incorporated within the tracks and droves of the settlements it serves (Salway 1970, 5). The Cat's Water settlement seems to have been temporarily deserted from the mid-first century AD before being re-occupied briefly in the mid-second century (Hayes 1978). This period of abandonment might be seen to coincide with the road's two periods of use. Any causal connection between these events is at present, however, difficult to establish.

FINDS

POTTERY

CATALOGUE OF ILLUSTRATED POTTERY (FIG 89)

NOTE

The fabric types of nos 1-3 are those of Dr Williams (Chapter 2). Vessels 4-6 are described using Dr Williams' 'Iron Age' fabric description, which are described in the Fourth Report, Chapter 6. Grid references for individual finds could not be recorded in this subsite.

1. Rimsherd. Fabric 1.
   Undecorated.
   Area IV, ditch 8, layer 3, depth 0.40. 78:262
2. Collar sherd from Collared Urn-type vessel. Fabric 3.
   Decoration: horizontal and diagonal twisted cord impressions.
   Area VII, ditch 9, layer 2, depth 0.15. 78:26
3. Base angle, simple type. Weathered. Fabric 2.
   Undecorated.
   Area II, ditch 8, layer 1, depth 0.10. 77:6
4. Rimsherd of shouldered bowl (dia 110). Fabric IB (soft, with finely crushed shell temper). This vessel has been pierced by five borings, made after firing; those near the rim top give a coarse comb effect.
   Undecorated.
   Area II, pit F11, layer 1, depth 0.15. 77:15
5. Rimsherd of vessel with slightly concave neck. Fabric as no 4.
   Undecorated.
   Area II, pit F11, layer 1, depth 0.15. 77:21
6. Carinated wall sherd. Fabric IB (harder than no 4, above).
   Decoration: spaced fingertip impressions around belly/shoulder.
   Area II, pit F17, layer 1, depth 0.08. 77:43
7. Rim and wall sherds of Romano-British jar in dark grey sandy fabric (no shell).
   Decoration: three horizontal bands of wheel-made lines.
   Dr J. P. Wild suggests (pers comm) a late first/early second century date for this vessel.
   Area VII, F19 (Fen Causeway), layer 12, depth 0.10-0.15. 78:2-11

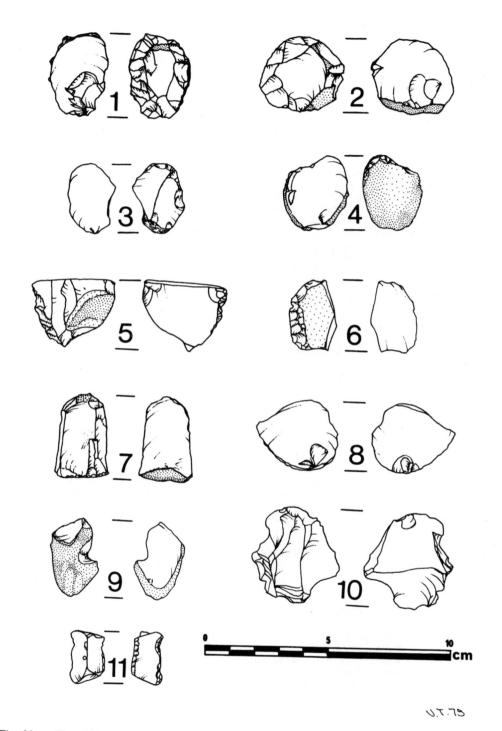

U.T.79

Fig. 90   Fourth Drove subsite, second millennium BC ditches: flints.

155

DISCUSSION

The wider significance of this small collection of material has been discussed under the appropriate heading above. It is sufficient to note here that nos 1-3 are from the second millennium ditches and are similar to contemporary vessels from Newark Road; nos 4-6 are from first millennium contexts and also compare closely with similar material from Newark Road. The dating of the Romano-British pot by Dr Wild is of considerable importance in view of its stratigraphic position within a possible surface of the Fen Causeway.

FLINT

CATALOGUE OF ILLUSTRATED FLINTS (FIG 90)

Scrapers (nos 1-9)
1. Short-end scraper on flake; edges worn.
    Area VII, ditch 9, layer 1, depth 0.25. 78:152
2. Short-end scraper on flake; slightly calcined.
    Area VII, ditch 8, layer 1, depth 0.06. 78:126
3. Short-end scraper on flake; one side damaged.
    Area VII, ditch 8, layer 1, depth 0.10. 78:129
4. Short-end scraper on flake; much cortex on dorsal surface.
    Area XVI, ditch 9, layer 1, depth 0.15. 78:265
5. End scraper on broken flake; fine invasive retouch.
    Area IV, ditch 8, layer 2, depth 0.20. 78:263
6. End/side scraper on broken flake.
    Area VII, ditch 9, layer 1, depth 0.25. 78:151
7. Long-end scraper on flake.
    Area X, ditch 8, layer 3, depth 0.10. 78:198
8. Short-end scraper or heavily utilised flake with steep retouch.
    Area X, ditch *i*, layer 1, depth 0.10. 78:179
9. Hollow scraper on flake.
    Area XV, ditch 10, layer 1, depth 0.30. 78:224

Denticulated Tools nos 10-11
10. Denticulated flake with slight unifacial retouch and worn points.
    Area X, ditch *i*, layer 1, depth 0.27. 78:185
11. Denticulated tool on a piece of irregular workshop waste; crudely retouched; points worn.
    Area IV, ditch 8, layer 1, depth 0.01. 78:280

DISCUSSION

The collection of flints from second millennium ditches on Fourth Drove was not large enough for metrical analysis. Qualitatively, however, it was closely similar to that from Newark Road, having many points in common with flints of Bradley's Group 4 (see Richards 1978, 17-19). A total of 67 flints were found and these could be classified as follows:

Implements (67.2% of total)
The 45 implements were of the following types:

		(percentage of total implements)
Scrapers 10		22.2
(Class A (i) Long-end	1	
Class A (ii) Short-end	5	
Class F Hollow ·	1	
Class E on broken flakes	2	
Scraper fragment	1)	
Denticulated tools 2		4.4
Retouched flakes (one broken) 2		4.4
Serrated flake................................ 1		2.2
Utilised flakes (6 broken;		
2 calcined) 30		66.6

Points of interest to note here include the high proportion of utilised waste flakes (30:14) and the generally high proportion of implements to by-products.

By-Products (32.8% of total)

The 22 by-products could be classed as follows:

		(percentage of total by-products)
Irregular workshop waste	8	36.4
Waste flakes................................	14	63.6
(No cores were found)		

CHAPTER 4: THE CAT'S WATER SUBSITE

INTRODUCTION (FIGS 91 and 92)

The Cat's Water subsite (FIG 3) was excavated in the seasons of 1975-78, and it will form the principal subject of the Fourth Report which will largely be given over to a detailed discussion of the Iron Age and Romano-British settlement (provisionally described in Pryor and Cranstone 1978). No proper consideration of the second millennium ditched enclosures on Cat's Water can be attempted *in vacuo*, outside the context of the later settlement; on the other hand, no full description of the Fengate second millennium enclosure system, as a whole, would be complete without the Cat's Water evidence. It has therefore been decided to devote this chapter to a general consideration of the Cat's Water ditches and to reserve the detailed treatment of sections, profiles and finds (which were few) for the Fourth Report. This chapter will also consider the inhumation at the junction of ditches F862 and 2, and the post-built round building, Structure 46.

The Cat's Water subsite, like Fourth Drove, had been flooded in Roman times, and later, and, as a result, carried a thick covering of heavy, clay-rich topsoil. This deposit not only made excavation difficult, but it also hid all but the latest features from the aerial camera (Taylor 1969, PL 1). Finds were effectively sealed beneath the surface by it, and although a few Romano-British sherds were brought up by the plough (Taylor 1969, 6, no 8), the presence of the Iron Age settlement and second millennium enclosure system could not be detected by simple inspection, whether from ground level or the air. The flood clay and modern plough-action combined together to give an impression of flatness (FIG 91); but removal of the clay revealed the original, undulating land surface (FIG 92).

THE SECOND MILLENNIUM BC ENCLOSURE DITCHES (FIG 93)

The rectilinear arrangement of ditches and droves is broadly similar to that found elsewhere at Fengate, and appears to disregard the slight rise and fall of the old land surface (FIG 92). This would argue against any suggestion that the primary function of the ditches was land drainage, for on a flat or near-flat landscape even the slightest, most gradual of slopes must be used to keep drain water flowing. Excavation in 1978, for example, showed that Iron Age and Romano-British ditches in the SW part of the excavated area were making use of a gradient of approximately 1 in 160.

The alignments of principal N-S and E-W ditches can be tied into the general Fengate system. These ditches may be seen to define at least four large and one small enclosure (that around structure 46). The large NW enclosure is defined on three sides: the northerly side is formed by ditch 5, which appears to be isolated, and not part of a droveway. Ditch 5 is pierced by a narrow (2.5m) entranceway at the NE corner of the enclosure, at which point its course is obscured by later features; it probably continued eastwards, out of the excavated area. Later features and problems with the geology made the relationship of ditch *iii* and ditch 5 obscure. The northern butt-end of

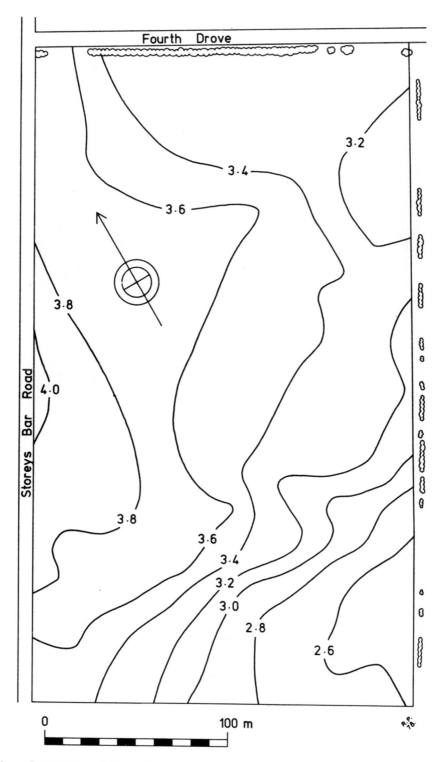

Fig. 91   Cat's Water subsite: surface contours in metres above OD.

159

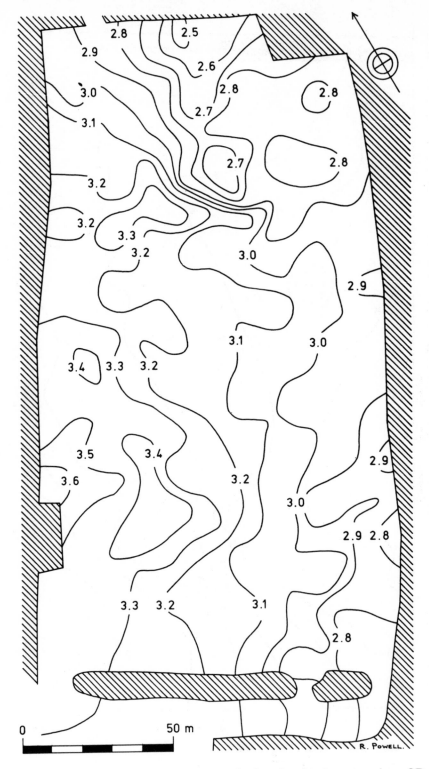

Fig. 92   Cat's Water subsite, main area: contours of stripped surface in metres above OD.

160

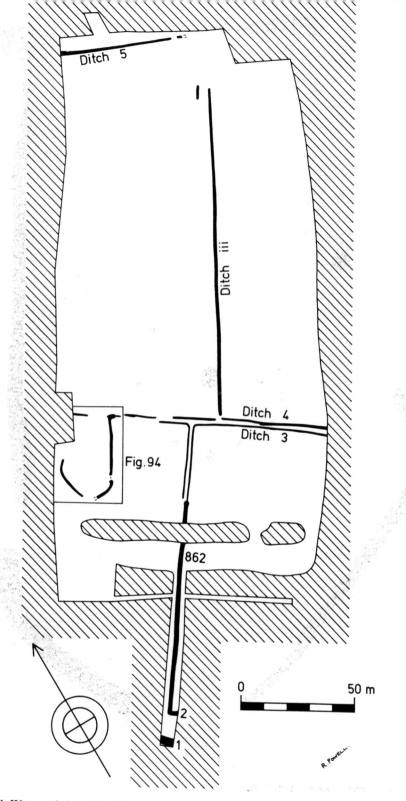

Fig. 93   Cat's Water subsite: plan of second millennium BC ditches (all other features omitted).

161

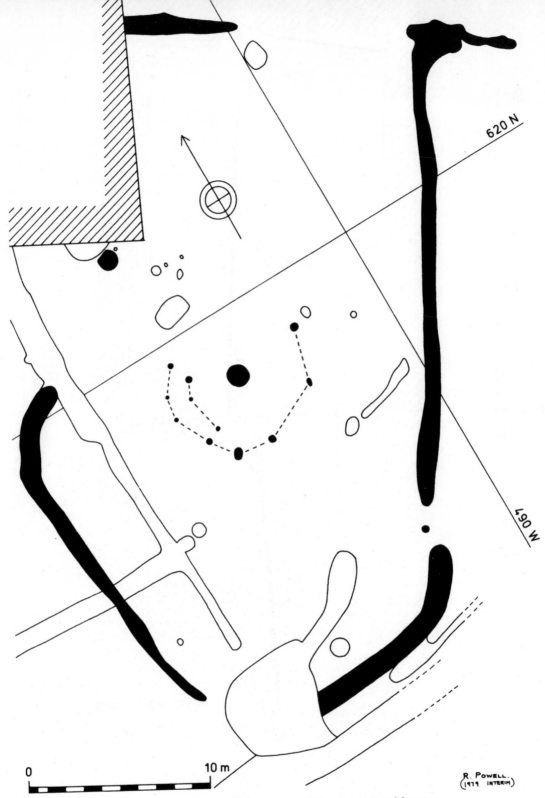

620 N

490 W

0   10 m

R. POWELL.
(1979 INTERIM)

Fig. 94   Cat's Water subsite, Areas VI and X: Structure 46 and associated features.

ditch *iii* is, however, fairly convincing, but the gap between it and ditch 5 is very wide (*c* 23m) and would probably have been reduced in some way. The short (6m) length of ditch parallel to the NE of ditch *iii*, and 4m W of it, was also difficult to excavate and interpret, due to later activity on the site (the more complex arrangement shown in Pryor and Cranstone (1978, FIG 5) is now considered less probable than that suggested here). Ditch *iii* is straight (length 140m) and shows no clear evidence for recuts, blocked entraceways or extension. It joins the E-W ditch 4 at a junction marked by two corner entranceways (from the easterly and westerly northern enclosures) into the E-W drove formed by ditches 3 and 4. There is some evidence (to be considered in the Fourth Report) that this three-way entrance complex had been modified during its period of use (cf FNG, FIG 13).

The E-W drove, formed by ditches 3 and 4, separates the northern from the southern enclosures; it is less regular than most other droveways at Fengate (its width varies from 1-2m) and shows some evidence for recutting and modification. The droveway runs off the excavated area to the E, but to the W breaks down into a series of discontinuous slightly offset ditches; the most westerly gap can be seen to form the entranceway for the sub-oval ditched enclosure surrounding the post-built house, structure 46, which will be discussed in greater detail below. The extreme S portion of the enclosure ditch was removed by a later, Iron Age and Romano-British, drove ditch, and the extreme (*c* 3-4m) W part of the excavated area at this point was seriously disturbed by modern sewer construction. The alignment of the enclosure around structure 46 suggests that it was added to the main ditched enclosure system after the latter had been in use for, perhaps, some time; it does not appear to have been laid out either before, or as part of, the original system.

The N-S droveway that leads into ditch F862, and with it serves to divide the two southerly enclosures, is 31m in length and *c* 1.5m wide. Its layout suggests that it was surveyed at the same time as the drove formed by ditches 3 and 4, which it joins at a T-junction. The easterly ditch of this N-S drove is massively enlarged, immediately south of the end of the drove, to form the major N-S ditch F862. The northern butt-end of ditch F862 is marked by a deep, pit-like expansion which extended well below the modern water-table. This expansion contained the lower trunk (with bark intact) and upper roots of a small oak tree, which has been submitted for radiocarbon assay (HAR-3204). Ditch F862 ran SW for 91m where it turned through a right-angle, to continue eastwards, towards the Fens, on the alignment of ditch 2 (see Chapter 1). A crouched inhumation, described below, was found on the NE side of the right-angled corner. The excavations were continued SW to locate ditch 1 which was duly found *c* 9.5-10m SW of ditch 2. This droveway is somewhat wider than others at Fengate.

STRUCTURE 46 (FIGS 94-96; Table 8)

This post-built structure was located in a small (*c* 20.5 x 35m) sub-oval enclosure immediately SW of ditch alignment 3/4 in Areas VI and X (FIG 94). A full discussion of the enclosure ditches must be reserved for the Fourth Report, but the interim plan (FIG 94) shows that it was served by at least four entranceways, one to the NE (width 9.2m); one to the SE (width 2.2m), also probably marked by a central post; one to the SW (width obscured by later, Iron Age activity); and one of indeterminable width to the N (this area was severely disturbed by recent sewer construction). Although the most

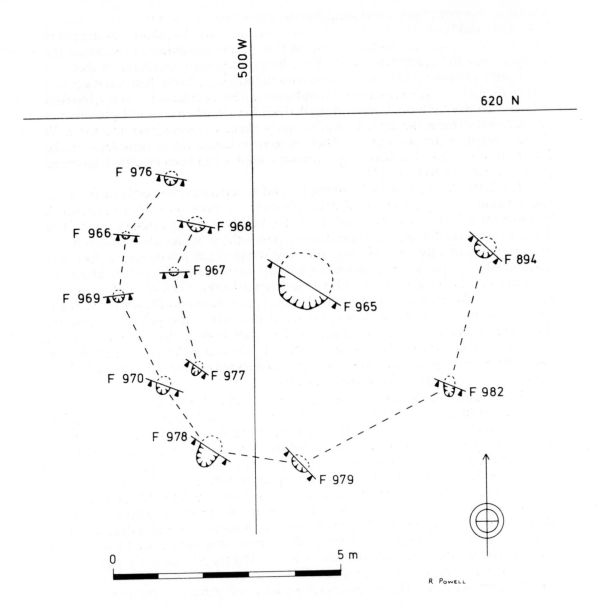

F 976

F 968

F 966

F 967

F 894

F 969

F 965

F 977

F 982

F 970

F 978

F 979

0
5 m

R Powell

Fig. 95   Cat's Water subsite, Areas VI and X: Structure 46.

northerly ditch could be shown to be contiguous with the main E-W second millennium ditch 3/4, and was, therefore, broadly contemporary with it, the other two ditches of the enclosure had no such direct links. No finds from their fillings were especially diagnostic (the wall sherd from F979 — 78:1803 — was somewhat harder than others of this period and may be of later date), as is often the case with ditches of this period at Fengate, but the pale colour of their fillings and their general arrangement strongly suggest an early date. All other features of later Iron Age and

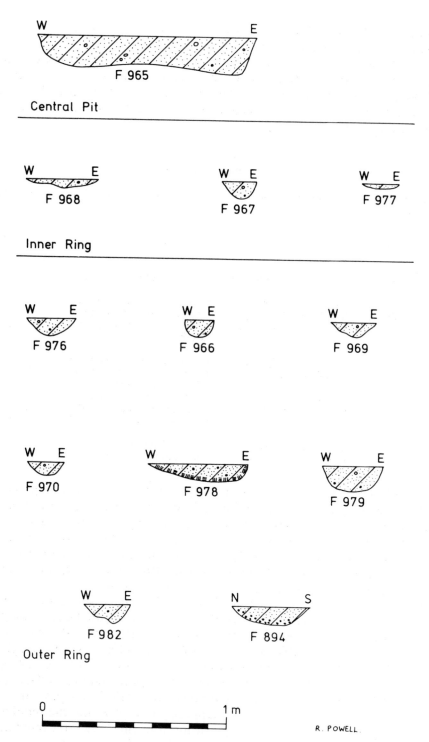

W   E
F 965

Central Pit

W   E   W E   W   E
F 968   F 967   F 977

Inner Ring

W   E   W E   W   E
F 976   F 966   F 969

W   E   W   E   W   E
F 970   F 978   F 979

W   E   N   S
F 982   F 894

Outer Ring

0   1 m

R. POWELL

Fig. 96   Cat's Water subsite: Structure 46 sections (for location of features and section lines see FIG 95).

Romano-British date could be clearly seen to cut them. It should also be noted here that the rarity of finds from the enclosure ditches was in sharp contrast to the quantity and variety of finds from the later features; this rarity of artifacts, moreover, far from arguing against a settlement function for the enclosure, finds a direct parallel in the Newark Road settlement of Area IV. The Fourth Report will show that Iron Age structures were almost invariably accompanied by an abundance of artifacts and discarded animal bones.

TABLE 8

Cat's Water subsite, Areas VI and X, details of features comprising structure 46 (see FIGS 95 and 96). All measurements in metres.

Feature Number (Order as in FIG 96)	Depth	Filling	Notes
Central Pit:			
965	0.20	Sandy loam (10YR 3/2)	Charcoal very rare; no finds.
Inner Ring:			
968	0.05	Silty loam (10YR 3/3)	Charcoal very rare; no finds.
967	0.09	Silty loam (10YR 3/3)	Charcoal very rare; no finds.
977	0.03	Silty loam (10YR 3/3)	Charcoal very rare; no finds; clear on surface, despite shallowness.
Outer Ring:			
976	0.20	Sand-silt (10YR 4/4)	Charcoal very rare; no finds.
966	0.19	Silty loam (10YR 3/3)	Charcoal common; no finds.
969	0.15	Silty loam (10YR 3/3)	Charcoal rare; no finds.
970	0.15	Loam (10YR 4/3)	Charcoal very rare; no finds.
978	0.20	Clay-loam (10YR 3/2)	Charcoal rare; lined with thin (0.05) clay layer; one scrap of pottery.
979	0.25	Silty loam (10YR 3/1)	Charcoal rare; one wall sherd.
982	0.20	Silty loam (10YR 4/3)	Charcoal absent; no finds.
894	0.10	Clay-loam (10YR 5/2)	Charcoal absent; no finds; thin 'rapid' at bottom (layer 2).

Turning now to the structure itself (FIG 95); it is composed of parts of two concentric rings of postholes (dia 7.2m and 5m respectively) arranged around a shallow circular pit, F965 (which shows no signs of having been used as a hearth). The fillings of the individual postholes are described in detail below, and their sections are drawn in FIG 96. None of the postholes, in common with most others from second millennium structures at Fengate, show signs of recutting or replacement, which might suggest that the house was built and used for just one period.

Parallels for this structure are not hard to find. A closely similar post-built structure (1) was found in the Newark Road subsite, Area IV; this building was formed by two concentric posthole rings (diameters 5.5 and 2.2m), within a shallow eaves-drip ring-gully (FIG 35). It is probable that the Cat's Water building has lost the slight traces of wall foundations and eaves-drip gully which only just survived at Newark Road. It should be noted that, with the exception of doorway/porch posts and the occasional central roof support pole, Iron Age round houses on Cat's Water generally seem to have been built without the aid of roof support posts set within the building itself (Pryor and Cranstone 1978). The weight of the roof, in these later buildings, was probably taken either by a ring-beam set atop the walls, or, in the case of smaller structures, by the walls themselves (eg Drury 1978, FIG 6). Second millennium

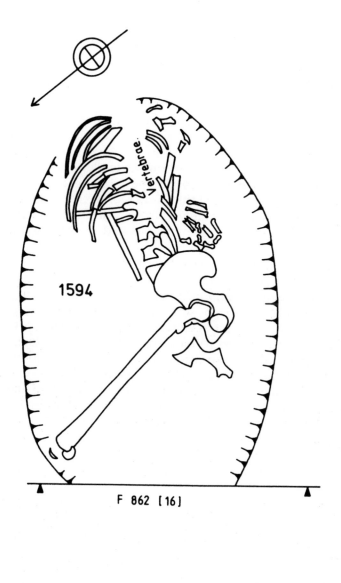

1594

Vertebrae.

F 862 [16]

0   50 cm

R. POWELL.

Fig. 97   Cat's Water subsite, Area XI: inhumation at intersection of ditch F862 and ditch 2 (Grid 523W/515N).

builders still found it necessary to take the weight of the roof on internal posts and thereby considerably reduced the useable space of their buildings.

INHUMATION (F1594) AT INTERSECTION OF DITCHES F862 AND 2 (FIG 97 and Appendix 9)

This inhumation was found at the intersection of ditches F862 and 2 in Area XI at Grid 523W/515N. The body lay in a shallow scoop (depth 0.05-0.10m) set in the NE side of ditch F862/2. Some bones extended into the ditch filling proper, and the shallow scoop of F1594 only became apparent once the bones had been fully revealed. There was no indication whatsoever that this burial had been inserted through the silted-up layers of the ditch filling. Rather, its location at an important junction, its orientation parallel to the ditch edge, and the fact that bones extended into the ditch filling, suggest that the burial was made when the ditch was open. The disturbed state of many of the bones nearer the surface suggest that they were removed or dislodged when the ditch was recut or cleaned out. Unfortunately, however, the ditch fillings in this part of the subsite were more than usually homogeneous and recuts could not be discerned stratigraphically.

This burial was excavated by Faye Powell, whose more detailed report on the bones appears below, as Appendix 9. Her observations on the state and condition of the bones are therefore of some importance. She notes that the major portion of the skeleton was complete, although several parts are missing, probably due to disturbance caused by prehistoric recutting of the ditch. The parts missing are the head, left scapula, right femur, both tibiae, right fibula and both feet. The burial was in the semi-crouched position, but the attitude of the skeleton would suggest a hurried or unceremonious burial: the upper part of the body was partially on its right side with the lower half twisted so as to rest on its back. The right arm was bent under the body with the right hand at the lower back. The left arm was also under the body, but twisted back and up, so that the left hand rested at the right shoulder.

CHAPTER 5: DISCUSSION

INTRODUCTION

This chapter is given over to a discussion of the ditched enclosure system, and its associated features. Features that pre- and post-date these enclosures have already been discussed in the appropriate chapters, above, and will not be considered further here.

The chapter is divided into six sections. The first considers, in brief summary, the general layout of the second millennium ditch system; the second discusses aspects of contemporary buildings, burial and wells; the third considers dating, both relative and absolute; the fourth discusses the origins of the system; the fifth attempts a reconstruction of the ancient economy and the sixth considers reasons for the system's demise.

It is inevitable, in a project as long-lived as that at Fengate, that much material will already have appeared in print. It is also inevitable that hypotheses will have changed and that new data will have caused old views to be modified substantially. In these circumstances, greater emphasis will be given to new explanation or interpretation, and previously published hypotheses which are still considered valid will be summarised as briefly as possible (the reader is advised to consult Chapter Six of the Second Report and pp 41-47 of Pryor 1976a).

1. THE LINEAR DITCH SYSTEM (FIGS 4 and 5)

This and the next section will attempt to summarise the considerable evidence for second millennium BC occupation at Fengate. No attempt has been made, however, to synthesise *all* the Fengate data, as the circumstances surrounding the discovery of the original Peterborough finds (Abbott 1910; Leeds 1922) make them unsuited for more than purely typological studies (Gibson, Appendix 10; Taylor 1969, 6). The Vicarage Farm subsite, of the present project, produced no significant finds or features that could belong to the second millennium, and the highly important, apparently bridged, rectilinear enclosure, excavated by Miss Mahany, is still only published in the briefest, interim, form (Mahany 1969). The material from the recent excavations will be summarised by subsite (FIG 3).

STOREY'S BAR ROAD

This subsite has been described at length in the Second Report. Although the pottery is all in the Grooved Ware style, with the exception of a Collared Urn cremation and a single sherd of Collared Urn from the bottom of the ring-ditch, and although the ditches of the rectilinear enclosures are, in general, somewhat slighter than those of the system described in this report, there are good reasons to believe that Storey's Bar Road forms an integral part of the same system. The evidence for and against the contemporaneity of the two systems will be briefly reviewed.

The best positive evidence is provided by the spatial arrangement of the Storey's Bar Road ditches which can be clearly seen to run parallel with the principal (N-S and

E-W) ditches of the main system; further, the slight divergence of ditch 1 and the most northerly ditch (FNG 2, FIG 6, ditch W23/R2) of the Storey's Bar Road system is entirely consistent with the divergence observed at Newark Road, Fourth Drove and Cat's Water. Additional evidence is provided by the spacing of the main E-W ditches which are laid out along the Fen-edge at, very approximately, one hundred metre intervals (FIG 4).

The radiocarbon dates, uncalibrated, from Storey's Bar Road suggest that the enclosures were laid out just before the beginning of the second millennium, but continued in use throughout the millennium. In other words, it is suggested here that the early date for the Storey's Bar settlement and enclosures is not particularly unusual and that it may merely reflect a slightly different method of ditch or hedge maintenance, a method which did not require frequent recutting of ditches. Speculation on the causes of this could be endless, but important factors would include local drainage; the subsoil clay content; the depth of the original topsoil cover; the success, or otherwise, of hedge planting and management and, of course, the species, age and herd size of livestock kept in each ditched enclosure. We shall see below (section 4) that there are good reasons to believe that other ditches of the larger system might be of similar antiquity.

The best argument against the broad contemporaneity of the Storey's Bar Grooved Ware enclosures and the main second millennium system is artifactual: datable material from the former is generally 'early' (for example: 'petit tranchet derivative' arrowheads; longer, larger waste and utilised flakes; larger scrapers; and Grooved Ware) and that from the latter is generally 'late' (barbed and tanged arrowheads; squat waste and utilised flakes; 'thumbnail' scrapers; denticulated tools; shale items of 'late' type: bronzework; coarse pottery in Collared Urn and 'Deverel-Rimbury' styles). These are good reasons, at face value, to doubt the contemporaneity of the two sets of ditched enclosures. If the main second millennium ditched enclosures had originated in the Late Neolithic, one might reasonably expect to find more 'early' material in the residual artifacts of the later recuts. This, however, presents problems, the main one being that of post-depositional survival, for there can be little doubt that much of the Grooved Ware from Storey's Bar Road would not have survived more than a few ditch recuttings. The survival argument has less force when it is applied to flints, but, again, the distorting effects of perhaps annual ditch maintenance over many centuries are, as yet, poorly understood. It should also be noted that much of the 'late' material is extraordinarily fragile and could not have survived long had it been disturbed: examples include the proposed salt mould with its thin, soft fabric; the delicate laminated shale pendant; the barely fired cylindrical loomweights and, of course, the poor quality shell-tempered pottery. Experimental archaeology would be a valuable means of monitoring some of these post-depositional processes and their effects.

Finally, detailed analysis of material from ditches hitherto thought to be Iron Age has shown that they too belong to the second millennium system. These ditches lie in the extreme NE end of Storey's Bar Road, Area I (FNG 2, FIG 5), and are clearly seen to be cut by ditches of the later Iron Age and Romano-British period. They will be described in detail in the Fourth Report Chapter 3 (ditches P18/70 and N1) and it should be sufficient to note here that they are laid out on the same alignment as other ditches of the main second millennium system.

PADHOLME ROAD (see Chapter 1)

The Padholme Road subsite was excavated at the commencement of the Fengate project, before techniques of stripping large areas had been developed, and as a result it is difficult to make any significant observations on the arrangement of ditches and enclosures. Ditches 1 and 2 were, in general, slighter and less regular, both in plan and section than ditches 3 and 4. Only one (N-S) ditch (F4/400) could be seen to link the two droveways. The alignment of both pairs of ditches is continued eastwards in the southern part of Cat's Water, where a better idea of the complexity of the system is provided by open-area excavation. No N-S ditches can be seen to link Padholme Road with Newark Road, but this is most probably the result of limited excavation, modern road and factory development north of Areas II, VII, VIII and XI, and geological disturbance immediately north of Padholme Road itself (see the discussion of ditch 5, Chapter 2).

NEWARK ROAD (see Chapter 2)

This subsite revealed the most complex arrangement of ditched droves and enclosures at Fengate. They could be seen to fall into two broadly-defined groups, corresponding to excavated Areas I-VI and VII (FIG 18). The former Areas contained enclosures arranged around the principal E-W ditches 5-10 (of which ditches 6-7 are of mid-Iron Age date and should therefore be disregarded for present purposes). These central-southerly enclosures could themselves be seen to fall into two groups: those between ditches 5 and 8, and those between ditches 9 and 10. Enclosures on either side of the main droveway formed by ditches 8 and 9 were clearly laid out on different, but internally consistent, lines. To the south of the main drove, where disturbance was a more critical factor than elsewhere, the enclosures were defined by smaller, narrower ditches.

Enclosure 1 was clearly intended to serve the well, and the ditches in its vicinity showed evidence for recut and blocked entranceways, indicating that this was an important area for livestock traffic. Enclosure 2 was more enigmatic, being seriously disturbed by the Fen Causeway and other factors; it would, however, appear to have been rectangular in shape and may once have reached into the Fourth Drove and Cat's Water subsites to the east. The large enclosure, 3, was also rather enigmatic, as the ditches defining it to N and S were shallow and, in the case of ditch 5, considerably disturbed. There was, however, some evidence for a post-built fenced drove, or droves, in its northeast corner, which was associated with a cluster of small pits, some of which contained settlement debris. These enclosures, like those to be described immediately below, could communicate with one another via internal entranceways and/or droves, without having to make use of the main E-W drove defined by ditches 8 and 9. The latter was not a reserved strip of boundary 'headland', however, since its ditches show good evidence for entranceways, many of which had been blocked and modified, and its surface and upper ditch sides were more than usually rich in phosphate (Appendix 6), which would suggest considerable livestock traffic.

North of the main E-W drove, between ditches 9 and 10, the land was divided into three rectilinear areas, of which only the central enclosure, B, was revealed on all four sides. Enclosure A, to the east, like enclosure B, showed no signs of internal occupation, but the numerous recuts of ditch 9 on its southern side suggest that access to the main drove was of some importance. The most westerly enclosure, C, showed evidence for settlement and at least two structures; the smaller, internal, ditch (*a* and *n*) appears to have silted up shortly after the abandonment of the settlement, and probably earlier than some of the larger ditches of the system (see Appendix 6).

The ditched enclosures of Areas I-VI were defined to the north by ditch 10, which, unlike any other substantial ditch of the system, showed no clear evidence for major recuts or entranceways. The lack of evidence for recuts is of importance, but should not be taken at its face value: most of the demonstrable recuts at Fengate could only be seen, in plan, at entranceways, because of the homogeneity of most second millennium ditch fillings. Ditch 10 then, was clearly a boundary of importance which was probably not broken by entranceways along its length, and which was generally maintained by deep recuts down to the gravel subsoil. It is suggested that the apparent absence of evidence for recutting could be taken to imply the very opposite, namely, that the ditch was frequently and thoroughly 'mucked out'.

North of ditch 10 the picture is less clear. The Newark Road subsite shows an open, apparently unenclosed, strip of land between the southerly enclosures of Areas I-VI and the northerly droves of Area VII. Area III of the Fourth Drove subsite, however, provides unambiguous evidence of a N-S ditch (F70) which forms a corner entranceway with an extension of ditch 10. Thus, the apparently unenclosed, reserved, strip of land, so clearly visible on Newark Road can be seen to form part of the larger ditched system.

The ditches of Area VII can be seen to define a series of N-S and E-W droves which show clear evidence for frequent off-centre recutting and modification. It should also be noted here that the southerly end of the western ditch of the main N-S drove is the result of geological disturbance which caused problems in determining correct excavation levels. This ditch may originally have continued further south, but there is no reason to suppose that it ran E-W, towards the 'industrial area'; this was positioned in the E corner of Area VII, was easily located at the correct level and only showed evidence for a single ditch (F254). The 'industrial area' itself is difficult to interpret. It consisted of a deposit of burnt limestone and charcoal from substantial boughs of Fen-type trees (Appendix 5). This deposit was dumped in an off-centre recut of ditch F254 and could be seen to extend for a few square metres around that ditch. The positioning of the 'industrial area' is midway between the sources of timber and charcoal and it is very tentatively suggested that the process involved was lime-burning.

FOURTH DROVE (see Chapter 3)

For various reasons, this subsite was excavated using long, narrow trenches, rather than open areas, and as a result, enclosures, *sensu stricto* cannot be properly defined. There are, however, indications that the general layout established on Newark Road Areas I-VI was continued eastwards, towards the Fens. The apparent absence of ditches running N-S between ditches 9 and 10 is in large measure explained by the presence of the Fen Causeway which runs diagonally across the subsite and which posed serious earthmoving problems. A small settlement was found immediately south of ditch 8 in Area VII, to the east. This Area was located along a modern drainage dyke whose low, wide bank afforded protection against plough damage. The north-east end of the Area was traversed by the Fen Causeway which, together with the modern drainage dyke bank, had raised the plough sufficiently to allow the preservation of the low, rounded bank which originally accompanied ditch 10. This, the lowest part of the site yet excavated, provided evidence for a pre-Roman freshwater flood, or floods, in the form of a clay-rich deposit (Appendix 4) which lay under the Fen Causeway, but which passed over the second millennium bank and into the partially silted-up ditch 10.

CAT'S WATER (see Chapter 4)

The large area stripped on the Cat's Water subsite provided sufficient lengths of ditch to allow secure connections (via alignments) to be made with the Padholme Road, Newark Road and Fourth Drove subsites. The two large enclosures between ditches 5 and 3-4 could perhaps have been further subdivided, but the area was severely disturbed in Iron Age times by the buildings and ditches of the large Cat's Water settlement (Pryor and Cranstone 1978). Padholme Road Areas XII and XIII, however, failed to produce any evidence for E-W ditches, as did the long trench, which was located outside the Iron Age settlement, to the east of the main excavated area. Further, although large, the later settlement was not total in its cover of the excavated area, and it is not, therefore, considered probable that the two large enclosures were further subdivided to any great extent by ditches.

The two large enclosures south of ditches 3 and 4 also showed no evidence for subdivision, with the exception of a small enclosure to the west, joined to ditch 3, which contained a post-built structure (46). A short length of N-S droveway at the centre of the excavated area gave way to a substantial single ditch (F862) which was traced in a narrow trench running south from the main excavation. The end of this trench located the easterly extension of the ditch alignment 1/2, from the Padholme Road subsite, to the west of Storey's Bar Road. It should be noted here that the large gap between the excavated lengths of ditches 1 and 2 was in great part determined by the location of modern buildings.

2. NON-LINEAR FEATURES OF SECOND MILLENNIUM DATE

STRUCTURES

Four structures of probable second millennium date have been found at Fengate. The largest and most complete building was located in Area IV of the Newark Road subsite. This round-house, Structure 1, formed part of the enclosure C settlement (FIG 34). Its main features included a four-post entranceway, a penannular eaves-drip gully which drained into a convenient nearby enclosure ditch, an insubstantially built wall (ie probably wattle-work rather than post-built), and two concentric circles of roof-support posts (FIGS 35-39). This building was similar in many respects to the post-built round house, Structure 46, from the Cat's Water subsite. The latter building was located inside a sub-oval ditched enclosure and was composed of two circles of posts; no evidence for an entrance or external eaves-drip gully survived, but this was almost certainly due to post-depositional factors (FIGS 94-96).

The other two second millennium BC structures, although also post-built, were of different type, and might well be connected with livestock (see Appendix 6). Both were constructed from quite substantial timbers (if the posthole, rather than the post-stain can be used as a guide) arranged in a D-shape, and spaced at broadly similar intervals (see FIG 81 for a comparison of the two buildings). The use of round, or probably round, structures as animal byres will be considered at greater length in the Fourth Report (but see also Bradley 1978b, 272).

These four structures raise a number of general points. First, they all appear to have been post-built. This method of construction is not commonly found in Iron Age contexts — excepting, of course, four post structures — at Fengate or elsewhere in the region, where the weight of the roof seems generally to have been taken by the walls which, where evidence survives, were built of stakes or wattle-work plates possibly tied together by a continuous ring-beam (Pryor and Cranstone 1978: 18; Harding 1974, 41-42; Dallas 1975). Contemporary parallels from the lowland zone north of the chalk hills of the 'Deverel-Rimbury' heartland are scarce, but Middle Bronze Age post-built structures are known from Codicote, Hertfordshire (Greenfield 1961) and Fisherwick, Staffordshire (C Smith 1975).

A second point of interest is that, unlike many of the Iron Age round-houses from Fengate, the second millennium structures show little, if any, good evidence for rebuilding. This might indicate that the buildings were erected for a short period of actual use. It has been suggested that the two round buildings (Newark Road Structure 1 and Cat's Water Structure 46) were used to house people and that the two D-shaped structures (Newark Road Structure 2 and Fourth Drove Structure 1) were for animals. The phosphate evidence from Newark Road (Appendix 6) strongly supports this interpretation, but it must nonetheless be noted that domestic rubbish was extraordinarily rare when compared with the vast amounts encountered on the Iron Age settlement (Pryor and Cranstone 1978; see also Hodder 1978 and Pryor 1979). It would, of course, be too simple to suppose that the rarity of rubbish indicates an absence of people, and some other explanation must be sought. It will be suggested below that the different patterns of rubbish survival in second millennium BC and Iron Age times does not merely reflect different methods of rubbish disposal (for example, incineration, transportation, or use as manure) but could be seen to have economic implications.

One final point of importance concerns the location of the structures. They would appear to be distributed around the ditch system in ones and twos and, given our non-random, approximately ten percent sample of the surviving system, they seem to be located without any pattern discernible to the modern eye. The figure of ten percent is a conservative estimate of the area stripped in the recent series of excavations, but it could be taken to indicate that 30-40 additional structures could await discovery at Fengate. This may, at first, seem a very high estimate until it is remembered that the ditch system was in use for a full millennium and that the buildings are not, therefore all contemporary.

BURIALS

Three burials were found in linear ditches of the enclosure system: one in ditch 1, Area IX, Padholme Road subsite (Appendix 8); one in ditch *f*, Area II, Newark Road subsite (Appendix 8) and one at the junction of ditches F862 and 2, Area XI, Cat's Water subsite (Appendix 9). All bodies had been placed in very shallow scoops at the bottom of ditches, without funerary offerings or grave goods of any sort. All, too, were buried in the crouched position and, with the exception of the burial in ditch *f*, Newark Road (which was in a substantially deeper than average length of ditch), all showed signs of post-depositional damage, most probably the result of subsequent ditch recutting. This could be taken to imply that the burials were made at an early stage in the ditch system's life, a hypothesis that finds support from the radiocarbon sample taken from around the Newark Road interment (HAR-780 1900 ± 120 bc). Certainly, crouched burial would not be out of place in earlier Bronze Age contexts.

The location of the burials is also of interest: one (Padholme Road) was placed in a straight length of ditch, not close to any obvious entranceway; one (Newark Road) was near a substantial entranceway and one (Cat's Water) was at the junction of two major ditches. All the burials were in suitably-sized ditches and there was no evidence for interment, perhaps under a low mound, in any of the smaller ditches. It is estimated that approximately 25% of the total length of suitably-sized second millennium ditches have been excavated and we have also noted that the total area stripped at Fengate represents, conservatively, about 10% of the surviving ditch system. If then we make the major assumption that bodies are evenly spaced throughout the ditch system and that the sample excavated at Fengate is representative of the whole, again a major assumption, then we might expect to find 120 burials in the surviving system at Fengate. Once more it should be emphasised, as in the case of the structure number estimates above, that these estimates are little more than informed guesses and are only intended to indicate orders of magnitude. They should not be used for population estimates, as they are based on non-random judgement samples of a ditched enclosure system of unknown original extent, fortuitously preserved by the irregular expansion of Peterborough towards the Fens. As a footnote, it is perhaps worth mentioning that the orientation of the burials is dictated by the alignment of the ditches in which they have been buried; they all lie longitudinally in the ditch: one aligned approximately N-S, one E-W and one on the corner of an E-W and N-S ditch. The dangers of inferring too much from burial alignments should, therefore, be obvious.

WELLS

Water would never have been far below the surface at Fengate — indeed, at the present time (April 1979) it is at, or just above, the stripped surface and rarely more than 0.5m below the modern, built-up ground level. This means that almost any small hole could have been used, particularly in wet seasons, to obtain water, and thereby constitute a well. Similarly, ditches would have provided readily accessible sources of water probably, in the case of the larger ditches, on a year-round basis. Under these circumstances it would be most unwise to attempt a spatial analysis of the obviously recognisable wells so far located; however, with the exception of two possible second millennium wells on the Cat's Water subsite (features 448 and 1551 in Areas V and X respectively) which produced early first millennium pottery from their lower filling (discussed in the Fourth Report), most of the features discussed in this report as wells seemed to have been located at important points in the ditch system, usually at entranceways, ditch junctions, or near settlement areas (Storey's Bar Road, feature B3 (FNG 2, Feature Division 2, FIG 6); Padholme Road, Area IX, F6 (FNG 1, FIG 19 and above, Chapter 1); Newark Road, F26 (FIGS 20-1)). An oak stake, almost certainly forming part of a wooden lining, was found at the bottom of the Cat's Water well F448, and the collapsed lining of the Storey's Bar Road well has been identified as *Corylus* (hazel) (FNG 2, Appendix 5).

It would appear that these large, lined, wells were in frequent use and that some care was taken both in choosing spots for their location and in their day-to-day maintenance. Certainly none of the excavated wells can be shown to have gone out of use while the enclosure system itself was still in use and the date of their abandonment should be taken as an important chronologico-economic horizon. If material from their filling can provide a *terminus ante quem* for their period of use, then the Fengate wells are indeed early (cf for example, Brongers and Woltring 1973, 13), and invite chronological (if not functional?) comparisons with Wilsford and Eaton Heath (Coles and Harding 1979, FIG 95; Wainwright 1973).

3. DATING

A. RELATIVE DATING

The relative dating of Early and Middle Bronze Age domestic pottery and flintwork is fraught with difficulties. The reason for this is, of course, that well-preserved and reliably dated vessels nearly always derive from funerary contexts, whereas settlement sites are rare and when excavated (or published) cannot be dated with the precision of a single-event grave group. This is not the place to reiterate the stylistic affinities of the Newark Road and Fourth Drove pottery (discussed at length in Chapters 2 and 3), but it quite clearly belongs within the second millennium, and probably within the first half. The same might also be said of the diagnostic flints, particularly the arrowheads and scrapers, although, again, the relative dating of local Early and Middle Bronze Age flintwork is still poorly understood.

The broad stylistic dating of artifacts from the ditches and their associated features would seem comparatively straightforward; but to what extent do these dates actually apply to the ditches and other features that produced the items? It must be assumed that the small pits which produced large quantities of pottery (eg FIG 59, no 27 and FIG 60, nos 35-38) had been deliberately back-filled with secondary refuse which is likely to be strictly contemporary, given the small size of the pits involved and the stylistic and technical similarity of the sherds within them (many of which can be joined together). It is, however, another matter to use these small pits to date the complete ditch system with its multifarious recuts, notwithstanding the close spatial relationship that exists between them in certain places (for example the pits and postholes at the NE corner of Newark Road enclosure 3). In view of the above, it has been decided not to attempt any more than the most general of relative dating for the ditches. All of the artifacts from the ditches would be at home in Middle and Early Bronze Age contexts, to use conventional teminology: the spearhead and spill are stylistically and metallurgically of pre-Late Bronze date; the cylindrical loomweights are not found in Iron Age features at Fengate and would appear to be clearly separated from them chronologically (Champion 1975, appendix); we have noted that the flintwork is early and that the pottery which is generally heavy and coarse does not belong to Barrett's 'post-Deverel-Rimbury' tradition (Barrett 1975; 1976) and, more positively, has stylistic affinities with Collared Urns, Food Vessels, and, less certainly, with an eastern 'Deverel-Rimbury' variant. On the other hand, the wells, particularly those on Newark Road and Cat's Water, have produced vessels in Barrett's 'post-Deverel-Rimbury' tradition, which are quite distinct in style and fabric from the wares just mentioned. Assuming that the wells were open up to the end of the ditch system's period of use — an assumption that can be perhaps justified on spatial grounds — and bearing in mind that very considerable lengths of ditch have been excavated, it would appear that a broad second millennium BC date is not only a conservative estimate of age, but may also be an indication of the length of time that the dich system was open and in use. We shall see below that this general picture is supported by the radiocarbon evidence.

B. ABSOLUTE DATING

Some of the problems that complicated the discussion of relative dating also apply to the radiocarbon dates. The principal problem concerns the association of the material sampled and the feature it is supposed to date. The distortions caused by frequent recutting of ditches and the filling of wells *after* their period of use, have been discussed at length above, and it was with these problems in mind that it was decided to take as many samples as possible. Four varieties of dates were sought; those which, on purely stratigraphic grounds, could belong to an early period of the ditch system's use; those which originated when the ditch system was in use; those which derived from secondary contexts and therefore provided a *terminus post quem* for the deposit in which they were found (note, not the ditch itself) and, finally, those which provided a *terminus ante quem* for any particular ditch.

Only one sample can be attributed stratigraphically to an early period in the ditch system's use, and that is HAR-780 (1900 ± 120 bc) which was taken around and below the burial in Newark Road, ditch *f* (the reader is referred to Appendix 12 for full details of all dates mentioned here).

Thirteen samples were taken from contexts which belong to a period when the ditch system was in use. Five of these are from small pits of the Storey's Bar Road settlement, described at length in the Second Report, which can be closely linked to the ditches on spatial grounds; these pits all belong to an early phase of the ditch system: (HAR-397) 2030 ± 100 bc; (HAR-399) 2020 ± 70 bc; (HAR-401) 2010 ± 90 bc; (HAR-404) 1930 ± 80 bc; (HAR-409) 1860 ± 150 bc. Sample HAR-774 was taken from the small backfilled pit F37, located in the NE corner of enclosure 3, Newark Road and gave a date of 2030 ± 100 bc. Samples which, on stratigraphic grounds, must post-date the initial digging of the ditches include the three from the recut 'industrial area' deposit of Newark Road, Area VII (HAR-1970: 960 ± 70 bc; HAR-1971: 1030 ± 70 bc; HAR-1972: 1000 ± 70 bc), and that from the junction of ditches 3 and F4 in Padholme Road Area VIII (UB-676: 1280 ± 70 bc). Finally, three samples were taken of twigs from waterlogged deposits either in wells (HAR-398: 1050 ± 70 bc) or from pit-like expansions of ditches that could have been used as wells or water-holes (HAR-785: 940 ± 60 bc; UB-677: 935 ± 135 bc). The latter three dates tend to support the hypothesis, discussed above, that wells continued in use until a very late stage in the ditch system's life. The range of dates obtained from deposits that are thought to have originated when the ditch system was in use spans the whole of the second millennium bc and, as such, corroborates the relative dating suggested by the artifacts.

A series of nine samples were taken from ditch fillings on the Newark Road subsite, to determine whether the enclosures had been substantially reused after the second millennium bc. These dates provide a useful check on the preceding series of samples and provide a *terminus post quem* for the accumulation of the secondary deposits. Samples were taken from ditch 8 (HAR-778: 1830 ± 90 bc); ditch 9 (HAR-781: 990 ± 90 bc; HAR-782: 980 ± 80 bc; HAR-783: 1040 ± 80 bc; HAR-784: 1040 ± 70 bc); ditch *b* (HAR-776: 1100 ± 80 bc; HAR-777: 1600 ± 200 bc); ditches *f* and *i* (HAR-779: 2240 ± 90 bc) and ditch *n* (HAR-775: 1170 ± 70 bc). Again, these samples are entirely consistent with a second millennium bc date for the use of the ditch system.

Finally, a sample was taken from a back-filled posthole containing pottery of early first millennium type (FIG 61, no 39) and which had been cut into the completely filled-in ditch *e*, Newark Road, Area II; this sample (HAR-773), which provides a *terminus ante quem* for the accumulation of the ditch filling, gave a date of 790 ± 80 bc. Although only a single date, it also provides support for the dating suggested above.

4. THE ORIGINS OF THE DITCHED ENCLOSURES

The explanation of the rise of this remarkable and early system of ditched enclosures is far from straightforward and must, in part, be sought in the explanation of their function during their main period of use. Aspects of the latter are treated in section 5, below. The evidence available suggests that the system, or important elements of it, came into use shortly before the onset of the second millennium bc. This presents an important difficulty, for it will be argued below that the ditched enclosures were laid out to parcel up flood-free winter grazing and that these land-management measures were made necessary, in part, by the size of the herds involved. The difficulty here is that there is little or no good evidence for occupation at Fengate in the second half of the third millennium bc (ie subsequent to the use of the house described in the First Report), and it is hard to envisage how a situation in which land should suddenly become scarce could arise in circumstances where the site was apparently unoccupied. A number of possible solutions to this problem can be offered.

First, as in the case of the apparent early first millennium 'gap', discussed below, it might be argued that our failure to find Middle Neolithic material merely reflects our inability to recognise it (see discussion in Pitts 1978a, 190). There is, however, a basic objection to this: Neolithic pottery, and especially that of the Grimston/Lyles Hill series, is known to be unreliable as a means of dating, and consequently radiocarbon samples have been taken wherever possible. No radiocarbon-dated settlement features have been found at Fengate to indicate substantial settlement during the period in question.

A second explanation, more plausible than the first, is that the type of economy practiced before the construction of the ditched enclosures was mobile, perhaps transhumant, and *extensive* in its use of winter pasture. We have seen that it has required the stripping of very large areas indeed merely to recover the partial remains of four small second millennium settlements and it could well be argued that the precursors of the ditched enclosures simply lie outside the limits of our excavation. Alternatively, it has been suggested (FNG 2, 158) that the type of building in use (perhaps only by a few communities) in the early years of the second millennium bc may not have left archaeological traces. Perhaps a combination of buildings of this sort and unenclosed, or simple hedged, fields would be impossible to detect using conventional archaeological techniques. Indeed, this problem strongly emphasises the need for an in-depth, multi-disciplinary study of one or more areas of the Fen and its Fen-edge, like that undertaken recently by Louwe Kooijmans (1974) in the Low Countries, for it is probable that the events preceeding the laying out of the ditched enclosures will only be understood by pollen analyses of peat in the nearby Fen. This is not the place to discuss future research, but a sufficient depth of Upper Peat could be preserved beneath the bank of Morton's Leam (dug in 1478), an artificial course of the river Nene 1 km south-east of Fengate.

A third possible explanation for the lack of archaeological evidence for settlement immediately prior to the establishment of the first ditched enclosures, is more simple. This hypothesis suggests that the site was largely abandoned during the latter half of the third millennium bc, at a time approximately coincident with the semi-marine incursions that laid down the Fen ('Buttery') Clay (FNG 2, 159-60 for a discussion of this hypothesis in more detail). This explanation is certainly attractive in many respects, but it still presents problems. First, it has not yet been reliably established whether the Fen Clay extended significantly towards Fengate beyond Dog-in-a-Doublet sluice, some 6 km east of the site. Second, the effects of such flooding on Fen vegetation this far inland, and the possible presence of raised bogs (David Hall, pers comm) which would have halted or seriously hindered invading flood waters, are still matters open to discussion. In view of these problems, it is probably best not to place too much weight on this otherwise attractive hypothesis. Similarly, the apparent abandonment of the site should not be seen in terms of retrenchment or population decline following the pioneer 'landnam' settlement(s) represented, in a later stage, by the Padholme Road house. Apart from the fact that the radiocarbon dates are too few and too recent to support such a suggestion, the palaeoenvironmental evidence is simply lacking. The answer to these problems probably lies in compromise: first, it must be recognised that there are no distinctive, securely-dated, Middle Neolithic artifacts; second, the type of extensive, small-scale pastoral economy which might have preceded the ditched enclosures would probably have left few archaeological traces and, thirdly, the Fen Clay incursions, at their height, would possibly have discouraged local communities from choosing Fengate as a permanent winter 'home base' in a Fen/Fen-edge transhumance cycle. It is not improbable that the antecedants of the ditched enclosures lay either further up the Nene valley, or on higher ground beneath modern Peterborough, and that their sudden appearance at Fengate merely reflects the incorporation of new ground into an expanding system of land management.

The frequent recutting of gravel-cut ditches makes it impossible to determine by stratigraphic means alone whether the enclosures were laid out in one or more large units or, alternatively, in smaller units piecemeal, over a longer period of time. The regularity of the Fengate enclosures, however, strongly suggests quite sophisticated methods of surveying, such as would be found in a *cohesive* system in which the major boundaries (ie the main E-W ditches) were established before the land between was subdivided according to need (Bradley 1978b, 268). If this analysis is accepted, it follows that the major E-W ditches were probably first dug in the latter years of the

Neolithic period (the problems of Late Neolithic 'continuity' are discussed, p.170A). It might also account for the different 'character' of enclosures between major E-W boundaries, seen so clearly on Newark Road.

5. ECONOMY AND SOCIETY

It was suggested in the Second Report (FNG 2, 157-163) that the mainstay of the Fengate economy in the later third and throughout the second millennium BC was livestock. The detailed arguments in support of this hypothesis need not be repeated here, but the principal evidence includes:

1. The layout of the ditched enclosures, especially:
   a) the positioning of entranceways at enclosure corners, and
   b) the location of a narrow 'sorting' drove along one side of an enclosure. This drove was laid out as an integral part of the original system.
2. The animal bone sample, although small, indicated that cattle, sheep and pigs were important and that cattle were generally too old at death to have been kept solely for meat production; dairy products would probably have played an important role in the economy (FNG 2, Appendix 7).
3. The macro-botanical and pollen evidence (FNG 2, Appendices 3 and 6), although from a late phase of the settlement, showed open country and there was no good evidence for cereal cultivation (and it must be recalled that the sample locations were within the enclosure system).
4. The absence of querns, rubbers, post-built 'granaries' or drying racks, storage vessels or grain impressions on pottery tended to emphasise the reduced role of cereals in the economy.
5. In such a deterministic environment as the Fen-edge one may reasonably examine the way in which more recent communities adapted their way of life to the undrained wetlands. Medieval and sixteenth century Fen-edge villagers made extensive use of the peat Fens on a seasonal basis (Darby 1940; Thirsk 1953). Livestock were taken out into the Fen meadows — often held in common — during the summer and returned to the Fen-edge 'home base' during the wetter months of winter. Hay was also cut for use over winter, and the wetlands provided an important source of winter protein in the form of fish, eels and wildfowl.

Let us now consider evidence for the economy of the communities that laid out and used the larger enclosure system discussed in this report. We have already noted that later Neolithic enclosures of the Storey's Bar Road subsite form an integral part of the larger system, and it would therefore be reasonable to expect that the two economies were broadly similar. All the archaeological evidence strongly suggests that this is, in fact, the case. This evidence may be summarised thus:

1. The layout of the ditched enclosures is entirely consistent with livestock management. There are numerous droveways and there is evidence from soil phosphate analyses that these droveways were used for livestock (Appendix 6). Although not proof against livestock on their own, there is now evidence to show that the ditches may well have been accompanied by banks (FIG 128; PL 15); if a laid hedge was placed on top of the bank, and if the ditches extended below the winter water table, as they do today, then even the smaller ditches at Fengate would provide effective barriers to livestock (see Chapter 3).

2. The animal bone sample, although regrettably small, does support the main conclusions outlined above (Appendix 7); the presence of many loomweights hints at the increased importance of sheep which may also, perhaps, be seen in the bone sample.

3. The botanical material will be published in the Fourth Report as part of a general study of first and second millennium material from Fengate.

4. There was no positive evidence for the consumption or cultivation of cereals on the site, although it must be noted that the absence of, for example, querns or rubbers, in an area where suitable stone is not available, might suggest that they were 'curated' items of considerable value (Pryor 1979).

The Newark Road and Padholme Road subsites provided evidence for activities that were not represented at Storey's Bar Road. Briquetage (possibly crystallisation vessel supports), a possible salt mould or disposable container for subsequent 'trade' or distribution, and a sawn-through flat sherd of a type often found at salterns indicate that salt was being processed near ditches 1 and 2, in Area IX, Padholme Road (FIG 13). The precise nature of the process involved is difficult to establish, as salt can be extracted from sea water in many ways (de Brisay and Evans 1975). No large chunks of fired, or unfired, clay were found, however, so it might be supposed that the initial evaporation took place in clay tanks out in the Fens (it should be recalled that the Nene is tidal today as far inland as Dog-in-a-Doublet sluice, just 6 km east of the site). Perhaps it was the very wet salt solution, scooped out of the evaporation tanks, that was crystallised at Fengate (de Brisay 1978). The slight evidence available does not suggest that salt-production was a major, specialist, industry at Fengate; it was probably another part of the daily round, undertaken at times when other tasks were not too pressing (Bradley 1978a, 68; 1975b, 23).

The second activity is represented by the 'industrial area' on Newark Road. This has been discussed at some length in Chapter 2 where it was very tentatively suggested that the process involved was lime-burning. The principal use for this lime was thought, for want of a better explanation, to be connected with farming, but it was realised that there were most serious chronological arguments against this view (eg Dodgshon 1978), since the use of lime as a marl or fertiliser was a product of the Agricultural Revolution of the eighteenth century (!). It has been suggested above that agriculture, as such, was probably not practised on a large scale at Fengate, so it is assumed that the lime was, perhaps, spread to make good the depredations of over-grazing (eg Simmons 1974, PL 10). If over-grazing was a problem, it would have been most serious in some of the smaller enclosures which would also have lost much grass through trampling (this has been suggested for the drove surfaces (Appendix 6)). As a postscript it is, perhaps, of interest to note that in their review of farm life in a Yorkshire dale Long and Davies (1948, 32) observe 'The cows grazed the spring and summer flush of grass which produced a flow of milk with properties well suited to the production of cheese. Incidentally great stress was laid on the grassland obtaining an adequate supply of lime and as evidence of this a great number of disused kilns are to be seen in the dale.'[1]

---

1. I am indebted to Andrew Fleming for this reference.

181

The third activity which can be shown to have taken place on site was the smithing of metal. This is indicated by the closely similar composition of the metal in the spearhead and the small spill of bronze (Craddock, Chapter 2). Both were found in ditches of the south-central Newark Road system, although a considerable distance apart, and it is reasonable to suppose that the smith worked near the spill (rather than the broken spearhead) in which case the most obvious location for his workshop would be the settlement area of enclosure C. Archaeological evidence for a large workshop is lacking and it is not altogether improbable that metalworking, like salt production, took place during slack periods of the farming cycle. Both activities could have been performed by individuals who also 'participated in the general economy by owning fields, animals etc, which (they) and (their) family maintain'. (Rowlands 1971, 213).

We will return to more general considerations raised by the interpretation of the Fengate second millennium economy later. At this point it is appropriate to consider the site in the light of recent research elsewhere, and we will start by reviewing the evidence from eastern England.

The linear ditches recognised from the air by Pickering (1978) and found by him to cover large areas of the East Midlands and Lincolnshire are considered to form a series of boundaries associated with the Jurassic Spine. These ditches are seen to form tribal boundaries and are thought by Pickering to date from the Middle Bronze Age to the Early Iron Age. This is not the place to offer a detailed critique of this paper which contains a number of points which the present author finds difficult to accept. Suffice it to say that some assertions lack data to support them, for example, that a number of parallel ditched alignments were 'originally constructed as banks and converted to trackways in the Romano-British period' (*ibid*, 142). The principal drawback of this paper, however, is that it assumes that the many lengths of ditch mapped from the air all formed part of the *same* system, despite gaps of many miles between different lengths. Although, no doubt, some stretches of parallel double ditches were used to provide material for a bank in between, this should not be assumed in every case. But while shortcomings in Pickering's interpretation of his aerial photographs may be demonstrated, the importance of the underlying data cannot be ignored. It is suggested here that the reason why these linear features appear to respect the lie of the land (as reflected in the title of Pickering's paper) is simply that they are fragments of field systems, intended to divide the land either into manageable units or into different categories of 'land use potential' (for example Ellison and Harriss 1972, FIG 26). Thus the ditched fields at Billingborough (mentioned by Pickering) and the ditched enclosures at Fengate run at right angles to the Fens, evenly apportioning land on wet Fen, skirtland, Fen-edge and upland. Pickering's map (*ibid*, 141) is important, then, as it indicates the known extent of ancient fields between the upper reaches of the Nene and the Humber. Further research, both in the air and on the ground, is urgently required.

Turning now to excavated evidence, the linear field system at Billingborough, once thought to be of Late Bronze Age date (Chowne 1978) is now considered, on artifactual and stratigraphic evidence, to belong within the Iron Age (P Chowne, pers comm). Despite this, Chowne's (1977) evidence for large-scale settlement along the Fen-edge in the Bronze Age is most impressive and further excavation is required to determine whether the known ditched field systems are all of this late date, or whether, as in the case of Fengate, the latest recuts, by removing earlier layers, are giving a falsely young date to the features themselves.

Moving south of Fengate, the best parallels are to be sought at Mucking, Essex. Here Mrs Jones' most recent excavations have revealed rectilinear ditched enclosures which include one ditched drove. These are stratigraphically linked with at least one Bronze Age barrow (no 3) and two others (nos 4 and 5) appear to have been used as sighting points for the enclosure ditches (Jones 1976; and pers comm).

Before leaving south-east England, mention should be made of the remarkable series of parallel ditched 'trackways' which McMaster (1975, 13) has noted are often associated with ring-ditches. These trackways and single linear ditches traverse large tracts of countryside in south-east Essex on the low-lying flat land between the rivers Stour and Colne. The area is, of course, known to have been the scene of considerable prehistoric activity at, for example, Lawford (unpublished) and Ardleigh (Erith and Longworth 1960). The countryside around the Stour/Colne valley and the Fen-edge at Peterborough is very similar and further work is required to determine whether the Essex cropmarks are comparable with the Fengate ditch system. Present indications, however, are certainly favourable.

The 'concave landscape' of the Somerset Levels (Coles 1978) is closely comparable with that at Fengate and although fields or enclosures have yet to be discovered, the importance of the marsh edge 'where mineral nutrients and the moss peats combined to create ideal conditions for fodder production, or for seasonal intensive use by animals' (Coles 1978, 148) has been rightly emphasised. The marsh-edge zone at Fengate would probably have been less critically important, as the Fens are, in general, quite well supplied with nutrients from the base-rich waters which drain into them (Godwin 1941, 300 ff). Oligotrophic peats, including a substantial raised bog are, however, known to have been in existence in the first half of the second millennium bc at Holme Fen, just 6 miles south of Fengate. This important site shows evidence for upland clearance leading to soil erosion into the Fen at about 1450 bc (Godwin and Vishnu-Mittre 1975), and it is, perhaps, tempting to view this clearance in terms of Coles 'concave landscape' model (Coles 1978, FIG 1). At Holme Fen the marsh edge zone of fodder production would have been especially important, and it is interesting to note that Godwin and Vishnu-Mittre (1975, 588) state that two bands of clay which washed into the Fen probably came from 'upland near Holme village'. The clay bands are thought to represent wash from clay soils exposed to erosion after clearance of the covering woodland. The area around Holme village corresponds well with Coles' zone of cereal production which was set back from the zone of fodder production, on slightly higher ground.

The undrained wetlands of the Somerset Levels and the Fens would only have been available for grazing on a seasonal basis (FNG 2, 161; Coles and Hibbert 1975, 17); much of this land was traditionally held in common and medieval records make it clear that pasture, hay gathering, turbary (peat cutting), fishing and fowling were strictly regulated activities (Darby 1940). Indeed, the land divisions at Fengate indicate that, even in prehistoric times, flood-free winter pasture was also a closely controlled resource. A broadly similar situation prevails on the highlands of Dartmoor. Here, seasonally available summer grazing was apportioned, or controlled, by a series of linear reaves (Fleming 1978 with refs). Some of the reave systems, for example the Dartmeet parallel reaves (Fleming 1978, FIG 4), bear a striking resemblance to the Fengate ditched enclosures, perhaps reflecting functional similarity. Both systems show chronological depth, although the available evidence suggests that the reaves may be slightly more recent (*ibid*, 110).

This brief review of comparable material demonstrates that, despite its early date, the Fengate ditched enclosure system was by no means unique in Britain. Ireland (Caulfield 1978) and the mainland of Europe (Bradley 1978b) also have early field or enclosure systems, but their apparent rarity in the Low Countries, in an environment similar to that discussed here, is a matter of some interest (Brongers and Woltring 1973; for recent work see Bakker *et al* 1977).

Some of the interpretive hypotheses offered in this report, in the Second Report and in other publications (Pryor 1974b; 1976a) are suitable for further examination. First, it has been stated (FNG 2, chapter 6; Pryor 1976a) that the ditched enclosures which run at right angles to the Fen were intended as a form of pasture management. Winter pasture was slow growing and the large herds of livestock returning from the lush meadows of the wetlands required careful control on the limited grazing of the Fen-edge. An alternative view might be that the ditched droveways between and around enclosures were intended to guide livestock through arable plots, in the manner of the classic infield/outfield system where droves led from a central settlement, through the surrounding gardens and arable plots, and into the open pastures beyond the infield. This hypothesis has a number of shortcomings, however.

The principal objection is that every drove at Fengate is broached by numerous entranceways into neighbouring enclosures. This arrangement is quite unlike that of the large ditched drove which runs ESE from the Romano-British yards of the Cat's Water subsite, presumably through agricultural land (FIG 4); it is also unlike the pattern in the Roman Fenland, where the droves are usually continuous (Hallam 1970). The placing of wells in various enclosures, and usually not associated with human settlement, might be taken to indicate that it was livestock that was being watered. It is also perhaps worth noting that a ditch, bank and hedge are wasteful of agricultural land (but less so of pasture), and that when cereal agriculture becomes important in the latter part of the first millennium, ditched fields are no longer used. A more theoretical objection to the hypothesis is that the Fengate enclosures are extraordinarily variable in size (compare, for example, Newark Road enclosure B with those on the Cat's Water subsite (FIGS 19 and 93)) and there is no evidence for the modular arrangement of agricultural plots seen in Gotland (Lindquist 1974) or, indeed, on the chalk hills of the downland (Bradley 1978b). The preferred plot size at Gotland was about 600 sq m which Lindquist interprets as a single day's ploughing for one man. In view of these objections, the original, stock-management, hypothesis still fits the Fengate evidence best.

At first glance the neat, surveyed, arrangement of the ditched enclosures seems to suggest the pesence of a powerful controlling authority and hence of a stratified, heirarchical society (Pryor 1976a, 42). An alternative, perhaps preferable, view is, however, possible. The development of prehistoric culture at Fengate can be seen in three, very broadly defined stages, roughly equivalent to the final three millennia bc. The first and last stages (for convenience, earlier Neolithic and Iron Age) are easier to describe than the middle ('Bronze Age') stage. The first stage has been interpreted as a pioneer, perhaps 'landnam' stage of single family settlement, approximately equivalent to the 'log cabin' settlers of North America (eg Coles 1976). Unfortunately, the dating of the earlier Neolithic house is not well established, but the two dates available would suggest that the building itself belongs to a final stage of this initial phase.

The third stage sees the beginnings of large-scale mixed farming and of nucleated settlement (Pryor and Cranstone 1978). The available evidence from the Nene Valley suggests a considerable increase in population during the first millennium BC (eg Brown and Taylor 1978) and this is reflected at Fengate by the known location of at least four settlements, of which one (Cat's Water) was substantial, one was larger than a simple family unit (Vicarage Farm — see FNG 1) and two were of unknown size (Padholme Road — see FNG 1 — and the Gravel Pits site(s) — Hawkes and Fell 1945; also Peterborough Museum collections).

The settlement and land use pattern of the second phase of culture at Fengate contrasts with the two just discussed. There is, moreover, no unambiguous evidence to suggest that all three stages are related in a crude evolutionary manner. We have already described the transition from the first to the second stage and have concluded that smooth evolution, on the site, is, on the whole, improbable. We will discuss the mechanism of change between the latter two stages in section 6, below, but here it is sufficient to note that the apparent economic and social metamorphosis could be the result of the natural processes of a highly deterministic environment.

The significance of the second millennium ditched enclosure system is that it represents a major intensification of land use. Settlements are small, non-nucleated, and appear to be spread around the enclosure system which, in all cases seems to have been laid out before the settlements were built. The settlements are striking, too, in that they seem so short-lived and, on the whole, insubstantial: there is no evidence for major rebuilding and domestic rubbish is very rare (but see Appendix 7). This picture accords well with what one might expect of a site seasonally occupied by folk whose most imprtant possessions were livestock.

Although the pattern of land-use was different, the intensive second phase of land-use at Gotland has many points in common with Fengate phase two (Lindquist 1974). Both areas show a transition from extensive, long-fallow (Boserup 1965, chapters 2 and 3) systems of farming in which 'the extensive, space-demanding exploitation of the land indicates that settlement and social relations were organised in some form of larger society, perhaps with a division of functions within the social groups (farmers, herdsmen, craftsmen etc). Society must have been organised in larger units than the extended family' (Lindquist 1974). The change from this to an intensive system sees, first of all, much greater importance given to land division: to fencing (Gotland) and ditching (Fengate). Both areas, during this second phase, show evidence for single family settlement units which are dotted around the fields or enclosures as effective, on-the-spot means of land control and management. The important point to emphasise is that a shift from extensive to intensive systems of land-use does not necessarily involve increased social stratification which may be reflected archaeologically by nucleation of settlement.

The economic model suggested above for stage two is of seasonal occupation of Fen-edge flood free grazing during the months of winter. During the drier months of summer a large proportion of the community, and its livestock, would make use of the rich peat Fen pastures. Fleming (1978, 112) has observed that 'the meeting of diverse groups in such zones of common land must have offered absorbing opportunities of cultural contact and possibly political development'. Perhaps these seasonal meetings might be the key to the social changes that must have taken place in the initial years of the first millennium at Fengate.

Finally, it is sometimes necessary to step back from economic interpretation and from models of cultural ecology. Despite the fact that the Fenland is a highly deterministic environment, the human, cultural, element ultimately determines the course of a society's development. At this point, then, it is appropriate to consider how Fengate would have appeared to contemporary communities in the centuries prior to the great drainage works of the last three hundred years. Writing of Peterborough, the eleventh century chronicler Hugh Candidus notes it is 'built in a fair spot, and a goodly, because on the one side it is rich in fenland, and in goodly waters, and on the other is has abundance of ploughlands and woodlands, with many fertile meads and pastures. On all sides it is beautiful to look upon and easy to approach on foot, save only on the eastern side where there is no coming to it save in a boat' (Mellows 1966, 2). Hugh's abbey grew and prospered (King 1973), as did the two other important Fenland religious houses, Ely (Miller 1951) and Ramsey (Raftis 1957). The abbeys at Thorney and Crowland were, however, much less fortunate (Raban 1977). Each of the five establishments had adequate early grants of land and capital; all were founded at very approximately the same period and were positioned in closely comparable locations on flood-free land near the peat Fen-edge. Simple environmental determinism will not explain why two of these houses fared so much worse than the others; the explanation of this state of affairs is complex, and not yet fully understood, but one thing is reasonably certain: whatever the explanation, it is *cultural* and not environmental (Raban 1977, 88-91), and has to do with local, national and ecclesiastical politics, grants, legacies, endowments and personalities. As levels of socio-cultural integration increase and multiply (Steward 1955, chapter 3) in the latter two millennia BC, the cultural element must become increasingly significant, even in such a deterministic environment as the Fen-edge.

6. THE DEMISE OF THE DITCHED ENCLOSURES

Radiocarbon dates (section 3B, above) quite clearly demonstrate that the enclosure system, its associated wells, and settlements, had gone out of use by, or very shortly after, about 1000 bc. The evidence of the radiocarbon dates also suggests that this was a fairly rapid process; certainly no excavated ditch had been used, or re-used, in full Iron Age times and no pottery of early first millennium type was found in any of the ditch fillings. It could, however, be argued, against this hypothesis, that the use of the ditched enclosures, as simple hedged fields, continued long after their apparent abandonment, in the suggested manner of Phases 3 and 4 of the Storey's Bar Road subsite (FNG 2, 66-8). This could, indeed, have been the case in areas which were not excavated, but it should be recalled that there was good evidence for the Storey's Bar second millennium use of the enclosures, both in their modification, and in their recutting through the naturally weathered deposits of the earlier ring-ditch (FNG 2, Feature Division 4). The large pit, W17 and the well, too, provided evidence that the use of the enclosures extended beyond the period of their initial, two phase, setting-out and construction. If substantial first millennium use of the ditched enclosures is to be suggested, evidence must be found to support it. The only early first millennium features on Newark Road (FIG 44, B) can be shown stratigraphically to post-date the latest tertiary (Appendix 3), filling of the enclosure ditches.

Further evidence for clear chronological separation is provided by the layout of first and second millennium features on the Cat's Water subsite, where the ditches and structures of the Iron Age settlement pay no heed to the underlying second millennium ditches (Pryor and Cranstone 1978, FIG 5). It is perhaps, of interest to note here that the E-W ditch 5 which appears to bound the Iron Age settlement to the north, but which is cut by an Iron Age ditch, could represent the line of a much overgrown hedge which the occupants of the later settlement found convenient to retain. Such a screen of trees, perhaps formed by elm suckers (Pollard *et al* 1974, PL 7) would have provided much-needed protection against the bitterly cold north-easterly winds which blow from the flat Fenland in wintertime.

It was suggested in a previous publication that an important factor in the demise of the ditched enclosure system was increased wetness (Pryor 1976a, 46). This hypothesis finds independant support in the discovery, at the north-east end of Fourth Drove Area VII, of a pre-Roman freshwater flood deposit which dips into ditch 10 at this point, the lowest yet excavated at Fengate (FIG 86; also Appendices 2 and 4). It should also be noted that the turn of the first and second millennia is a time of generally increased climatic wetness which would have had the effect of raising the local water table, probably quite substantially (Piggott 1972; Godwin 1975, 472; Coles and Harding 1979, 475 ff). Other local indications of wet conditions include the formation of Whittlesey and Trundle meres in the Iron Age (Godwin and Vishnu-Mittre 1975), the construction of a wooden trackway, possibly in the early years of the first millennium, at Little Thetford, Cambridgeshire (Lethbridge 1935) and, perhaps, the discovery in 1950 of the Peterborough log boat (PL 16; Lethbridge *et al* 1951). The dating of this craft is, unfortunately, most uncertain: the pollen analyses at best provide a *terminus post quem* for the muds in which the boat was embedded (but see Smith and Pilcher 1973), and the potsherd, given the recent *comparanda* from Fengate, must be considered undiagnostic, although probably post-Neolithic. A radiocarbon date of recently located fragments of the boat, now re-housed in Peterborough Museum, could determine whether or not the vessel is of prehistoric age (McGrail 1978).

The palaeoenvironmental evidence for increased wetness in the Fens during the early years of the first millennium BC is, however, strong (recently summarised by Sir Harry Godwin (1978, chapter 9)). The results of the pollen analyses are fully supported by Sir Cyril Fox (1923) whose distribution maps, although covering the Fen just to the south of Peterborough, show massive use of the Fen in Bronze Age times — clearly reflecting drier conditions — and the virtual abandonment of the peats in the Iron Age.

The generally increased wetness is reflected at Fengate by the deposit of freshwater alluvium beneath the Fen Causeway which is also associated with ditch 10 and its bank. Evidence for erosion is slight, and the site is, perhaps, best seen as lying within a zone of deposition where floodwaters, carrying clays and silts in suspension are unable to drain to the sea (Vita-Finzi 1969; Turnbaugh 1978). The flood deposit at Fourth Drove should not, however, be seen as a single isolated event; given a wetter climate and, perhaps, silting around river outfalls to the sea the 'flooding (with attendant effects) constitutes a natural *process* routinely at work, rather than an anomalous or capricious *event*' (Turnbaugh 1978, 605 (author's italics)). Under these circumstances a way of life which depended *absolutely* on the annual availability of summer grazing would be most seriously affected.

The apparently sudden demise of the ditched enclosure system has important social implications. The picture of economic and social life at Fengate in the second millennium BC, as painted here and in the Second Report, is one of order and stability. The very maintenance, largely unmodified, of a single network of ditches for a thousand years, must indicate considerable social stability, with well-regulated systems for the descent of land, property and livestock. Under these circumstances it is possible to speak of a climax system of largely pastoral transhumance intimately geared to a rich and varied environment (Clarke 1978, 351 ff). The extent, and careful maintenance, of the ditch system, when allied to its long use-life, strongly indicate that the size of the local population would have been near the carrying capacity of the most limiting element of the economic cycle, which, in this case, would have been the availability of winter pasture. Much communal effort must have been expended in managing the efficient use of this limited resource, as it is doubtful whether the peat Fen pastures would ever have required, or been amenable to, large-scale cooperative public or private works. Once the Fenland water table had begun to rise, there would be little that prehistoric communities could have done to arrest the process; had, however, the critical element in the economic cycle been the availability of *Fen* resources (hay, grazing, winter protein), rather than winter grazing, it is probable that Fen-edge communities would have adapted to the environmental changes faster, and with less disruption, as part of their normal adaptation to a changing environment.

The apparently sudden demise of the ditched enclosures could be seen as the almost catastrophic response of a highly specialised society to a small, but critical change in the environment. The events that took place at about 1000 bc at Fengate illustrate Sahlins and Service's (1960, 97) 'law of evolutionary potential' which has been restated in archaeological terms by Plog (1974, 52): 'The more specialised a population in acquiring some resource, the lower the probability that the strategy will survive a change in some conditioning environmental variable; the less specialised, the greater the probability'. Plog goes on to add the necessary qualification that in more specialised societies, size of population is important: the larger the population, the greater its chance of surviving a major environmental change. If our interpretation of events at Fengate is correct, then the adaptive response of a dispersed, highly specialised community to the changes in local environment was indeed drastic: the archaeological evidence suggests that land management methods, in use for over a millennium, were quite suddenly abandoned; the settlement pattern changed and the basis of the economy changed with it.

Although highly specialised, the communities of the late second/early first millennium BC were able to successfully adapt to the new conditions, as the scale of subsequent, Iron Age, occupation attests. The early years of the first millennium must, however, have been difficult times for the inhabitants of Fengate, and it cannot be mere coincidence that well-dated material of the Late Bronze/Early Iron Age is rare; nor is it surprising to discover a molluscan fauna indicative of scrub cover in the secondary deposits of the abandoned second millennium ditches of Newark Road (Appendix 4).

Finally, as we have already noted, areas prone to flood are subjected to a continuing process. In the Fenland this process has been, hopefully, controlled in recent times. But the medieval Fen-edge villager, although exercising very limited control of the higher Fen near his village, was still more or less at the mercy of the elements. Even these later communities were forced to adapt their economies to changing conditions, and although perhaps less specialised than the second millennium BC groups at Fengate, the changes they were forced to undergo were serious and far-reaching. Thus Ravensdale (1974, 156), discussing two Fen-edge villages (Landbeach and Waterbeach) of the southern Fenland notes: 'the vagaries of the fen in conjunction with the force of the Medieval population explosion, multiplied the demand for arable on the old sheep-lands of Landbeach. Its earlier phases we can only arrive at by inferences: when we can see a little into its operation near the end of the thirteenth century, expansion is almost over and the invasion of the black waters is turning assarting into a more desperate struggle for survival'.

APPENDIX 1

METHODS OF EXCAVATION 1975-78

This brief note is intended to supplement the fuller account of Fengate methods of excavation given in the Second Report (FNG 2, Appendix 1). In general, methods of excavation remained substantially the same in the latter four seasons as in the initial four years, the only exception to this being the first season (1971) when excavation techniques were still being developed. The changes of the last four years have been quantitative rather than qualitative: we have tried to excavate more features, faster and at less cost, than in previous seasons, but at the same time we have been at pains to ensure that standards of recovery have remained similar. The efforts taken to attempt a more-or-less uniform standard of data recovery are outlined in the Second Report (FNG 2, 169) and the significance of these attempts is illustrated when the finds' distributions are analysed in detail, above (cf FIGS 25, 51-2).

It is perhaps worth mentioning here that the weather played a more than usually important role in the latter part of the Fengate project. First, the extremely dry conditions of the 1976 summer hampered work considerably. Temperatures of over 100°F were recorded on the Newark Road subsite and the sand-silts of the second millennium ditch fillings baked so hard that pick-axes had to be used. Despite efforts to standardise methods of digging, these conditions probably adversely affected the rate of artifact recovery. On the other hand, the persistence of the hot, dry conditions (over 20 weeks without a rain shower) may have aided our efforts at standardisation of data recovery.

The season of 1978 was unusually cold and damp, and while this may not have seriously affected the results obtained, it did mean that rather less, quantitatively speaking, was achieved than in the previous three or four years.

The principal development in mechanical methods of excavation was the greater use of paired machine working. The main pairing employed was that of the self-elevating scraper (usually a 9cu yd International E200 Payscraper) which was combined with a 360° tracked hydraulic excavator (a Hy-Mac 580C with extended boom and dipper and 2m toothless ditch-cleaning blade). The scraper was used to lower the upper 0.20m of the *plaggen* soil (cf Appendix 2), before the hydraulic excavator was employed to remove the remaining overburden, which varied in thickness, depending on height above OD. The excavator's loose earth was deposited to one side in a low, flat heap, which was then picked up and removed by the scraper. Attempts were made to employ tractor and trailer units to remove this loose earth without double handling, but the productivity of the excavator, and the travelling distances involved, required the use of at least five such units and this soon proved not to be cost-effective. The use of larger dump trucks was not thought advisable in view of the damage that their tyres would have caused in wet weather (it should be recalled that the scraper's tyres were safely separated from the archaeological horizon by the loose earth it was scraping). The whole of the Cat's Water subsite main area and most of Newark Road (Areas III-VII) were stripped in this way. Fourth Drove Areas I, II and VII were cleared using paired machines, but the remaining, smaller, areas were cleared using the hydraulic excavator alone. This machine was fitted with wide flat tracks to prevent compaction and, with its extended reach, could excavate a circle of diameter 22m.

Methods of hand excavation remained substantially the same as in previous seasons, but greater use was made of the ¼-inch mesh dry shaker sieves (FNG 2, PL 14). A comparison of these half-metre 'control' lengths of sieved ditch filling with lengths excavated in the traditional way is given in FIG 25. Finally, despite many practical difficulties, fine mesh wet sieves were employed on undisturbed primary and secondary rubbish deposits of the Cat's Water Iron Age settlement; these experiments will be discussed in the Fourth Report (Cat's Water Structure 54).

APPENDIX 2

A SEDIMENT ANALYSIS OF THE SECOND MILLENNIUM BC DITCHES AT NEWARK ROAD SUBSITE, FENGATE, PETERBOROUGH

C A I French

INTRODUCTION

The ditch deposits at Fengate are the major source of environmental data relating to the site's history. Consequently it is important that the possible origins and composition of the sediments which comprise the ditch fills are understood. The techniques of particle size analysis and a statistical examination of the results, the determination of soil pH and of the alkali-soluble humus and free iron contents were used to gain some idea of the possibilities involved. No definite statements on the origin and modes of transport of the sediments could be made, however, unless a mineralogical analysis was undertaken.

MODERN SOIL PROFILE

The modern soil profile overlying the Nene valley terrace gravels consists of an upper clay loam (0-17cm) which merges into a clay horizon (17-26cm) and then into a sandy loam (26-42cm). The alkali-soluble humus and free iron contents decrease with depth, and indicate a moderately well leached soil.

As this soil has been subjected to the dumping of night soil in post-medieval times, it is believed to be of a thin plaggen type (after Limbrey 1975) and to be representative of most of the site. A consequence of this process is that nutrients derived from a much wider area will have been concentrated on the site.

Variations do occur, however. For example, there is clay loam with a very high organic matter content in a slight depression in the north-west corner of the Fourth Drove subsite. This may represent a former shallow pool or marshy area. On the eastern edge of the same subsite there is a clay loam which may equate with the flood clay on the adjacent Cat's Water subsite. These profiles suggest that there was widespread and intermittent flooding in the area of the Fen-edge, and that the margin landscape was not as uniform as it appears today.

SECOND MILLENNIUM DITCH PROFILES

Two series of samples were taken from the same two ditch sections which had been analyzed for molluscs, that is ditch 10 (62W/34N) and ditch 9 (39W/87N) (FIG 108). Both ditches form part of the extensive second millennium BC system.

Soil description terms of the United States Dept of Agriculture (1951) were used.

A section through ditch 10 showed the following stratigraphy after c. 50-60cm of topsoil had been removed (FIG 108):

Depth below machined surface (cm)	Layer	
0-25 } 25-50 }	(1)	Sandy loam with scattered gravel pebbles. 10YR 5/6.
50-60 } 60-75 }	(2)	Sandy loam with scattered gravel pebbles, with a zone of loamy sand at the 50-60cm level. Gravel content increases from the 50-75cm level to the base of the profile. 10YR 5/4.
75-90	(3)	Loamy sand with a high gravel content and containing much organic material. 10YR 3/3.
90+		Sand-gravel slip. 10YR 5/4. Nene valley terrace gravel.

A section through ditch 9 showed the following stratigraphy after c. 50-60cm of topsoil had been removed (FIG 108):

Depth below machined surface (cm)	Layer	
0-25 } 25-50 }	(1)	Sandy loam which becomes a loamy sand, with scattered pebbles. 10YR 5/6.
50-70 } 70-80 }	(2)	Sandy loam which becomes a loamy sand, with scattered gravel pebbles. There is some organic material at the base of this layer. 10YR 4/4.
80-85		Sand-gravel slip. 10YR 5/4.
85+		Nene valley terrace gravel.

Soil pH

The soil pH measures the concentration or activity of hydrogen ions. Measurements were taken of two dilutions, water/soil and potassium chloride/soil using a pH meter (Avery and Bascomb 1974; Bunting and Campbell 1976).

191

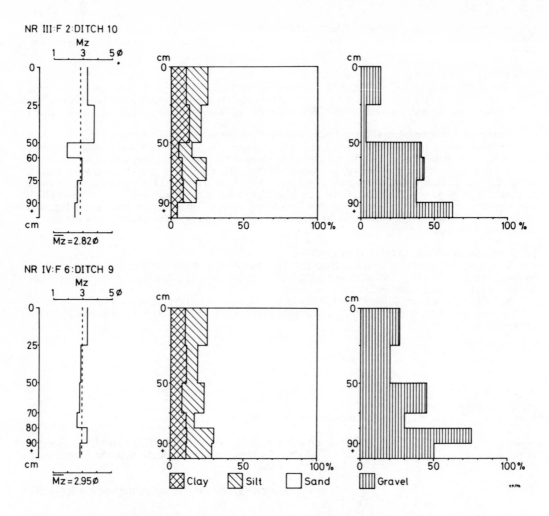

NR III:F 2:DITCH 10

NR IV:F 6:DITCH 9

Clay   Silt   Sand   Gravel

Fig. 98   Appendix 2: histograms showing mean particle size; sand, silt and clay percentages and gravel content.

The pH readings for both ditch profiles range from *c* 6 to 9, and indicate that the sediments are circum-neutral to calcareous. Due to leaching of the upper part of the profile by percolating rain-water and the influence of calcareous ground-water, the pH increases from the top to the bottom of both profiles.

PARTICLE SIZE ANALYSIS OF DITCHES 9 AND 10 (FIGS 98-104)

The size grades of the US Dept of Agriculture (1951) were used to differentiate the sediments. The results then enabled the calculation of the four graphic measures of mean size, standard deviation, skewness and kurtosis, based of the formulae of Folk and Ward (1957). The hydrometer method of particle size analysis was used to determine the silt and clay fractions (after Shackley 1975). The sand fraction was obtained by dry sieving.

The sediments of both ditches will be considered together. The most notable feature of both ditches is the general uniformity in the composition of the ditch fills. They consist primarily of sandy loam or loamy sand, and an admixture of gravel.

The gravel fraction of the ditch sediments constitutes the second most common fraction in terms of percentage by weight after the sand fraction. It is composed of gravel (2mm-10mm) and small stones (10mm-50mm) originating from the terrace gravels. The gravel content is greatest in the primary and lower secondary fills, when the infilling processes would have been most rapid, and the ditch sides, edges and possible adjacent banks were relatively unstable. Above the 50cm level, the gravel content declines.

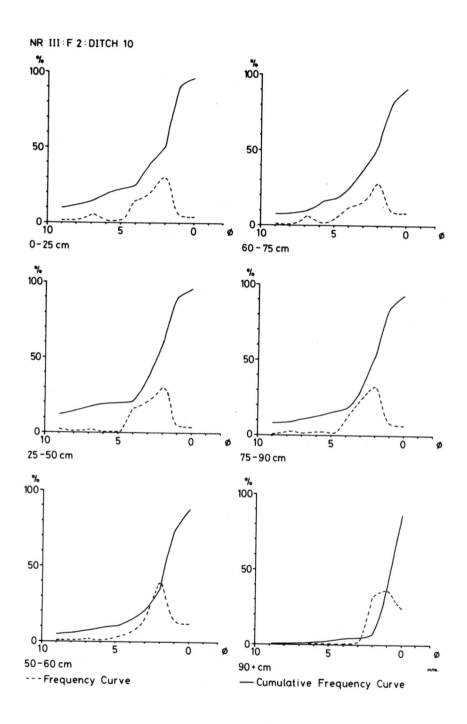

Fig. 99   Appendix 2: ditch 10, sand, silt and clay fractions.

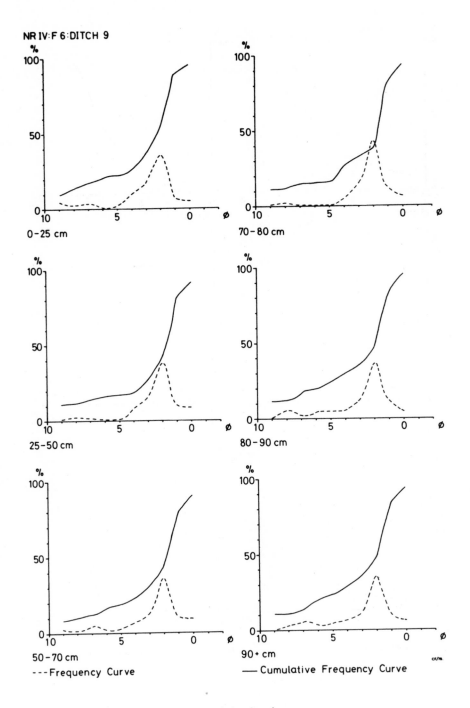

Fig. 100   Appendix 2: ditch 9, sand, silt and clay fractions.

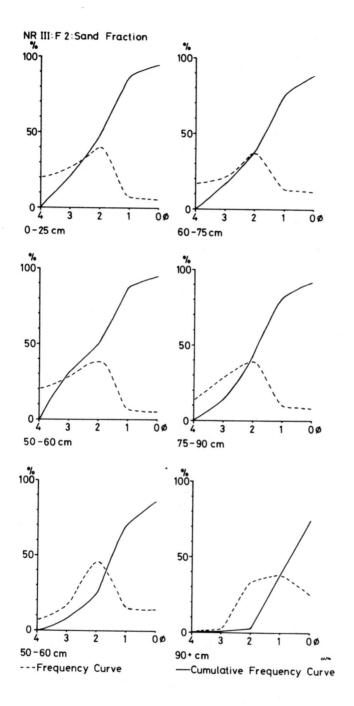

Fig. 101 Appendix 2: ditch 10, sand fraction.

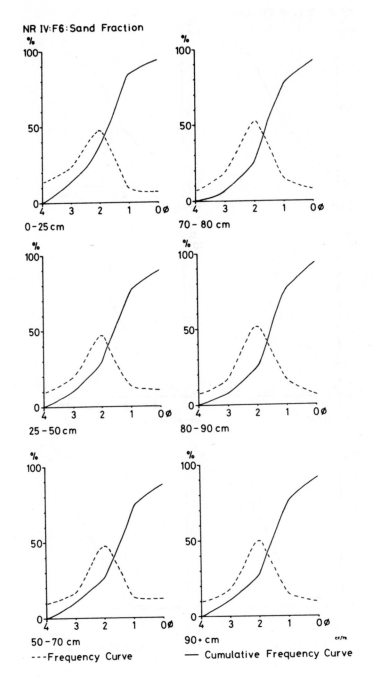

Fig. 102   Appendix 2: ditch 9, sand fraction.

196

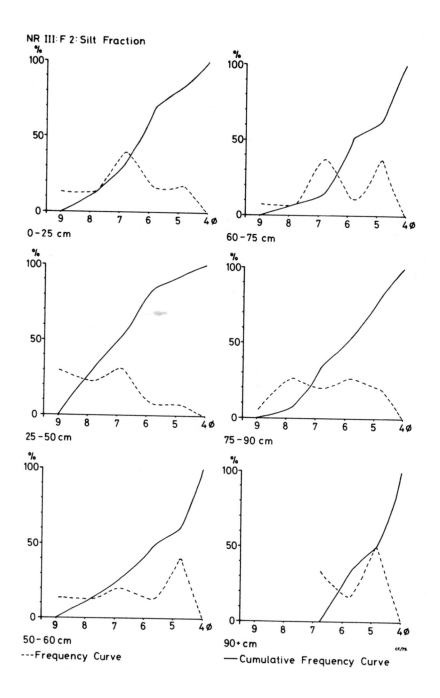

NR III: F 2: Silt Fraction

0 – 25 cm

25 – 50 cm

50 – 60 cm

60 – 75 cm

75 – 90 cm

90+ cm

---Frequency Curve

—Cumulative Frequency Curve

Fig. 103   Appendix 2: ditch 10, silt fraction.

197

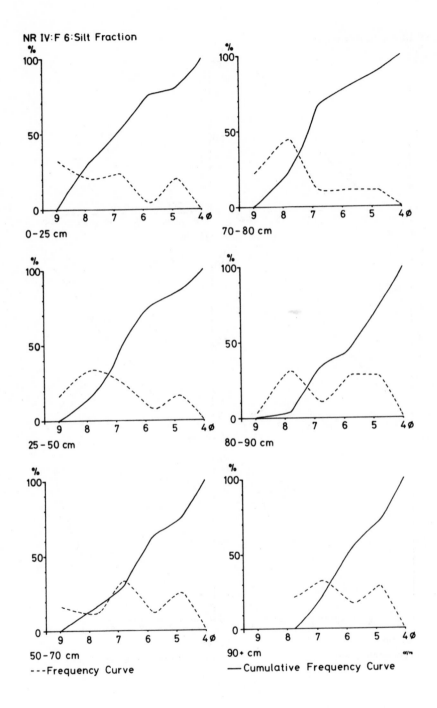

Fig. 104　　Appendix 2: ditch 9, silt fraction.

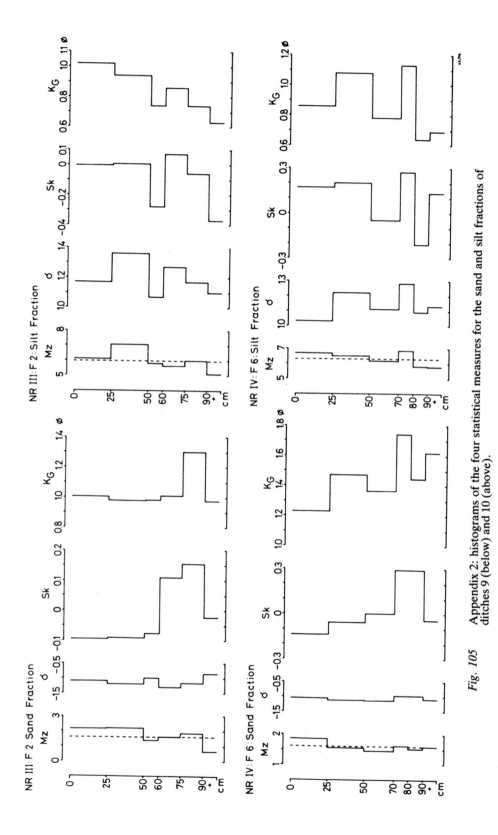

Fig. 105   Appendix 2: histograms of the four statistical measures for the sand and silt fractions of ditches 9 (below) and 10 (above).

199

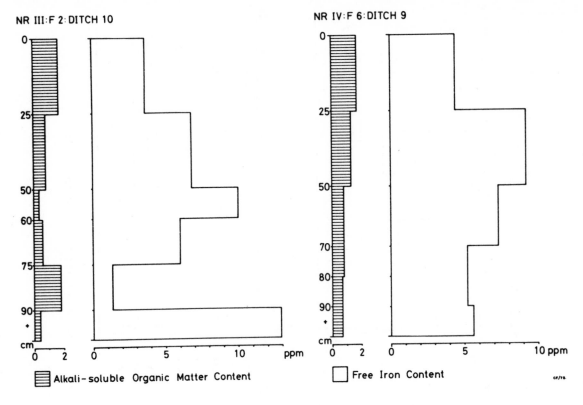

NR III:F 2:DITCH 10

NR IV:F 6:DITCH 9

▤ Alkali-soluble Organic Matter Content

☐ Free Iron Content

Fig. 106   Appendix 2: histograms showing alkali-soluble humus and free iron content.

The sand fraction is dominant throughout (FIGS 98-102) with a mean size of c 1.60 (FIG 105). Medium sand (1-20; 0.5-0.25mm) predominates, and fine sand (2-30; 0.25-0.125mm) is the next most commonly occurring size grade. The basal layer of both ditches contains a greater proportion of coarse sand (−1 −10; 2.0-0.5mm) than the overlying sediments. This is indicative of the initial rapid weathering of the ditches.

The statistical estimates (Folk and Ward 1957) were calculated separately for the sand and silt fractions (FIG 105), since the size distributions of the sediments were open-ended, in that they contained a proportion of unanalyzed fines. The sorting of the sand fraction is relatively uniform which suggests that the rate of infilling was relatively constant. There may, however, have been some sorting and mixing in the 'new' ditch environment. Below the 50cm level the skewness values suggest a considerable degree of environmental mixing (Folk 1966). The skewness values also indicate that there was an increasing amount of sand coarser than the sand mean size towards the base of the ditch. Leptokurtic kurtosis values occur in the lower secondary fill of ditch 10, and the primary and secondary fills of ditch 9. They imply that part of the sediment achieved its sorting elsewhere, and it was transported with its size character relatively unchanged into another environment, where it underwent mixing with another type of material (Folk and Ward 1957), in this case mainly gravel and sand.

The silt fraction, although much subordinate to the sand and gravel fractions, is a constant feature of the ditch fills (FIGS 98, 103 and 104). The mean size of the silt fraction is c 60, or the medium silt size grade, and the coarseness of the silt increases slightly with depth (FIG 105). The sorting is irregular, and worsens the finer the silt becomes (FIG 105). There may have been some sorting and mixing of the silt fraction in the 'new' ditch environment. In particular, the worst sorting occurs at the 70-80cm level in ditch 10, which corresponds to the highest skewness values and suggests that a zone of environmental mixing occurred in the lower secondary fill. The kurtosis values are mesokurtic and platykurtic, which suggests that there was little sorting of the silt fraction elsewhere, before its deposition. This implies that the silt was not transported any great distance.

The clay fraction is consistently present, but only as a minor component of the ditch fills. It may have been present naturally in the subsoil. There has been little clay formation *in situ*, but possibly some downward movement of clay in suspension through the profile from the overlying clay loam topsoil, although no clay skins were visible.

ALKALI-SOLUBLE HUMUS CONTENT

The alkali-soluble humus content was determined by using the sodium hydroxide and colorimeter method (Hesse 1971; Shackley 1975).

The humus content of the sediments of both ditches is consistently low (FIG 106). The slight increase in the humus content of the primary fill of ditch 10 is probably due to the natural accumulation of leaf litter and twigs in the ditch bottom. This may have aided the creation of waterlogged conditions in the ditch. This apparently did not occur, however, to any great extent in ditch 9. There is no evidence of any former turf lines to represent standstill horizons in the process of the infilling of the ditches.

FREE IRON CONTENT

The free iron was extracted using the dithionite and colorimeter method (Avery and Bascomb 1974).

The varying free iron content in both ditch profiles (FIG 106) is responsible for the orangey-brown colour of the sediments and the formation of iron-pan, especially on the bottom and sides of the ditches. Consequently, the ditches must have been subject to periods of drying-out. Furthermore, severe iron-pan formation in the ditch bottoms could have hindered their usefulness as drainage ditches, and could possibly have been a contributory cause of their abandonment. The increase in iron content at the 25-60cm level of ditch 10 and 25-50cm level of ditch 9 may suggest that the half-infilled ditches remained open for a time at the stage between secondary and tertiary fills, and may have been subject to a period of alternating dry and very damp conditions. Nevertheless, there is the possibility that the concentrations of iron may be post-depositional.

CONCLUSIONS

The dominant gravel and sand fractions of the sediments in the ditches indicate at least two local sources of infill material. First, their incorporation may have been caused by water-scouring of the ditch by slowly running water carried in the ditch and by run-off down the ditch sides. The former action was confined to the primary and lowermost secondary fill of ditch 10. Consequently the ditch became waterlogged, with its bottom and edges subject to iron-pan formation. On the other hand, the somewhat shallower ditch 9 was not so much affected by waterlogging.

The second source for the sand and gravel was from the ditch sides and edges, by frost weathering, exposure and gravitational forces. These sources were dominant throughout the period of deposition of the secondary fill in the ditches. Another source of material may have been from a possible adjacent bank. A second millennium ditch (10) and associated bank have been found in a sealed context of the Fourth Drove subsite (Chapter 3). Banks may once have been a common occurrence, but have since been destroyed by ploughing. There is, however, no evidence of any deliberate backfilling of the ditches.

There are three possible sources for the silt fraction. Most probably the silt was already present as a component of the subsoil. It may also have been derived from local wind-action and water run-off from exposed or broken ground. It is least probably derived from wind-blowing from the surrounding area. The silt fraction may have undergone some sorting by the action of the water carried in the ditch. The coarser silt, sand and gravel would tend to remain, whereas the finer silt and clay may have been subject to transport in suspension.

The phases of infilling of the ditches are suggested as follows:

1) The ditch bottoms were subject to the action of intermittent, slowly moving water. This may have contributed to the erosion of some sand and gravel, the sedimentation of the coarser silt, and the removal of the finer silt and clay in suspension. Sand and gravel also became incorporated into the ditches from the ditch sides and edges, and possible banks. There was the accumulation of some dead and decaying plant material. These components comprise the primary ditch fill (75-90+cm in ditch 10; 80-85cm in ditch 9).

2) Sand and gravel continued to infill the ditch quite rapidly, and dominate the secondary ditch fill (25-75cm in ditch 10; 25-80cm in ditch 9). Small silt and clay components also contribute to the ditch fills. This period of infilling may have undergone varying rates of deposition, with the faster phases corresponding to greater amounts of sand and gravel in the ditch sediments. The lowermost secondary fill was still subject to the influence of waterlogging.

3) This was followed by relative slowing in the rate of deposition probably caused by the increased stabilization of the ditch edges by vegetation. The gravel content decreases, and there is a slight increase in the silt component. These components comprise the lower tertiary fills of both ditches (0-25cm).

4) The upper part of the tertiary fills has been truncated and disrupted by modern ploughing and manuring, but has now stabilized and developed into a sandy to clay loam.

Both ditches thus underwent gradual and natural processes of infilling largely with locally derived sediments subsequent to their abandonment possibly in the 10th century BC. The evidence is insufficient to say that the waterlogging represents a change in ground-water regime severe enough to have caused the abandonment of the site. But intermittent freshwater flooding, of which there is evidence on the Fourth Drove subsite, may have been a contributing reason.

ACKNOWLEDGEMENTS

I would like to thank Professor G W Dimbleby, Dr K D Thomas and Mr P Taylor of the Institute of Archaeology for their help and advice in preparing this report.

APPENDIX 3

DESCRIPTION OF THE TERMS USED TO DESCRIBE THE MATRIX COMPOSITION OF FEATURE FILLINGS AT FENGATE

C A I French

1. THE FOUR MAJOR SEDIMENT TYPES

The US Dept of Agriculture classification of sediment particles has been used (USDA 1951).

Gravel
The gravel fraction consists of those particles greater than 2mm ($-1.0\,\emptyset$) in diameter. At Fengate, this fraction is composed of angular flints and pebbles mainly derived from the river gravel terrace on which the site is situated. The two size ranges commonly present are 2-10mm and 10-50mm. The percentage of gravel present in the topsoil varies from *c* 0% to 32%. The percentage of gravel present in the sediments infilling the archaeological features varies from *c* 0% to 83%.

Sand
The sand fraction consists of those particles between 2mm ($-1.0\,\emptyset$) and 0.063mm ($4.0\,\emptyset$) in diameter. There are three sand size grades: very coarse/coarse sand (2.0mm-0.5mm; $-1.0\,\emptyset$-$1.0\,\emptyset$); medium sand (0.5mm-0.25mm; $1.0\,\emptyset$-$2.0\,\emptyset$); and fine/very fine sand (0.25mm-0.063mm; $2.0\,\emptyset$-$4.0\,\emptyset$). The medium sand size grade is the dominant sand component of the sediments. The percentage of sand present in the topsoil varies from *c* 17%-61%. The percentage of sand present in the sediments infilling the archaeological features varies from *c* 21%-96%.

Sand and gravel are the two major components of the infilling sediments on the Newark Road, Fourth Drove and Cat's Water subsites at Fengate.

Silt
The silt fraction consists of those particles between 0.063mm ($4.0\,\emptyset$) and 0.002mm ($9.0\,\emptyset$) in diameter. There are three silt size grades: coarse silt (0.063mm-0.032mm; $4.0\,\emptyset$-*c* $5.0\,\emptyset$); medium silt (0.032mm-0.008mm; *c* $5.0\,\emptyset$-$7.0\,\emptyset$); and fine silt (0.008mm-0.002mm; *c* $7.0\,\emptyset$-$9.0\,\emptyset$). The medium/fine silt size grades are the dominant silt components of the sediments. The percentage of silt present in the topsoil varies from *c* 7%-39%. The percentage of silt present in the sediments infilling the archaeological features varies from *c* 3%-38%.

Silt is a relatively minor, but consistently occurring, component of the infilling sediments.

Clay
The clay fraction consists of those particles less than 0.002mm ($9.0\,\emptyset$) in diameter. It forms a minor component of the infilling sediments. The percentage of clay in the sediments infilling the archaeological features varies from *c* 0%-25%. The 'flood clay' which overlies many features and partially infills some of the Late Iron Age features on the Cat's Water subsite has a clay component of *c* 52%. The percentage of clay in the topsoil varies from *c* 17%-44%, and exhibits a well-developed blocky ped structure.

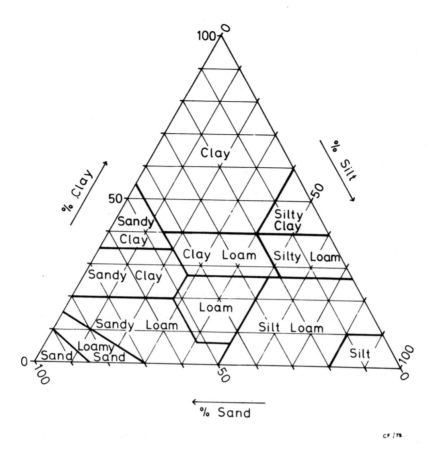

CF /78

Fig. 107   Appendix 3: soil texture triangle.

2. CORRELATIONS BETWEEN THE SITE RECORD (LAYER CARD) MATRIX DESCRIPTIONS AND THE TEXTURAL DESCRIPTIONS OBTAINED FROM THE SEDIMENT ANALYSES OF APPENDIX 2

The only major correlation required is for the term 'sand-silt'. It essentially equates with the terms 'sandy loam' and 'loamy sand'.

A descriptive term that was not used on the standard site layer cards was 'sandy clay loam', but was an uncommon occurrence. Otherwise, the descriptive terminology used for the matrix composition was satisfactory.

The major problem was the varying experience of the excavators in describing the feature infills correctly. But the general similarities of the sediments found in the archaeological features across the site made recognition easier, and enabled a good degree of consistency to be obtained.

The most common matrix types, as detailed in the sediment analysis, were loamy sand and sandy loam with varying gravel contents. This reflects the importance of locally derived sediments in determining the composition of the infilling deposits in the archaeological features. The silt and clay fractions were relatively minor in terms of percentage composition of the sediments, except in the topsoil and areas influenced by the 'flood clay'.

The character of the sediments was described using the triangular textural diagram (FIG 107). The textural descriptions and the percentage range of each fraction are given in Table 9. The size grades of the US Dept of Agriculture (1951) were used to differentiate the sediments, and the appropriate phi (θ) values were obtained from Page (1955). The key to the symbols used in the section drawings is given in Figure 10.

TABLE 9
TABLE 9
Textural Description of the Sediments at Fengate

Textural Description	% Sand Minimum/Maximum		% Silt Minimum/Maximum		% Clay Minimum/Maximum	
Clay	0	45	0	40	40	100
Sandy Clay	45	65	0	20	35	55
Silty Clay	0	20	40	60	40	60
Clay Loam	20	45	15	52	27	40
Sandy Clay Loam	45	80	0	28	20	35
Silty Clay Loam	0	20	40	72	27	40
Loam	25	52	28	50	7	27
Sandy Loam*	45	85	0	50	0	17
Silt Loam	0	50	50	88	0	27
Silt	0	20	80	100	0	15
Loamy Sand*	70	90	0	30	0	15
Sand*	85	100	0	15	0	10

(For convenience, the same textural descriptions have been used to describe the sediments as would be used for the description of soil types.)
*Sediment types commonly found in the infilling of archaeological features on the Newark Road and Cat's Water subsites at Fengate.

APPENDIX 4

AN ANALYSIS OF MOLLUSCS FROM TWO SECOND MILLENNIUM BC DITCHES AT THE NEWARK ROAD SUBSITE, FENGATE, PETERBOROUGH

C A I French

INTRODUCTION

Two series of samples were taken from the second millennium BC field system on the Newark Road subsite. On archaeological evidence, this field system was abandoned quite suddenly sometime after c 950-900 bc (Chapter 5). Thus, the time period represented by the molluscs in the infilling of the abandoned ditches is probably the early 1st millennium bc or the Late Bronze Age.

Five contiguous samples were taken from ditch 10 where it is intersected by the major N-S ditch b (which separates enclosures B and C; 62W/84N) (FIGS 19 and 108). These samples were analysed for land and freshwater snails (Table 10), and the results presented in the form of a relative histogram (FIG 110). It was hoped that the results of the analysis might reflect the ditch history, as well as, perhaps, that of enclosure B, and the large archaeologically sterile area to the north of ditch 10, just before and during abandonment.

Four contiguous samples were also taken from ditch 9, which is situated parallel and to the south of ditch 10, on the south side of enclosure C (39W/87N) (FIGS 19 and 108). These samples were also analysed for land and freshwater snails (Table 11), and the results presented in the form of a relative histogram (FIG 109). It was hoped that the analysis might reflect activities on the droveway between ditches 8 and 9, as well as in enclosure C, and give more information about the infilling processes of the ditches.

Enclosures B and C, and ditches 8, 9 and 10 are thought to be of one, more or less contemporary, system (Chapter 5). Thus, the results of the analyses may be comparable.

Ideally, the analysis of more ditch section profiles would have been valuable, but the two sections analysed were the only two sections excavated which provided sufficient numbers of molluscs to make any analysis worthwhile. The low molluscan abundance is probably due to insufficient upward movement of calcium carbonate from the terrace gravel subsoil into the ditch sediments. The soil reaction of pH of the sediments in the two ditches ranges from c pH 6.7 to c 8.5, and shows a general tendency to increase or

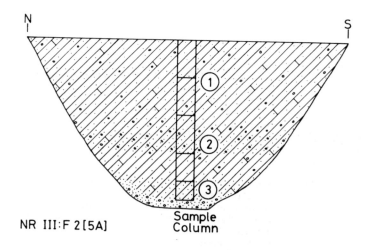

NR III:F 2 [5A]

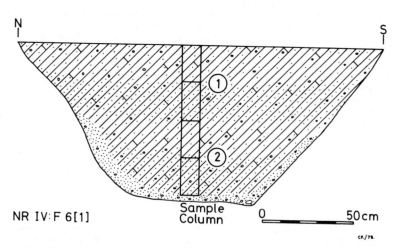

NR IV:F 6[1]

Sample Column

0   50cm

cr./71.

Fig. 108   Appendix 4: Newark Road subsite, sections through second millennium BC ditches showing location of sample columns for mollusc and sediment analyses (Ditch 10 at Grid 62W/84N and ditch 9 at Grid 39W/87N).

become more basic from the top to the base of the ditch profile (compare Appendix 7; also FNG 2, 170). Consequently, the preservation is better in the bottom half or so of the ditch fills. The increasing alkalinity of the soil towards the base of the ditches is probably due to the influence of alkaline ground water and the movement of bases down through the ditch fill by percolating rainwater.

THE PROFILES
    A section through ditch 10 (F2) showed the following stratigraphy after *c* 60cm of topsoil had been removed (FIG 108):

Depth below machined surface (cm)	Layers	
0-20 ⎫ 20-40 ⎭	(1)	Sandy loam (75%-79% sand*) with scattered gravel pebbles. 10YR 5/6.
40-60 ⎫ 60-75 ⎭	(2)	Sandy loam (75%-79% sand) with scattered gravel pebbles, with a zone of loamy sand (85% sand) at the 50-60cm level. Gravel content greatly increases from 50-75cm and may be deliberate back-fill. 10YR 5/4.

*The sediment analysis is discussed in detail in Appendix 2.

Depth below machined surface (cm)	Layers	
75-85	(3)	Loamy sand (82% sand) with high gravel pebble content containing much organic matter. 10YR 4/4.
85-90	(4)	Sand-gravel slip. 10 YR 5/4.
90+		Nene valley terrace gravel.

A section through ditch 9 (or F6) showed the following stratigraphy after *c* 60cm of topsoil had been removed (FIG 108).

Depth below machined surface (cm)	Layer	
0-20 } 20-40 }	(1)	Sandy loam (74% sand), which becomes a loamy sand with scattered gravel pebbles. 10YR 5/6.
40-60 } 60-80 }	(2)	Sandy loam (77% sand) which becomes a loamy sand (83% sand) with scattered gravel pebbles. There is some organic material at the base of the layer. 10YR 4/4.
80-85		Sand-gravel slip. 10YR 5/4.
85+		Nene valley terrace gravel.

The particle size analysis of the sediments in both ditches (Appendix 2) has helped to confirm both the uniformity of the deposits infilling the ditches and the similarity between the fills of the two ditches.

The primary fill of both ditches consists of sand-gravel slip from the ditch sides and edges, and the natural accumulation of organic material. The primary fill of ditch 10 (75-90cm) has remained waterlogged and anaerobic since its accumulation. Consequently, drainage was impeded and a semi-aquatic environment was created in the ditch. It is therefore rich in organic remains, whereas snails are few. The small numbers of snails suggest that they were accidentally incorporated, rather than being the remains of snails once living in the ditch, except the few freshwater species which had just begun to establish themselves. On the other hand, ditch 9 (F6), which is somewhat shallower, slightly farther inland from the Fens, was not so much affected. It therefore, contains little preserved organic material.

The secondary fill of both ditches consists largely of sandy loam to loamy sand sediments, which are dominated by sand. In ditch 10, the lower secondary fill (40-75cm) is still very much under the influence of local ground water and/or gently flowing or standing water, resulting from the abandonment and impedence of the ditch as a drain. In its upper secondary fill (20-40cm), this influence has almost disappeared. Thus, the snails contained in the secondary ditch fill may better reflect the ditch habitat than the adjacent areas. In ditch 9 the secondary fill (20-80cm) is little affected by waterlogging or even partial waterlogging. Consequently, the snails contained in this fill may be more indicative of the fields' enclosure adjacent to the ditch. But because the matrix is less basic and more subject to leaching, the abundance of molluscs falls quite rapidly towards the top of the profile.

Despite the presence of earthworms in these profiles today, their activity has apparently not been great enough to cause the creation of stone-free horizons. The small gravel pebbles are more or less randomly scattered throughout the ditch fills. It is suggested that the distinction between the layers in the ditch fills results merely from possible standstill phases in the process of infilling. Otherwise, the uniformity of the sand, silt and clay fractions in the ditch sediments suggests the quite rapid, more or less continuous and natural infilling of both ditches, although under the influence of a changing vegetational environment. However, the high gravel content (*c* 40%) at the base of layer 2 (50-75cm) and in layer 3 (75-85cm) in ditch 10 and the concentration of gravel towards the south side of the ditch, suggests that there may have been some deliberate infilling. Perhaps an adjacent bank was levelled out. This possible infilling does not appear to have been deliberately carried out along the whole length of the ditch.

The tertiary fills of both ditches (above 20cm) are devoid of molluscs. This is probably because of leaching, post-depositional weathering, conditions of relatively low pH (*c* 7.0) and possible disturbance by modern ploughing and the dumping of 'night soil' (Horton *et al* 1974).

MOLLUSCAN INTERPRETATION
Ditch 10 (F2)
Three ecological groups were recognised: one major group was comprised of freshwater species which were living in and around the water's edge within the ditch; a second major group was comprised of obligatory marsh species living just above the water's edge, and of other terrestrial species able to tolerate very damp and wet conditions; and a major group was comprised of 'woodland' terrestrial species, and of catholic or intermediate terrestrial species, perhaps living on the upper sides and edges of the ditch, and possibly also reflecting the adjacent environment on either side of the ditch.

The molluscs from the primary fill (75-85cm), although of low abundance for the reasons given above, are dominated by three freshwater species (35%), and *Vallonia costata* (23%). The former are

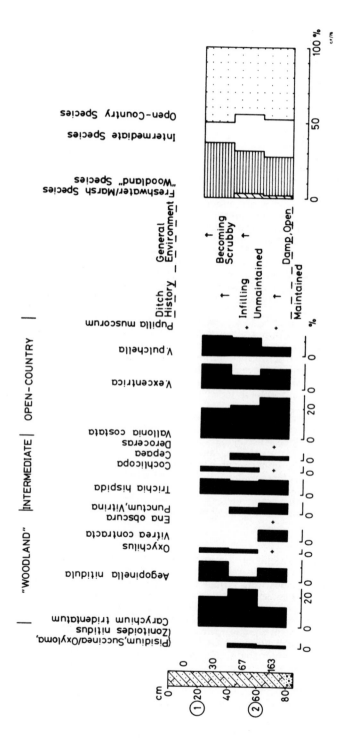

Fig. 109   Appendix 4: Newark Road subsite, Area IV, ditch 9 (F6), relative histogram of the molluscs.

207

probably living on the dead vegetation in the ditch base as it became waterlogged. Slow-moving water choked with vegetation is regarded as a poor habitat for freshwater snails (Boycott 1936). One must also allow sufficient time for the dispersal of freshwater species to the 'new' habitat locus. The presence and abundance of *Vallonia costata* may reflect two aspects of environment. First, despite commonly being found in an environment of short-turfed grassland in many Neolithic and Bronze Age sites in Britain, it may be found living in damp situations. It occurred in swamp carr and fen carr conditions at Wheatfen, Norfolk (Ellis 1941), and it may inhabit marsh and swamp environments (Evans 1972; Kerney *et al* 1964). Secondly, the presence of *Vallonia costata* may also be reflecting the mainly open, grassland environment of the adjacent enclosures which would have still obtained, given the archaeological interpretation that the enclosures had been used for winter pasture.

The composition of the molluscan assemblage found in the two samples taken from the lower secondary fill (60-75 and 40-60cm) is composed of representatives of three major ecological groups. Freshwater species comprise 59% and 44% respectively of the total assemblage. *Anisus vortex* (42% and 27%) is the predominant species, which favours hard, gently flowing water with some plants and weeds present at the water's edge (Boycott 1936). The two other freshwater species present, in much lower abundance, *Lymnaea stagnalis* and *Lymnaea peregra*, will tolerate similar water conditions to *Anisus vortex* such as, for example, water subject to stagnation.

Secondly, there is a small group of obligatory marsh species (6% and 7%) and a larger group of normally terrestrial species but which are able to tolerate wet and marshy conditions (19% and 26%). All of these live on vegetation above the water level and on either side of the ditch. *Succinea/Oxyloma* spp. and *Zonitoides nitidus* are obligatory marsh dwellers, and prefer open conditions (Boycott 1936). *Vallonia pulchella* (1.3% and 1.6%) is included in the group because it is one of several terrestrial species which, more often than not, may occur in marsh habitats (Evans 1972). Also included in this group are three land snails species — *Vallonia excentrica* (2% and 1.6%), *Vallonia costata* (9% and 17%) and *Carychium tridentatum* (7.5% and 6.5%), all of which may tolerate marshy habitats (Boycott 1934; Ellis 1941; Evans 1972). In particular, *Vallonia costata* exhibits a marked decline in abundance between two maxima (23% to 9% to 17%) in the lowermost secondary fill when the influence of slow-running water was most felt and the species' tolerance for wetness was surpassed. Its presence throughout suggests that the adjacent areas were quite open.

Thirdly, there is the group of terrestrial molluscs comprising 17.5% and 22% respectively, of the lower secondary fill assemblages. This includes six 'woodland' species (8% in both samples), with *Aegopinella nitidula* as the dominant species. Although none of them are restricted to 'woodland' *per se* they perhaps suggest unkempt, somewhat scrubby conditions on the ditch sides and edges. Numerous elderberry seeds found in the samples from the lower secondary fill suggest the presence of at least a few bushes nearby. There is also a group of six catholic or intermediate species (9.5% and 14%) all of which are tolerant of most terrestrial habitats, and probably indicate conditions similar to those suggested by the 'woodland' species.

Thus, the molluscs from the lower secondary fill of ditch 10 suggest that the ditch held some slow-moving water with some low vegetation on the ditch sides, and generally open but somewhat scrubby conditions on either side of the ditch. This vegetation resembles that of the unmaintained ditches and unkempt 'bush hedges' found around the site today and on the margins of Wicken Fen.

The molluscan assemblage from the upper secondary filling is dominated by terrestrial species (96%), to the almost complete exclusion of freshwater and obligatory marsh species. In particular, there is a marked increase in the abundance of *Carychium tridentatum* (35%) and *Trichia hispida* (16%), along with a general increase in abundance of the intermediate species group to 36.5%. This suggests a slowing down in the rate of infilling of the ditch, with damp, unkempt, somewhat scrubby vegetation on either side of the ditch.

Ditch 9 (F6)

The character and composition of the molluscan assemblage from the secondary fill of ditch 9 is much more limited than that of ditch 10. Due to the almost complete absence of freshwater and marsh-dwelling molluscs, the terrestrial genera and species were grouped according to convention into 'woodland' intermediate or catholic and open-country species. Furthermore, the assemblage is believed to reflect not only the environment of the ditch itself, but the adjacent surroundings.

Initially, the ditch may possibly have held some water, but apparently it never became sufficiently choked with organic matter to create a semi-aquatic environment, as occurred in ditch 10. Even if the ditch did hold water, a freshwater habitat did not exist for a sufficient period of time to allow the establishment of a community of freshwater snails. The few obligatory marsh dwellers present — *Succinea/Oxyloma* spp and *Zonitoides nitidus* — were probably living in and around puddles in the base of the ditch.

The genera and species present in the secondary ditch fill suggest an environment of damp, generally open, but rather unkempt and scrubby ground. *Carychium tridentatum* (13.5%, 25%, 20%) and the three

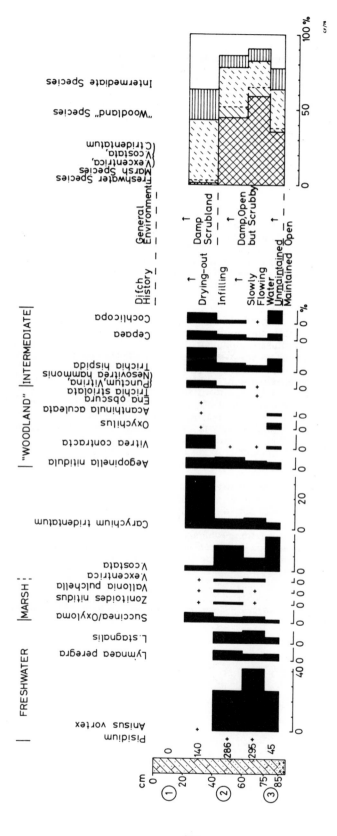

Fig 110   Appendix 4: Newark Road subsite, Area III, ditch 10 (F2): relative histogram of the molluscs.

species of *Vallonia* (47%, 43%, 50%) predominate. The former species favours undisturbed, sheltered and very humid habitats such as at the base of tall grass (Evans 1972). The three species of *Vallonia* suggest open, fairly damp, grass-covered ground. The predominance of *Vallonia costata*, and the occurrence of *Pupilla muscorum*, another open-country species, suggest that there was some unstable ground in the area, certainly on the ditch sides, and perhaps also on the adjacent 'droveway'.

Thus, one can visualize a ditch environment of a gradually infilling, and drying, ditch, with some grass and weed cover, and the occasional bush. Although the ditch no doubt served as a drain as well as an enclosure and droveway-demarcating ditch, it did not support a freshwater/marsh mollusc community, unlike ditch 10. The surrounding area, both in enclosures C and 3, was of largely open, but unmaintained, damp grassland, which possibly became more scrubby with time. The decrease in abundance of snails from the bottom to the top of the profile is probably due to a combination of post-depositional weathering and increased vertical distance from calcareous ground water, rather than impoverishment of the molluscan environment.

Fourth Drove Subsite

Samples were also taken from the Fourth Drove subsite (FIG 86). Molluscs (Table 12) were only preserved in a loamy sand with clay horizon (layer 3) sealed beneath the Roman Fen Causeway. This material also formed the tertiary fill of ditch 10. The molluscs suggest that it is a freshwater flooding horizon. Although this flooding horizon is not, apparently, continuous over the whole site, and it may only be generally dated to the 1st millennium BC, intermittent flooding of this kind may have been a contributory reason for the abandonment of the ditched enclosure system (see Chapter 5).

GENERAL IMPLICATIONS

Sometime after 950-900 bc ditch 10 ceased to be actively maintained. It became waterlogged, probably held slowly flowing water, and supported a marshy vegetation. The ditch waterlogging was probably due to a combination of the abandonment of the ditch and perhaps a localised 'ponding-up' of water in the deeper parts of the ditch system. What was once maintained winter pasture in enclosures A, B and C, to the south, became very unkempt, damp, open scrubland. In effect, the vegetation was gradually reverting to the natural fen-margin environment of fen carr. As the process of ditch infilling continued, the ditch environment became relatively dry, and was surrounded by a damp, more scrubby environment.

The molluscan evidence from ditch 10 is insufficient to postulate that all the ditches on the enclosure system became waterlogged. Nor is there sufficient evidence to suggest a locally higher water table. Nevertheless the increasing wetness associated with the 'climatic deterioration' of the first half of the first millennium BC, the formation of Whittlesey and Trundle Meres (Godwin and Vishnu-Mittre 1975) a few kilometres to the east, and/or a rise in sea level (Willis 1961) affecting the River Nene, which is tidal today to within *c* 6km of Fengate, may have been contributing reasons for the abandonment of the Bronze Age field system at Fengate.

Following the abandonment of the enclosure system, there was certainly localised waterlogging in some parts of the ditch system (as in ditch 10), while other lengths of ditch remained relatively dry (as in ditch 9). The molluscan evidence from both ditches suggests that they generally filled-in naturally, and quite rapidly, and provided a suitable molluscan habitat of wet, grassy-weedy vegetation with the occasional bush. There is, as yet, no definite evidence for the existence of hedges alongside the ditches and possibly upon banks, but the idea does not seem unreasonable. The once maintained open grassland enclosures between ditches 9 and 10 soon became unkempt, with a scrubby vegetation, following the abandonment of the ditch system.

ACKNOWLEDGEMENTS

I would like to thank Dr K D Thomas of the Institute of Archaeology for his help and advice in preparing this report.

TABLE 10
Newark Road subsite, Area III, molluscs from ditch 10

Dry weight . . . 2kg.

Depth below surface (cm.)	0-20	20-40	40-60	60-75	75-85
Carychium tridentatum (Risso)	—	49	19	22	2
Lymnaea stagnalis (Linnaeus)	—	—	23	30	2
L.peregra (müller)	—	—	19	13	2
Anisus vortex (Linnaeus)	—	2	82	128	12
Succinea/Oxyloma spp.	—	—	11	13	1
Cochlicopa lubrica (Müller)	—	—	1	1	—
C.lubricella (Porro)	—	—	—	—	1
Cochlicopa spp.	—	11	6	3	3
Acanthinula aculeata (Müller)	—	1	—	—	—
Vallonia costata (Müller)	—	5	51	28	10
V.pulchella (Müller)	—	2	5	4	—
V.excentrica Sterki	—	1	5	6	—
Ena obscura (Müller)	—	1	—	—	—
Cepaea spp.	—	9	11	5	2
Trichia striolata (C Pfeiffer)	—	—	—	4	—
Trichia hispida (Linnaeus)	—	24	17	13	4
Punctum pygmaeum (Draparnaud)	—	2	1	—	—
Vitrea contracta (Westerlund)	—	14	1	4	1
Oxychilus spp.	—	1	—	—	1
Nesovitrea hammonis (Ström)	—	2	2	1	—
Aegopinella nitidula (Drapernaud)	—	11	22	16	2
Zonitoides nitidus (Müller)	—	2	5	1	1
Vitrina pellucida (Müller)	—	3	2	1	—
Pisidium spp.	—	—	3	3	—

TABLE 11
Newark Road subsite, Area IV, molluscs from ditch 9

Dry weight . . . 2kg.

Depth below surface (cm.)	0-20	20-40	40-60	60-80
Carychium tridentatum (Risso)	—	6	17	22
Succinea/Oxyloma sp.	—	—	1	1
Cochlicopa spp.	—	1	2	2
Pupilla muscorum (Linnaeus)	—	—	1	1
Vallonia costata (Müller)	—	6	15	45
V.pulchella (Müller)	—	4	8	10
V.excentrica Sterki	—	5	6	22
Ena obscura (Müller)	—	—	—	2
Cepaea spp.	—	—	3	6
Trichia hispida (Linnaeus)	—	3	6	16
Punctum pygmaeum (Drapernaud)	—	—	—	2
Vitrea contracta (Westerlund)	—	—	—	5
Oxychilus spp.	—	1	2	1
Aegopinella nitidula (Drapernaud)	—	4	2	15
Zonitoides nitidus (Müller)	—	—	1	1
Vitrina pellucida (Müller)	—	—	3	10
Deroceras sp.	—	—	—	1
Pisidium sp.	—	—	—	1

TABLE 12
Fourth Drove subsite, Area VII, molluscs from ditch 10

Sample weight (kg.) . . . 1kg. Depth (cm.).	45-55	55-65	65-75
Succinea/Oxyloma spp.	—	31	—
Bithynia tentaculata (Linnaeus)	1	4	—
Lymnaea truncatula (Müller)	—	115	—
L.stagnalis (Linnaeus)	—	1	—
L.peregra (Müller)	—	11	—
Lymnaea spp.	—	2	—
Anisus leucostoma (Millet)	—	1	—
A.vortex (Linnaeus)	—	2	—
Bathyomphalus contortus (Linnaeus)	—	1	—
Gyraulus albus (Müller)	—	2	—
Hippeutis complanatus (Linnaeus)	—	14	—
Planorbarius corneus (Linnaeus)	—	7	—
Pisidium spp.	—	2	—

APPENDIX 5

A REPORT ON CHARCOAL FROM THE 'INDUSTRIAL AREA', NEWARK ROAD SUBSITE, DITCH 254

Maisie Taylor

Four bulk samples of one bucketful each were taken, and the charcoal was extracted by simple flotation in the field; as well as the pieces of charcoal which were retained by the sieves [⅛″ mesh] there was a much more finely divided material which was not retained. The samples considered here were taken from a section which was laid along the grid line 18W (FIG 45), but samples taken from other parts of the ditch, although not examined in such detail, showed very similar results.

Four samples were taken from the recut, layer 1, but it proved difficult to give precise depths because of the amount of limestone present. These samples produced 78gm of charcoal. Starting from the top of the deposit, and working down, the quantities of charcoal from each sample were as follows (in gm):

Sample 1 : 47
   2 : 17
   3 : 6
   4 : 8

The samples were then initially sorted under a low powered microscope to extract the *Quercus* sp (oak). The amount of oak present was unusually small:

Sample 1 : 2%)
   2 : 6%) (by weight)
   3 : 12.5%)
   4 : 33%)

Although samples 3 and 4 show higher proportions of oak, this is a distortion, as the samples were smaller and the oak consisted of one or two very large pieces.

The remaining charcoal was then examined under the microscope at x50 and x100 magnification. All the charcoal was in large pieces and extremely hard and undistorted, so that, except for Sample 4, the proportion of pieces that was unidentifiable was nil. In Sample 4 there were two large pieces which were knots and unidentifiable. These two pieces were 33% of the original sample by weight.

Two other points emerged from the closer examination of the samples. Firstly, a very high proportion of the material came from wood which had originally been from good-sized logs; there was very little twiggy material, and one or two pieces appeared to have come from large tree trunks. Other than these few pieces, however, most of the material seemed to have been derived from logs at least 200-300mm diameter.

The second point to emerge was that once the oak had been extracted from the sample, the remaining pieces were of a very limited number of species. Except for one piece of *Ilex* sp. (holly) from Sample 4, the rest of the sample formed two categories of almost equal size:

1. *Populus/Salix* sp (poplar/willow)
2. *Alnus/Corylus* sp (alder/hazel)

It was not possible to further narrow the identification of the poplar/willow group, which are notoriously difficult to separate (Godwin 1975, 282). Both are Fen species and would very likely have been growing close to the area where they were burned. Poplar is a very slow burning wood (Wilkinson 1973, 60) whereas willow, if well dried, makes a very good fuel which is nearly smokeless (Wilkinson 1973, 114). Presumably the two, if burned together, would make a satisfactory combination.

In the other group (alder/hazel), it was not possible to identify the pieces with more accuracy. No pieces were specifically identified as hazel, while several were definitely identified as alder. Certainly, bearing in mind the close proximity of the Fen, it would seem more likely that there would be a plentiful supply of alder. Hazel might well have been growing on the higher, limestone land behind the site and hazel nuts have been found on the site in other contexts. It is also important to note that hazel can grow to a good-sized tree even though it is usually only seen as a shrub today (Godwin 1975, 272). Hazel has been much used as a fuel, whereas alder is generally considered to be slow burning and poor as a fuel (Wilkinson 1973, 22 and 48). Finally, it will be recalled that although holly is barely represented in the samples, it is a very fine fuel wood, but it does not give off a great amount of heat (Wilkinson 1973, 53). Oak is well-known as an excellent fuel wood and oak charcoal has been extensively exploited in the past as a fuel (Wilkinson 1973, 55).

The proportion of the various species obtained and identified was as follows (percentage by weight):

	Sample 1 (47gm)	Sample 2 (17gm)	Sample 3 (6gm)	Sample 4 (8gm)
Quercus sp (oak)	2	6	12.5	33
Populus/Salix (poplar/willow)	49	47	43	17
Alnus/Corylus (alder/hazel)	49	47	44.5	16.5
Ilex (holly)	—	—	—	0.5
Unidentifiable	—	—	—	33
	100.0	100.0	100.0	100.0

The total percentages from the four samples were:

Quercus	13.4%
Populus/Salix	39.0%
Alnus/Corylus	39.2%
Remainder	8.4%

The author was not present when the original samples were taken and processed. In view of the fact that Fen species were so heavily represented it was decided to take a further sample as a control. A fifth bulk sample was taken from the same location and gently wet sieved through 1.7mm mesh. The charcoal thus recovered was divided into 100gm lots. Four of these were examined and were found not to deviate significantly from the relative proportions of Samples 1, 2, and 3. It was considered, therefore, that the above figures represent a reasonable picture of the species present and their relative proportions.

It is interesting to note that approximately a dozen very small (ie less then 6 x 4mm) burnt and unburnt flint flakes were found in each 100gm sample examined.

APPENDIX 6

THE SOIL PHOSPHATE SURVEY AT THE NEWARK ROAD SUBSITE, FENGATE.
Dr P T Craddock

INTRODUCTION

The practice of using the variation of the phosphate content of soil at archaeological sites as an indicator of the nature and degree of occupation is well established, especially in Scandinavia (Provan 1971). Food remains, bone, urine, and faeces are rich in phosphate which, unlike the other organic constituents of the products listed above, is relatively indestructable; thus a high local concentration of phosphate in the soil may be used as an indicator of occupation. Even in quite acid soils phosphate is only very slowly leached away. Dr M J Hughes of the British Museum Research Laboratory has developed a field technique primarily for use on the Museum's excavations at Grime's Graves (Sieveking *et al* 1973). Preliminary results there suggested little occupation and it was decided to carry out a similar survey of an area of another archaeological site known to be rich in prehistoric occupation. The Fengate area of

Peterborough was admirably suited for this purpose; an additional advantage of the site was that the excavations could be used to check any conclusions drawn from the phosphate survey. A phosphate survey of topsoil, the details of which are to be published separately, was accordingly done on the Cat's Water (Roman and Iron Age) subsite, and this resulted in the discovery of the large Iron Age settlement (Pryor and Cranstone 1978). Following the success of this operation, it was decided to extend the use of soil phosphate analysis beyond the determination of previously unknown sites to their interpretation, when excavated. The complexity of the series of fields and trackways at the Newark Road subsite suggested that they may have been used for cattle management over a long period of time (see main text). If this was the case, then one could expect the animals to have created along the droveway a bare muddy surface rich in phosphate, succinctly described in the Cornish expression 'a piss-mire'! Accordingly, a series of samples was taken from the excavated surface of the drove and from the bottom of the flanking ditches (FIG 111). Control samples were taken from the adjacent enclosures and from the section of the well, from top to bottom (FIG 21).

In one of the enclosures adjacent to the trackway, the circular drip gully of a house was found, linked to a series of small ditches around the enclosure (FIG 31). If the house had been occupied for any length of time then there should be a relatively high phosphate content in the soil in its immediate vicinity, and also in the adjacent ditches. To investigate this, samples were taken on a five metre grid over most of enclosure C, with 'controls' north of ditch 10 and south of ditch 8. In addition, approximately a hundred further samples were taken from the shallow ditches and gullies associated with the hut (FIG 112). The pH of the soil is between 5.5 and 6.5.

METHOD

Soil samples were collected from freshly excavated surfaces using a clean trowel. About twenty grammes were taken and stored in self-seal polythene bags. The phosphate content was estimated colorimetrically using the standard molybdenum blue method of Murphy and Riley (1962). Full details of the method are given in Sieveking *et al* (1973), and also in Hughes *et al* (1976). The phosphate was released from the subsoil by digestion with 2N hydrochloric acid in a water bath for 20 minutes. This releases most of the available phosphate but it must be stressed it does not give the total phosphate; further these soils were not dried or otherwise treated before analysis and thus the results are only semi-quantitative. However, the methods which were developed for use in the field do enable up to three hundred samples to be analysed per day. Also, since the aim is to identify areas of abnormally high available phosphate, such as might result from man's activities, the determination of total phosphate content is not strictly required. For these reasons individual figures expressed in the conventional manner, as mgm per 100gm of soil, are not quoted, only the limits within which the figures lie being presented (see FIGS 111 and 112).

Very valuable phosphate work using a much more precise method to separately determine the organic and inorganic phosphates is being undertaken elsewhere to answer questions of different land use (Eidt 1978). Our method, although only approximate, is, however, ideally suited to field conditions, and quickly provides results sufficiently accurate (and reproduceable) to answer the problems we are concerned with here.

DISCUSSION

The samples taken from the surface of the main E-W drove (between ditches 8 and 9) are considerably higher in phosphate than the corresponding samples from the surfaces of the surrounding enclosures (see FIG 111). Only five of the 135 field samples have more than 25mgm P per 100gm soil, and some have more than 50mgm P per 100gm soil, yet seventeen of the eighteen droveway samples have more than 25mgm P per 100gm soil, and three have more than 50mgm P per 100gm soil. Secondly, at nine places along the droveway a sample from the surface and the bottom of the ditches at each side was taken. In seven cases the average phosphate content of the ditches was lower than the trackway surface above them, which suggests the trackway surface was receiving phosphate which only slowly percolated into the ditch. This is borne out at two places (A and B on FIG 111) where samples were taken at several points from the edges of sections across the ditch. Both sections show a markedly high phosphate concentration on the side *towards* the droveway surface, suggesting phosphate was running in from the track surface. Other sections show uniform phosphate concentration horizontally, but increasing with depth (FIG 111 sections C, D and Well).

This evidence suggests that the droveway received much phosphate on its surface during its period of use and the most likely source of this phosphate was from animals.

The phosphate evidence for occupation in and around the two structures is also fairly strong (FIG 112). The circular drip gully of Structure 1 links up with a shallow ditch system which runs around the enclosure, except to the east where it is interrupted by an entranceway. The drip gully itself has only a moderate phosphate content (only one of the four samples having more than 25mgm P 100gm soil). This is understandable, as there is no reason why rain water pouring off the roof should be phosphate-rich. However, the rest of the gully, and small ditch system, have a phosphate content much higher than the immediately adjacent main drove ditches. Of the nineteen samples taken along ditch 9, thirteen

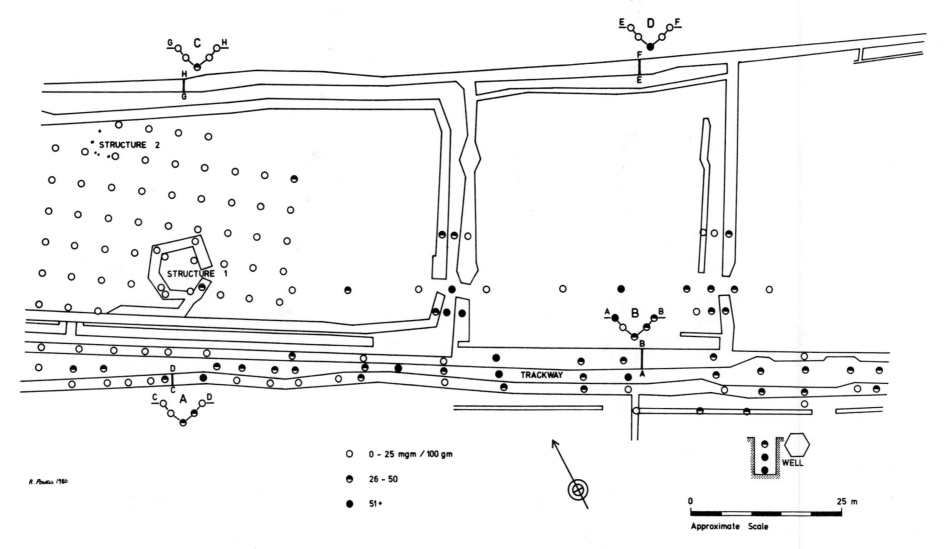

Fig. 111   Appendix 6: Newark Road subsite, Area IV, schematised ditch plan showing sample locations. Concentrations in mgm per 100gm of soil.

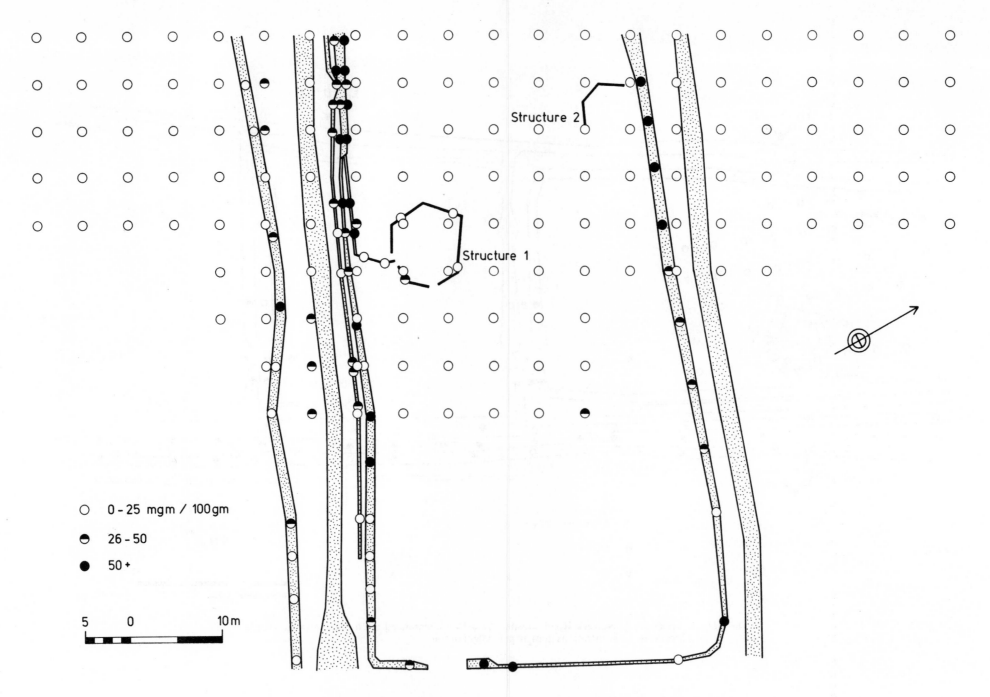

Fig. 112   Appendix 6: Newark Road subsite, Area IV, schematised plan of the settlement area, showing sample locations. Concentrations in mgm per 100gm of soil.

Structure 2

Structure 1

○ 0 - 25 mgm / 100gm

◐ 26 - 50

● 50 +

5   0   10 m

contained 25mgm (or under) P per 100gm soil; five were between 25 and 50, and only one was over 50mgm P per 100gm soil. By contrast, of the 53 samples taken from the shallow ditch system around the house, twelve contained 25mgm (or under) P per 100gm soil; twenty-one were between 25 and 50, and twenty samples were over 50mgm P per 100gm soil. Further, two thirds of the high values (including two over 100mgm P per 100gm soil) were from ditches of the western half of the enclosure, in the occupation area.

The two highest phosphate values of 180 and 250mgm P per 100gm soil lie immediately adjacent to Structure 2, and independently confirm its interpretation as a hut. The phosphate content of samples from around the two structures is no higher than that in other, presumably unoccupied, enclosures; this suggests that phosphate in these areas did not penetrate to the *subsoil* but was absorbed by grass and other plants, and that only the phosphate in the contaminated muddy water, which flowed into the shallow ditches, could be directly fixed in the soil. The high P values from the shallow ditches when compared with the enclosure surface samples (and indeed the main drove ditch samples), suggest that they silted up with phosphate-rich debris transported by surface water. The numerous recuts of the shallow ditch near Structure 1 suggest that much silting up was taking place during the occupation of the site. By contrast, the lower phosphate content of the main ditches suggests they were open for longer, and only silted up when occupation (and use of the trackway) had ceased; by this time there was little available soluble phosphate to wash into the ditch.

The Iron Age settlement at the Cat's Water subsite was also sampled, and there the phosphate content was generally much higher (from ditches and surfaces) than Newark Road (see FNG4, Appendix 4).

The archaeological evidence suggests that the Cat's Water settlement is a much more substantial occupation of longer duration (Pryor and Cranstone 1978) and this is confirmed by the greater build up of phosphate. It is also important to note that both the Iron Age settlement and the second millennium droveway had relatively high phosphate counts, probably due to extensive long term use; this would have removed grass and other plant cover, together with much topsoil, allowing the soluble phosphate to percolate directly into the subsoil and become fixed near the surface. The absence of surface phosphate in the vicinity of the two structures suggests the occupation there was of a much shorter and more ephemeral nature than on either the Iron Age site, or indeed, the droveway.

ACKNOWLEDGEMENTS

I wish to thank M J Hughes for discussions with him on all aspects of this work, and to Dawn Stevens for her help in taking and analysing the samples.

APPENDIX 7

ANIMAL BONES FROM THE SECOND MILLENNIUM DITCHES, NEWARK ROAD SUBSITE, FENGATE

Kathleen Biddick

1. INTRODUCTION

The bone sample discussed here was excavated during the seasons of 1974-77. The excavation methods are discussed in Appendix 1. No wet sieving control samples were taken in view of (a) practical difficulties (b) the secondary (and distorted) nature of the deposit and (c) the rarity of bone in the ditch fillings (compare FIGS 115-117). A rough control was provided by the dry sieving of half-metre 'control' sections of ditch through ¼" mesh screens.

It should be emphasised from the outset that the bone derived from naturally accumulated deposits of ditches that were open and in use for a millennium. This fact severely restricts the usefulness of the sample for comparative purposes; as in the case of the artifacts, it is not correct to talk of an *assemblage* of bone from Newark Road, in the sense of a closely associated group of material (see Chapter 2). Despite these major qualifications, the site is still important, and it has therefore been decided to present the data in greater detail than might, at first, appear necessary.

Observations on natural and cultural modifications to the bone were made on the 585 pieces which could be identified to species. When unidentifiable fragments had sufficient evidence of bone wall thickness and projected length, they were tentatively placed within a species size range. Remaining unidentifiable material was sieved into metric ranges (>20mm; >15mm; >10mm; >5mm) and weighed. Freshly broken identified pieces were glued together where possible. The degree of identification for the whole sample is difficult to quantify since the identified material was not weighed. In spite of methodological difficulties with the *Wiegemethode* (Casteel 1978), weighing was contemplated as a means of establishing the proportions of identified and unidentified material. The variable degree of iron-pan accretion precluded this, however.

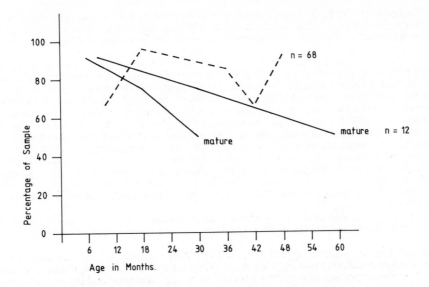

Fig. 113   Appendix 7: Newark Road subsite, cumulative percentage graphs of cattle age. Dashed line: epiphyseal data (from Table 16). Solid line: mandible data; top, 19th century (after Silver 1969); bottom, modern.

    Bone preservation was generally poor. Eighty-two measurements of soil pH were taken from the filling of linear ditches of Areas II, III and IV. These gave a median value of 7.93, a mean of 7.69 and a standard deviation of .67. This uniformly slightly base-rich soil pH is broadly similar to that observed on the Storey's Bar Road subsite (see FNG 2, Appendix 2) and may have been caused by modern lime-spreading (FNG 2, 170). Six percent (34) of the bone sample showed advanced weathering with exfoliation. Iron-pan accretion, common to this and most other Fengate subsites, affected 5% (29) of the bone over 50% of their surface area. The prevalence of iron-pan on both bone and artifacts argues for ancient soil acidity, either locally in ditch fillings, or over the site as a whole, of a higher order than that noted here (Limbrey 1975). The iron-pan encrustation influenced the visibility of gnawing, butchery and burning traces and often rendered pieces unmeasureable. Efforts to remove it chemically and physically were unsuccessful.

    Gnawing was observed on 7% (37) of the identified sample, and 90% (33) of these instances were judged to be carnivore traces (Miller 1969). Most of the gnawed bone was found in E-W ditches on either side of the Area IV settlement.

    Heat exposure was observed in 23 (4%) instances, ranging from partial carbonisation through various combinations and stages, to full calcination. Nine tentative observations of heat exposure were made on dental material. Only 4% of the total sample showed any evidence for heat exposure and 78% of these occurred on cranial and podial pieces. The distribution of heat affected material was similar to that of gnawed bone, ie near the Area IV settlement.

2. SPECIES IDENTIFICATION AND AGEING

    Bearing in mind the limitations of the collection, a few tentative observations may be offered.

A. Fragment Count

    Table 13 lists numbers and percentages of indentified bone fragments per species; this table also includes lists of species and fragment-size ranges, discussed above. Table 14 gives the skeletal elements counted to arrive at the totals given in Table 13. Cattle predominate the fragment count as they did the later Neolithic sample described by Mary Harman in the Second Report (FNG 2, Appendix 7). Although comparisons of the two subsites are of dubious worth, cattle form 75.5% of the Newark Road domestic animal collection (as opposed to 70% at Storey's Bar Road); perhaps more significantly, pig only form 5% of the Newark Road material (23% at Storey's Bar Road). Given the nature of the sample, further quantification of relative abundance of species through minimum number of individuals (Chaplin 1971) would be misleading.

B. Ageing

FIG 113 is a cumulative percentage graph of cattle epiphyseal fusion and mandibular tooth eruption and wear data presented in Tables 16-18. Both tables are based on modern standards suggested by Silver (1968). The sample size is small and the graph and tables should, accordingly, be treated with caution; this warning applies particularly to the mandibles where no index of internal wear association, based on variable states for M1, M2, M3 could be constructed from the sample. The data for pig and sheep are too inadequate for discussion or graphical display and fusion records are simply listed in Table 16.

Ideally, sexual distribution should be considered in conjunction with age profiles. This is impossible for the Newark Road sample. Only one pelvic fragment could be judged, on visual inspection, to be from a cow; the larger cattle metacarpal and horncore (Table 19) may be from a castrate.

C. Measurements

The collection of measurable material from Newark Road is tabulated in full in Table 19. The standardised measurements proposed by von den Driesch (1976) were employed. Withers height for cattle and sheep were calculated with the factors advocated by von den Driesch and Boessneck (1974). Dog, horse and pig material were too fragmentary to allow these calculations. A more summarised presentation was impossible as no element for any species has more than 10 values per measurement.

D. Butchering/Consumption and Distribution Patterns (FIGS 115-7)

Bone with clear evidence for butchering is too rare for detailed quantification and analysis. Indeed, even under the best of circumstances it is difficult to distinguish between butchery and consumption bone debris, and the sample size makes it impossible here. A few tentative observations on the butchery/consumption (hereafter referred to simply as 'butchery') debris, can, however, be attempted.

Butchery probably involved the breaking or smashing of long bones, as can be seen in the large number of shaft fragments, compared with the end (proximal and distal) fragments (Table 18) (Yellen 1977). This pattern should be considered in conjunction with Table 13 which expresses the effect of natural properties of element survival at work in the sample, namely those dependent on variability in bio-degradation of bone (Brain 1969; Binford and Bertram 1977). Only 24 butchery marks were observed, and 21 of these were on cattle bones. These observations are briefly recorded below.

Skull and mandible. Butchery marks were observed on 5 pieces of cranial and mandibular bone. The skull was removed by strong cleaving in the basioccipital area. The remains of a dull crushing mark in the nasal fragment probably resulted in the separation of the facial area from the rest of the skull to gain access to the brain. One to three sharp, heavy cuts occur laterally under the condyle of two mandibles.

Vertebrae and Ribs. Five light cut marks on the dorsal anterior surface of the atlas were probably made to loosen tendons prior to skull disarticulation. Sharp cuts on the neural spine of a thoracic vertebrae are problematic. Slicing away the slender muscles along the vertebral column after the rib section had been disarticulated might produce such a pattern. Alternatively the vertebral column could have been separated in this area. It is hard to see how this would produce a transverse cut. The treatment of the brisket cannot be reconstructed. Only one rib shaft fragment was marked with a fine cut.

Forelimb. No marks have been located on the scapulae. From its fragment distribution it is not clear whether it was chopped at the neck during forelimb removal, or if the flesh was freed from the upper quarter by chopping the lateral and medial tuberosities of the humerus. One piece with the glenoid fossa intact had been fractured while the bone was fresh, producing a spiral fracture pattern. Transverse cut marks located medially above the distal end of the humerus most probably refer to secondary flesh removal. A longitudinal spirally fractured medial fragment of a humerus also displays these fine flesh-removing marks. Two metacarpal fragments have transverse knick-like marks along the anterior surface. These are attributable to skinning(?).

Hindlimb. No butchering marks were located on the very fragmented femora pieces. Tibiae have high incidences of spiral fracturing and flaking along the fracture line. Other marks, classified as hack and chip marks, also located along the fracture lines, are thought to have been made during utilisation in the butchering process. The fracture pattern and impact marks along the fracture lines are being studied in detail (Biddick and Tomenchuk 1975). One metatarsal has fine cut-marks from skinning. The short, sharp marks in the proximal medial area of the astragalus were produced during severance of the tendons to permit the hind leg to relax.

Bone Distribution

Cranial, edible and podial fragments (Carter 1975) of cattle, sheep, pig and 'other' bones are plotted along the excavated sections of certain enclosure ditches (FIGS 115-7). The area illustrated is around the Area IV settlement, and it also includes a portion of ditch 10 to the east. The reader is reminded of the low density of bone finds when studying FIGS 115-7.

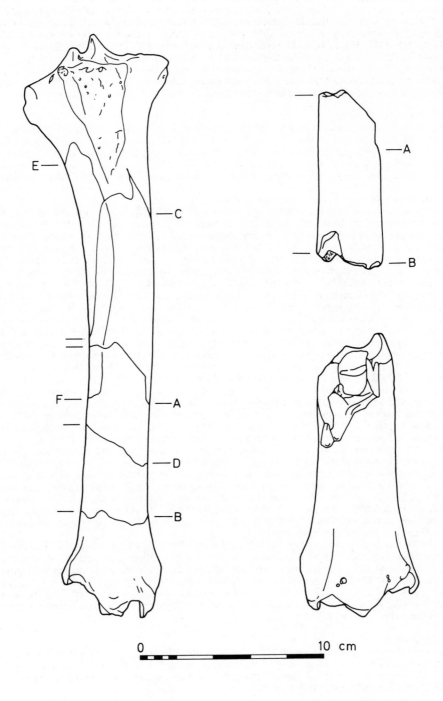

Fig. 114   Appendix 7: location of breaks on cattle tibiae with position of individual breaks shown on
the left.

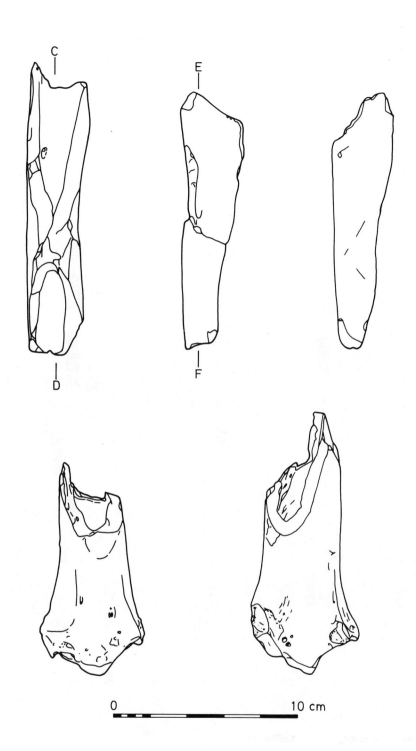

C

D

E

F

0   10 cm

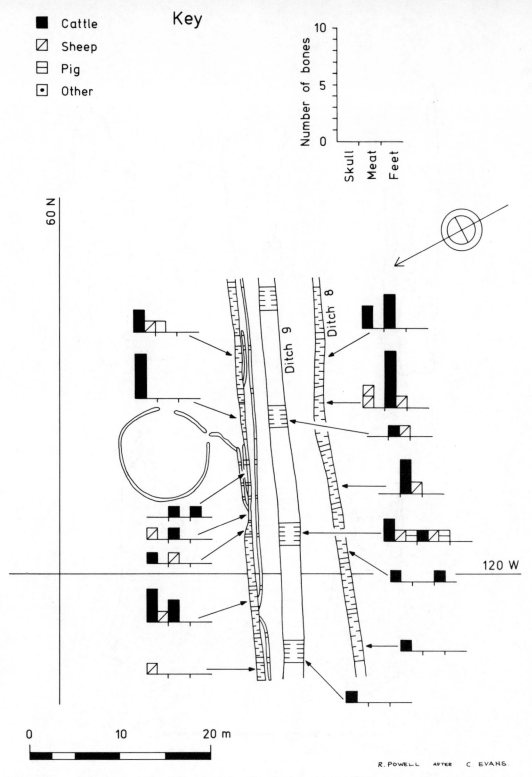

Key

- ■ Cattle
- ▨ Sheep
- ⊟ Pig
- ⊡ Other

Fig. 115 Appendix 7: Newark Road subsite: distribution of animal bones in some second millennium ditches.

R. POWELL AFTER C. EVANS.

222

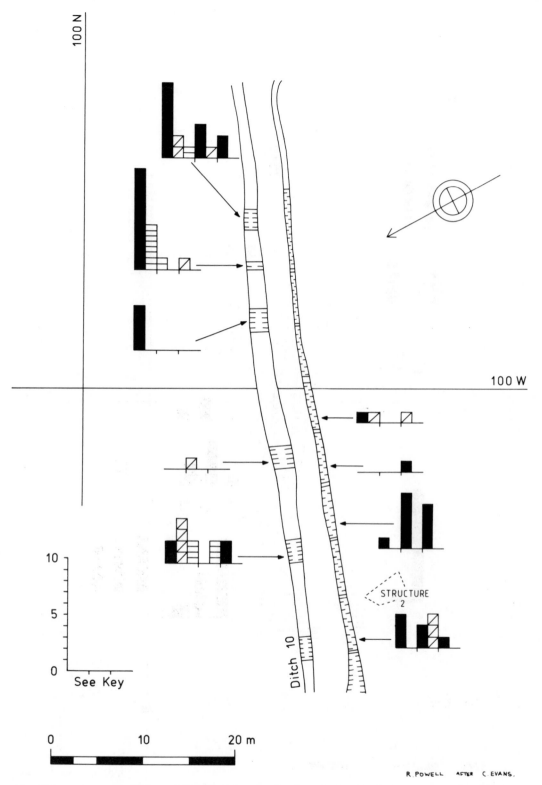

100 N

100 W

See Key

10

5

0

Ditch 10

STRUCTURE
2

0   10   20 m

R. POWELL   AFTER   C. EVANS.

Fig. 116   Appendix 7: Newark Road subsite: distribution of animal bones in some second millennium
ditches. For key to symbols used see FIG 115.

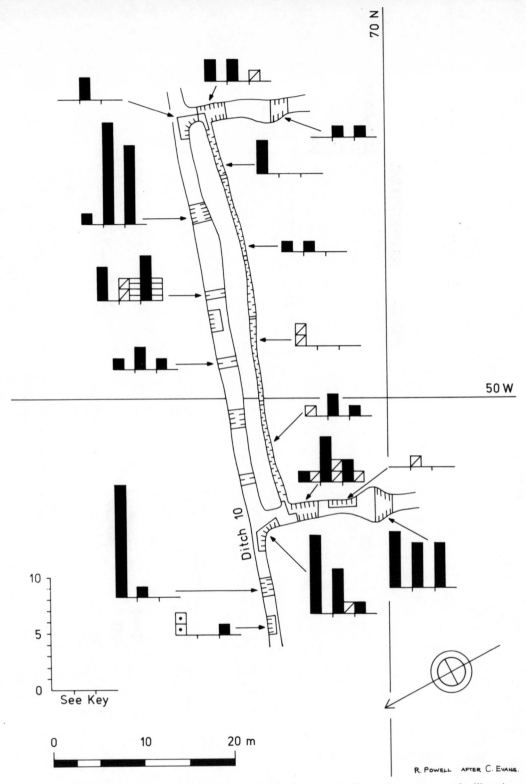

70 N

50 W

Ditch 10

10

5

0

See Key

0   10   20 m

R. POWELL AFTER C. EVANS.

Fig. 117   Appendix 7: Newark Road subsite: distribution of animal bones in some second millennium ditches. For key to symbols used see FIG 115.

224

Structures 1 and 2 are focal points for butchering activities. The association of species is highest here, and cranial and podial elements cluster in the vicinity of Structure 2. Long bone elements have a wide distribution. Secondary processing activities (marrow extraction?) have a southerly distribution towards ditch 8, a ditch which has a high incidence of fractured long bone fragments. Of the 37 observations of gnawing, 25 were on cattle bones (of which 88% were long bones). A second area where butchery and associated activities seem to have taken place is the NE corner of enclosure C and, perhaps, the NW corner of enclosure B (FIG 117). This area is marked by a predominance of cattle material; species diversity is low and cranial, edible and podial material occur together.

TABLE 13

Part 1: Bone fragments for each species, Newark Road

	total	%
dog (*Canis familiaris*)	12	2.1
horse (*Equus caballus*)	7	1.2
pig (*Sus domesticus*)	28	4.9
sheep/goat (*Ovis aries/ Capra hircus*)	108	18.8
cattle (*Bos taurus*)	420	73.0
Total domestic species	575	100.0
badger (*Meles meles*)	4	
wolf (Canis lupus)	1	
fox (Vulpes vulpes)	2	
red deer (*Cervus elaphus*)	2	
Total wild species	9	
bird *Anser* sp.	1	
unidentifiable fragments in ranges		
dog to sheep range	21	22.3
sheep to deer range	2	.2
sheep to cattle range	11	12.7
deer to cattle range	60	63.8
Total unidentified bone with assigned range	94	
unidentifiable bone: sieved and weighed		
.5cm	130gm	
1.0cm	460gm	
1.5cm	585gm	
2.0cm	1275gm	
	2450gm	

Table 13 (continued)

Part 2: Mean survivorship of anatomical elements: cattle and sheep, Newark Road

	Cattle		Sheep	
	MNI	%	MNI	%
skull	4.50	16.9	0	—
mandible	26.50	100.	3.50	100
vertebrae	1.30	4.9	.07	2.0
ribs	.38	1.4	.03	.85
scapula	3.50	13.2	1.00	28.5
humerus p.	1.50	5.6	0.50	14.2
humerus d.	5.00	18.8	1.00	28.5
radius p.	5.50	20.7	1.00	28.5
radius d.	2.00	7.5	0	—
MC p.	7.50	28.3	1.50	42.8
MC d.	3.0	11.3	.50	14.2
pelvis	8.0	30.1	3.50	100.
femur p.	2.0	7.5	0	—
femur d.	0.5	1.8	0	—
Tibia p.	2.5	9.4	0	—
Tibia d.	5.5	20.7	2.00	57.0
MT p.	3.5	13.2	1.00	28.5
MT d.	1.5	5.6	.50	14.2
astragalus	6.0	22.6	.50	14.2
calcaneus	4.5	16.9	.50	14.2
phalanges	0.37	1.3	0	—
		357.7		487.65
mean survival percentage		17%		23%

TABLE 14

Specification of the skeletal elements: totals and percentages

	dog *Canis familiaris* %	horse *Equus caballus* %	pig *Sus domesticus* %	sheep/goat *Ovis aries/ Capra hircus* %	cattle *Bos taurus* %	wolf *Canis lupus* %	red deer *Cervus elaphus* %	badger *Meles meles* %	fox *Vulpes vulpes* %
horn core	—	—	—	—	6 1.4	—		—	—
antler	—	—	—	—		—	1 100	—	—
skull	6 50	—	1 3.5	—	23 5.5	—	—	—	—
mandible	—	1 14.2	2 7.1	7 6.4	53 12.6	—	—	—	—
teeth	3 25	1 14.2	14 50.	40 37	85 20.2	—	—	—	—
vertebrae	2 16.6	—		2 1.8	34 8.1	—	—	—	—
ribs	—	—	1 3.5	2 1.8	10 2.4	—	—	—	—
scapula	—	—	2 7.1	2 1.8	7 1.6	—	—	—	—
humerus	—	—	1 3.5	7 6.4	27 6.4	—	—	1 25	—
radius	—	—		8 7.4	20 4.6	—	—	1 25	1 50
ulna	1 8	1 14.2	—	1 .9	8 1.9	—	—	—	1 50
pelvis	—	—	2 7.1	7 6.4	16 3.8	—	—	—	—
femur	—	1 14.2	1 3.5	2 1.8	17 3.9	—	—	1 25	—
tibia	—	2 28.5	—	16 14.8	28 6.5	1 100	—	1 25	—
carpals/ tarsals	—	—	2 7.1	—	25 5.9	—	—	—	—
metapodia	—	—	2 7.1	14 7.2	52 12.1	—	—	—	—
phalanges	—	1 14.2	—	—	9 2.1	—	—	—	—
other	—	1 14.2	—	—	—	—	—	—	—

226

TABLE 15

Proportions of parts of long bones present: Cattle

Part	humerus no	%	radius no	%	ulna no	%	MC no	%	femur no	%	tibia no	%	MT no	%
p. + 1/4	0	—	4	20	2	25	3	16	4	24	2	7	2	8
p. > 1/4	0	—	4	20	0	—	6	32	0	—	0	—	3	13
d. + 1/4	2	7	0	—	0	—	0	—	0	—	3	11	1	4
d. > 1/4	5	19	1	5	0	—	0	—	1	6	5	18	0	—
shaft < 50%	5	19	1	5	3	38	0	—	4	24	6	21	4	17
shaft > 50%	8	30	4	20	3	38	3	16	6	35	3	11	8	33
longi- tudinal 95%	4	15	3	15	0	—	1	5	2	12	6	21	3	13
complete 100%	3	11	3	15	0	—	3	16	0	—	3	11	2	8
complete	0	—	0	—	3	16	0	—	0	—	0	—	0	—
Totals:	27		20		8		19		17		28		24	

p = proximal
d = distal

TABLE 16

Epiphyseal Fusion Record: Newark Road

	Pig fused	unfused	Sheep fused	unfused	Cattle fused	unfused
scapula	—	—	1	—	2	—
pelvis	—	—	—	—	—	1
d. humerus	1	—	3	—	7	—
p. radius	—	—	1	1	8	—
1st phalanx	—	—	3	—	5	—
2nd phalanx	—	—	1	—	3	1
d. metacarpal	—	—	1*	—	4	3
d. tibia	1	—	2	1	9	—
d. metatarsal	—	—	1	1	4	—
olecranon	1	—	1	—	—	1
calcaneum	—	1	1	—	3	1
p. femur	—	—	—	—	2	2
d. radius	—	—	—	—	4	—
p. humerus	—	—	—	—	2	—
d. femur	—	—	—	—	3	—
p. tibia	—	—	1*	—	2	1
Total	3	1	16	3	58	10

* growth line visible

TABLE 17

Percentage of epiphyseal fusion for different age stages

Stage	Sheep fused	unfused	%	Stage	Cattle fused	unfused	%
6-10	1	0	100	7-10	2	1	66 2/3
10	4	1	80				
13-16	4	0	100	12-18	23	1	96
18-24	3	1	75				
20-28	1	1	50	24-36	17	3	85
30-36	2	0	100	36-42	5	4	56
36-42	1	0	100	42-48	11	1	92

TABLE 18

Tooth wear stages for mandibular cattle teeth (stages after Grant 1975, FIG 220) and mandibular sheep teeth (stages after Payne 1973)

Cattle Mandible	PM4	PM4	M1	M2	M3	Possible Age Stage	(Silver 1969)
1	d		b			5-6 months	
2			k	g		24-30 +	
3				b	erupt.	24-30	
4	j			b		24-30	
5			o	l		mature	
6		g	k	h	f	mature	
7				l	m	mature	
8	l		h	a		>15-18<24-30	
9	j		f	b	erupt.	24-30	
10	j		h	c		24-30	
11			k	k	j	mature	
12				g	b	24-30	

Loose teeth: Cattle	PM4	PM4	M1	M2	M3		
		h	erupt.	c(3x)	erupt.		
			j (2x)	d	d		
			k	e	f		
				k	h		
				o	j		
					k		

Sheep			M1	M2	M3		(Payne 1973)
1			h	f		stage E	
2			h	f		stage E	
3			h	d		stage E	
4					g	stage E	
5			h	k	j	stage E	

TABLE 19

Measurements (mm)[1] (after von den Driesch 1976)

Badger
  Humerus
    breadth distal   28.0
    breadth trochlea   14.5
    minimum width diaphysis   9.0
    breadth proximal   20.2
    depth proximal   24.3
  Ulna
    breadth process coronarii   8.8
    depth process anconeus   15.4
    minimum depth of olecranon   14.6
  Femur
    breadth proximal   26.7
    depth caput   12.4
  Tibia
    breadth proximal   22.7
    minimum width diaphysis   18.0
    breadth distal   19.1
    depth distal   12.0
    greatest length   110.0

[1]approximate measures appear in parentheses

TABLE 19 (continued)

Wolf
   Tibia
      breadth distal   26.9
      depth distal   20.6

Fox
   Humerus
      breadth distal   17.3
      breadth trochlea   13.2
      minimum width diaphysis 7.2

Dog

Skull	Ind.1	Ind.2
height occipital triangle	41.2	
skull height	58.2	
length molar row	18.2	
length P_4	18.1	16.9
breadth P_4	10.4	9.1
length M_1	12.1	10.1
breadth M_1	17.3	15.0
Mandible	12.2	
length P_4	12.2	
breadth P_4	7.6	
Ulna		
breadth process coronarii	12.3	

Horse
   Ulna
      breadth process coronarii 34.8
      depth process anconeus   51.4
      minimum depth olecranon 41.6
   Tibia
      minimum width diaphysis 32.1
      breadth distal   60.0
      depth distal   37.1
   Patella
      length greatest   58.0
      breadth greatest   54.0
      depth greatest   30.3

Pig

Mandible		
length molar row	66.7	
length M_3	32.9	33.6
breadth M_3	15.3	(15.8)
stage wear M_3	c	g
Humerus		
minimum width diaphysis	17.7	
Ulna		
breadth process coronarii	16.8	
depth process anconeus	29.4	
Tibia		
breadth distal	29.1	
depth distal	24.9	

TABLE 19 (continued)

Sheep/Goat
  Mandible

length tooth row	65.5				
length molar row	44.2				
length premolar row	21.0				
smallest height diastema	10.4				
height in front of M_1	18.3				
height behind M_3	(29.2)				
length M_3	18.0	21.0	21.9		
breadth M_3	(7.1)	7.7	8.7		
wear stage M_3	g	i	j		
Humerus					
breadth distal	25.8	30.1			
breadth trochlea	25.0				
minimum width diaphysis	12.4				
Radius					
breadth proximal	22.1	22.3	27.6		
minimum width shaft	12.4	12.1	15.6		
breadth proximal articular surface	26.9				
Ulna					
breadth process coronarii	16.4				
depth process anconeus	25.0				
minimum depth olecranon	20.5				
Metacarpal					
breadth proximal	20.2	21.0	18.3(juv.)		
depth proximal	15.5	15.4	14.0		
minimum width diaphysis		12.5			
breadth distal		22.9			
depth distal		14.5			
greatest length		125.0			
withers height (factor 4.85)		60.6			
Tibia					
minimum width diaphysis	12.0	12.7	13.6	14.3	
breadth distal	22.0		23.3		22.2
depth distal	16.5		18.2		17.9
Astragalus					
length lateral	26.5				
length medial	24.2				
depth lateral	14.4				
depth medial	15.6				
breadth caput	(16.6)				
Calcaneus					
greatest breadth	17.9				
Metatarsus					
breadth proximal	16.6	16.7			
depth proximal	16.7	17.7			
minimum width diaphysis			9.9		

Phalanx I				Phalanx II
breadth proximal	11.1	11.2	11.5	10.1
minimum width diaphysis	9.6	9.5	9.5	9.1
breadth distal		10.5	10.3	8.0
greatest length	31.7	32.5	32.2	20.8
depth proximal	(12.9)	(12.9)	(12.9)	11.5
smallest depth	8.4	8.5	8.2	9.7
depth distal		(9.6)	(10.1)	10.3

TABLE 19 (continued)

Cattle

Horn Core

greatest diameter base	41.0							
least diameter base	31.5							
basal circumference	111.7							
outer curvature	116.1							
inner curvature	(86.3)							

Atlas

width cranial	72.8
width caudal	71.8
greatest length	83.5

Axis

length corpus	90.8
width cranial	89.1

Teeth mandibular

length M_3	26.8	33.7	34.7	35.6	36.1	37.5	38.8
breadth M_3	15.8	13.5	14.3	15.9	15.3	12.9	16.8
wear stage	k	j	j	m	j	f	k

Scapula

smallest length collum	46.9	48.3	
greatest length process articularis	53.9	64.1	60.7
greatest length distal	60.9	53.1	56.6
breadth distal	45.0	46.7	42.3

Humerus

breadth distal	57.0	66.5	67.2	73.2	77.7	80.5		
breadth trochlea	53.3	56.5	65.3	65.0	70.7	71.4	59.4	
minimum width shaft		28.2		30.5	31.1	36.4		29.0
depth proximal				94.6	(95.0)			
length (from caput)				219.0	233.7			

Radius

breadth proximal	62.2	65.4	69.1	75.2	76.2	81.7		
minimum width diaphysis		30.7	37.1	37.0	37.6	44.0	33.0	41.2
breadth distal		(62.0)		68.0		75.2		
greatest length		238.0		270.0		299.0		

Ulna

breadth process coronarii	37.0	37.1	
depth process anconeus			58.2

Metacarpal

breadth proximal	(38.7)	46.2	47.4	50.4	50.6	51.3	54.2	64.5
depth proximal	27.3		29.0	30.6	29.0	32.1	32.7	39.1
minimum width diaphysis	26.7		27.0	28.3	28.7		29.5	
breadth distal			51.4				53.3	
greatest length			169.0				187.0	
withers height (factor 6,6.3)			(101.4-106.4)				112.2-117.8	

Metacarpal cont

minimum width shaft	27.0	
breadth distal		55.6

Pelvis

length acetabulum	55.0	59.1	64.7
breadth acetabulum	46.0	59.3	

Femur

breadth proximal	33.5				
depth caput	25.6	40.5			
minimum width diaphysis	13.1		27.1	29.0	29.5

Tibia

breadth proximal	79.6							
minimum width diaphysis	33.5	30.5	30.5	31.5	(33.9)	35.0	36.8	
breadth distal	55.9							50.7
depth distal	42.3							39.2
greatest length	308.0							

TABLE 19 (continued)

Tibia cont

breadth distal	56.8	62.5
depth distal	43.6	49.3

Astragalus

length lateral		50.5	57.3	57.9	58.7	60.0	60.0	61.0	62.2
length medial	52.1	54.1	54.9	50.6	54.1	54.5	58.3		55.1
depth lateral		34.7	31.5	39.3	32.7		34.8	35.5	36.0
depth medial	29.0		31.2	32.3	33.9	32.6	35.3		34.6
breadth caput	(38.4)	41.2	(34.8)	36.6	(37.6)			43.0	39.0

Calcaneus

greatest breadth	40.2

Metatarsus

breadth proximal	40.0	41.5	43.5				
depth proximal	36.2		34.4				
minimum width diaphysis	22.0		22.1	18.0	20.2	23.0	24.2

Phalanges

	I	I	I	I	II
breadth proximal	24.3	26.0	26.2	27.5	26.4
minimum width diaphysis	22.0	23.2	23.0	24.5	21.3
breadth distal	24.5	25.5		25.5	22.0
depth proximal			27.6		(27.5)
smallest depth	15.7	17.1	18.2		20.2
depth distal	(17.5)	(18.0)	20.1		

APPENDIX 8

A NOTE ON TWO HUMAN SKELETONS FROM DITCHES OF THE SECOND MILLENNIUM BC SYSTEM AT FENGATE

Calvin Wells

NOTE

This report went to press after the sad decease of Dr Wells who was unable therefore to correct proofs or comment on the few minor alterations suggested by the main author and Mrs Powell, who wrote the report on the other burial from the second millennium BC ditch system (Appendix 9).

1. INHUMATION FROM THE PADHOLME ROAD SUBSITE, AREA IX, DITCH 1 (PL 4; FIG 7 for location)

This consists of some exceedingly disintegrated remains of a lightly built skeleton. No cranial fragments are present but many post-cranial elements are identifiable. These include parts of clavicle, scapula, humerus, ulna, radius, metacarpals, femur, tibia, fibula, patella and calcaneus. All these are grossly fragmented and incomplete. A few doubtful scraps of vertebrae and other bones of hands and feet are present also. Virtually no firmly identifiable pelvic fragments survive.

There is very little which can be said about these remnants. All the long bones, including the clavicles, are very lightly built and slender. Their muscle markings are inconspicuous. These features, together with the small size of surviving articular elements make it almost certain that this was a woman. A fragment of right femoral shaft can be measured to give the Meric Index:

Fe D1	19.8
Fe D2	31.3
Index	63.2 (Hyperplatymeric)

Hyperplatymeria is common in archaic British material but its significance is still not well understood.

A length of femoral shaft has a weakly developed linea aspera and this, with its small circumference, suggests that this person had no great development of the thigh muscles. However, in comparison with what can be seen of the very slender upper limbs, the thighs and legs seem to be disproportionately sturdy.

Her age is extremely difficult to estimate. She was fully adult, but not enough survives to justify greater precision than this.

The absence of cranial fragments is interesting. Although the state of these remains is bad, enough post-cranial material survives from most parts of the body to suggest that parts of the skull would also have done so, unless it had been deliberately removed before the body was buried, or removed by subsequent recutting of the ditch.

2. INHUMATION FROM THE NEWARK ROAD SUBSITE, AREA II, DITCH F (FIG 27; PL 12)

This consists of a severely smashed skull, with the mandible in fairly good condition. Post cranial remains include: all vertebrae (damaged); about 60 fragments of ribs; the pelvis; all long bones; most bones of hands and feet; a few other scraps. All bones are damaged, defective and much eroded by soil action.

The sex of this skeleton is not easy to determine. It has the male features of moderately heavy mastoid processes, rather narrow sciatic notches, a somewhat rounded superior orbital margin and a steepish fall of the posterior part of the iliac crest. Other features, especially in the pelvis, are ambiguous. Others point much more strongly towards its being female. These include: negligible brow ridges, a small frontal sinus, very slender, straight clavicles, very small articular surfaces, eg scapula and long bones, and an overall gracility of the skeleton. On balance the evidence suggests that it was a female.

Her age is fairly narrowly determined by epiphyseal evidence as being about 20-23 years.

The skull is too smashed and defective to permit reliable reconstruction. The frontal bone, which is metopic, can be reconstructed to give a minimum frontal breadth (B') of 104.2mm and a maximum breadth (B") of about 128mm. These are both high values, and when some parietal fragments are tentatively added, a strong subjective impression is obtained of a broad, rather globular, skull.

Both zygomata survive and, though damaged, can be articulated cautiously with the frontal. When this is done the orbits appear to be unusually small with orbital breadth (0_1) close to 39.0mm and orbital height (0_2) about 30.6, giving an Orbital Index of 78.5. Cranial length is too uncertain to measure but the skull was almost certainly brachycranial.

The jaws are the best preserved part of the skeleton. They show the following dental state:

$$\begin{array}{c} \text{P} \\ 8\ 7\ 6\ 5\ 4\ 3\ 2\ 1\ \big|\ 1\ 2\ 3\ 4\ 5\ 6\ 7\ 8 \\ \hline 8\ 7\ 6\ 5\ 4\ 3\ 2\ 1\ \big|\ 1\ 2\ 3\ 4\ 5\ 6\ 7\ 8 \\ \text{C} \\ \text{P} \end{array}$$

P = periodontal abscess
C = caries

Dental attrition is very light with no exposure of dentine, except on the incisors, and little erosion of the cusp height except on the 1st molars. This is slightly greater on the right than the left. The very light attrition suggests that this woman's basic diet was fairly soft: perhaps she lived largely on milk, cheese, porridges and similar food, with fish rather than tough beef or mutton. The slightly greater attrition of her right molars may indicate that she occasionally chewed bones (and was right handed in the holding of them?). The disproportionate, but still slight, attrition of her incisors may indicate that she used these teeth as tools — to split or hold willow for basketry, thongs for leather work, etc.

Periodontal abscess cavities around the roots of 5⌋ and 6⌊. The mandibular one is presumably the result of a large caries cavity which is present interstially distally on the molar. Light deposits of tartar are present on most teeth. Enamel hypoplasia is present, but not severely, on the lateral incisors and canines. This indicates the occurrence of some illness or, perhaps, episode of malnutrition in early childhood. There is considerable overcrowding of the teeth in both jaws, especially in the mandible and in the region of 4̅3̅2̅1̅. This, to some extent, supports the above suggestion that she normally had a softish diet that was not functionally demanding.

The mandible was relatively narrow and, with her globular head, must have given this young woman a chin-pinched, elvish look.

The post-cranial skeleton is not well preserved and this limits what can be learned from it.
The following measurements were taken on the long bones (in mm):

	L	R
FeL1	—	438.2
FeD1	—	20.7
FeD2	—	31.2
Meric Index	—	66.3
TiDi	31.2	—
TiD2	21.3	—
Cnemic Index	68.2	—

This corresponds to a stature of about 1633mm (5ft 4¼ inches.). The Meric Index is hyperplatymeric; the Cnemic Index is mesocnemic. This combination, which is very common is early British material, indicates that the antero-posterior flattening of the femoral shaft is relatively greater than the side-to-side flatterning of the tibia. The significance of this is not fully known.

233

Other long bone lengths and articular diameters can be obtained with a considerable measure of uncertainty.

These limb bones are of moderately light build but muscle markings are fairly well developed, though not strong. They are more marked on the lower limbs than the arms.

Apart from the metopism there are no anatomical variants of any note. And apart from her dental disease there is no evidence of any pathology.

APPENDIX 9

A NOTE ON THE HUMAN SKELETON FROM A DITCH OF THE SECOND MILLENNIUM BC SYSTEM (CAT'S WATER SUBSITE)

F V H Powell

The inhumation described below was located in a shallow grave (F1594) at the north-east corner of the intersection of ditch 862 and ditch 2 in Area XI of the Cat's Water subsite at Grid 523W/515N (FIG 97). The condition and arrangement of the bones are described in detail in Chapter 4.

This was a disturbed crouched burial of an adolescent female of about 15 to 16 years. The sex was based on the slightness of the long bones and the wide angle of the sciatic notch, the presence of a pre-auricular sulcus, and the sub-pubic angle of the pelvis. The age was based on the presence of unfused epiphyses of the phalanges of the right hand; the presence of unfused epiphyses of the innominates; and the fused proximal epiphysis of the left femur but with an unfused distal epiphysis.

MEASUREMENTS: (in mm)

Left Humerus:	Minimum diameter of shaft — 13
	Maximum diameter of shaft — 19
Right Scapula:	Maximum Glenoid Fossa Breadth — 26
Right Ulna:	Height of Radial Facet — 11
Left Femur:	Anterior/posterior diameter — 22
	Transverse diameter — 29
	(Platymeric Index — 75.8)
	Maximum diameter of head — 42
Left Patella:	Maximum length — 37

APPENDIX 10

SOME BEAKER POTTERY FROM THE G WYMAN ABBOTT COLLECTION IN PETERBOROUGH MUSEUM

Alex M Gibson

The G Wyman Abbott collection of Beaker pottery at Peterborough comprises over 350 sherds, of varying sizes, of fine and rusticated wares, all of which have been drawn by the writer, except in the few cases where more than one sherd are demonstrably from the same vessel; in these cases only the most informative sherd, or sherds, have been drawn. All rims and bases have been illustrated, together with a representative collection of wall sherds.

The collection is the product of emergency salvage operations by Mr Wyman Abbott during gravel quarrying at Fengate, and as a result, stratigraphic details are usually missing (Abbott 1910). Numerous sites were explored during these operations, and the collection probably derives from several different settlements on the Fen-edge; but is has, unfortunately, been impossible to provenance the sherds more precisely than 'from Fengate', since the collection was already in a confused state when obtained by the museum. It is, however, known that some Beaker sherds were recovered from Williamson's Pits, but the actual sherds are unknown. The subject of this report, therefore, is a large, essentially unstratified collection of pottery from the Late Neolithic/Early Bronze Age transitional period, from roughly the same region on the Fen-edge.

As stated earlier, all the sherds have been drawn, but only a representative selection has been illustrated here due to lack of space. As can be seen from FIGS 121-127, the size of the sherds varies considerably from about 70mm square to little more than thumb-nail size, the average being about 30mm square. The fabric varies slightly in colour from buff through pink to light brown, only occasionally grey, on both surfaces; is unburnished, and sometimes has some slight grit protruding, as in the case of FIG 126, 17, FIG 127, 1, or else has a slightly pitted surface (FIG 125, 3). On the whole, however, the surfaces are smooth. The fabric itself is filled with medium-sized to finely-crushed shell which appears to be the only added tempering. Small amounts of natural flint, quartz, haematite and fossiliferous limestone are also visible in thin section but appear to have been already in the clay. The fabric is quite fine, hard, and well fired, and even the generally coarser rusticated pottery does not have large-sized grits and closely resembles the fine wares microscopically.

The fabric and appearance of all the sherds was very similar indeed, and the group is markedly homogeneous; this made the task of sorting the pottery into individual vessels virtually impossible. Some sorting was nevertheless attempted, but with success only in a very few instances, particularly among the rusticated sherds, where the fabric differences were still slight, but significant. In the latter instance, 25 or 30 vessels are thought to be represented. On the basis of the quantity of sherds, and in view of the way in which fine ware sherds greatly outnumber coarse ware rusticated sherds, an estimate of about 50 or 60 fine beakers would be conservatively indicated.

The bar graph (FIG 118) of formal traits present among the sherds shows that by far the most common are convex belly sherds, with convex neck and rim sherds following a close second and third respectively. There are 29 base sherds and a modest nine cordoned sherds and three sherds with both neck and belly traces. One sherd appears to be from a straight neck just below the rim, but the dotted lines imply that there may be more of these among the formally featureless sherds of which there are about 190.

A breakdown of the 36 rims on the second bar graph (FIG 119) shows that simple rounded rims are the most numerous, with inturned rounded rims and cordoned rims occurring the least frequently.

Few sherds are large enough to display more than two motifs so the diagram of frequency of motif combinations is significant. This diagram is read across: for example, cross hatching occurs on its own 97 times; fingernail impressions, twice with metoped decoration, and three times on its own. The motifs are not very varied, and on the whole fairly simple, the most elaborate being the metoped decoration (FIG 123,5), and the fine all-over decoration of FIG 124, 6. Excluding, temporarily, the rusticated sherds, most of the decoration is by impressed comb, fingernails are sometimes used, in the case of FIG 121, 7, and also fingertips (FIG 126, 16; 127, 7). Corded decoration is absent. The rusticated sherds are mainly fingernail decorated, with the decoration consisting of pinched, paired impressions (FIG 125, 15, 16; FIG 126, 4, 8). Single rows of fingernail impressions are also present (FIG 126, 3), and other rustication techniques include stabbing (FIG 126, 5, 9), cordons, and incision (FIG 126, 6). It is possible that FIG 126, 6 may be a sherd from a Food Vessel, but it would be unwise to make a positive identification in view of the minute size of the sherd.

The motifs used all fall into Clarke's Basic European, Southern British and Metoped or Panelled groups (groups 1, 4 and 5 respectively), the metoped decoration appearing to be Clarke's motif No 38 (Clarke 1970). In the Basic European group, motifs 1-5, and 7, are all included in the Fengate material, and in the Southern British group motifs 29, 32 and 34 are all employed. Despite the Basic European motifs present, there are few, if any, early Beakers in the group, the exception probably being FIG 124, 14 and FIG 125, 2, which are the only sherds that have zones of medium width, as well as early motifs. The rest of the sherds are late, and can be placed in Lanting and Van der Waals' (1972) steps Four or Five, on the slight evidence for accentuated necks and metopic decoration. The cylindrical neck and globular body of FIG 121, 1, and the two broad zones of decoration are even later features, and assign this vessel to step Six.

The sherds are unusual in that they do not show the amount of variation that is commonly found in Beaker pottery assemblages from domestic sites in the Fen area, where rusticated sherds are usually present in greater proportions, and where there is often some unclassifiable material among the pottery. With the exception of the rusticated ware (and even this is comparatively fine) and of a few large vessels, such as FIG 121, 7, and FIG 123, 5, all the Beaker pottery might pass for funerary material. No mention, however, is made of skeletal material being found with the Beakers, and although they were salvaged and not excavated *sensu stricto*, Abbott does mention animal bones. Under these circumstances it is likely that human bones would be noticed too. The broken nature of the pottery is also evidence in favour of the pits being receptacles for refuse of a domestic nature. It is, of course, possible that the pits had a 'ritual' function and that breaking the vessels was a part of the ritual (especially in view of the high percentage of fine wares).

Weathering, often a characteristic of domestic rubbish, has only affected a few sherds, and it seems probable that the material must have been covered up soon after breakage. Generally domestic sites produce a large proportion of abraded pottery. The Grooved Ware sherds from the recent excavation on the Storey's Bar Road subsite (FNG 2) are certainly abraded, but they had probably been on the surface for some time in antiquity. The pottery found by Abbott had been tidily dumped.

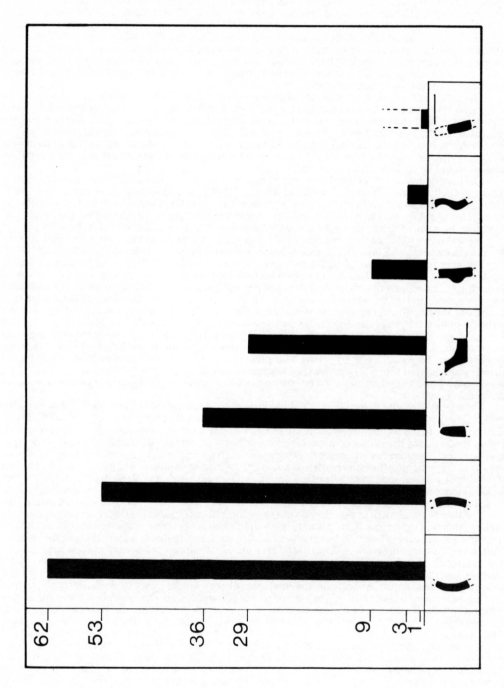

Fig. 118   Appendix 10: histogram showing frequency (in nos) of formal traits.

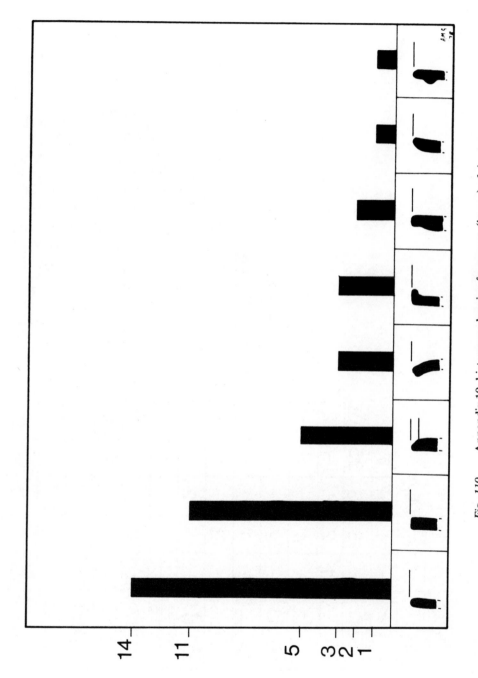

Fig. 119   Appendix 10: histogram showing frequency (in nos) of rim types.

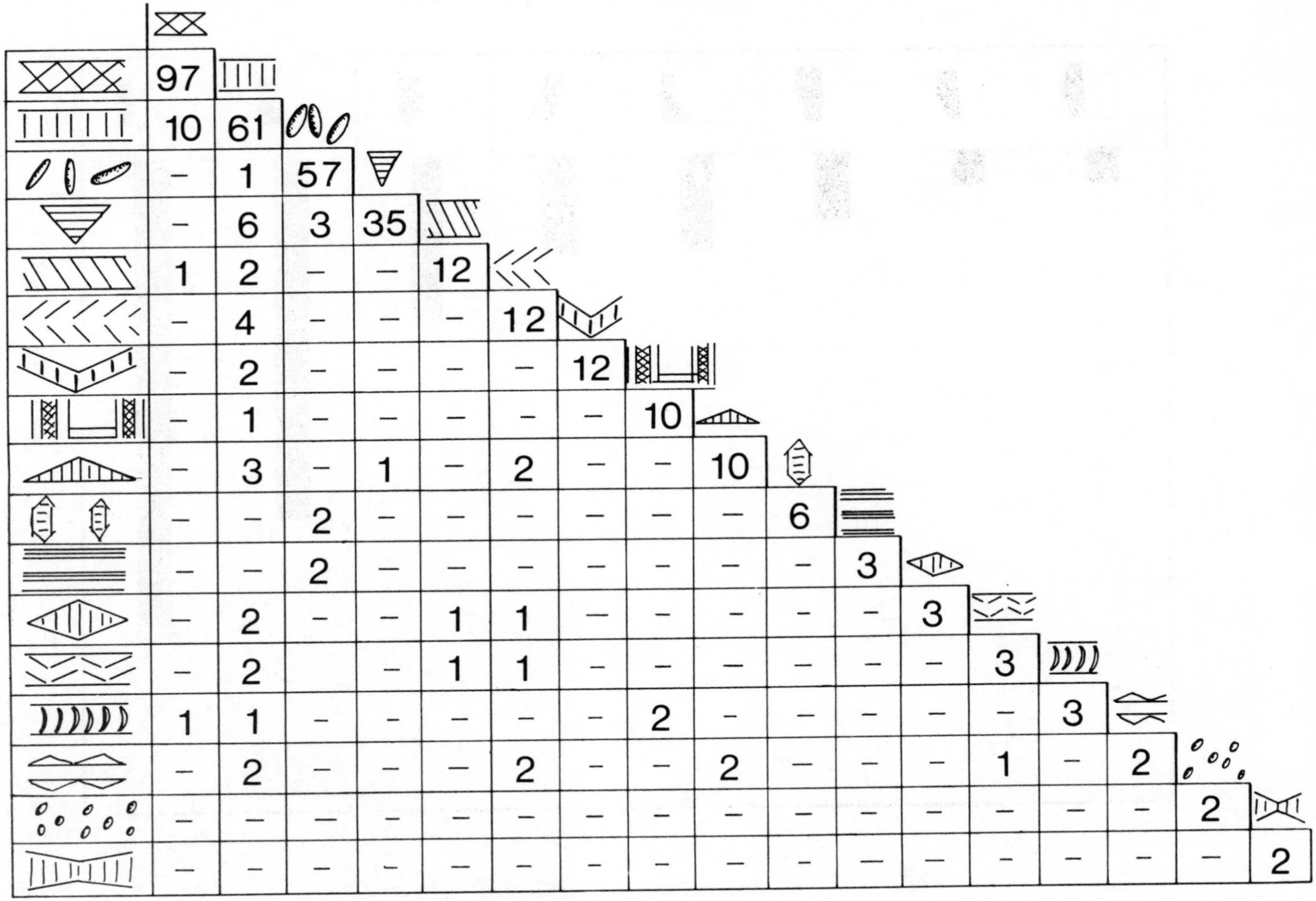

Fig. 120   Appendix 10: chart showing frequency of motif combinations.

238

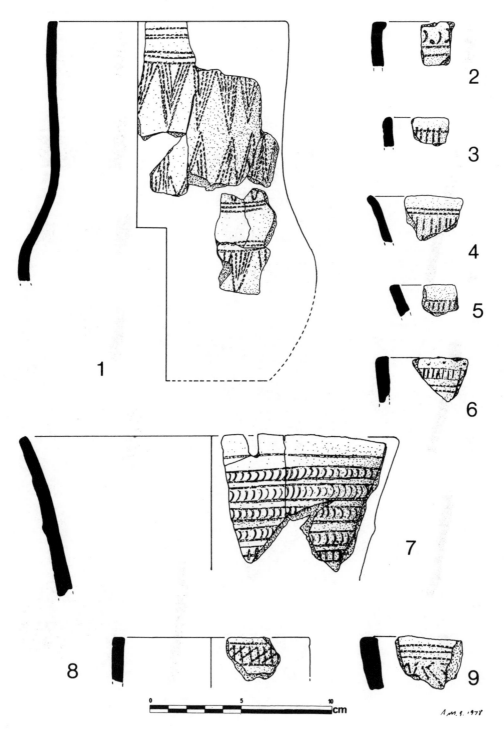

1

2

3

4

5

6

7

8

9

0   5   10
cm

A.M.S. 1978

Fig. 121   Appendix 10: Beaker pottery.

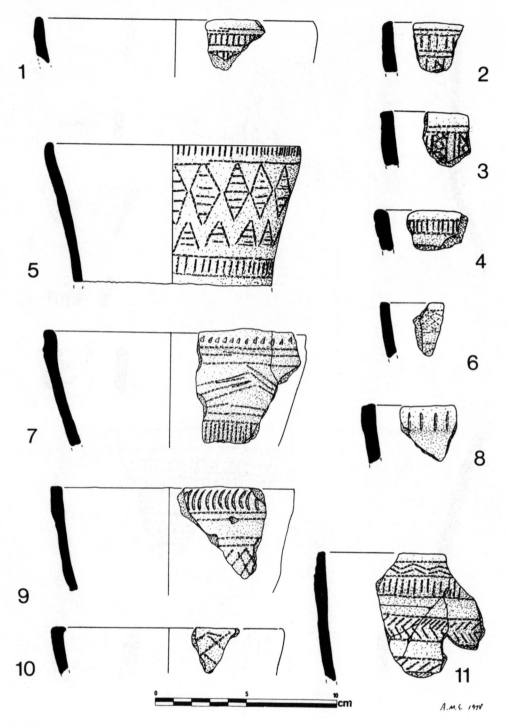

Fig. 122   Appendix 10: Beaker pottery.

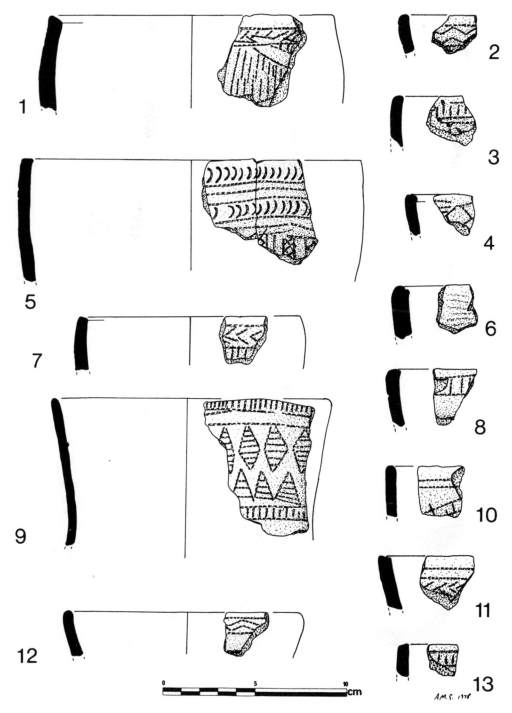

Fig. 123 Appendix 10: Beaker pottery.

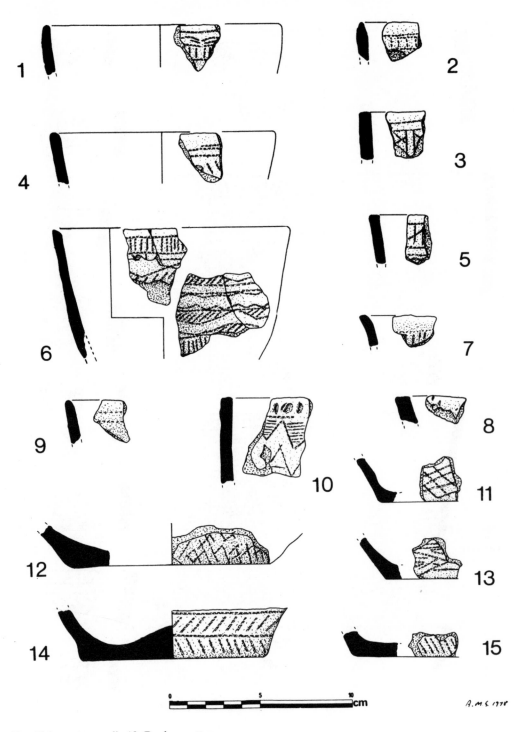

Fig. 124   Appendix 10: Beaker pottery.

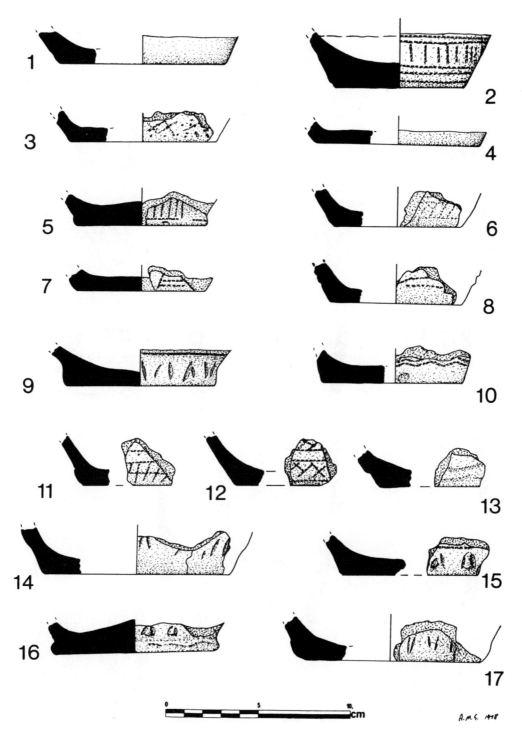

Fig. 125　　Appendix 10: Beaker pottery.

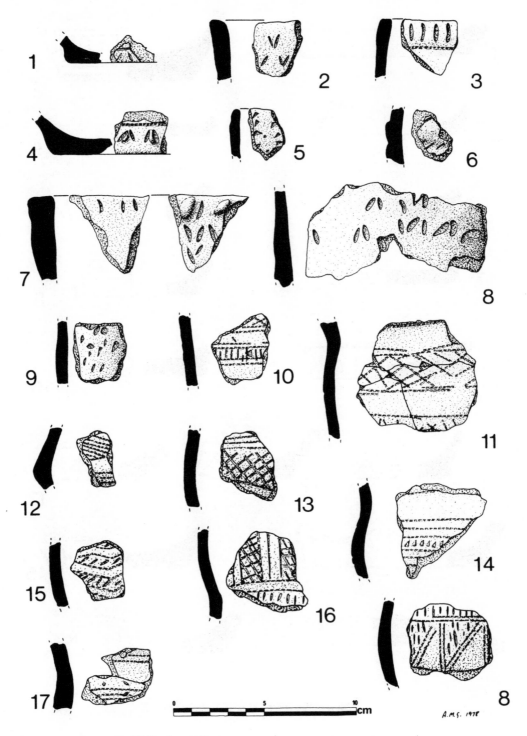

Fig. 126   Appendix 10: Beaker pottery.

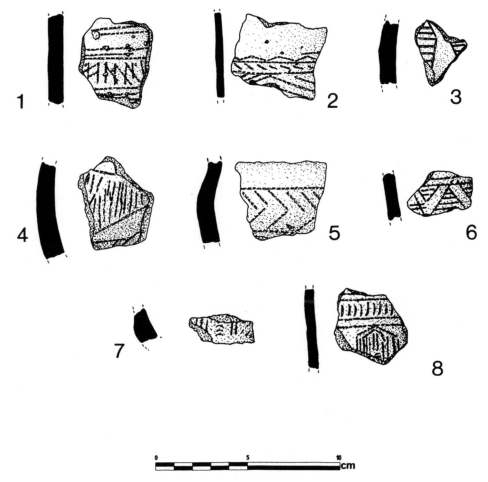

Fig. 127   Appendix 10: Beaker pottery.

This material compares favourably with that recently discovered at Fengate (Chapters 1 and 2, above) which is, if anything, in a slightly poorer condition than that in the museum; but this is probably due to more extensive weathering or different soil conditions. The rusticated pottery (FIG 60, 36) is rather more coarse than the Wyman Abbott material, and more typical of the coarse varieties of finger rusticated pottery which is common among Peterborough assemblages and often confused with the rusticated ware in Beaker fabrics, as seen, for example in FIG 50, 30.

ACKNOWLEDGEMENTS

I would like to thank Francis Pryor who gave me the idea of writing up this material and who allowed me to examine the recent material from Fengate: I also wish to thank Martin Howe (and his tube of glue) at Peterborough Museum for letting me borrow and play with the pottery. Ann Woods at Leicester University, Department of Archaeology, examined the thin sections, and was kind enough not to laugh at my early miserable attempts at fabric description.

APPENDIX 11

CONCORDANCE LIST OF FIELD AND PUBLICATION DITCH DESIGNATIONS

PADHOLME ROAD SUBSITE:

As Published	As Dug (see FNG 2: Appendix 11)
Ditch 1	FNG 71, Area IX, F2; FNG 71, Area X, F2.
Ditch 2	FNG 71, Area IX, F1; FNG 71, Area X, F1.
Ditch 3	FNG 71, Area II, F2; FNG 71, Area VII, F2; FNG 71; Area VIII, F2; FNG 72, Area I, F7; FNG 72, Area III, F3.
Ditch 4	FNG 71, Area II, F1; FNG 71, Area VII, F1.

Note Published and recorded Area numbers did not require alteration after the season of 1972 (FNG 2, Appendix 11).

NEWARK ROAD SUBSITE:

Areas I-VI only (Area VII numbers not changed):

Ditch 8	FNG 76, F7; FNG 74, F2; FNG 76, F359.
Ditch 9	FNG 76, F6; FNG 74, F3; FNG 76, F356; FNG 76, F357; FNG 76 358.
Ditch 10	FNG 76, F1; FNG 75, F2.
Ditch *a*	FNG 76, F2; FNG 75 1 (1-4); FNG 74, F56.
Ditch *b*	FNG 74, F55 (1-2); FNG 75, F7.
Ditch *c*	FNG 75, F8.
Ditch *d*	FNG 76, F320; FNG 76, F116.
Ditch *e*	FNG 74, F9 (1-5); FNG 75, F16.
Ditch *f*	FNG 74, F10 (1-5); FNG 75, F17.
Ditch *g*	FNG 76 no number (plan only).
Ditch *h*	As *g*, above.
Ditch *i*	FNG 74, F10 (5-10).
Ditch *j*	FNG 74, F4.
Ditch *k*	FNG 74, F9 (6-7).
Ditch *l*	FNG 74 no number (plan only).
Ditch *m*	FNG 74, F55 (4-5).
Ditch *n*	FNG 74, F56 (S3-13); FNG 76, F5.
Ditch *o*	FNG 74, F57; FNG 76, F109 (1-15).
Ditch *p*	FNG 76, F111.
Ditch *q*	FNG 76, F5 (10-15) and north.
Ditch *r*	FNG 76, F109.
Ditch *s*	FNG 74, F1 (S6-S10).
Ditch *t*	FNG 74, F5 (1-7).
Ditch *u*	FNG 74, F1 (1-6); FNG 76, F360 (1-Butt).
Ditch *v*	FNG 76, F361 (1-S2).
Ditch *w*	FNG 74, F6 (S2-1).
Ditch *x*	FNG 74, F6 (S3-6).
Ditch *y*	FNG 76, F379; FNG 76, F378.
Ditch *z*	FNG 74, F5 (8-9); FNG 76, F375 (1-5).

FOURTH DROVE SUBSITE:

Ditch 8 (E-W):	Area VII: F44, 26, 23, 22; Area XVI: F82; Area X: F60; Area V: F81; Area IV: F72, 73, 75; Area II: F10.
Ditch 9 (E-W):	Area VII: F24; Area XVI: F83; Area X: F61; Area V: F78; Area IV: F77.
Ditch 10 (E-W):	Area VII: F20; Areas XV-XII: F65; Areas II-III: F43.
Ditch *i*	Area X: F52.
Ditch *ii*	Area X: F53.
Ditch *iii*	Area I: F1; Area IV: F69.

CAT'S WATER SUBSITE (N-S):

Ditch 5	F115.
Ditch *iii*	F566, 537, 483, 815.
Ditch 3/4	F810, 838, 837, 836.
Ditch 3	F870, 912, 960.
Ditch 4	F860, 997, 905.
N-S ditches between	
Ditches 2 and 3	F836, 852, 862.
Ditch 2	F1591.
Ditch 1	F1592.

APPENDIX 12

RADIOCARBON DATES

The radiocarbon dates listed here include, for ease of reference, those samples which have been published in full in the first two reports (FNG 1, 38; FNG 2, 226-7). Dates are given using the 5568 half-life for carbon-14, as recommended in the journal *Radiocarbon*, and ± figures are to one standard deviation.

GaK-4196 Charcoal, 4960 ± 64 bp (*c* 3010 bc). Possibly residual charcoal from foundation trench of earlier Neolithic house (Padholme Road subsite, Area XIII, F39C). *See First Report.*

GaK-4197 Charcoal, 4395 ± 50 bp (*c* 2445 bc). From corner post of earlier Neolithic house (Padholme Road subsite, Area XIII, F59). *See First Report.*

GaK-4198 Wood from collapsed wattle lining of well, 2300 ± 46 bp (*c* 350 bc). Well had been backfilled with secondary rubbish including Iron Age scored pottery (FNG 1, FIGS 20-22) (Padholme Road subsite, Area XI, F3b, layer 5). *See First Report.*

HAR-397 Charcoal, 3980 ± 100 bp (*c* 2030 bc). From small pit in the Late Neolithic settlement, Storey's Bar Road subsite (B24). *See Second Report.*

HAR-398 Wood from collapsed (?) lining of well, 3000 ± 70 bp (*c* 1050 bc). Gives *terminus ante quem* for Late Neolithic settlement (Storey's Bar Road subsite, B3, layer 5). *See Second Report.*

HAR-399 Charcoal, 3970 ± 70 bp (*c* 2020 bc). From small pit in the Late Neolithic settlement, Storey's Bar Road subsite (B61). *See Second Report.*

HAR-400 Charcoal, 3410 ± 120 bp (*c* 1460 bc). Contents of Collared Urn from ring ditch enclosure, Storey's Bar Road subsite. *See Second Report.*

HAR-401 Charcoal, 3960 ± 90 bp (*c* 2010 bc). From pit in the Late Neolithic settlement, Storey's Bar Road subsite (Y4). *See Second Report.*

HAR-404 Charcoal, 3880 ± 80 bp (*c* 1930 bc). From small pit in the Late Neolithic settlement, Storey's Bar Road subsite (Y12). *See Second Report.*

HAR-406 Wood, from stake in bottom of large pit, 3290 ± 80 bp (*c* 1340 bc). Storey's Bar Road settlement (pit W17, layer 5). *See Second Report.*

HAR-407 Wood, twigs, 2670 ± 90 bp (*c* 720 bc). Storey's Bar Road settlement (pit W17, layer 5). *See Second Report.*

HAR-409 Charcoal, 3810 ± 150 bp (*c* 1860 bc). From small pit in the Late Neolithic settlement, Storey's Bar Road subsite (W32). *See Second Report.*

HAR-770 Charcoal, 4460 ± 130 bp (*c* 2510 bc). From small pit (P10) probably *not* associated with the main Storey's Bar Road Late Neolithic settlement. Small sample. *See Second Report.*

HAR-771 Charcoal, 3960 ± 70 bp (*c* 2010 bc). From small pit containing Grooved Ware, but probably *not* part of the main Storey's Bar Road Late Neolithic settlement (pit P59). *See Second Report.*

HAR-773 Charcoal, 2740 ± 80 bp (*c* 790 bc). From posthole cut into layer 1 of the second millennium BC ditch *e* (FIG 44: B); the charcoal is associated with the fresh sherds of pottery shown in FIG 61, no 39. *Newark Road subsite, Area II, F17, layer 1 (Grid 22W/63N).*

HAR-774 Charcoal, 3980 ± 100 bp (*c* 2030 bc). From small backfilled pit at NE corner of enclosure 3 and closely associated with rusticated potsherds in a possible variant of the Deverel-Rimbury tradition (FIG 60, nos 35-37). *Newark Road subsite, Area II, F37, layer 1 (Grid 33W/32N).*

HAR-775	Charcoal, 3120 ± 70 bp (c 1170 bc). From ditch n, c 22m E of Structure 1, in Newark Road Area IV. The sample came from layer 2 of the ditch at depth 0.50m, from a deposit very rich in charcoal and probably backfilled with debris derived from the settlement area to the W (see Appendix 6 for a discussion of the small ditches of enclosure C). *Newark Road subsite, Area II, ditch n, layer 2, depth 0.50m (Grid 81W/41N)*.
HAR-776	Charcoal, 3050 ± 80 bp (c 1100 bc). From ditch b near its butt-end, where layers 3 and 4 were exceptionally rich in charcoal, as in the case of HAR-775 (above), possibly derived from nearby settlement. The large amounts of charcoal would support such a hypothesis, but none of the material had been burnt in the ditch itself. *Newark Road subsite, Area II, ditch b, layers 3 and 4, depth below 1.05m (Grid 60W/59N)*.
HAR-777	Charcoal, 3550 ± 200 bp (c 1600 bc). Harwell notes that the small size of the sample accounts for the larger than normal standard deviation figure. As HAR-776 (above), but from layer 2. A similar source for this material would seem probable. *Newark Road subsite, Area II, layer 2, depth 0.30-1.05m (Grid 60W/59N)*.
HAR-778	Charcoal, 3780 ± 90 bp (c 1830 bc). This sample was taken from a number of locations in ditch 8, Newark Road subsite, Area II, from layers 1 and 2, depth below 0.20m. The charcoal derives from occupation debris which has slipped into the ditch during processes of natural weathering. It therefore provides a *terminus post quem* for the ditch's final period of use. *Newark Road subsite, Area II, ditch 8, layers 1 and 2, depth below 0.20m*.
HAR-779	Charcoal, 4190 ± 90 bp (c 2240 bc). This sample, like that above (HAR-776), was taken to provide a *terminus post quem*, but for ditches f and i. It was taken from charcoal from layers 1 and 2, below 0.20m. *Newark Road subsite, Area II, ditches f and i, layers 1 and 2, depth below 0.20m*.
HAR-780	Charcoal, 3850 ± 120 bp (c 1900 bc). This sample, which also included small twigs, was taken around (but not above), and immediately below, the crouched inhumation in Newark Road ditch f. *Newark Road subsite, Area II, ditch f, layers 3 and 4, depth below 0.85m (Grid 17W/59N)*.
HAR-781	Charcoal, 2940 ± 90 bp (c 990 bc). *Newark Road subsite, Area II, ditch 9, layer 1, depth 0.20-0.40m*. (Discussed below).
HAR-782	Charcoal, 2930 ± 80 bp (c 980 bc). *Newark Road subsite, Area II, ditch 9, layer 2, depth 0-20-0.55m*. (Discussed below).
HAR-783	Charcoal, 2990 ± 80 bp (c 1040 bc). *Newark Road subsite, Area II, ditch 9, layer 2, depth 0.20-0.70m*. (Discussed below).
HAR-784	Charcoal, 2990 ± 70 bp (c 1040 bc). *Newark Road subsite, Area II, ditch 9, layer 3, depth 0.55-0.90m*. (Discussed below).
HAR-785	Wood (twigs), 2890 ± 60 bp (c 940 bc). *Newark Road subsite, Area II, ditch 9 (at junction with ditch i at Grid 15W/45N), layer 4, depth below 0.85m*. (Discussed below).

The five dates listed immediately above (HAR nos 781-5), were all obtained from samples taken from ditch 9, directly south-west of enclosure B, between ditches i and the N-S length of ditch n. The samples were taken both to provide a *terminus post quem* for the last period of the ditch's use and to determine, if possible, whether the ditch had been substantially recut. Each of the four samples HAR-781 to -784 was taken from charcoal recovered from a separate ten metre length of ditch filling. Sample HAR-785 was taken from waterlogged twigs within layer 4 of ditch 9 at its junction with ditch i (see FIG 24). These twigs must have accumulated after the final substantial recutting of the ditch and therefore serve to date its latest period of use. The range of these five determinations (1040-940 bc, mean values; 1120-880 bc, at one standard deviation; 1200-820 bc, at two standard deviations) is surprisingly small, given the uncertainty of their stratigraphic context. They compare well with the more tightly stratified group of samples from the 'industrial area' (below, HAR nos 1970-1973).

HAR-786	Wood, 2800 ± 80 bp (c 850 bc). Twigs from waterlogged layer 5 of the large pit W17, of the Storey's Bar Road subsite. *See Second Report*.
HAR-1970	Charcoal, 2910 ± 70 bp (c 960 bc). From the 'industrial area': *Newark Road subsite, Area VII, F254, layer 1, depth 0.20-0.25m*. (Discussed below).
HAR-1971	Charcoal, 2980 ± 70 bp (c 1030 bc). From the 'industrial area': *Newark Road subsite, Area VII, F254, layer 1, depth 0.20-0.30m*. Samples taken from 3m of ditch E of HAR-1970. (Discussed below).
HAR-1972	Charcoal, 2950 ± 70 bp (c 1000 bc). From the 'industrial area': *Newark Road subsite, Area VII, F254, layer 1, depth 0.20-0.25m*. Same length of ditch as HAR-1971 (above). (Discussed below).

The three samples HAR-1970-71 were all taken from charcoal which derived from the filling of the recut layer 1 of ditch 254 in the 'industrial area' of Newark Road, Area VII. The charcoal is best seen as a by-product of the process, or processes, which involved the burning of limestone which, together with the charcoal, formed the bulk of this deposit. The three dates therefore provide a *terminus ante quem* for the use of the ditch prior to the final recut. The very narrow range of the three dates tends to support the hypothesis that the charcoal involved was the by-product of a specific, and perhaps short-lived, industrial activity. A larger range of dates might be expected if this material had derived from undisturbed or redeposited secondary settlement debris (compare, for example: HAR nos 397, 399, 401, 404 and 409).

UB-676   Charcoal, 3230 ± 70 bp (c 1280 bc). This sample was taken from a dense concentration of charcoal, animal bones, burnt stones etc at the *junction of ditch 3 and the N-S ditch F4 in Area VIII of the Padholme Road subsite* (see section, FIG 12, for location).

UB-677   Birch twigs, 2885 ± 135 bp (c 935 bc). From a waterlogged deposit in a well, or pit-like enlargement of ditch 1. *Padholme Road subsite, Area X, F4, layer 5* (see section, FIG 12, for location).

UB-822   Twigs, 2290 ± 125 bp (c 340 bc). From waterlogged wood in the bottom of a rock-cut pit or water-hole in the Early Iron Age settlement of the *Vicarage Farm subsite, Area I, F6, layer 4.* This pit produced the black burnished bowl with the wrapped wooden handle and other EIA pottery (FNG 1, FIG 14, 1-3, for pottery from layer 4). *See Second Report.*

BIBLIOGRAPHY

Abbott, G W,
    1910   The discovery of prehistoric pits at Peterborough, *Archaeologia*, 62, 332-52
Annable, F K, and Simpson, D D A,
    1964   *Guide catalogue of the Neolithic and Bronze Age collections in Devizes Museum*, Devizes, Wiltshire
Avery, B W, and Bascomb, C L, eds,
    1974   *Soil survey laboratory methods*, Soil Survey Technical Monograph No 6.
Baker, F T,
    1960   The Iron Age salt industry in Lincolnshire, *Lincolnshire Architectural and Archaeological Society Reports and Papers*, 8, 26-34
    1975   Salt making sites on the Lincolnshire coast before the Romans, in de Brisay and Evans 1975, 31-32
Bakker, J A *et al*
    1977   Hoogkarspel-Watertoren: towards a reconstruction of ecology and archaeology of an agrarian settlement of 1000 BC, in B L van Beek, R W Brandt and W Groenman van Waateringe (eds), *Ex Horreo*, 189-225, Amsterdam University.
Barrett, J C,
    1974   Four Bronze Age cremation cemeteries from Middlesex, *Transactions of the London and Middlesex Archaeological Society*, 24, 111-34
    1975   The later pottery: types, affinities, chronology and significance, in R J Bradley and A Ellison, *Ram's Hill*, 101-117, *British Archaeological Reports*, 19, Oxford
    1976   Deverel-Rimbury: problems of chronology and interpretation, in Burgess and Miket, 1976, 289-308
Biddick, K, and Tomechuk, J,
    1975   Quantifying continuous lesions and fractures on long bones, *Journal of Field Archaeology*, 2, 239-49

Binford, L, and Bertram, J,
    1977   Bone frequencies and attritional processes, in L Binford, (ed) *For theory building in archaeology,* 77-135, Seminar Press, London

Boserup, E,
    1965   *The conditions of agricultural growth*, Aldine, Chicago

Boycott, A E,
    1934   The habitats of land mollusca in Britain, *Journal of Ecology*, 22, 1-38
    1936   The habitats of freshwater mollusca in Britain, *Journal of Animal Ecology*, 5, 116-87

Bradley, R J,
    1970   The excavation of a Beaker settlement at Belle Tout, East Sussex, England, *Proceedings of the Prehistoric Society*, 36, 312-79
    1975a   The flint industry, in R J Bradley and A Ellison (eds), *Ram's Hill*, 83-7, *British Archaeological Reports*, 19, Oxford
    1975b   Salt and settlement in the Hampshire Sussex borderland, in de Brisay and Evans 1975, 20-25
    1978a   *The prehistoric settlement of Britain*, Routledge and Kegan Paul, London
    1978b   Prehistoric field systems in Britain and North-west Europe — a review of some recent work, *World Archaeology*, 9, 3, 265-80

Brain, C K,
    1969   The contributions of Namib Desert Hottentots to an understanding of australopithecine bone accumulations, *Scientific Papers of the Namib Desert Research Station*, 39, 13-22

Brewster, T C M,
    1963   *The excavation of Staple Howe*, Scarborough

British Standards,
    1969   *British standard 410, test sieves*

Bromwich, J I',
    1970   Freshwater flooding along the Fen Margins south of the Isle of Ely during the Roman Period, in Phillips 1970, 114-26

Brongers, J A, and Woltering, P J,
    1973   Prehistory in the Netherlands: an economic-technological approach, in *Berichten van de Rijksdienst voor het Oudheidkundig Bodermonderzoek*, 23, 7-47

Brown, F, and Taylor, C C,
    1978   Settlement and land use in Northamptonshire: a comparison between the Iron Age and the Middle Ages, in B W Cunliffe and R T Rowley, eds, *Lowland Iron Age communities in Europe*, 78-79, *British Archaeological Reports*, S48, Oxford

Browne, D M,
    1978   Roman Cambridgeshire, in J J Wilkes, and C R Elrington, eds, *Cambridge and the Isle of Ely*, Victoria County History, 7, London

Burgess, C B,
    1968   The later Bronze Age in the British Isles and North-western France, *Archaeological Journal*, 125, 1-45

Burgess, C B, Coombs, D, and Davies, D G,
           The Broadward Complex and barbed spearheads, in C B Burgess and F Lynch, eds, *Prehistoric man in Wales and the West*, 211-284, Bath

Burgess, C B, and Miket, R, eds
    1976   *Settlement and economy in the third and second millennia BC, British Archaeological Reports*, 33, Oxford

Burgess, C B, and Shennan, S J,
    1976   The Beaker phenomenon: some suggestions, in Burgess and Miket, 1976, 309-31

Burgess, C B, and Varndell, G,
    1978   Some notes on the chronology and development of collared urns, *Northumberland Archaeological Group Newsletter*, 2, 24-33

Butzer, K W,
    1978   Toward an integrated, contextual approach in archaeology: a personal view, *Journal of Archaeological Science*, 5, 191-93

Bunting, B T, and Campbell, J A,
    1976   *Pedology laboratory manual*, McMaster University, Hamilton

Calkin,
    1955   'Kimmeridge coal money:' the Romano British shale armlet industry, *Proceedings. Dorset Natural History and Archaeological Society*, 75, 45-71

Carter, H H,
1975   The animal bones, in R Bradley and A Ellison (eds), *Ram's Hill*, 118-22, *British Archaeological Reports*, 19, Oxford

Casteel, R W,
1978   Faunal asemblages and the 'Wiegemethode' or weight method, *Journal of Field Archaeology*, 5, 71-77

Caulfield, S,
1978   Neolithic fields: the Irish evidence, in H C Bowen, and P J Fowler, eds, *Early land allotment*, 137-43, *British Archaeological Reports*, 48, Oxford

Champion, T C,
1975   Britain in the European Iron Age, *Archaeologia Atlantica*, 1, 127-45

Cherry, J F, Gamble, C, and Shennan, S,
1978   *Sampling in contemporary British archaeology, British Archaeological Reports*, 50, Oxford

Chowne, P,
1977   Some recent finds of Bronze Age pottery from South Lincolnshire, *South Lincolnshire Archaeology*, 1, 24-25
1978   Billingborough Bronze Age settlement: an interim note, *Lincolnshire History and Archaeology*, 13, 15-24

Clarke, J G D,
1932   The curved flint sickle blades of Britain, *Proceedings of the Prehistoric Society of East Anglia*, 7, 67-81
1933   Report on an Early Bronze Age site in the South-Eastern Fens, *Antiquaries Journal*, 13, 264-96
1934   Derivative forms of the *petit tranchet* in Britain, *Archaeological Journal*, 91, 32-58
1936   Report on a Late Bronze Age site in Mildenhall Fen, West Suffolk, *Antiquaries Journal*, 6, 29-50
1948   The development of fishing in prehistoric Europe, *Antiquaries Journal*, 28, 45-85.
1960   Excavations at the prehistoric site at Hurst Fen, Mildenhall, Suffolk, 1954, 1957 and 1958, *Proceedings of the Prehistoric Society*, 26, 202-45

Clarke, D L,
1970   *Beaker pottery of Great Britain and Ireland*, Cambridge University Press, 2 vols
1972   A provisional model of an Iron Age society and its settlement system, in D L Clarke, ed, *Models in archaeology*, 801-70, Methuen, London
1978   *Analytical archaeology*, 2nd ed, Methuen, London

Coles, J M,
1972   *Field archaeology in Britain*, Methuen, London
1976   Forest farmers: some archaeological, historical and experimental evidence relating to the prehistory of Europe, in S J De Laet, ed, *Acculturation and continuity in Atlantic Europe*, 59-66, Bruges
1978   The Somerset Levels: a concave landscape, in H C Bowen and P J Fowler, eds, *Early land allotment, British Archaeological Reports*, 48

Coles, J M, and Harding, A F,
1979   *The Bronze Age in Europe*, Methuen, London

Coles, J M, and Hibbert, F A,
1975   The Somerset Levels, in P J Fowler, ed, *Recent work in rural archaeology*, 12-26, Moonraker Press, Bradford-on-Avon, Wiltshire

Coles, J M, and Jones, R A,
1975   Timber and radiocarbon dates, *Antiquity*, 49, 194, 123-5

Coombs, D G,
1975   Bronze Age weapon hoards in Britain, *Archaeologia Atlantica*, 2, 49-81

Craddock, P T,
1978   Deliberate alloying in the Atlantic Bronze Age, *Proceedings of the Fifth Atlantic Colloquium*, ed Ryan, Dublin

Cunliffe, B W, and Phillipson, D W,
1968   Excavations at Eldon's Seat, Encombe, Dorset, England, *Proceedings of the Prehistoric Society*, 34, 191-237

Dallas, C,
1975   A Belgic farmstead at Orton Longueville, *Durobrivae*, 3, 26-7

Darby, H C,
    1940   *The medieval Fenland*, David and Charles, reprinted 1974
Davey, P J,
    1973   Bronze Age metalwork from Lincolnshire, *Archaeologia*, 104, 51-127
Davey, P J, and Knowles, G C,
    1971   The Appleby hoard, *Archaeological Journal*, 122, 154-161
de Brisay, K W,
    1978   The excavation of a Red Hill at Peldon, Essex, with notes on some other sites, *Antiquaries Journal*, 58, 31-60
de Brisay, K W, and Evans, K A, eds,
    1975   *Salt: the study of an ancient industry*, Colchester
Dodgshon, R A,
    1978   Land improvement in Scottish farming: marl and lime in Roxburghshire and Berwickshire in the eighteenth century, *Agricultural History Review*, 26, 1-14
Donaldson, P, Kinnes, I A and Wells, C,
    1977   The excavation of a multiple round barrow at Barnack, Cambridgeshire 1974-1976, *Antiquaries Journal*, 58, 197-321
von den Dreisch, A,
    1976   *Das Vermessen von Tierknochen aus vor — und frühgeschichtlichen Siedlungen*. Institut f. Paläoanatomie, Domestikationsforschung und Geschichte der Tiermedizin, München
von den Dreisch, A, and Boessneck,
    1974   Kritische Anmerkungen zur Widerristhohenberechnung aus Längemassen vor- und fruhqeschtlicher Tiernocken, *Svagtirkunde Hilteilungen*, 22, 325-48

Drury, P,
    1978   Little Waltham and pre-Belgic Iron Age settlement in Essex, in B W Cunliffe and R T Rowley, eds, *Lowland Iron Age communities in Europe*, 43-76, British Archaeological Reports, S48, Oxford
Ehrenberg, M,
    1977   Bronze Age spearheads from Berkshire, Buckinghamshire, and Oxfordshire, *British Archaeological Reports*, 34, Oxford
Eidt, R C,
    1977   Selection and examination of anthrosols by phosphate, *Science*, 197, 1327-33
Ellis, A E,
    1941   The mollusca of the Norfolk Broads, *Journal of Conchology*, 21, 224-43
Ellison, A, and Harriss, J,
    1972   Settlement and land use in the prehistory and early history of southern England: a study based on locational models, in D L Clarke, ed, *Models in Archaeology*, 911-62, Methuen, London
Erith, F H, and Longworth, I H,
    1960   A Bronze Age urnfield on Vinces Farm, Ardleigh, Essex, *Proceedings of the Prehistoric Society*, 26, 178-92
Evans, J G,
    1972   *Land snails in archaeology*, Seminar Press, London
Farrar, R A H,
    1975   Prehistoric and Roman saltworks in Dorset, in de Brisay and Evans 1975, 14-19
Fasham, P J, and Ross, J M,
    1978   A Bronze Age flint industry from a barrow site in Micheldever Wood, Hampshire, *Proceedings of the Prehistoric Society*, 44, 47-67
Fell, C, and Coles, J M,
    1965   A reconsideration of the Ambleside hoard and the burial at Butts Beck Quarry, Dalton-in-Furness, *Transactions of the Cumberland and Westmorland Antiquarian and Archaeological Society*, 65, new series, 38-52
Fleming, A,
    1978   The prehistoric landscape of Dartmoor Part 1; South Dartmoor, *Proceedings of the Prehistoric Society* 144, 97-123
Folk, R L,
    1966   A review of grain-size parameters, *Sedimentology*, 6, 73-93
Folk, R L, and Ward, W C,
    1957   Brazos River bar: a study of grain-size parameters, *Journal of Sedimentary Petrology*, 27, 1, 3-26

Fox, C,
    1923   *The archaeology of the Cambridge region*, Cambridge University Press
Godwin, H,
    1941   Studies of the post-glacial history of British vegetation: parts III and IV, *Philosophical Transactions of the Royal Society, London, B*, 230, 233-303
    1975   *The history of the British flora*, 2nd ed, Cambridge University Press
    1978   *Fenland: its ancient past and uncertain future*, Cambridge University Press
Godwin, H, and Vishnu-Mittre,
    1975   Flandrian deposits of the Fenland margin at Holme Fen and Whittlesey Mere, Hunts, *Philosophical Transactions of the Royal Society, London, B*, 270, 561-608
Grant, A,
    1975   The use of tooth wear as a guide to the age of domestic animals, in B Cunliffe, *Excavations at Portchester Castle I: Roman,* Society of Antiquaries Research Report 32, 437-50
Green, H S,
    1974   Early Bronze Age burial, territory and population in Milton Keynes, Buckinghamshire, and the Great Ouse Valley, *Archaeological Journal*, 131, 75-139
    1976   The excavation of a late Neolithic settlement at Stacey Bushes, Milton Keynes, and its significance, in Burgess and Miket 1976, 11-28
Greenfield, E,
    1961   The Bronze Age round barrow on Codicote Heath, Hertfordshire, *St Albans and Hertfordshire Architectural and Archaeological Society Transactions*, 5-20
Hallam, S,
    1970   Settlement round the Wash, in C W Phillips, ed, *The Fenland in Roman times*, Royal Geographical Society Research Series No 5, London
Halstead, P, Hodder, I and Jones, G,
    1978   Behavioural archaeology and refuse patterns: a case study, *Norwegian Archaeological Review*, 11, 118-31
Harcourt, R A,
    1974   The dog in prehistoric and early historic Britain, *Journal of Archaeological Science*, 1, 151-75
Harding, D W,
    1974   *The Iron Age in lowland Britain*, Routledge and Kegan Paul
Hawkes, C F C, and Fell, C I,
    1945   The Early Iron Age settlement at Fengate, Peterborough, *Archaeological Journal*, 100, 188-223
Hawkes, C F C, and Smith, M A,
    1955   Bronze Age hoards in the British Museum, *Inventaria Archaeologica, GB*, 9-13
Hayes, J W,
    1978   A group of Roman pottery from Fengate, *Durobrivae*, 6, 12-13
Hesse, P R,
    1971   *A textbook of soil chemical analysis*, John Murray, London
Holden, E W,
    1972   A Bronze Age cemetery-barrow on Itford Hill, *Sussex Archaeological Collections*, 110, 70-117
    1975   Itford Hill flint artifacts, *Sussex Archaeological Collections*, 113, 187
Horton, A, Lake, R D, Bisson, G, and Coppack, B C,
    1974   *The geology of Peterborough*, Report of the Institute of Geological Sciences, 73/12, London
Hughes, M J, Cowell, M R, and Craddock, P T,
    1976   Atomic absorption techniques in archaeology, *Archaeometry*, 18, 19-37
Jackson, D A,
    1976   The excavation of Neolithic and Bronze Age sites at Aldwincle, Northamptonshire, 1967-71, *Northamptonshire Archaeology*, 11, 12-70
Jockenhövel, A,
    1975   Zum Beginn der Jungbronzezeitkul tur un Westeuropa, *Jahresbericht des Instituts für Vorgeschichte der Universität Frankfurt A M*

Jones, M U,
1976　　The Mucking excavations 1976, *Panorama*, Journal of Thurrock Local History Society, 20, 34-43

Kenny, E J A,
1933　　A Roman bridge in the Fens, *Geographical Journal*, 82, 434-41

Kerney, M P, Brown, E H, and Chandler, T J,
1964　　The late-glacial and post-glacial history of the chalk escarpment near Brook, Kent, *Philosophical Transactions of the Royal Society, B*, 248, 135-204

Kerrich, J E and Clarke, D L,
1967　　Notes on the possible misuse and errors of cumulative percentage frequency graphs for the comparison of prehistoric artefact asemblages, *Proceedings of the Prehistoric Society*, 33, 57-69

King, E,
1973　　*Peterborough Abbey 1086-1310: a study in the land market*, Cambridge University Press

Kinnes, I A,
1977　　The finds (from Barnack), in Donaldson *et al* 1977, 209-216

Lanting, J N and van der Waals, J D,
1972　　British Beakers as seen from the Continent, *Helinium*, 12, 20-46

Leaf, C S,
1935　　Report on the excavation of two sites in Mildenhall Fen, *Proceedings of the Cambridgeshire Antiquarian Society*, 35, 106-27

Leeds, E T,
1922　　Further discoveries of the Neolithic and Bronze Ages at Peterborough, *Antiquaries Journal*, 2, 220-37

Lethbridge, T C,
1935　　Investigation of the ancient causeway in the Fen between Fordy and Little Thetford, Cambridgeshire, *Proceedings of the Cambridgeshire Antiquarian Society*, 35, 86-9

Lethbridge, T C, Fell, C I, and Bachem, K E,
1951　　Report on a recently discovered dug-out canoe from Peterborough, *Proceedings of the Prehistoric Society*, 17, 229-33

Limbrey, S,
1975　　*Soil science and archaeology*, Academic Press, London

Lindquist, S O,
1974　　The development of the agrarian landscape on Gotland during the Early Iron Age, *Norwegian Archaeological Review*, 7, 6-32

Long, W H, and Davies, G M,
1948　　*Farm life in a Yorkshire dale*, Dalesman Publishing Company, Clapham

Longworth, I H,
1961　　The origins and development of the primary series in the collared urn tradition in England and Wales, *Proceedings of the Prehistoric Society*, 27, 263-306

Longworth, I H, Wainwright, G J, and Wilson, K E,
1971　　The Grooved Ware site at Lion Point, Clacton, in G de G Sieveking, ed, *Prehistoric and Roman Studies*, 93-124, British Museum, London

Louwe Kooijmans, L P,
1974　　The Rhine/Meuse delta: four studies on its prehistoric occupation and Holocene geology, *Analecta Praehistorica Leidensia*, 8

Mahany, C M,
1969　　Fengate, *Current Archaeology*, 17, 156-7

Manby, T G,
1974　　Pottery from Weldon, Northamptonshire, *Northamptonshire Archaeology*, 9, 11-12

Margary, I D,
1957　　*Roman roads in Britain*, Vol 2, Oxford University Press

May, J,
1970　　Dragonby: an interim report on excavations on an Iron Age and Romano-British site near Scunthorpe, Lincolnshire, *Antiquaries Journal*, 50, 222-45
1976　　*Prehistoric Lincolnshire*, History of Lincolnshire Committee

McGrail, S,
1978　　*Logboats of England and Wales*, parts i and ii, *British Archaeological Reports*, 51, Oxford

McMaster, I,
1975　　A further four years aerial survey 1970-1974, *Colchester Archaeological Group Quarterly Bulletin*, 18, 12-27

Mellows, W T,
1966   *The Peterborough chronicle of Hugh Candidus*, Peterborough Museum Society
Mercer, R J,
1976   Grimes Graves, Norfolk — an interim statement on conclusions drawn from the total excavation of a flint mine shaft and a substantial surface area in 1971-2, in Burgess and Miket 1976, 101-111
Miller, E,
1951   *The abbey and bishopric of Ely*, reprinted 1969, Cambridge University Press
Miller, G J,
1969   A study of cuts, grooves and other marks on recent and fossil bone: I animal tooth marks, *Tebiwa*, 12, 20-26
Moore, W R G, and Williams, J H,
1975   A later Neolithic site at Ecton, Northampton, *Northamptonshire Archaeology*, 10, 3-30
Mortimer, J R,
1905   *Forty years researches in British and Saxon burial mounds of East Yorkshire*, 1st edition, Brown, London
Murphy, J, and Riley, J P,
1962   A modified single solution method for the determination of phosphate in natural waters, *Analitica Chimica Acta*, 27, 31-6
Page, H G,
1955   Phi-millimetre conversion table, *Journal of Sedimentary petrology*, 25, 4, 285-92
Payne, S,
1973   Kill-off patterns in sheep and goats: the mandibles from Asvan Kale, *Anatolian Studies*, 23, 281-303
Phillips, C W,
1970   *The Fenland in Roman times*, Royal Geographical Society Research Series No 5, London
Pickering, J,
1978   The Jurassic spine, *Current Archaeology*, 64, 140-43
Piggott, S,
1972   A note on climatic deterioration in the first millennium BC in Britain, *Scottish Archaeological Forum*, 4, 109-13
Pitts, M W,
1978a   Towards an understanding of flint industries in post-glacial England, *University of London Institute of Archaeology Bulletin*, 15, 179-197
1978b   On the shape of waste flakes as an index of technological change in lithic industries, *Journal of Archaeological Science*, 5, 17-38
Pitts, M W, and Jacobi, R M,
1979   Some aspects of change in flaked stone industries of the Mesolithic and Neolithic in Southern Britain, *Journal of Archaeological Science*, 6, 163-78
Plog, F T,
1974   *The study of prehistoric change*, Academic Press, London
Pollard, E, Hooper, M D, and Moore, N W
1974   *Hedges*, New Naturalist Series, 58, Collins, London
Provan, D M J,
1971   Soil phosphate analysis as a tool in archaeology, *Norwegian Archaeological Review*, 4, 37-50
Pryor, F M M,
1974a   Two Bronze Age burials near Pilsgate Lincolnshire, *Proceedings of the Cambridgeshire Antiquarian Society*, 68, 1-12
1974b   Fengate, *Current Archaeology*, 46, 332-38
1974c   *Excavations at Fengate, Peterborough, England: the first report*, Archaeology Monograph 3, Royal Ontario Museum, Toronto
1976a   Fen-edge land management in the Bronze Age: an interim report on excavations at Fengate, Peterborough 1971-4, in C B Burgess and R Miket, 1976, 29-49
1976b   A Neolithic multiple burial from Fengate, Peterborough, *Antiquity*, 50, 232-3
1977   Fengate 1976, *Durobrivae*, 5, 14-16
1978a   *Excavations at Fengate, Peterborough, England: the second report*, Archaeology Monograph 5, Royal Ontario Museum, Toronto
1978b   Three new bronze Age weapons, *Durobrivae*, 6, 14-16
1979   Will it all come out in the wash? Reflections at the end of eight years' digging, *paper presented to a conference on later Bronze Age settlement in Britain, held at Leeds, January 1979*, to be published in *British Archaeological Reports*, Oxford

Pryor, F M M, and Cranstone, D A L,
    1978   An interim report on excavations at Fengate, Peterborough 1975-77, *Northamptonshire Archaeology*, 13, 9-27

Raban, S,
    1977   *The estates of Thorney and Crowland*, University of Cambridge Department of Land Economy Occasional Paper no 7

Rahtz, P, and ApSimon, A M,
    1962   Excavations at Shearplace Hill, Sydling St Nicholas, Dorset, England, *Proceedings of the Prehistoric Society*, 28, 289-328

Radley, J,
    1969   A shale bracelet industry from Totley Moor, near Sheffield, *Transactions of the Hunter Archaeological Society*, 9, 264-68

Raftis, J A,
    1957   *The estates of Ramsey Abbey*, Pontifical Institute of Medieval Studies, Toronto

Ravensdale, J R,
    1974   *Liable to floods*, Cambridge University Press

Richards, J C,
    1978   *The archaeology of the Berkshire Downs: an introductory survey*, Berkshire Archaeological Committee Publication 3, Reading

Rowlands, M J,
    1971   The archaeological interpretation of prehistoric metalworking, *World Archaeology*, 3, 210-24
    1976   *The production and distribution of metalwork in the Middle Bronze Age in Southern Britain*, 2 vols, *British Archaeological Reports*, 31, Oxford

Sahlins, M, and Service, E,
    1960   *Evolution and culture*, University of Michigan Press, Ann Arbor

Salway, P,
    1970   The Roman Fenland, in Phillips 1970, 1-21

Schiffer, M B,
    1976   *Behavioural archaeology*, Seminar Press, London

Shackley, M L,
    1975   *Archaeological sediments: a survey of analytical methods*, Butterworth, London

Sieveking, G de G, Longworth, I H, Hughes, M J, Clark, A J, and Millett A,
    1973   A new survey of Grime's Graves, Norfolk, *Proceedings of the Prehistoric Society*, 39, 182-218

Silver, I A,
    1969   The ageing of domestic animals, in D R Brothwell, and E S Higgs, eds, *Science in archaeology*, 283-302, Thames and Hudson, London

Simmons, I G,
    1974   *The ecology of natural resources*, Arnold, London

Simpson, D D A,
    1968   Food Vessels: associations and chronology, in J M Coles and D D A Simpson, eds, *Studies in ancient Europe*, 197-212, Leicester University Press

Simpson, W G,
    1976   A barrow cemetery of the second millennium BC at Tallington, Lincolnshire, *Proceedings of the Prehistoric Society*, 42, 215-40

Smedley, N, and Owles, E,
    1962   Pottery of the Early and Early Middle Bronze Age in Suffolk, *Proceedings of the Suffolk Institute of Archaeology*, 29, 175-97

Smith, A G, and Pilcher, J R,
    1973   Radiocarbon dates and vegetational history of the British Isles, *New Phytologist*, 72, 903-14

Smith, C A,
    1975   Second report on excavations at Fisherwick, Staffordshire. 1973. Ice-wedge casts and a Middle Bronze Age settlement, *Transactions of the South Staffordshire Archaeological and Historical Society*, 16, 1-17

Smith, I F,
    1956   *The decorative art of Neolithic ceramics in South-Eastern England and its relations*, unpublished PhD thesis, Institute of Archaeology, London
    1965   *Windmill Hill and Avebury: excavations by Alexander Keiller 1926-39*, Oxford University Press

Smith, M A,
    1959   Some Somerset hoards and their place in the Bronze Age of Southern Britain, *Proceedings of the Prehistoric Society*, 25, 144-187

Speth, J D,
    1972   Mechanical basis of percussion flaking, *American Antiquity*, 37, 34-60

Steward, J S,
    1955   *Theory of culture change: the methodology of multilinear evolution*, paperback edition, 1977, Illinois University Press, Urbana

Taylor, C C,
    1969   *Peterborough New Town, a survey of the antiquities in the area of development*, Part 1, Royal Commission on Historical Monuments, London

Thirsk, J,
    1953   *Fenland farming in the sixteenth century*, Department of English Local History Occasional Papers, no 3, Leicester University Press

Tringham, R, Cooper, G, Voytek, B, and Whitman, A,
    1974   Experimentation in the formation of edge damage: a new approach to lithic analysis, *Journal of Field Archaeology*, 1, 171-96

Turnbaugh, W A,
    1978   Floods and archaeology, *American Antiquity*, 43, 4, 593-607

USDA,
    1951   *Soil survey manual*, United States Dept of Agriculture Handbook No 18

Vita-Finzi, C,
    1969   Fluvial geology, in D R Brothwell, and E S Higgs, eds, *Science in archaeology*, 2nd edition, 135-50, Thames and Hudson, London

Wainwright, G J,
    1973   Prehistoric and Romano-British settlements at Eaton Heath, Norwich, *Archaeological Journal*, 130, 1-43

Wainwright, G J, and Longworth, I H,
    1971   *Durrington Walls: excavations 1966-68*, Society of Antiquaries Research Report 29, London

Waterbolk, H T,
    1977   Walled enclosures of the Iron Age in the North of the Netherlands, *Palaeohistoria*, 19, 97-172

Whittle, A W R,
    1977   *The earlier neolithic of Southern England and its continental background*, British Archaeological Reports, 35, Oxford

White, D A and Reed, R,
    1971   The excavation of a bowl barrow at Oakley Down, Dorset, 1968, *Procedings of the Dorset Natural History and Archaeological Society*, 92,159-66

Wilkinson, G,
    1973   *Trees in the wild*, Stephen Hope Books, London

Willis, E H,
    1961   Marine transgression sequences in the English Fenland, *Annals of the New York Academy of Science*, 95, 369-76

Yellen, J E,
    1977   Cultural patterning in faunal remains: evidence from the ! Kung Bushmen, in D W Ingersoll, J E Yellen and W Macdonal eds, *Experimental Archaeology*, 271-331, Columbia University Press, New York

Plate 1 Padholme Road subsite: cropmarks. Padholme Road joins Storey's Bar Road at a T-junction, top left. Ditches 1–2 follow the darker field boundary; top right; ditches 3–4 pass under the building, lower right. *Photo by J. K. St. Joseph: Cambridge University Collection, copyright reserved.*

Plate 2 Padholme Road subsite, Areas IX and X, ditches 1 (right) and 2 (left), looking south-east.

Plate 3 Padholme Road subsite, Area VIII, ditch F4, section at south edge of excavation.

Plate 4   Padholme Road subsite, Area IX: crouched inhumation in ditch 1. Left scale in centimetres; right in inches (black) and centimetres (grey).

Plate 5   Padholme Road subsite, Area VII, ditch 4, notched oak log (see also FIG 15).

Plate 6 Newark Road subsite: cropmarks, looking north-east. The Fen Causeway shows as a negative mark obliterating ditches 5–7; the dark 'blotches' represent clay deposits. *Photo by J. K. St. Joseph: Cambridge University Collection, copyright reserved.*

Plate 7   Newark Road subsite and Cat's Water subsite (right), looking north-east, 1976 season. *Photo by S.G. Upex: Nene Valley Research Committee.*

Plate 9 Newark Road subsite, looking south, with Area VII in the foreground. *Photo by S. G. Upex, Nene Valley Research Committee.*

Plate 8 Newark Road subsite, Areas I-VI, looking south-east, with Storey's Bar Road at the top. *Photo by S. G. Upex, Nene Valley Research Committee.*

264

Plate 10 Newark Road subsite, Area II (1974), looking west along main drove.

Plate 11   Newark Road subsite, Areas IV and II (1976), looking south-east across main drove, with ditch 8 traversing the site diagonally.

Plate 12   Newark Road subsite, Area II: crouched inhumation in ditch *f*. Scales in half metres (top) and centimetres (bottom).

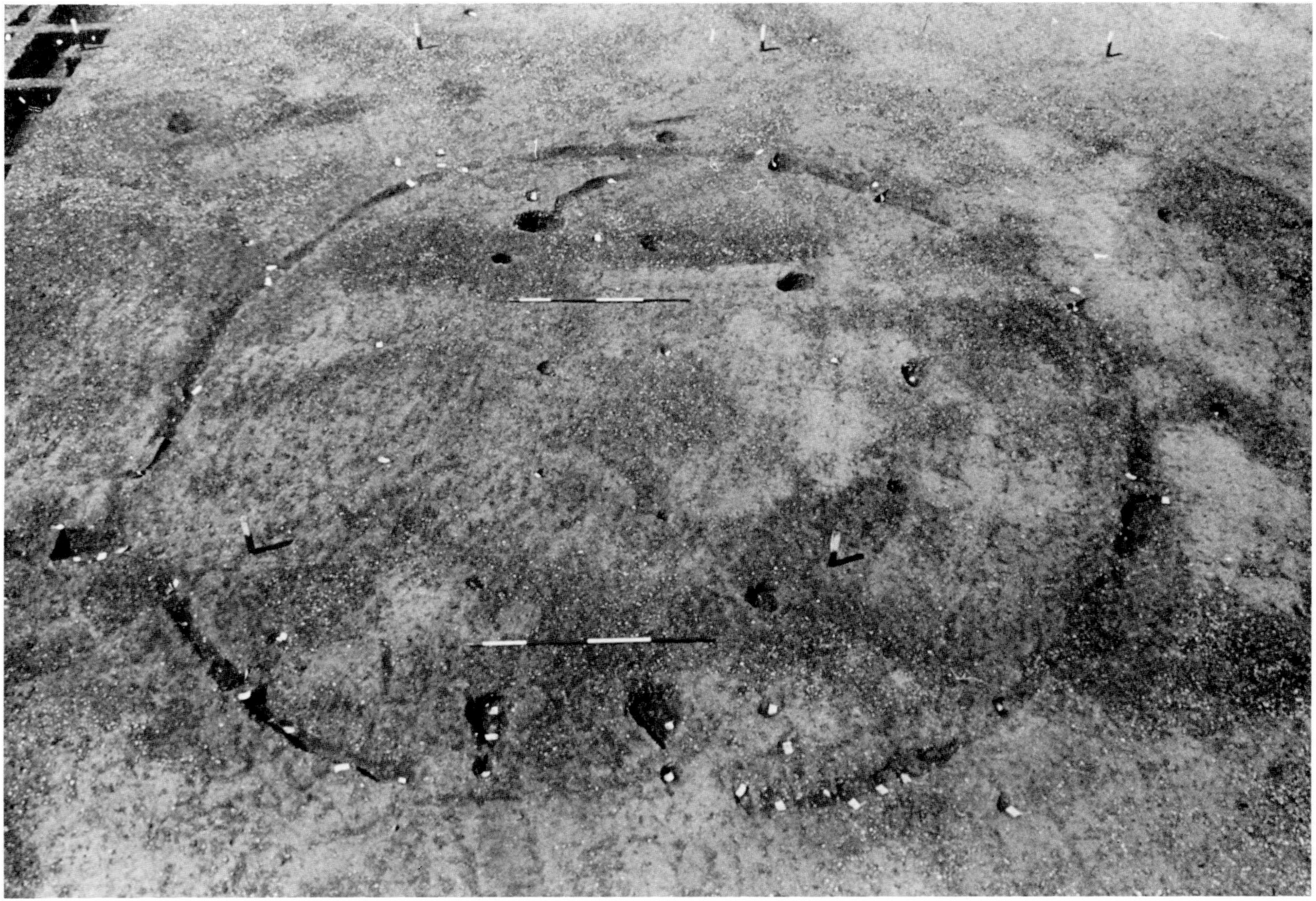

Plate 13 Newark Road subsite, Area IV, Structure 1, general view, with doorway and porch lower, centre. Scales in half metres.

Plate 14 Newark Road subsite, Area IV, looking south-west, showing arrangement of Structure 1 and associated droveway ditches. Scales in half metres.

Plate 15   Fourth Drove subsite, Area VII, north-east: ditch 10 and its associated bank. This photograph is explained in the accompanying Figure (128).

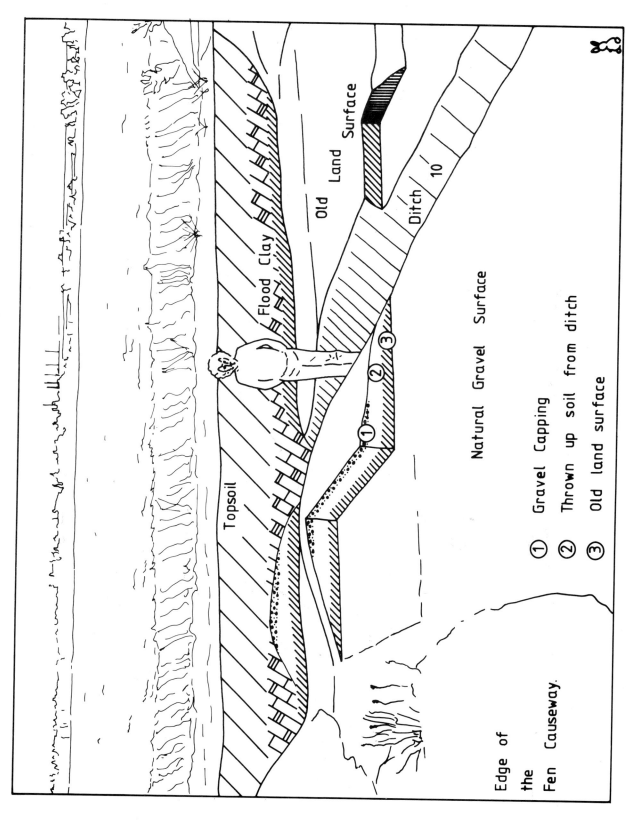

Fig. 128   Line drawing showing interpretation of PL 15.

Plate 16   The Peterborough logboat. Photograph taken in October 1950. Length *c*. 9.91m; beam (at stern, away from camera) 0.76m. *Photo provided by Peterborough Museum and reproduced by courtesy of Central Electricity Generating Board (South-East Region).*